SOURCES IN BRITISH POLITICAL HISTORY
1900-1951

Sources in British Political History 1900-1951

compiled for the British Library of Political
and Economic Science by
CHRIS COOK

with

Philip Jones
Josephine Sinclair
Jeffrey Weeks

Volume I

A Guide to the Archives of
Selected Organisations and Societies

First published 1975 by
THE MACMILLAN PRESS LTD
London and Basingstoke
Associated companies in New York
Dublin Melbourne Johannesburg and Madras

SBN 333 15036 8

Typeset in Great Britain by
COLD COMPOSITION LTD
Tunbridge Wells, Kent
Printed in Great Britain by
REDWOOD BURN LTD
Trowbridge and Esher

465133932

Contents

Foreword

This is the first of three volumes reporting the results of a survey of twentieth-century British political archives. It has been undertaken by the British Library of Political and Economic Science with the support of the Social Science Research Council.

The project originated from a meeting of archivists, historians and librarians, held in October 1967 on the initiative of Nuffield College, Oxford, which appointed a Political Archives Investigation Committee (whose membership is listed on p. ix) to explore the possibility of making a major effort to locate and list modern British political manuscripts and encourage their preservation.

With the assistance of a grant from the Social Science Research Council a two-year pilot project, directed by Dr Cameron Hazlehurst, was begun at Nuffield College in 1968, with the object of locating the papers of Cabinet Ministers who held office between 1900 and 1951. The same Committee acted as a steering committee for the project. This enquiry was an undoubted success; and Dr Hazlehurst's guide to the papers of Cabinet Ministers was published in 1974.*

In view of the favourable outcome of the pilot project, the Committee had no hesitation in recommending that a more comprehensive survey should be under-taken; and particularly bearing in mind the bibliographical facilities and geographical convenience of London, as well as the number of scholars active in relevant fields working in the London School of Economics, it proposed that this phase of the investigation should be carried out under the auspices of the British Library of Political and Economic Science.

A generous grant was accordingly made to the British Library of Political and Economic Science by the Social Science Research Council; and on 1 October 1970, a research team directed by Dr C. P. Cook began work on a five-year project intended to locate the papers of all persons and organisations influential in British politics between 1900 and 1951, encourage their preservation, and publish a guide.

In carrying out a project which has such very wide terms of reference combined with a fixed time-limit, priorities have inevitably had to be established. Whilst a comprehensive search is being made for the papers of all members of the House of Commons, the papers of individual members of other categories are being sought more selectively, on the basis either of their rank or of their known political activity. These categories include civil servants of, or above, the rank of Under-Secretary; diplomats; and field commanders and chiefs of staff of the armed services. The records of political parties, societies, institutions and pressure groups, with which this first volume is concerned, have similarly, of necessity, been treated with some degree of selectivity.

D. A. CLARKE

British Library of Political and Economic Science

---

*Hazlehurst, C. and Woodland, C. *A Guide to the papers of British Cabinet Ministers 1900-1951* (Royal Historical Society, 1974).

Members of the Political Archives Investigation Committee

Mr John Brooke, Historical Manuscripts Commission (1967-) (Chairman, 1972-)
Mr D. A. Clarke, British Library of Political and Economic Science (1967-)
Dr C. P. Cook, British Library of Political and Economic Science (1970-)
Mr Martin Gilbert, Merton College, Oxford (1967-70)
Dr R. M. Hartwell, Nuffield College, Oxford (Chairman, 1967-72)
Dr Cameron Hazlehurst, Nuffield College, Oxford (1967-70)
Professor A. Marwick, the Open University (1972-)
Dr H. M. Pelling, St John's College, Cambridge (1967-)
Mrs Felicity Strong, Historical Manuscripts Commission (1967-)
Dr John Roberts, Merton College, Oxford (1973-)
Mr A. J. P. Taylor, The Beaverbrook Library (1972-)
Professor D. C. Watt, London School of Economics and Political Science (1967-)
Dr Edwin Welch, Churchill College, Cambridge (1967-71)

Acknowledgements

This book could not have been compiled without a large grant from the Social Science Research Council and the help and guidance of Derek Clarke, the Librarian of the British Library of Political and Economic Science, and of his staff, among whom particular mention should be made of Geoffry Allen and David Bovey.

It would be impossible to thank by name all the people without whose help this volume either would not have appeared or would have looked very different. I am, however, especially indebted to the following: Maurice Bond, OBE, Clerk of the Records at the House of Lords; D. S. Porter of the Bodleian Library, Oxford; Christine Kennedy of Nuffield College, Oxford; Irene Wagner, Librarian to the Labour Party; Roy Garratt, Librarian of the Co-operative Union; A. E. B. Owen of Cambridge University Library; Daniel Waley, Keeper of Manuscripts at the British Library; A. J. P. Taylor at the Beaverbrook Library; J. K. Bates, Secretary of the National Register of Archives (Scotland); J. S. Ritchie at the National Library of Scotland; Sir John Ainsworth, Bt, at the National Library of Ireland; and B. G. Owens at the National Library of Wales. The section on Ireland received enormous help from Philip Bull of the Bodleian Library, Oxford. Ian MacDougall and Miss W. Schroeder supplied invaluable information about Scottish sources for labour history and the holdings of the International Institute of Social History at Amsterdam respectively.

I have relied heavily on suggestions, advice and information supplied by colleagues and friends, both at the London School of Economics and elsewhere. I should like to thank especially Joyce Bellamy and John Saville of the University of Hull, together with Paul Addison, John Barnes, George Bergstrom, Geoffrey Block, Martin Ceadel, Maurice Cowling, Roy Douglas, Catharine Hodges, Barry Hollingsworth, George Jones, Elie Kedourie, Stephen Koss, Mrs P. Larby, Iain Maclean, Ross McKibbin, Ted Milligan, Kenneth Morgan, Ian Nish, Gillian Peele, John Ramsden, David Rolf, Leonard Schapiro, Paul Shorter, Martin Sieff, D. H. Simpson, Richard Storey, Paul Sturges, Brenda Swann, Maureen Turnbull, Paul Wilkinson, Philip Woods and Ken Young.

Warm thanks are due to the officers of the organisations covered by this book. A particular debt is owed to Lord Fraser of Kilmorack at the Conservative Central Office, and to the Director of Organisation there, Sir Richard Webster.

Although this volume is relatively independent of the work done by Cameron Hazlehurst and Christine Woodland, their work complements it and their help has been greatly appreciated. I have also received continuous help and advice from members of the steering committee, both past and present, and especially from Mrs Strong and the staff of the Historical Manuscripts Commission, whose work is so closely associated with our own.

Last but by no means least, the compilation of this book has been a team effort, and my very warm thanks are due to my colleagues and co-authors, Philip Jones, Josephine Sinclair and Jeffrey Weeks. Most of the typing for the survey was done with unfailing energy and kindness by Eileen Pattison, with additional secretarial help from Jean Ali and Wendi Momen. The index was compiled by Beryl McKie.

CHRIS COOK

Introduction

1. *Contents*

This volume deals with the archives of organisations and societies active and influential in British politics between 1900 and 1951. Subsequent volumes will deal successively with the private political papers of senior public servants and Members of Parliament.

The great majority of entries in this volume relate to the archives of political parties, trade unions and other organisations directly involved in politics and political controversy. Also included are a number of other organisations whose activities are or were only marginally political. For example, many of the religious societies included, and the associations involved in the temperance movement and social work, were not primarily, or even partly, political organisations, yet their archives can be of value to the historian in putting political facts into context and tracing the interaction between politics and the people. For this reason, where information is available they have been included.

The period covered by the survey is 1900 to 1951, but many of the organisations included had a continuous existence from long before 1900, and others continued after 1951. Many, indeed, are still active. To mention only those archives which fall into the period of the survey would be misleading, and a brief account of pre-1900 material has therefore been given where appropriate. In a few instances organisations (such as the Campaign for Nuclear Disarmament), founded and active after 1951, have deposited their records. It was decided to include these organisations, although strictly speaking they fall outside the scope of the survey.

Every effort has been made to secure information about as wide and representative a range of organisations as possible. For a number of reasons, however, the records of certain organisations are omitted. Occasionally the organisation has been unwilling for an entry to appear, perhaps because of lack of facilities for students or because the records are confidential and are therefore necessarily closed at present. More often it reflects the difficulty of tracing the extant archives of long since defunct or disbanded organisations and pressure groups.

Where the archives of an organisation have been lost or destroyed, and no records survive, the volume includes references to private papers which may to a limited extent constitute an alternative source of information. For example, under the Liberal League the user is referred to the papers of the 5th Earl of Rosebery in the National Library of Scotland. References to such private papers are given, however, only where all other information is lacking.

2. *Arrangement*

The entries in this guide are, in general, arranged alphabetically, under the last known name of the organisation concerned, with a composite index to the names of all organisations listed and their predecessors. Each entry consists of a brief account of the history and aims of the organisation, followed by a survey of the records which survive and notes on their location and availability. In a few instances, however, a number of different organisations have for convenience been grouped under a single subject heading, instead of being scattered throughout the text. Examples of subjects treated in this way include Temperance, Women's Suffrage, Syndicalism and the Radical Right. Organisations omitted from the alphabetical sequence for this reason will be found in the index. The main section of the book is followed by short notes on relevant archives in Ireland, Scotland and Wales, together with a list of the postal addresses of the main libraries and record repositories mentioned in this book.

3. *Abbreviations*

In a book of this type, abbreviations of the titles of organisations and societies mentioned have been extensively used in order to save needless repetition. Normally, it is hoped that the abbreviation used will be self-evident from its context in a particular entry. The following abbreviations are extensively used throughout the book:

Ann. Reps.	Annual Reports.
A/cs.	Accounts.
B.L.P.E.S.	British Library of Political and Economic Science.
Exec. Comm.	Executive Committee.
F. & G.P.	Finance and General Purposes Committee.
M.B.	Minute Book.

4. *Further Information*

Many of the archives listed in this volume remain in the custody of the organisations which created them. Comparatively few have hitherto been deposited in record offices or public and university libraries, but the situation is apt to change. No book of this sort can ever be completely up-to-date: organisations move, officials change, records may be lost, destroyed, found or deposited. The user should be aware of all these possibilities, and is strongly advised to try to make his own checks before bothering the busy officers of organisations. Up-to-date addresses can be obtained from the *Directory of British Associations*, revised and updated regularly by CBD Research Ltd, Beckenham, Kent, or from *Whitaker's Almanack*. Recent deposits are recorded in the annual list of *Accessions to Repositories* published by H. M. Stationery Office for the Historical Manuscripts Commission. More detailed unpublished lists of archives both in repositories and libraries and in the custody of their originators may often be found in the National Register of Archives maintained by the Historical Manuscripts Commission, Quality House, Quality Court, Chancery Lane, London WC2A 1HP, where known alterations and additions to the information given in this volume will be recorded.

The present survey was not intended to include within its scope those governmental or similar organisations whose archives would usually be transferred to the Public Record Office, and consequently no detailed research on the contents of the Public Record Office has been attempted. However, the official records of government departments inevitably include correspondence with, and papers relating to, many of the societies and institutions dealt with in this volume. In many cases, where an organisation's formal archive has not been located, the Public Record

Office contains the most valuable collection of relevant source material. The reader should therefore use this book in conjunction with the various handlists and publications produced by the Public Record Office.*

It is hoped that the information in this volume is correct at the time of going to press, but apart from the possible changes mentioned earlier, it must be remembered that the details were often supplied by officers of the organisations whose knowledge of the older records was imperfect, or by scholars whose interests might be limited to certain aspects of their work. Both the British Library of Political and Economic Science and the Historical Manuscripts Commission would be grateful to be informed of alterations, additions and amendments.

---

*A description of the records, and of the principles upon which the classes are arranged, is provided in the *Guide to the Contents of the Public Record Office*, 3 vols (H.M.S.O., 1963-68), and in the typescript supplements available in the Search Rooms of the Public Record Office.

A Guide to the Archives of Selected Organisations and Societies

ABORTION LAW REFORM ASSOCIATION

22 Brewhouse Hill Wheathampstead Herts. AL4 8AG

Formed in 1936, the Association aims to obtain and publish information on the legal, social and medical aspects of abortion, to encourage research into these aspects and to secure such changes in relevant British law as may be considered necessary.

Papers

Most of the records still exist. However, they are uncatalogued and unsorted. The early material (1936-61) has been deposited with the Medical Sociology Research Unit of the Centre for Social Studies at Aberdeen. At present the papers are in vast numbers of box files and tea-chests and the work of sorting and indexing has just begun. Also in Aberdeen are the press cutting records for the years 1961-69.

Availability

Enquiries should be addressed to the Secretary at the Aberdeen Medical Sociology Research Unit.

ABYSSINIAN ASSOCIATION

The Association was formally established in April 1936, with Professor H. S. Jevons as Hon. Secretary. Its declared aims were to collect and publish correct information on conditions in Abyssinia, to answer pro-Italian propaganda, and to render direct assistance to the Abyssinian Government by pressing for effective sanctions and financial assistance. After the Italian conquest of Abyssinia the Association continued with the first of these aims. It sponsored the Abyssinian Loan, designed to give assistance to Haile Selassie's Government.

Papers

Certain records relating to the activities of the Association and of the Anglo-Ethiopian Society, together with other material on Abyssinia, can be found in the Herbert Stanley Jevons Collection, National Library of Wales. A schedule of this collection is available there. The relevant papers include files of cyclostyled notes on the planning of the Association, typescripts of articles, memoranda, etc., 1935-51, together with certain pamphlets. In addition, there is material on the Anglo-Ethiopian Society, of which Jevons was Treasurer, 1948-55; account books of the Ethiopian Fund, 1940-42, and of the Anglo-Ethiopian Society, 1953-55.

Other relevant material in the Jevons Collection includes correspondence with Haile Selassie, 1937-53.

Availability

Access to the Jevons papers is restricted; the permission of the depositor, Mrs. R. Kõnekamp, is needed. Further information may be obtained from the National Library of Wales.

See also *Abyssinian Refugees Relief Fund*.

ABYSSINIAN REFUGEES RELIEF FUND

The Fund was inaugurated in 1937 to receive the unexpended balance of moneys raised by various organisations for the relief of suffering during the war in

Abyssinia and to raise further funds. Its treasurer was F. Livie-Noble of the *London Group on African Affairs* (q.v.).

Papers

A useful collection of papers concerning the Fund is contained within the archives of the London Group on African Affairs, deposited in Rhodes House Library, Oxford.

The papers include general correspondence (1937-42) dealing with such items as the organisation of refugee camps, minutes and committee papers (March 1937-July 1939), a variety of financial correspondence, receipts and accounts. There are also assorted press cuttings, together with summaries of the work done by the A.R.R.F. for 1938 and 1939.

Availability

Apply to the Librarian, Rhodes House Library, Oxford.

AGE CONCERN: NATIONAL OLD PEOPLE'S WELFARE COUNCIL
Bernard Sunley House 60 Pitcairn Road Mitcham Surrey CR4 3LL

Age Concern was founded in August 1940 as an independent associated group of the National Council of Social Service under the name of the National Old People's Welfare Committee, which name it retained until 1955 when it became the National Old People's Welfare Council. In 1970 it became fully independent of the N.C.S.S. and in 1971 it added Age Concern to the title.

Papers

Age Concern has retained most of its records back to the date of foundation. These records include minute books of the National Committee and the various sub-committees of Age Concern. In addition there are the results of surveys carried out by Age Concern from 1949. Age Concern keeps most of its correspondence with only routine correspondence having been destroyed. The earlier correspondence between 1940 and 1959 has been catalogued and is in box files. In addition there are annual reports from 1941 and National Conference reports dating from foundation. A complete run of the journal of Age Concern, *Age Concern Today* (*Quarterly Bulletin* until 1972) from 1948 to the present is also kept.

Availability

Access is given on written application to the Information Officer.

AGRICULTURAL PARTY

Inaugurated at Norwich in January 1931, the Agricultural Party was founded by J. F. Wright of the Norfolk branch of the National Farmers' Union. By 1932 the party had over 140 branches all over the country. Its clear-cut policy called for the introduction of taxes on imported food to protect British agriculture. The Executive included Lord Rothermere (Hon. President) and Lord Beaverbrook (Senior Vice-President), who supported the party in his newspapers and gave financial assistance to the short electoral campaign to win 'direct parliamentary representation' for British agriculture. Although some Conservative M.P.s backed the party programme, no Agricultural Party candidate was returned to Parliament.

By 1932 the party was already in demise: relations with the National Farmers' Union were embittered, and the National Government's policies proved disappointing. Two years later, even Beaverbrook abandoned the party, if not the cause.

Papers

Two boxes of papers relating to the Agricultural Party are included in the Beaverbrook Collection at the Beaverbrook Library, 33 St. Bride Street, London EC4A 4AY. The main files are labelled 'Correspondence: J. F. Wright and the National Farmers' Union'. The papers begin in January 1931 with letters relating to the launching of the Agricultural Party. The file includes minutes of various party meetings, including those of the meeting of 27 March 1931, attended by Neville Chamberlain and Sir Patrick Gower. The main series of papers continues to 1949 based on Beaverbrook's correspondence with Wright, but covering the organisation of the party, and its relations with the Conservative Party, the Government and the National Farmers' Union. Correspondence with other party notables and with party branches is filed separately, as is correspondence relating to the campaign on behalf of British poultry farmers, 1932-33. Only a small proportion of the papers dates from the period after 1934.

Availability

Applications should be addressed to the Director of the Beaverbrook Library.

AIMS OF INDUSTRY
5 Plough Place Fetter Lane London EC4A 1AN

Aims of Industry was founded in 1942 by Lord Perry of Stock Harvard. It was the first, and is still the only, organisation established exclusively to foster understanding of free enterprise, its contribution to the economy, its responsibilities and its problems. Aims of Industry is not involved in party politics, but presses the cause of free enterprise, right or wrong.

Papers

Aims of Industry does keep files of correspondence, but not for very long. It also keeps minutes of Council meetings, but as this is equivalent to a board of directors, they are not available for general scrutiny.

Copies of the many Aims of Industry booklets are of course available.

AIR LEAGUE
142 Sloane Street London SW1X 9BJ

Founded in 1909 as the Aerial League of the British Empire, it changed its name in 1920 to the Air League of the British Empire, and in 1965 it adopted its present title. The League works for: greater national awareness of the key role of successful aviation; aerospace activity in Britain's overall technology, overall trade, overall communications and overall defence.

Papers

No papers are available at the League's offices.

ALL SOULS FOREIGN AFFAIRS GROUP

Convened by Sir Arthur Salter and the Hon. Harold Nicolson in December 1937, the Group met for weekend conferences at All Souls College, Oxford, and occasional short meetings in London. Members included Lord Allen of Hurtwood, Sir Norman Angell, H.A.L. Fisher, Lionel Curtis, Harold Macmillan, Arnold Toynbee, B. H. Liddell Hart and A. L. Rowse.

Papers

Many collections of private papers contain material relating to the Group's work. Lord Allen's papers are in the University of South Carolina; Norman Angell's papers in Ball State University, Indiana; Lionel Curtis's papers are now deposited in the Bodleian Library; the Harold Nicolson diaries are in Balliol College, Oxford; the Liddell Hart papers will eventually be available at King's College, London; Lord Salter, Harold Macmillan and A.L. Rowse still retain their papers. A. L. Rowse used his journals of the late 1930s to prepare *All Souls and Appeasement* (1961).

AMALGAMATED SOCIETY OF BOILERMAKERS, SHIPWRIGHTS, BLACKSMITHS AND STRUCTURAL WORKERS
Lifton House Eslington Road Newcastle upon Tyne NE2 4SB

Amalgamation into the present union was effected in 1966, and the records of the constituent unions are best treated under three headings.

Shipwrights' Union

The Associated Shipwrights' Society, known after 1907 as the Shipconstructives' and Shipwrights' Association, was formed by Alexander Wilkie in 1882. Its nucleus was the Glasgow Shipwrights' Society of which Wilkie was Secretary.

Papers

A good assortment of records is preserved at Lifton House. However, the material has not been catalogued and only a rough guide to the papers can be given.

Associated Shipwrights' Society. A bound rule book dates from February 1882, when members from several ports and districts met at Glasgow and adopted the Society's rules and regulations; the rule book extends to 1900. A substantial collection of the Society's reports, papers and circulars for the years 1882-1907 is preserved; this material is bound up together in a separate series from the annual reports (1882-1907). A group of four special bindings contains records of demarcation arbitrations, e.g. Tyneside 1889-90, and papers entitled 'Circulars and Votes on Labour Representation, 1891-1903'. Financial reports (1882-85) of the A.S.S. constitute an additional item. Other interesting material includes an arbitration of 1877 between the Clyde Shipbuilding Employers' Association and the Clyde Associated Shipwrights, and a large number of old piece-rate cards, relating to the affairs of various unions and employers' associations.

Some papers of the Glasgow Shipwrights' Society and the Associated Shipwrights of Glasgow have survived for the years 1879-82; the material relates to the calling of meetings, and includes financial reports, draft rules, membership forms and some correspondence of the union leader Alexander Wilkie.

Quarterly and annual reports (1893-1900) of the National Society of Drillers and Holecutters are bound in one volume. In addition, there are annual reports with some quarterly and monthly reports of the Shipconstructives' and Shipwrights' Association, 1908-66.

Reports, papers and circulars of the S.S.A. for 1908-17 are extant, together with three volumes of Executive Committee minutes, Jan. 1909-Nov. 1910. E.C. minutes continue in series up to 1966. Amongst other records are a minute book of the Southwick branch of the Shipconstructives, 1915-39, a cash book marked 'Contingent Fund Account', 1913-25, and an agreement of 9 September 1891, marked 'Shipwrights and Joiners Demarcation of Work together with Decisions of S. J. and E. Standing Committee'. Two copies of D.C. Cummings's 1905 history of the Boilermakers and Iron and Steel Ship Builders' Society (1834-1904) are kept with this material.

Much of the material in this collection relates to Wilkie, who was M.P. for Dundee, 1906-22. Among the more personal items are certain papers relating to Dundee elections, 1905-10 (including a cash book, 1909-10, and an election address).

Among his papers, Wilkie bound up conference reports of an earlier grouping of separate Shipwrights' societies, at which he had been a delegate from the Glasgow Shipwrights' Society. The grouping was named the United Kingdom Amalgamated Society of Shipwrights. Formed some time around 1850, it was not a national union or formal amalgamation, but more of a loose federation of separate port societies.

The annual proceedings of the U.K. Amalgamated Society of Shipwrights for the years 1870-91 are all bound together. They comprise rules and regulations (1870) with annual revisions, lists of the affiliated independent port societies and names of representatives attending conferences, membership figures, accounts of meetings and of discussions regarding reform into a national union with centralised funds.

Blacksmiths' Union

The Scottish United Operative Blacksmiths' Protective and Friendly Society, formed in 1857, was the first of the numerous Blacksmiths' associations, which gradually drew together and in 1924 took the name Associated Blacksmiths, Forge and Smithy Workers' Society.

Papers

The records are at present in the care of Mrs. Angela Tuckett, 5 Liddington Street, Swindon, who is writing a history of the Blacksmiths' unions. The papers will eventually be returned to Lifton House.

The material consists in the main of bound volumes of financial and similar reports dating back to 1857:

Scottish United Operative Blacksmiths' Protective and Friendly Society, 1857-72;

Associated Blacksmiths' Society of Scotland (formed 1872), 1873-85;

Associated Blacksmiths' Society (formed 1885), 1886-1909;

Associated Blacksmiths and Iron Workers' Society of Great Britain and Ireland (1915) (annual and monthly reports), 1910-24;

Associated Blacksmiths, Forge and Smithy Workers Society (annual, quarterly and organisers' reports), 1925-61.

From 1873-80 very useful minutes of the Central Executive Board are bound together in two volumes. These minutes for the years 1881-1909 are at present missing; but from 1910-24 they are printed in the monthly reports.

The reports gradually extend in scope, with remarks by the General Secretary and at some stages quite good organisers' quarterly reports. In later years they took the form of *The Anvil*, the Blacksmiths' magazine. The general continuity of the reports in some way makes up for the lack of original minute books and correspondence. A useful feature are eight benefit books (1857-1905, 1909-19), with original entry of members, age, cause of death, date and detail of cause of exclusion, and details of wife's death for funeral benefits. Other material includes bound rule books from 1857; confidential Federation notes verbatim (1913); a printed letter on 'Procedure . . . if called to the Colours' (1918); a recruiting appeal to youths and apprentices (1941); a note on the admission of women, with the result of a ballot (1943); an anlaysis of contributions and wages in 1900 and 1944, etc.

Also preserved with these records are the following:

Federation of Engineering and Shipbuilding Trades, Treasurer's cash books, 1909-23, 1923-29. The Blacksmiths' General Secretary was usually the Federation's Treasurer.

Amalgamated Union of Shipbuilding, Engineering and Constructional Workers, three minute books, 1921. These are the proceedings of the attempted amalgamation between the Blacksmiths, Shipwrights and Boilermakers, which was finally consummated in 1966.

Boilermakers' Society

The records are now at Lifton House. Full details are unfortunately not available. However, the main series are bound annual reports and monthly reports. The earliest records of the Society are provided in the form of rule books, to which are attached records of the debate about particular rules. Later records were kept in a very comprehensive manner.

Availability

Persons wishing to see the records should apply to the General President of the Amalgamated Society.

AMALGAMATED SOCIETY OF OPERATIVE LACE MAKERS AND AUXILIARY WORKERS

Lace-making in the Nottingham area dates from 1760, and the Amalgamated Society of Operative Lace Makers was formed in 1874 to embrace earlier associations of the trade.

Papers

The records of the Amalgamated Sociey are deposited in Nottingham University Library. They include: accounts, 1876-1947; benefit registers, 1909-42; conciliation records, 1874-1918; contribution books, 1867-1948; correspondence, 1876-84, 1929-48; minutes, 1877-1948; rules (including constituent societies), early 19th century to 1933. N. H. Cuthbert's *The Lace Makers* (1960) provides a history of trade unionism in the British lace industry, 1760-1960.

Availability

Applications should be addressed to the Librarian at the University of Nottingham.

AMALGAMATED UNION OF ENGINEERING WORKERS

The first engineering societies appeared in the early years of the 19th century, and by 1851 a number of amalgamations had occurred which resulted in the establishment of the Amalgamated Society of Engineers, Machinists, Smiths,

Millwrights and Patternmakers, a new type of union in Britain which served as a 'model' for other national societies. The A.S.E. promoted further amalgamations of all workers in the engineering industry and in 1920 it succeeded in bringing together nine unions to form the Amalgamated Engineering Union. The nine unions covered the Steam Engine Makers, the United Machine Workers, the Smiths and Strikers, the Brassfounders' Society, the North of England Brass Turners, the London Metal Turners, the East of Scotland Brassfounders, the Instrument Makers, and the Toolmakers' Society. Since 1920 there have been several further amalgamations: the Amalgamated Society of Glassworkers Engineers (1944), the Amalgamated Society of Vehicle Builders, Carpenters and Mechanics (1945), the Amalgamated Machine, Engine and Iron Grinders and Glaziers Society (1956), the Leeds Spindle and Flyer Makers' Trade and Friendly Society (1958), the United Operative Spindle and Flyer Makers' Trade (1962), the Turners, Fitters and Instrument Makers' Union (Scotland) (1965). The Amalgamated Union of Foundry Workers joined them in 1966. The present name of the union was adopted in 1971, the occasion of the amalgamation with the Construction Engineering Union and the Draughtsmen's Allied Technicians' Association.

Engineering Section
110 Peckham Road London SE15

Full minutes of the A.S.E. and A.E.U., and rule books, are kept in the strongroom at the union headquarters. These are not open to researchers.

The important records of the union are the monthly, quarterly, half-yearly, annual and abstract reports and levies, which are printed in bound volumes dating from 1851. A full set is housed in the Research Library at union headquarters. Disputes, amalgamations, legal matters, etc., are all covered in these reports. A further set of bound volumes contains shorthand notes of central and special A.E.U. conferences from 1924 to the present. The A.E.U. *Journal*, dating from 1920, contains sections of the reports. Original correspondence has not usually survived, and the union's policy is now to destroy correspondence, press cuttings, pamphlets, etc., after a few years. Two odd box files found in the Library, however, contain papers and correspondence relating to (*a*) war production, dilution (1939-44), and (*b*) post-war reconstruction.

An assortment of records of the early engineering workers' societies is also available. These include registers of members of various societies from the early and mid-19th century, e.g. Todmorden branch; contribution books, e.g. the Greenock branch of the Journeyman, Steam Engine, Machine Makers and Millwrights' Friendly Society (*c*. 1851); minutes (1844-90) of the Wigan branch, and assorted bound reports (1882-1920) of the Steam Engine Makers' Society; a minute book (1841-48) of one of the A.S.E. constituent unions; several minute books of A.S.E. local (and some general) Executive Council meetings (1850s); A.S.E. quarterly returns from branches (1851), a letter book (1854-56) and general information schedules from branches (1876); and photocopies of the first minute book of the A.S.E. Executive Council (1851), and rule books of the Millwrights' Friendly Society (1845) and the Mechanics' Friendly Society (1824).

It would appear that the records of most of the amalgamated societies were never handed over to the A.E.U./A.U.E.W., and it can be assumed that most papers were destroyed. However, it is possible that some materials may survive in the A.U.E.W. divisional offices. Certain local records have already been located. Minute books (1915-44) of the A.S.E./A.E.U. Edinburgh District Committee are available at the National Library of Scotland, together with papers of the Lock-Out Committee (March-June 1922) and the Social Committee (1932-35). Minute books, from 1915, of the Manchester District are kept in their offices. For the records at union headquarters, enquiries should be addressed to the General Secretary.

Foundry Section
16 Chorlton Road Manchester 16

The Amalgamated Union of Foundry Workers (A.U.F.W.) stems directly from the formation of the Friendly Iron Moulders' Society (F.I.M.S.) in 1809. In the mid-19th century the many associations of English and Scottish iron moulders began consolidation into centralised craft unions with a national organisation and funds. But not until 1920 was amalgamation effected between the Friendly Society of Iron Founders (F.S.I.F.), the Amalgamated Iron Moulders of Scotland (A.I.M.S.) and the Associated Society of Coremakers (A.S.C.) to form the National Union of Foundry Workers (N.U.F.W.). In 1946 this was joined by the Ironfounding Workers' Association (I.W.A.) and the United Metal Founders' Society (U.M.F.S.) to form the A.U.F.W., which in 1966 merged into the Amalgamated Union of Engineering and Foundry Workers.

Many of the Foundry section's records are now in the care of the Modern Records Centre, University of Warwick Library. The main series of minute books dates from 1856 and relates successively to the F.I.M.S., F.S.I.F., N.U.F.W. and A.U.F.W. A few branch minutes are also available. Other series include minutes of the Scottish Iron Moulders' Union (later A.I.M.S.) from 1840, the Scottish Iron Dressers (1856-67), the Central Iron Moulders' Association (1889-98), the London United Brassfounders' Society (1890-1909, 1914-41), and the Associated Iron, Steel and Brass Dressers of Scotland (1917-41). The papers of the A.U.F.W. collection include: founding documents; miscellaneous 19th-century material of F.S.I.F.; special circulars; voting papers, etc., of A.I.M.S. and an actuarial report of 1912; N.U.F.W. documents relating to the reconstruction and amalgamation movement; and press cuttings. Among the printed union records are: F.I.M.S. (F.S.I.F.) periodic reports, 1838-1919; S.I.M.U. (A.I.M.S.), an assortment of accounts and reports from the period 1851-1919; C.I.A. (I.W.A.), printed records, 1898-1946; A.S.C., printed records, 1902-19; N.U.F.W., journals (1919-46), etc.; S.B.U., reports for 1930s and national agreements and information (1922-54); National Engineering Joint Trades Movement, memorandum on 'Post-War Reconstruction in the Engineering Industry' (1946); A.E.U., 'Amalgamation: Report of Meeting of Trade Unions in the Engineering Industry' (1956). A number of rule books relating to many of the foundry workers' associations, and dating from 1809, has also been preserved.

A large assortment of Scottish records from 1840-1946 is housed in the National Library of Scotland. These comprise papers of the Scottish Iron Moulders' Union (later the Associated Iron Moulders of Scotland), Central Ironmoulders' Association (later known as the Ironfounding Workers' Association), the Scottish Iron Dressers' Union (later Associated Iron, Steel and Brass Dressers of Scotland), and a few local records of the National Union of Foundry Workers. For the records at union headquarters, applications should be made to the General Secretary of the A.U.E.W. (Foundry Section). The Scottish records are open to bona fide students.

Constructional Section
Construction House 190 Cedars Road Clapham London SW4 0PZ

The Constructional Engineering Union was formed in 1924, from a section of the British Iron, Steel and Kindred Trades Association (see under *Iron and Steel Trades Confederation*). Many records were destroyed by bomb damage in World War II. However, minutes of the Executive Committee (with gaps) have survived, together with copies of the union's journal, and three original enrolment books. Records of conferences, held since 1944, have also been retained. Enquiries should be addressed to the General Secretary of the A.U.E.W. (Constructional Section).

Technical and Supervisory Section
Onslow Hall Little Green Richmond Surrey TW9 1QN

The Association of Engineering and Shipbuilding Draughtsmen was formed in Glasgow in 1913, and in 1960 took the name Draughtsmen's and Allied Technicians' Association. Records are retained at the T.A.S.S. headquarters. They include some committee minutes, verbatim reports of conferences from the union's foundation, an assortment of pamphlets and copies of the Association's journal *The Draughtsman*. Correspondence is not retained. For recent years, copies of *The Vacancy List* and *T.A.S.S. News* are available. J. E. Mortimer's *A History of the Association of Engineering and Shipbuilding Draughtsmen* appeared in 1960. Persons wishing to see the records should apply to the General Secretary.

ANGLO-GERMAN FELLOWSHIP

Originally founded after World War I to improve the relationship between Great Britain and Germany, it fell into abeyance after the return of the Nazis to power, but was reconstituted in 1935 by those who saw Germany as a bastion against Bolshevism. It supported the Munich agreement, and included among its subscribers members of both Houses of Parliament and directors of the Bank of England. Lord Mount Temple, Chairman of the Anti-Socialist and Anti-Communist Union, was Chairman of the Fellowship until November 1938.

Papers

The papers of Lord Mount Temple at the Hampshire Record Office include correspondence, pamphlets and news cuttings, etc., concerning his membership of the Anglo-German Fellowship. A small collection of papers of the late Professor T. P. Conwell-Evans has been promised to the Bodleian Library.

ANTI-SLAVERY SOCIETY FOR THE PROTECTION OF HUMAN RIGHTS
56 Weymouth Street London W1

The Anti-Slavery Society, formed in 1839, merged in 1909 with the Aborigines' Protection Society. In 1957 the Society's present name was adopted. The aims of the Society, in accordance with the principles of the United Nations Declaration of Human Rights of 1948, are the eradication of slavery, the abolition of forced labour resembling slavery, and the protection and advancement of primitive peoples.

Papers

The archives of the Anti-Slavery Society are sent at periodic intervals to Rhodes House Library, Oxford. The papers fall into the following categories:

(1) The main series of general 19th-century correspondence has been arranged in volumes under the names of the officers of the societies receiving them. The societies comprise the Committee on Slavery, formed in 1823, and the British and Foreign Anti-Slavery Society that developed from it; the National Freedmen's Aid Society and the Aborigines' Protection Society, formed in 1838. Letters from Prime Ministers, government offices, foreign legations, etc., and miscellaneous correspondence are preserved in parallel series. In addition to a schedule to these volumes, a card index of the letters is available.

9

(2) The 20th-century letters up to 1960 are again grouped under the name of the Secretary receiving them, with parallel series of letters from government offices and official bodies. A large proportion of the material relates to the career of Sir John Harris.

(3) The next section is rather mixed but includes material relating to the Mico Charity (West Indies schools); minute books of the Committee on Slavery and of the British and Foreign Anti-Slavery Society, 1823-1925, with three volumes consisting of the 1840 minutes of the General Convention for Anti-Slavery, and 1839-43 and 1843-53 memorials and petitions; Anti-Slavery Society 'out' letters, 1869-99; account books, cash books and ledgers, 1846-50, 1866-88, 1899-1941; assorted notes and rough minute books.

(4) A large body of papers covering both the 19th and 20th century is arranged according to the territory to which each group of papers refers, or in a few cases to the subject-matter. Areas represented include the Americas and the West Indies, Asia and the Far East, Africa and Australasia. Subjects take in the various conferences and congresses on slavery, and the activities of the League of Nations and the United Nations.

(5) This section consists of the records of the Committee for the Welfare of Africans in Europe, which was formed during World War I to care for the welfare of the native labour contingents in France and for the fighting forces. These records extend to 1944.

(6) Other items include: a collection of press cuttings, printed papers and boxes of photographs; photographs relating to an expedition to the Congo and São Tomé, 1911-12; engraving plates, blocks and slides used for the Society's publications and lectures; financial records.

Also deposited at Rhodes House Library are the papers of Kathleen, Lady Simon, D.B.E., wife of Sir John Simon and joint President of the Society from 1944-45. The papers are directly connected with her work for the Society, the lectures she gave on slavery and the articles she wrote. A few papers relevant to other interests, including the Zionist movement, are included. The papers comprise correspondence, notebooks, newspaper cuttings and 'territorial' papers.

Availability

Persons wishing to use the papers should apply to the Librarian at Rhodes House.

ANTI-SOCIALIST AND ANTI-COMMUNIST UNION

The Anti-Socialist Union of Great Britain was formed in 1908 as a non-party organisation with the object of exposing the fallacies of Socialists and promoting and supporting measures of 'true Social Reform'. The Union defended the Constitution, the Monarchy, the rights and liberty of the individual, the right to private property, and the sanctity of the home and family life.

Papers

The official records of the Union have not been located. However, a mass of published books, pamphlets and leaflets is available, together with copies of the A.S.U. newspaper *Anti-Socialist* (later known as *Liberty*) which was published 1908-12. Otherwise, material relating to the A.S.U. can be found in certain collections of private papers. These include the Mount Temple MSS. at the Hampshire Record Office, the Blumenfeld papers at the Beaverbrook Library, and the papers of Lady Askwith (wife of the 1st Baron Askwith) with Mrs. Miller-Jones, 8 Egerton Terrace, London SW3. The papers of Walter Long at the Wiltshire

Record Office may be useful. A copy of the conference report inaugurating the A.S.U., and called the 'Conference on the progress of Socialism, 27 October 1907', is deposited at the Guildhall Library, London.

Availability

Persons wishing to see the Mount Temple papers need the permission of the Trustees of the Broadlands Archives Settlement. Enquiries should be addressed to the Hampshire County Archivist. The Blumenfeld papers may be seen by arrangement with the director of the Beaverbrook Library.

ANTI-WASTE LEAGUE

Founded by Lord Rothermere in 1921, the League called for reductions in taxation and government spending. Originally in 1919 Rothermere intended forming an Anti-Waste Party to fight the Coalition Government. Instead the campaign was fought mainly within the Unionist Party, with the League sponsoring candidates at by-elections. Esmond Harmsworth, Rothermere's son, was elected to Parliament in November 1919 on a 'Stop the Waste' ticket, and in June 1921 James Erskine secured an Anti-Waste victory at St. George's, Westminster.

Papers

No League archive as such has been located, and few papers of the 1st Lord Rothermere have survived. The present Lord Rothermere (Esmond Harmsworth), however, does retain some material. Papers relating to the election campaigns of Sir James Erskine are with his granddaughter, Mrs. John Delaney, of Haywards Heath, Sussex.

ARMENIA

A number of British groups and organisations, now defunct, has been involved in the affairs of Armenia and its people. Few archives have been located, but certain papers may be mentioned.

James Bryce was the founder and first President of the Anglo-Armenian Society. The main collection of his papers, which contains a substantial amount of material relating to Armenia, is deposited at the Bodleian Library. Two minute books and other papers (1915-38) of the British Armenia Committee can be found with the *Anti-Slavery Society* (q.v.) collection at Rhodes House, Oxford.

An interesting assortment of papers concerning Armenia is retained at Friends House Library (see under *Society of Friends*). The Friends Armenia Committee was established in 1924 and records extend up to *c.* 1938, including minutes (1925-33), correspondence, accounts, etc., (1926-34), and proceedings of yearly meetings. The private papers of M. N. Fox (1872-1949) contain reports on his work with Armenian refugees (1924-34).

At the British Library, the papers of Dudley Stafford Northcote comprise accounts of Armenia and correspondence and papers (1918-26) relating to his work as Relief Officer for the Armenian Refugees Lord Mayor's Fund. (Add. Mss. 57559-61).

For these and many other organisations concerned with Armenia, printed material is available and other information can be gleaned from other collections of private papers, from the press and from official files at the Public Record Office.

ARMY LEAGUE

The League was active in the 1930s among a group of private individuals with political, military and business experience, who had become increasingly concerned at the weakness of the British Army. The League entered upon a public campaign in favour of rearmament. Among other activities it set up the Citizens Service League to campaign for compulsory National Service. A further campaign to educate public opinion on the need for armaments was launched in the early 1950s.

Papers

The papers of Sir Basil Liddell Hart are the most valuable source so far located. These are at present being catalogued and are to be deposited at the Centre for Military Archives, King's College, London.

The Liddell Hart Collection is supplemented by certain papers (1950s) of Julian Amery, M.P., also at the Centre for Military Archives.

Availability

Applications should be made to the Archivist, C.M.A., King's College, London.

ASSOCIATED SOCIETY OF LOCOMOTIVE ENGINEERS AND FIREMEN
9 Arkwright Road London NW3 6AB

The union was founded in 1880.

Papers

Unfortunately very few records have survived. Over the years, historical records and documents have either become mislaid or been destroyed, and little is retained at the union offices.

ASSOCIATION OF BRITISH CHAMBERS OF COMMERCE
68 Queen Street London EC4

The Association was formed in 1860.

Papers

A substantial archive has been deposited in the Guildhall Library, London EC2P 2EJ. The records comprise the following: minutes of the Executive Council, 1860-1953, with attached drafts; correspondence, reports, memoranda, circulars, rules and regulations, printed Acts of Parliament, newspaper cuttings, etc., 1876-1949; minutes of the President's Advisory Committee, 1921-28; minutes, 6 June 1923, of a Special Committee on the improvement and extension of the Association's work, with a report on members' views about the Committee's recommendations; minutes of the Finance and Taxation Committee, 1921-52, with attached correspondence, notes, etc.; minutes of the Home Affairs and Transport Committee, 1921-51; typescript agenda for meetings of the Home Affairs and Transport Committee, with MS. annotation on proceedings, 1922-30; loose papers relating to these records; miscellaneous committee minutes (subjects include transport, patents and Anglo-Russian trade); typescript agenda for meetings of the

Transport Sub-committee, with MS. annotations, 1922-27; minutes of the Foreign and Colonial Affairs Committee, becoming (May 1928) the Overseas Committee, 1921-52 (vol. 3, 1930-35, is missing); minutes of the Postal Committee, 1925-39. Copies of the annual report are available at the Association's offices.

Availability

Persons wishing to see the records should apply to the Keeper of Manuscripts at the Guildhall Library.

Chambers of Commerce (including, in various cases, Industry and Shipping)[1]

Birmingham. Full set of minutes of the Council from 1900; complete set of volumes of the Chamber's *Journal* from 1903. The records are available to approved researchers, though minutes of the last ten years are confidential.

Bradford. Minutes of Council and committees date from 1851; copies of monthly *Journal* are also retained.

Bristol. The Chamber was founded in 1823, and there is an important set of records from then (although minutes were kept irregularly during the early years), including the minutes of the Council, committees, and various organisations which were affiliated with it, together with annual reports, the earlier issues of which, up to World War I, included statistical material relating to the Port of Bristol and reviews of the year in many of the main manufacturers and trades.

Broadstairs. Minutes, 1903-32, have been deposited in Kent Archives Office.

Cardiff. Records dating from 1850 have been deposited in the Glamorgan Record Office. The records include those of the Cardiff Incorporated Chamber of Commerce, the Cardiff and Bristol Channel Shipowners' Association, the South Wales Coal Exporters' Association, and in general cover the details of coal, shipping and railway activities in South Wales during the past century.

Coventry. This Chamber of Commerce has had a chequered history: it was founded in 1856 and was active until 1889, when it ceased to exist for fifteen years. It was resurrected in 1903. No records of this period survive, however; all the Chamber's books and records were destroyed in 1940.

Derby. Records have been deposited in Derby Public Library.

Devonport Mercantile Association. Minutes date from 1876.

Leeds. Records 1851-1938 have been deposited in the Brotherton Library, Leeds University. They include a full run of minutes, and bound volumes of the more important correspondence. Minutes from 1938 onwards are held by the Chamber but will eventually go to the Brotherton Library. No files are discarded until anything which is likely to be of historical importance has been extracted and filed or bound for the purposes of historical research.

Leicester and County. Minutes of monthly Council meetings survive since the formation of the Chamber in 1860. The Chamber also has copies of yearbooks, issued occasionally from 1921.

London. The Chamber has retained a large amount of records, which can be divided into the following main categories:

(1) Minutes of the Executive Committee, General Purposes Committee and the Finance Committee. The earliest date from 1885.

(2) A whole series of minute books for the furtherance of trade in particular areas of the world, e.g. an East African minute book for 1891, Western Australian for 1896; there are several score minute books of this sort. They are uncatalogued.

---

[1] Except where stated, records are retained by the Chamber concerned.

(3)   Minutes of sub-committees concerned with specific trades, e.g. Silk, Textiles, Canned Goods, etc. Again, these volumes are unsorted and amount to several dozen.

(4)   A variety of records of organisations that have chanced to leave their records at Cannon Street. These include:

    (i)   A minute book of the British-Roumanian Chamber of Commerce.

    (ii)   Minutes of the British Zinc Smelters' Conference, 29 August 1918-24.

    (iii)   A minute book of the Nigerian Chamber of Mines.

    (iv)   Minutes of the London Waterside Manufacturers' Association, 3 volumes: 1903-05, 1905, 1905-20.

In addition, there are extensive records of the Timber Trade Federation, which include general minutes, 1892-1923, Executive Council minutes, 1920-25, attendance books, 1925-28, and the minutes of various committees, including Foreign Importers, 1892-1927, Hardwood Section, 1904-20, Softwood Section, 1920-26, Plywood Propaganda, 1925-28, Retail Section, 1917-28, South-East Section, 1919-25.

Manchester. The older records were deposited with Manchester Central Library in 1935 and the Chamber agreed to deposit further records at eight-yearly intervals. They are made available to accredited students. The deposits have largely been of minute books and include those of the Society of Merchants, 1794-1801, the Manchester Commercial Association, 1845-58, the Manchester Association of Importers and Exporters, 1907-35, and the Manchester Chamber of Commerce from 1821. These latter records include proceedings, board and general minutes, minutes of committees, etc.

Merseyside Chamber of Commerce and Industry (Liverpool Chamber of Commerce). The Liverpool Chamber was founded in 1850, and records dating from 1860 are deposited in Liverpool Central Library. These include minute books of the Council, 1860-64, 1883-1904, 1907-25, and of various committees, e.g. Arbitration, 1914-45, Commercial Law, 1897-1922, the Executive, 1902-25, Finance, 1871-1909, General Purposes, 1882-1925, General Trade, 1900-24; minutes of various country sections, e.g. African trade from 1902, East India and China from 1891, Russia from 1902; and minutes of various industry sections, such as Animal and Meat Trades, Canned Goods, Coal, Motor Trade, Tea Trade, Timber Trade, Tobacco. Other records deposited by the Council include minutes of the Union of Tobacco Manufacturers of Great Britain and Ireland (later Northern Tobacco Manufacturers' Association), 1908-55, and of the Liverpool and Manchester Districts Coal Exporters' Association, 1920-25. Annual reports from 1850 are held at the Chamber's offices, as are copies of the *Journals* issued by the Chamber from 1902.

North Staffordshire. Records dating back to 1875 have survived, comprising minutes, press cuttings and printed yearbooks. The records are unsorted and have suffered from damp.

Southampton. Copies of annual reports date back to 1872. The minutes go back to the 1930s.

Swansea. Although the Chamber was founded in 1846, records date back no further than 1945; older records were destroyed during the war.

Warrington. Records (1876-1915) have been deposited in Warrington Municipal Library.

ASSOCIATION OF CONSERVATIVE CLUBS LTD.
32 Smith Square London SW1

Founded in 1894, the organisation embraces Conservative Clubs throughout the country. The Association aims to promote Conservatism through the medium of member clubs and to encourage close liaison with other Conservative Party organisations.

Papers

Records are housed at the Association's headquarters. They include minute books for the Governing Body from foundation, and for its successors from 1948. A substantial amount of correspondence is retained, but the overwhelming majority of it relates to the services which the A.C.C. provides for its affiliates. There are files relating to the Council and the Executive Committee, but these add little to the minutes. A complete set of bound copies of the *Conservative Clubs' Gazette* from foundation in 1895 to suspension in 1941 is also preserved. The *Clubman* and the *Conservative Clubs' Magazine* are the post-war successors of the *Gazette*.

Availability

Applications should be made to the Secretary.

ASSOCIATION OF EDUCATION COMMITTEES
10 Queen Anne Street London WIM 0AE

The Association was founded in 1903 at a meeting of the new Education Committee established by the 1902 Education Act. Its objects are:

(*a*) to act as a medium of communication between Local Education Committees and the Department of Education or other relevant Government Departments;

(*b*) to consider and take action in respect of any proposed legislation or administrative procedure affecting the powers of Local Education Authorities;

(*c*) to promote interchange of opinion on educational matters;

(*d*) and to take relevant action regarding matters relating to education.

Papers

From foundation to 1932 all that survives is a set of signed minutes of the Association's Executive Committee, and a set of bound volumes of annual reports, together with material of a purely domestic nature, e.g. the acquisition by the Association of a publishing company. No correspondence of this earlier period seems to survive.

From 1932 to the present the Association retains the Executive Committee's minutes, together with all other printed documents. In addition there is a growing volume of correspondence.

Availability

Research facilities are limited and the correspondence is not made available for research purposes; it is received on the basis of complete and lasting confidentiality.

Minutes are published and are available in public libraries.

ASSOCIATION OF PATTERNMAKERS AND ALLIED CRAFTSMEN
15 Cleve Road London NW6 1YA

The union was founded in 1872, as the United Patternmakers' Association. The name was changed in 1968.

Papers

The Association has kept records from 1872, in the form of monthly reports, annual reports and Executive Committee minutes.

Availability

Applications should be addressed to the General Secretary.

ASSOCIATION OF PROFESSIONAL, EXECUTIVE, CLERICAL AND COMPUTER STAFF
22 Worple Road London SW19

The union was established in 1890 as the National Union of Clerks. The words 'and Administrative Workers' were added to the title in 1920, and in 1940 it adopted the name Clerical and Administrative Workers' Union. The present name was adopted in 1972.

Papers

These are housed at the headquarters of the union and include the following: minute books, 1893-98, 1898-1904, 1910-12; minutes of the General Trustees' meeting, 1911; minutes of annual conference, 1898-1907; annual conference agenda, 1913; annual reports, 1907 to date; account books, 1906-10; rules, 1898, 1905, 1907, 1911, 1912 and to date; press cuttings for 1898-1907, 1910, 1911-12; a run of *The Clerk* from 1908 to date; and various other assorted papers for the 1900s.

In addition, certain records of the Association of Shorthand Writers and Typists, later the Association of Women Clerks and Secretaries, survive with the above. These include Executive Committee agenda and minutes, 1903-40, when amalgamation with the Clerical Workers took place; annual reports, 1903-17; rules from the 1900s; press cuttings from 1912; and various documents and papers from about the same period.

Availability

Application should be made to the General Secretary.

ASSOCIATION OF SCIENTIFIC, TECHNICAL AND MANAGERIAL STAFFS
10-26A Jamestown Road London NW1 7DT

The Association was established in 1968 as an amalgamation of the Association of Scientific Workers (A.Sc.W.) (founded in 1918 as the National Union of Scientific Workers) and the Association of Supervisory Staffs, Executives and Technicians (ASSET, formed in 1917 as the National Foremen's Association and later known as the Association of Supervisory Staffs and Engineering Technicians). In 1971 the Medical Practitioners' Union (founded in 1912 as the State Medical

Service Association, and known as the Panel Medico-Political Union, 1914-19, and the Medico-Political Union, 1919-21) amalgamated with A.S.T.M.S. and since that date staff associations and unions, particularly in the finance sector, have joined the Association.

Papers

Records of A.S.T.M.S., ASSET and the Medical Practitioners' Union are presently retained at A.S.T.M.S. Head Office. Also retained at Jamestown Road are extensive records of the Guild of Insurance Officials and the Union of Insurance Workers. Many records of the A.Sc.W. are in the care of the History and Social Studies of Science Division of the University of Sussex. These include minutes of the Executive Committee, 1918-51, of the Council, 1919-68; papers relating to University Activities, 1943-57; conference papers 1942-6; correspondence files for the 1920s and 1930s; branch papers of the North Woolwich branch, and the Central London branch; papers collected by Dr Amicia Young for a proposed history of the A.Sc.W.; and copies of rules, etc.

Availability

For information concerning A.S.T.M.S. and ASSET enquiries should be directed to the Research Department of A.S.T.M.S.; enquiries concerning the records of the Medical Practitioners' Union should be directed to the Medical Secretary; and enquiries concerning A.Sc.W. papers should be addressed to the Secretary, History and Social Studies of Science Division, University of Sussex.

ASSOCIATION OF UNIVERSITY TEACHERS
Bremar House Sale Place London W2

The Association was founded in 1919.

Papers

A number of box files of pre-1945 correspondence has been placed on permanent loan in the Modern Records Centre, University of Warwick Library.

Availability

Enquiries should be directed to the Archivist, Modern Records Centre.

AUTOMOBILE ASSOCIATION
Fanum House Basing Hill Basingstoke Hants

The Automobile Association (A.A.) was founded in 1905 to provide a comprehensive service for motorists. It provides information to motorists, breakdown services and road patrols, technical and legal services, etc.

Papers

The A.A. has retained many records. The minutes of committees are on microfilm and are not available for study. Members of the staff are empowered to answer specific enquiries. The following records are in the care of the Publicity Department: modern files, originating from the Publicity Department, on organisation and work; press cuttings books from 1931 (earlier books were given as salvage during World War I); cuttings books of comment on recent A.G.M.s; press statements, brochures and publications, including annual reports from 1906, and monthly reports to Committee; a complete set of the A.A. house journal, *Fanum Fare*, and the news circular, *Fanum News* and *A.A. News;* alphabetical files of information on motoring topics; alphabetical files on other motoring and transport organisations, e.g. Transport Trust.

Although separate from the A.A. records, the W. Rees Jeffreys collection at B.L.P.E.S. should be noted. This collection contains useful information on the activities of the Motor Union and the Roads Improvement Association.

Availability

Enquiries should be directed to the Publicity Department of the A.A. Enquiries concerning the Rees Jeffreys Papers should be directed to the Librarian, B.L.P.E.S.

BAKERS' UNION
3rd Floor Station House Darkes Lane Potters Bar Herts.

The union was founded in 1849 as the Amalgamated Union of Operative Bakers, Confectioners and Allied Workers; it assumed its present name in 1964.

Papers

These are housed at the union headquarters and include minutes (which include relevant correspondence) from 1914, membership and certain branch records from 1926, records of important wage agreements and runs of the journal, *Journeyman Baker Magazine*, from 1885. The latter has been known as the *Bakery Worker* since 1969, and contains the annual reports.

Availability

By previous appointment with the General Secretary.

BALKAN COMMITTEE

Formed in 1903 by Noel Buxton, the Committee provided a forum for persons concerned with Balkan affairs and the freedom of the Balkan peoples from Turkish rule. James Bryce was the first President, and members included G. P. Gooch, J. D. Bourchier, H. Nevinson and T. P. Conwell Evans (see under *Anglo-German Fellowship*). The Committee continued its work into the inter-war period.

Papers

No formal archive has been located, but material relating to the Committee and its work can be found in various collections of private papers. The papers of Lord Noel-Buxton are in three sections. A substantial amount of material on Balkan affairs (1896-1943) is at present with Professor H. N. Fieldhouse at McGill University, Montreal, Canada; a press cuttings collection is at Duke University, Durham, North Carolina; and the remaining correspondence (c. 1915) is with the Hon. Mrs. J. C. Hogg at Brenchley in Kent. The papers of G. P. Gooch are with Professor Frank Eyck at the University of Calgary, Alberta, and the Nevinson diaries are at the Bodleian Library. As with most foreign affairs pressure groups, the Foreign Office files at the Public Record Office are a rich source of material, and the Committee published reports, leaflets, etc. Other organisations concerned with Balkan affairs include the Serbian Society of Great Britain, the Serbia Relief Fund (World War I), and the Yugoslav Society of Great Britain, for all of which material exists in the papers of R. W. Seton-Watson at the School of Slavonic and East European Studies, University of London.

BAPTIST MISSIONARY SOCIETY
93 Gloucester Place London W1

The Society was founded in 1792 and has been active in Africa, Asia and the Americas up to the present day.

Papers

A very large collection of records is preserved at the Society's headquarters, and a detailed index to the papers has been compiled. Records in the 'Home' section include minutes of the General Committee, 1792-99, 1815-1914 and 1940-44, and minutes and papers of various sub-committees. Letters are carefully arranged by correspondent. Papers relating to finance and property, candidates, medical work and women's work are grouped separately.

The records of the Society relating to its work overseas are arranged according to geographical area. The Africa papers comprise a general collection of minutes, reports and correspondence, and collections relating to the Cameroons, Congo, Angola and Sierra Leone. The records relating to Asia are divided into a general series, and special categories covering Ceylon, Malaya, Japan and Pakistan: the papers relating to India and China constitute two further series of considerable extent.

A further section of the archives relates to the West Indies, and papers relating to Canada, France, Germany, Italy and Scandinavia are all sorted into separate categories. The final section of the archive relates to auxiliaries and other societies, and also includes a variety of unofficial papers.

Availability

The archives may be seen at the Society's headquarters on written application to the Librarian.

BI-METALLIC LEAGUE

Apart from the published literature on bi-metallism, the best sources for the League are certain collections of private papers. Among these, the more important include the A. J. Balfour papers at the British Library (Add. Mss. 49683-49962) and with the family at Whittingehame; the papers of Morton Frewen at the Library of Congress; the R. L. Everrett Collection (to be deposited at the Ipswich and East Suffolk Record Office); and the papers of Henry Chaplin, about which enquiries should be addressed to the Keeper of the Northern Ireland Public Record Office. In addition, a small collection of correspondence between William J. Walsh, Roman Catholic Archbishop of Dublin, and W. R. Moss, 1892-95, concerning Bi-Metallism, is available at the Bodleian Library (ref. MS. John Johnson 13).

BISHOPSGATE INSTITUTE
230 Bishopsgate London EC2

Printed material and two collections of papers at the Bishopsgate Institute are important sources for the development of working-class radicalism in the 19th century. The manuscript collections are described below.

1. *George Jacob Holyoake Papers*

This collection includes a muster roll of Garibaldi's British Legion, with related correspondence, 1860-61; Central Garibaldi Committee, minute book, August

1860-March 1861; MS. and news cutting minutes of the Travelling Tax Abolition Committee, 1877-98; London Atheistical Society, rules, 1842-43, and index of *c.* 5,000 letters from Holyoake, 1845-48; a notebook containing brief notes of lectures, etc., 1838-39; odd pages of a diary for 1845, and diaries, 1849, 1850, 1853-63, 1865-77, 1879-81, 1882-1905; Holyoake's 'Cash Book of the Fleet Street House', 1858-61; letters relating to Collett's *History of the taxes upon knowledge,* 1898-99; copy of an article entitled 'Self-Culture - Uses of Books'; logbooks (i.e. chronological autobiographical notes), 1831-40, 1845; and a diary-cum-notebook, 1847-52.

2. *George Howell MSS*

The collection consists of letter books, 1865-79, 1883-84; industrial notes on engineering, 1909-10; Howell's personal diaries, 1864-73, 1875-83, 1885-89, 1895-97, 1899, 1900, 1902, 1903, 1908, and diaries of Howell's son, George Washington Taviner Howell, 1873-80; George Howell's autobiography (6 volumes).

Trades Union Congress records include: T.U.C. Parliamentary Committee, minutes and reports, 1872; notes on the 3rd annual T.U.C., 7-11 March 1871; notes on the 4th and 5th T.U.C.s, 1872 and 1873; T.U.C. Parliamentary Committee, financial reports and balance sheets, 1871-76.

The Plimsoll Seamen's Fund Committee reports, correspondence, etc., cover the years 1873-75.

Reform League papers include Executive Committee minute books, 1865-69; Executive agenda book, 1867-69; Council minutes, 1866-69; Finance Committee minutes, 1866-68; cash book, 1865-69; account book, 1865-68; Secretary's petty cash book, 1865-66; ledger, 1865-67; Bazaar Committee, 1866; notes, 1865-66; list of departments and branches; branch election reports, 1868.

Other papers include Howell's incoming correspondence, 1865-1911; School Board Election Committee, minute book and letters, 1879; Crystal Palace, Mansion House Committee, minutes, notes, miscellaneous letters, 1877; biography of Ernest Jones, the Chartist; personal diaries of Ernest Jones with notes by Howell, 1840-47; box file of MS. notes, cuttings and other material for the biography of Jones.

Also in this collection are minutes of the International Workingmen's Association, 1866-69, and a history of the Association dated 1900.

Availability

Enquiries concerning these collections should be directed to the Reference Librarian, Bishopsgate Institute.

BOARD OF DEPUTIES OF BRITISH JEWS
Woburn House Upper Woburn Place London WC1

Established in 1760, the Board is the representative body of British Jewry and is recognised by H.M. Government. Synagogues and secular organisations are represented on the Board, which is a deliberative body aiming to watch over the interests of British Jewry, to protect Jews against any disability which they may suffer by reasons of their creed and to take such action as may be conducive to their welfare.

Papers

A mass of material, relating to the Board and its committees, survives in the offices of the organisation. The papers are due to be sorted in the near future but no detailed description is available except by general subject matter. In all the archive is probably equivalent to a 400 foot shelf run.

One section of the records has been sorted into labelled file boxes, with an index. These papers cover the years c. 1915-42 and comprise correspondence, duplicated material and general historical files on world Jewry. A very wide range of subject matter is represented, with files on, for example, national and local organisations, the American Jewish Foreign Affairs Committee (1907-31), South Africa, the 1931 census, the Children's and Young Persons Bill (1929-32), the Slaughter of Animals Bill (1911-23), Unemployment, the Sheerness Disused Cemetery, etc.

A second section of the archive consists of Bound Minute Books, in several series.

Thirdly, there is a mass of more recent files, as yet without an index. Other unsorted material goes back to c. 1930. The records are known to include material relating to anti-semitism, the attitudes of British Jewry towards Nazism and attitudes towards refugees. Many of the documents are of national and international importance.

Finally, the Board holds a range of printed publications.

Availability

At present access to the archives can only be obtained on request. It is hoped however to have the records indexed and easily accessible in due course. Enquiries should be addressed to the Secretary.

BREWERS' SOCIETY
42 Portland Square London W1

The Brewers' Society was formed in 1904 as a result of the amalgamation of the Country Brewers' Society, the London Brewers' Society and the Burton Brewers' Society. Its aim is to promote the interests of the brewing trade.

Papers

The minutes of the former Country Brewers' Society are complete from its foundation in 1822 and there is also one surviving letter book for the early 1870s. No other material prior to 1904 seems to have survived.

After 1904 there are minutes and annual reports to date. Files of correspondence begin in the early 1930s and are full thereafter. Circulars from the Society to its members exist from World War I onwards.

Availability

Applications to see this material should be made to the Secretary. There is no automatic access.

BRITISH AND FOREIGN BIBLE SOCIETY
146 Queen Victoria Street London EC4V 4BX

A product of the Evangelical revival of the 18th-19th centuries, the British and Foreign Bible Society was founded on an inter-denominational basis in March 1804, in order to encourage a wider circulation of the Holy Scriptures at home and abroad. Formed in response to an appeal for Bibles for Wales, it soon widened its scope to supply the countries of Europe and to aid the production of new translations being prepared on the mission field. During the 19th century it established its agencies all round the world, and inspired the formation of many other Bible Societies. This century has seen the development of national Bible

Societies, which co-operate to carry on the work begun by the B.F.B.S. The Bible Societies have published some portion of the Bible in more than a thousand languages.

Papers

The archives of the Society, dating from 1804, are housed at its London headquarters and are open to researchers at the discretion of the Committee. They consist principally of the Committee minutes, correspondence, and financial papers of the parent Society, though records of a few 19th century auxiliary societies are also preserved. The 19th century correspondence, both home and foreign, is arranged chronologically and the letters are indexed by name of writer. The incoming correspondence is missing entirely from 1857-1900. 20th century correspondence is arranged in subject files, and is not fully organised, but it appears that a great deal has been lost. An exception to this is material relating to the translations published by the Society, for which records survive throughout the whole period.

Some local records are preserved at the National Library of Wales, Aberystwyth. These comprise minute books of the Llandysul Auxiliary, 1943-49, and minute books of the Lleyn and Eifionydd (later Pwllheli) Auxiliary, 1823-1938.

Availability

Application should be made to the Society's archivist.

BRITISH AND FOREIGN SCHOOL SOCIETY
7 Stone Buildings Lincoln's Inn London WC2

The Society was formed in 1808 by Joseph Lancaster and others. They aimed to promote educational interests according to the precepts of the Nonconformist churches. The Society flourished in the 19th century and has been active up to the present day.

Papers

Most of the records of the British and Foreign School Society were destroyed in the Temple by bombing in World War II. The surviving material at Lincoln's Inn comprises two MS. minute books, 1809 and 1810, and a book of letters from Lancaster to William Allen. Copies of the annual reports from 1834 are also available. Earlier reports may be seen at the Library of Borough Road College, Isleworth, Middlesex, and at the British Library, which has a complete set from 1809. The College also holds several hundred letters, 1820-45, mainly from South America, and a collection of pamphlets and other printed material relating to the Society and the College, chiefly 19th century. The published history, *A Century of Education, 1808-1908* by R. Bryan Binns, may be supplemented by a thesis, written in the 1930s, using the Society's records and held by the Secretary.

Availability

Researchers wishing to use the records should apply to the Secretary of the Society, or to the Librarian at Borough Road College.

BRITISH ASSOCIATION FOR THE ADVANCEMENT OF SCIENCE
Fortress House 23 Savile Row London W1

The British Association was formed in 1831 with the aim of promoting the study of scientific research and the spread of scientific knowledge.

Papers

A full and important set of minute books exists for the Council and Executive Committee from 1831. Correspondence has not been retained.

Availability

Access to the records of the Association is normally granted on application to the Secretary.

BRITISH ASSOCIATION OF COLLIERY MANAGEMENT
B.A.C.M. House 317 Nottingham Road Old Basford Nottingham

The Association is a registered trade union established in 1947 to cater for the needs of those engaged in the management, scientific development and administration of the coal industry and its ancillary undertakings. It was founded with the co-operation of the National Association of Colliery Undermanagers, the Institute of Mining Surveyors, the National Association of Colliery Managers and the Association of Mining Electrical and Mechanical Engineers.

Papers

The Association has retained its records from its formation in 1947, including minutes and reports and copies of its regular *News Letter.* Correspondence, press cuttings and other material is kept for a period of seven years only.

Availability

Applications should be made to the General Secretary.

BRITISH ASSOCIATION OF MALAYSIA AND SINGAPORE

The Association was founded in 1868 as the Straits Settlements Association by businessmen and others with interests in that area. Later names were the Association of British Malaya (1920) and the British Association of Malaya. The present name was adopted in 1964 and the Association was dissolved in 1973.

Papers

The record books and minute books of the Association are deposited in the India Office Library and in the Library of the Royal Commonwealth Society. The material is of a varied nature and includes correspondence with the Colonial Office, etc., and documents relating to proposals for the constitutional future of Malaya in the immediate post-war years.

Also preserved with this collection is a wide range of material relating to British activities and experiences in Malaya from 1801. The private papers of some civil servants in Malaya, e.g. Sir George Maxwell (1871-1959), and documents relating to the two world wars, are included.

Availability

Applications should be addressed to the Deputy Keeper of the India Office Library and to the R.C.S. Librarian.

BRITISH BROADCASTING CORPORATION

Since its inception in 1926 the British Broadcasting Corporation (from 1922-26 the British Broadcasting Company) has occupied a central position in British public life. Professor Asa Briggs is currently engaged in writing a comprehensive *History of Broadcasting in the United Kingdom*, of which the first three volumes have already appeared.

Papers

The B.B.C. departments (including Television and External Services) have deposited their early papers in the Written Archives Centre, Caversham Park, Reading RG4 8TZ. The period covered at present is 1922-54, and the pre-1927 items are well catalogued with cross-references.

The voluminous archive contains an immense amount of material, including scripts, news bulletins, minutes of meetings, memoranda, personal files and correspondence with writers, speakers and artists. The various aspects of broadcasting at home and overseas, the founding of the B.B.C., broadcasters' personal dealings with the B.B.C., the institutional history of the Corporation and its committees are all covered, together with the full minutes and papers of meetings of the Board of Governors and of other top-level management and departmental meetings, and of the various advisory committees. There are invaluable files concerned with dealings with outside individuals and bodies, including politicians, the press, government departments, and radio and listeners' organisations. Internal memoranda and letters, full daily programme sheets and the records of the *Radio Times* are also preserved. For the World War II period, there are over 7,000 files, with new categories of material including intelligence papers and reports, monitoring digests and special papers written by monitors. Unfortunately a great deal of primary material has been destroyed, particularly concerning the B.B.C.'s Overseas Services, and many files of key papers are incomplete.

Some departments within the Corporation have retained some of their records. For example, the Play Library of sound drama scripts, the Television Drama Script Library, the Recorded Sound Archives and the *Radio Times* Hulton Picture Library are all outside the responsibility of the Written Archives Centre. The Centre does hold B.B.C. publications and a vast collection of press cuttings, relating to broadcasting and the Corporation, and this is supplemented by the more general holdings of the separate News Information Service.

Availability

The material at Caversham Park, with certain limitations, notably copyright, is now open to bona fide researchers. The B.B.C. charges for access at a daily rate with special terms for season-ticket holders. A fee is also charged for research undertaken by the staff. Students wishing to use the Centre should apply in writing to the Written Archives Officer. In the case of materials held by other departments, enquiries should be addressed to the appropriate officer.

BRITISH COMMONWEALTH PEACE FEDERATION

Founded in 1932, the Federation was an association of voluntary members, formed to unite the Empire for world peace and progress; to promote on the part of the Governments of the Empire the initiation and pursuit of policies that would make for international co-operation and peace, and to advance such policies in the Parliaments of the Empire and at international conferences.

Papers

The records of the organisation, apart from the Federation's publications, have not been located. Some references to the Federation, however, occur in the Vyvyan Adams papers at the B.L.P.E.S. Any surviving papers of Walter Ayles, one-time M.P. and Secretary of the Federation, would undoubtedly be of value.

Availability

For the Adams papers, applications should be addressed to the Librarian.

BRITISH COMMONWEALTH UNION
6-14 Dean Farrar Street London SW1

Founded in 1915 as the British Empire Union, the association aims to secure a closer union commercially, politically, socially or otherwise (*a*) between the United Kingdom and all parts of the Commonwealth, and (*b*) between the British Commonwealth and all friendly states. Further, the B.C.U. aims to safeguard British commerce, industry and labour from unfair competition. The Union has worked to counter alien policies and movements opposed to the liberty of the individual and to strengthen the belief in free enterprise.

Papers

A very interesting assortment of records has survived in the B.C.U. offices. The bound minute books are as follows: Executive Committee, 1915-16 and 1916-17; Grand Council, 1917-27; Finance Committee, 1918-20 and 1920-28; A.G.M.s, 1923-67; Finance and General Purposes Committee, 1929-35; Board of Management, 1917-27, 1927-39 and 1939-49. In addition there is an assortment of papers, files and printed material, all in brown paper parcels. The more interesting records include papers relating to the Socialist Sunday School movement in the 1920s and 1930s. The B.C.U. compiled lists of schools, names and addresses of organisers, circulars and articles, published pamphlets and collected speakers' notes (e.g. 'The Church and Socialism', 'Sedition') and pamphlets, news cuttings, etc., relating to the Socialist Sunday Schools and to Socialist activities in general. Other papers include 'Recruiting Campaign Appeal 1937', a file on the Duchess of Atholl, M.P., B.C.U. protests to the B.B.C., registers of members, scripts for films, material for the B.C.U. pamphlet *Danger Ahead*, Empire Day booklets, ball programmes, balance sheets and leaflets. More recent papers and correspondence are retained, in unsorted parcels, e.g. assorted papers, typed minutes, etc., 1954-64, Board minutes and correspondence, 1962-64, and material relating to Rhodesia (1960s). Copies of the annual reports for 1921 and 1928-58 are available, together with bound copies of the journal *Empire Record*.

A large assortment of B.C.U. papers is also included in the papers of Sir Patrick Hannon (one-time Director of B.C.U.) at the Beaverbrook Library. These papers comprise numerous files relating to prospective parliamentary candidates supported by the B.C.U. in elections *c.* 1918-25, assorted committee minutes and papers (e.g. Industrial Group), financial records and legal papers.

Availability

The papers in the B.C.U. office may be seen by arrangement with the Director. Applications to see the Hannon Collection should be addressed to the Director of the Beaverbrook Library.

BRITISH FEDERATION OF BUSINESS AND PROFESSIONAL WOMEN

The British Federation grew out of the Council of the Federation of British Business and Professional Women's Clubs, whose first meeting was held in 1933. It was agreed in January 1935 that membership of professional groups so organised would qualify for membership of the International Federation of Business and Professional Women, and the British Federation was founded later the same year. The Federation has now been dissolved.

Papers

Various papers have been deposited in the Fawcett Library. These date from the early 1950s and include: minutes of the Executive and other committees, 1953-69, minutes and reports of the A.G.M., 1958-71, minutes of the Bridge Committee, 1953-65, financial statements, 1958-71, correspondence dating from the 1950s, various International Federation papers, and copies of the *Newsletter* and the journal, *Women at Work*.

Availability

Enquiries should be directed to the Librarian, *Fawcett Society* (q.v.).

BRITISH FEDERATION OF MASTER PRINTERS
11 Bedford Row London WC1R 4DX

Formed in 1900, the organisation encourages the efficiency and profitability of the general printing industry.

Papers

Minutes of the Council, 1925 to date, survive in the Federation's offices. Also retained are minutes of major committees: Labour and Legislation, from 1927; Technical, from 1930; and Education, from 1957. Copies of the monthly journal, 1902 to date, and the annual reference book, from 1920, are useful. Two published histories may be consulted: Mary Sessions, *The Federation of Master Printers — How it began (1950)*, and Ellic Howe, *B.F.M.P. 1900-1950 (1950)*.

The Society of Master Printers in Scotland and the Edinburgh Association of Master Printers, now integral parts of the British Federation, have retained their records at 10 York Place, Edinburgh. The Society of Master Printers had been founded in 1910 as the Scottish Alliance of Employers in the Printing and Allied Trades, later the Scottish Alliance of Master Printers and in 1960 the final name. Records include full minutes, correspondence, diaries, etc.

Availability

The records of the British Federation are available for reference by approved applicants. Enquiries should be addressed to the Secretary. Enquiries concerning records of the Society of Master Printers in Scotland should be directed to the Secretary, National Register of Archives (Scotland).

BRITISH HOSPITALS CONTRIBUTORY SCHEMES ASSOCIATION
30 Lancaster Gate London W2 3LT

Formed in 1930 to co-ordinate the work of the Hospital Saturday Funds and other contributory schemes, which were collecting to help support the voluntary hospitals. In 1948, with the advent of the National Health Service, the aims of the Association were changed. The present Association provides contributors to the member schemes with benefits supplementary to those offered by the National Health Service.

Papers

An assortment of records has been deposited in the British Library of Political and Economic Science. The papers date from 1930, but most relate to more recent years. The material is in two batches, sorted into boxes. The first set of files includes conference proceedings, 1930-38, reports, 1931-48, Executive Committee minutes, 1946-49, register of members, attendance lists, minutes of Special Purpose Sub-committee, Publicity Sub-committee, Planning Sub-committee, etc., and also several regional area minute books. The second batch of recent records comprises further minutes and papers of various committees, correspondence, 1948-67, circulars, 1948-67, broadsheets and papers of the British League of Hospital Friends.

Availability

Applications should be addressed to the Librarian at B.L.P.E.S.

BRITISH HOUSEWIVES' LEAGUE
33 Ashley Road Epsom Surrey

Formed in 1947, the organisation stands in defence of family life, and against rising prices. It has worked consistently to inform British housewives of the economic consequences of British membership of the European Economic Community.

Papers

Minutes and other records remain confidential to the League. Some material, however, is available: this includes memoranda on the Common Market, a letter to the Prime Minister (1961) and the reply; pamphlets; and copies of the journal *Housewives Today*, published independently but in support of the B.H.L.

Availability

Enquiries should be addressed to the Secretary.

BRITISH HUMANIST ASSOCIATION
13 Prince of Wales Terrace London W8

Ethical societies were formed in Britain in the late 19th century to disentangle moral ideas from religious doctrines, metaphysical systems and ethical theories, and to make them an independent force in personal life and social relations. In 1896 the societies came together to form the Ethical Union, which was incorporated in 1928, and an International Ethical Union was founded in Zurich, also in 1896. The British Humanist Association was formed in 1963 as a front organisation by the Ethical Union and the *Rationalist Press Association* (q.v.). On the withdrawal of the R.P.A. from this new organisation in 1965, the Ethical Union changed its name to the British Humanist Association.

Papers

Records of the B.H.A. and its predecessor the Ethical Union are retained in the Association's offices. They include minute books, annual reports and copies of the various humanist journals.

Availability

The B.H.A. Library is at present being reorganised. Enquiries should be directed to the General Secretary.

BRITISH MEDICAL ASSOCIATION
B.M.A. House Tavistock Square London WC1H 9JP

The Association developed out of the Provincial Medical and Surgical Association, founded in Worcester in 1832 by Charles Hastings. It moved to London in 1855, when it changed its name to the British Medical Association. The B.M.A. is a voluntary association of doctors, forbidden by its articles to take any action which would make it a trade union. Its objects are 'to promote the medical and allied sciences and to maintain the honour and interests of the medical profession'.

Reference should be made to: Ernest Muirhead Little, *History of the British Medical Association, 1832-1932* (1932); and Paul Vaughan, *Doctors' Commons* (1959).

Papers

The records of the Association are retained at B.M.A. House. Several assorted minute books survive covering the early activities of the Association, e.g. single minute books of the Eastern Provincial Medical and Surgical Associations for the 1830s, the Newton (Merseyside) Association, 1837, and the North Staffs. Medical Society, 1863-64.

Fuller minutes of the Association run from about 1860, and particularly since the establishment of the Medical Secretariat in 1909 the records of all committees and of Council have been maintained, viz. minutes, agenda, documents, etc. Committee documents have been, in most cases, individually indexed. Very little original correspondence survives before 1919. What has survived has been card-indexed. Since 1919 correspondence of historical importance has been preserved. With the establishment of the Central Registry in 1947 this correspondence has been more systematically filed, and is arranged under subject headings.

The Association has a complete run of its journal, the *British Medical Journal*, since its inception in 1840, and this is a valuable source of the B.M.A.'s history, including reports of various committees and the annual report of Council (now published as a supplement to the *B.M.J.* in March of each year). The Association Library also has full copies of *The Lancet* and a very good collection of the journals of fellow medical associations throughout the world.

Availability

Applications to use the records should be made in writing to the Secretary, and each application will be considered on its merits.

BRITISH RED CROSS SOCIETY
9 Grosvenor Crescent London SW1X 7EJ

The British Red Cross Society was founded in 1870 as the National Society for Aid to the Sick and Wounded in War. The International Committee of the Red

Cross had been founded earlier in Geneva, in 1863. In 1898 the permanent Central Red Cross Committee was established to draw together the work of the National Aid Society, the St. John's Ambulance Association and the Army Nursing Reserve; and in 1905 the Central British Red Cross Council, as it was now called, amalgamated with the National Aid Society to form the British Red Cross Society. This was granted a Royal Charter of Incorporation in 1908. This declared the aim of the Society as to furnish aid to the sick and wounded in time of war; and in 1919 this was widened to include the improvement of health, the prevention of disease and the mitigation of suffering throughout the world.

Papers

The British Red Cross has established its own archives centre at its National Training Centre, Barnett Hill, Wonersh, near Guildford, Surrey. The records held here include historical reports relating to wars in which service has been given to the sick and wounded since 1870; minute books, from 1905, of the Council's Executive Committees; more than 500 card index boxes containing the personal war service records of members of the Society both in World Wars I and II. Also retained here is a considerable amount of printed material emanating from Geneva, concerning the International Committee and the League of Red Cross Societies. Most correspondence is destroyed at regular intervals. Current correspondence is filed at the Central Filing Department in London; similarly, international correspondence is retained by the International Relations Department. Certain papers, relating to the Society's work in World War I are deposited in the Imperial War Museum.

The British Red Cross has published a journal, known as *Red Cross* from 1914 to the 1930s, then as *News Review,* and since 1971 as *Cross Talk.*

Availability

All enquiries concerning the archives of the British Red Cross should be directed to the archivist at the National Training Centre; or to the Keeper of Documents at the Imperial War Museum.

BRITISH SHIPPING FEDERATION
Shipping Federation House 146-150 Minories London EC3N 1ND

The Federation was formed in 1890, at a time of embittered industrial conflict, to promote better relations between shipping employers and sea-going personnel. Membership extends at the present time to almost 200 shipowners and ship managers. The work of the Federation falls into three broad divisions: the regulation of employment conditions throughout the Merchant Navy and the representation of members in negotiations with the various seafarers' organisations; recruitment, training and the supply of crews for ships in the Merchant Navy; and daily services to individual shipowners.

Papers

The records of the Federation back to 1890 are housed at the Federation's offices. The papers are largely uncatalogued and unsorted. However, the collection includes such items as minutes of the main committee meetings, annual reports, and circulars of general interest to shipowners. Each year from 1890 to about 1951 all the important (mostly printed) papers were bound together into so-called 'Grey Books'. Correspondence is retained on a selective basis. Important subjects have their own series of papers.

Availability

Although the Federation does not have the facilities of a library and records officer, it does on occasions arrange for persons undertaking research to go through the records. Applications should be made in writing to the Secretary.

BRITISH-SOVIET FRIENDSHIP SOCIETY
36 St John's Square London EC1

The Society was founded in 1946 as a successor to the Anglo-Soviet Friendship Committee, formed in 1940. Earlier predecessor organisations were the Russia Today Society, founded in 1934, and the Friends of the Soviet Union, established in 1930. The Society aims to strengthen peace and friendship, understanding and trade between Great Britain and the U.S.S.R., to promote and develop friendly association between the peoples and organisations of the two countries, and to act as a source of factual information on the two countries.

Papers

Nearly all early correspondence and other records were lost in 1958 when the offices of the Society were transferred. However, some minute books of the Society and its predecessors exist, and the Society possesses a rich collection of leaflets, pamphlets and similar material. Many of these are not to be found elsewhere.

Availability

Any application to see the records of the Society should be addressed to the General Secretary. All applications will be considered on their merits.

BRITISH TEXTILE EMPLOYERS' ASSOCIATION (COTTON, MAN-MADE AND ALLIED FIBRES)
5th Floor Royal Exchange Manchester M2 7ED

Formed in 1969, the Association incorporates the former Federation of Master Cotton Spinners' Associations, the British Spinners' and Doublers' Association, the U.K. Textile Manufacturers' Association and the Textile Finishing Trades' Association. The organisation acts on behalf of employers in the trade to protect their interests in the commercial, economic and industrial fields.

Papers

The Association holds annual reports of the employers' associations on the spinning side of the industry back to 1892, and minutes of meetings, etc., of the weaving organisations back to the 1870s. Copies of all the statistical information connected with the industry published by the now defunct Textile Council and its predecessor organisations are also preserved by the Textile Statistics Bureau (Cotton, Man-made and Allied Fibres) Ltd., 5th Floor, Royal Exchange, Manchester M2 7ER.

Further interesting records of the cotton-spinning industry are included in the Barber-Lomax Collection at the Lancashire Record Office. As well as recent annual reports, etc., of the Federation of Master Cotton Spinners' Associations (and its successors) and of the Bolton Master Cotton Spinners' Association, the collection comprises drafts, notes, reports and papers relating to the cotton-spinning industry produced by the employers' associations and by various government departments, dating back to 1930. Full records (1870-1970) of the Oldham and District Textile Employers' Association have been deposited in Manchester University Library. These include letter books, reports, papers on wage bargaining, industrial conditions, etc.

Availability

Enquiries should be addressed to the Secretary of each organisation as appropriate.

BRITISH VIGILANCE ASSOCIATION and NATIONAL COMMITTEE FOR THE SUPPRESSION OF TRAFFIC IN PERSONS

The National Vigilance Society was founded in 1885, with the aim of suppressing 'traffic in persons' and protecting young people. It amalgamated with the National Committee for the Suppression of Traffic in Women in 1953 to form the British Vigilance Association. This was disbanded in 1972.

Papers

Various unsorted and uncatalogued records, including minutes, correspondence and reports, have been deposited in the Fawcett Library. At the time of writing no detailed examination of this collection had been made.

Availability

Applications to be made to the Librarian, Fawcett Library.

BRITISH WOOL CONFEDERATION
Lloyds Bank Chambers Hustlergate Bradford BD1 1PH

The Confederation was formed in 1973 from the old British Wool Federation (1904) and the Woolcombing Employers' Association, founded in 1910.

Papers

Many of the B.W.F. records have been destroyed, but copies of circulars issued since 1938 and minute books from the early 1920s have survived. All the more important records for the W.E.A., along with those of its 'daughter', the Woolcombers' Mutual Association Ltd. (formed in 1933), are retained in the Confederation's offices.

Availability

All enquiries concerning the records should be addressed to the Secretary.

BRITISH WORKERS' LEAGUE

The British Workers' National League was formed in 1916, by Victor Fisher (1870-1954), A. M. Thompson (1861-1948), and others, as a successor to the Socialist National Defence Committee (1915). This organisation of patriotic labour received support from several Members of Parliament, and financial assistance from Lord Milner. The League's aims embodied many of Milner's views on Socialism and the Empire. It called primarily for mobilisation of working-class opinion behind the war effort, and democratic federation and commercial preference within the British Empire. In 1917 the League began to adopt prospective parliamentary candidates, and the following year formed the National Democratic Party as a patriotic working-class party in support of the Coalition. 20 Victor Fisher candidates received the Lloyd George 'coupon', and 10 were elected to Parliament. In the following years, however, support for the N.D.P. was not sustained, with most losses to the Labour Party. The B.W.L. journal *Empire Citizen* ceased publication in 1927.

Papers

The official records of the League and the N.D.P. have not been located. However, copies of the published journals, *Clarion, British Citizen and Empire Worker* and *Empire Citizen* (1921-27), are available. Other material exists in the Milner Collection at the Bodleian Library and in the Lloyd George papers at the Beaverbrook Library. The Bonar Law Collection in that Library also includes some relevant papers. No papers of Victor Fisher appear to have survived, but the correspondence of A. M. Thompson is housed at Manchester Central Library.

Availability

The journals can be found at the British Library. For the personal papers, scholars should apply to the relevant Librarian, and for the Milner papers to the Warden at New College, Oxford.

BUILDING SOCIETIES ASSOCIATION
14 Park Street London W1Y 4AL

The Association was founded in 1869, as the National Association of Building Societies. Its work includes the assembly and dissemination of information, advisory services, collective advertising, and negotiations with the Government.

Papers

The records of the above organisation are housed in the Association's offices. Apart from minutes of the Association, which are complete, there is a series of letter books for the early 1930s. In addition, a complete set of all circulars, memoranda, etc., sent out by the Society exists in the Secretary's office. Otherwise there is no surviving archival material.

Availability

Applications should be addressed to the Secretary.

CAMPAIGN FOR NUCLEAR DISARMAMENT
14 Gray's Inn Road London WC1

Founded in 1958, the movement called in the first instance for unilateral nuclear disarmament. Militant members of the Campaign later formed the Committee of 100.

Papers

An assortment of records has been deposited at the B.L.P.E.S. which is at present arranged in approximately 40 box files and parcels, and over 70 loose files. The material includes minutes of Council and the Executive Committee, a very large collection of correspondence, duplicated leaflets and handouts, press cuttings and copies of the various C.N.D. publications, e.g. the journal *Sanity* (1961-70), *Youth Against the Bomb* and *Resurgence*. Other files relate to the annual conferences (1959-70), Easter Campaigns, the National Committee, the youth movement, administration, advertising, finance, material for magazines, Vietnam, the 'Ministry of Disarmament', the Committee of 100 and other peace groups.

A further collection of C.N.D. papers and printed material, accumulated by Dr. Mansel Davies as Secretary of the Aberystwyth Nuclear Weapons Committee, has been deposited at the National Library of Wales. The papers include a minute book (1958-60) of the Committee, correspondence, Davies's notes and typescripts, scientific papers, pamphlets and posters, press cuttings and journals.

Availability

Applications should be addressed to the Librarian, B.L.P.E.S.

CANNING HOUSE
2 Belgrave Square London SW1X 8PJ

The institution incorporates the Hispanic Council and the Luso-Brazilian Council, which were both founded in 1943 and which aim to promote closer relationships between the United Kingdom and the countries of Latin America, Spain and Portugal. These Councils were merged into one in 1973, when a further Canning House Economic Affairs Council Ltd. was established for the purpose of furthering economic and trade relations with Latin America.

Papers

Annual reports of the two Councils from 1943 have been retained. Collections of economic, statistical and cultural reviews on Latin America are available.

Availability

Enquiries should be addressed to the Librarian.

CARLTON CLUB
69 St. James's Street London SW1

Founded in 1832, the Carlton is both a social club and a political institution, which has included in its membership lists all the great names of the Conservative Party.

Papers

Unfortunately many records were destroyed during the war when the Club was bombed. Researchers should refer to the revised history of the Club: Sir Charles Petrie, *The Carlton Club* (1972).

CATENIAN ASSOCIATION
8 Chesham Place London SW1X 8HP

Founded in 1908 as the Chums' Benevolent Association, the society brings together Roman Catholic laymen in the professions, business and public service for social and charitable activities.

Many records were destroyed upon the Association's removal from its Manchester offices in 1947. However, recent records and such records as survived, which include all the minute books of the Grand Council, copies of the yearbook and journal, are preserved at the Association's headquarters.

Availability

Enquiries should be addressed to the Grand Secretary.

CATHOLIC EDUCATION COUNCIL FOR ENGLAND AND WALES
41 Cromwell Road London SW7

Founded in 1847 as the Catholic Poor Schools Committee, the organisation was re-established in 1905 under the present name. The Council promotes the development of Catholic education in England and Wales.

Papers

Apart from annual reports which are extant from 1847, only the most recent records have survived. Minutes, correspondence and printed material are complete from 1949, with press cuttings from 1935.

Availability

The records are housed in the head office. Limited access is granted by arrangement with the Secretary.

CATHOLIC RECORD SOCIETY
Hon. Secretary, c/o 114 Mount Street London W1

The Society was founded in 1904 by a group of scholars under Archbishop Francis Bourne, Archbishop of Westminster. The Society's objects were stated to be 'the transcribing, printing, indexing and distributing to its members, of the Catholic Register of Baptisms, Marriages and Deaths and other old Records of the Faith, chiefly personal and genealogical, since the Reformation in England and Wales'. From 1952, when the constitution of an educational charity was adopted, the aim became 'the advancement of education in connection with the history of Roman Catholicism in England and Wales since the Reformation'.

Papers

The Society has retained its minute books and correspondence from 1904. The minutes are often brief and formal, and the correspondence is not yet indexed. Papers were assembled annually and filed alphabetically according to subject-matter or correspondent. A complete run of the annual reports also exists: these were not always printed and sometimes contain lists of subscribers and members of Council.

Availability

The papers are housed at the library in Mount Street. Access is restricted. Written applications should be addressed to the Society's Secretary, and the Council will consider each individual case on its merits.

CATHOLIC TRUTH SOCIETY
P.O. Box 422 38-40 Eccleston Square London SW1V 1PD

Founded in 1868 by Dr. (later Cardinal) Vaughan, the Society aims to spread the Catholic faith and practice by the promotion of knowledge about it.

Papers

The Society possesses minute books from 1884, and a printed index covering the 1884-1938 minutes.

Availability

These records are private. A pamphlet setting out the history of the Society can be obtained from the General Secretary.

CATHOLIC UNION OF GREAT BRITAIN
18 The Boltons London SW10 9SY

Founded in 1872, the Catholic Union of Great Britain is an association of members of the English, Welsh and Scots Catholic laity set up to express and defend Catholic principles and interests and the Christian standpoint in public affairs, irrespective of political party. Its special field of activity is the representation, where necessary, of Catholic interests in Parliament, to Ministers of government departments, and to other public authorities or national bodies. A Parliamentary Sub-committee of the Standing Committee, which is composed of Roman Catholic members of both Houses of Parliament and certain Catholic legal experts, keeps the Union informed of all Bills coming before Parliament which appear likely to affect the Christian conscience.

Papers

An assortment of early records has been deposited at the Westminster Archives, Archbishop's House, London SW1P 1QJ. These papers include minutes, annual reports and subject files. All other records are retained by the Secretary. These include a large amount of correspondence on a variety of subjects, e.g. birth control and euthanasia. The Union's published material includes *Your Death Warrant*, ed. Jonathan Gould and Lord Craigmyle (1971).

Availability

The papers are not generally open to researchers, but enquiries should be addressed to the Secretary who will consider any application on its merits.

CHEMICAL INDUSTRIES ASSOCIATION LTD.
Alembic House 93 Albert Embankment London SE1 7TU

The Association was formed as recently as 1966, from the merger of the Association of British Chemical Manufacturers and the Association of Chemical and Allied Employers.

Papers

All the records of the constituent associations, dating back to about 1917, are preserved at the Association's offices. They are not catalogued, but papers are classified under their numbers in the original filing systems of the two associations.

Availability

Application should be made to the Economic Intelligence Officer of the Association.

CHINA ASSOCIATION
18 Diamond House 37-38 Hatton Garden London EC1N 8EB

The Association was established in 1889 by a group of businessmen with interests in China. Two associated societies have recently been formed, the Japan Association in 1950 and the Hong Kong Association in 1961. The Association aims to represent, express and give effect to the opinion of the British mercantile community in their political and commercial relations with the Chinese and Japanese; to promote and protect British trade, commerce, shipping and manufacturers in the Far East; to promote or oppose legislative or other measures affecting such trade; and to act as a charitable and social organisation for persons interested in the China trade.

Papers

A substantial collection is at present kept at Diamond House. The former Secretary is compiling a detailed index of the main subjects, in date order, in every report, minute and letter. Minute books of the Association are continuous from 1889, with Executive Committee minutes for the years 1943-45, 1956-61. Annual reports are also in series from foundation. These records are complemented by a letter book, 1893-97, circulars to members, 1907-28, 1946-54, and committee papers, 1927-45, 1956-66. A parcel of correspondence with the Foreign Office (1945-67) is of particular interest. Other special files relate to Civil War in China, 1948-49, relinquishment of extraterritorality, 1943, a new treaty of commerce and navigation, 1944-46, Hong Kong textiles, 1958, and the establishment of the Japan Association in 1950. A large press cuttings book, 1940-47, is available, together with a number of photograph albums. The archive also includes a good selection of branch records, e.g. Tientsin, A.G.M. minutes, 1936-39, 1941; Shanghai, A.G.M. minutes, 1920-23, and assorted reports; Hankow, reports, 1919-20; and some papers (1909) of the Association's Incorporated School of Practical Chinese. Finally, certain British Chamber of Commerce records survive: Shanghai, minutes, circulars and some correspondence, 1946-52, reports, 1948-51; Tientsin, minutes and circulars, 1947-52; Hankow, minutes, 1947-52.

Availability

Applications should be addressed to the Secretary.

CHRISTIAN ACTION
2 Amen Court London EC4

Christian Action was founded in 1949 to encourage involvement of Christians as Christians in social and political affairs. One of the offshoots of Christian Action is the Defence and Aid Fund, originally established in the 1950s as a 'treason fund' for defendants accused of treason in South Africa.

Papers

Christian Action has retained all its minutes back to the date of its foundation. Also, most of its correspondence has been kept since the early 1950s. Christian

Action has additionally maintained press cutting files about its activities; these are very full for the period 1949-69 but are rather less full for subsequent years.

Availability

The records may be seen on written application to the Secretary.

CHRISTIAN SOCIAL UNION

Formed in 1889 by Scott Holland, Charles Gore and Bishop B. F. Westcott, the C.S.U. stands with the Anglo-Catholic Guild of St. Matthew (1877) and the *Church Socialist League* (q.v.) among Anglican Christian Socialist groups. The Union was, however, less 'Socialist' in outlook than the others, more narrowly sectarian than the League, and generally was the organisation of the clerical, public school and intellectual wing of the movement. Rooted in the Oxford Movement, the 'sacramental Socialists' owed much to F. D. Maurice as also to non-religious stimuli, but had for their cause a firm theological foundation, drawing on the Bible, the tradition and doctrines of the Church and the 'immanentalist' argument to affirm loudly that one is a Socialist by the very fact that one is a Christian. By the late 1890s the radical spirit of the C.S.U. had already waned, the organisation appeared anaemic and narrow and, though not disbanded until the 1920s, the Union was superseded by the League.

Papers

Some records have been deposited at Pusey House Library, Oxford. These comprise annual reports and occasional letters, 1905-13, and papers of the Oxford University branch. These include minutes, 1889-1923, reports, lists of members and pamphlets. For the years 1920-23, the organisation was called the Industrial Christian Fellowship. Other material is available with the Community of the Resurrection, Mirfield, Yorks., and in the published journals and literature of the Christian Socialist movement.

Availability

Applications should be addressed to the Librarian at Pusey House.

CHURCH ARMY
185 Marylebone Road London NW1 5QL

Founded by Prebendary Wilson Carlile in 1882, the Army is an Anglican body of Evangelists. Among its activities the Church Army runs welfare hostels, youth centres, old people's homes and has a workshop for the disabled. The Evangelists work in prisons, hospitals and with the armed forces, among drug addicts, and in the sphere of moral welfare. Many officers work with clergy in the parishes and others hold missions. Earlier in the century much work was undertaken among the unemployed.

Papers

The published records, journals, etc., of the Church Army, from commencement to the present day, are open for inspection. Minute books and other original materials are retained, but they remain confidential to the society and are not available. However, specific questions relating to matters previous to 1940 may be answered.

Enquiries should be addressed to the Archives Officer.

CHURCH MISSIONARY SOCIETY
157 Waterloo Road London SE1

The Society was founded in 1799 under the auspices of the Church of England for world-wide missionary work. The C.M.S. has enjoyed an active history to the present day.

Papers

The very large collection of records at the Society's headquarters has been carefully catalogued.

1. *Home*

(a) *General Secretary's Department.* Committee minutes and general correspondence date from 1799. A number of special categories include the correspondence relating to conferences (1910), education (1910), finance (1860, 1917), medical work (1935-65) and political and religious matters (1911). The series entitled 'Outside Organisations' (1872-81, 1911) includes correspondence with the Conference of British Missionary Societies and the International Missionary Council. The Department also embraces correspondence with missions overseas. The overseas correspondence, which is mostly 20th century, is sorted according to geographical area and country.

(b) *Candidates Department.* The records comprise minutes of the Candidates Committee (1906), papers and letters. Correspondence with the Overseas Education Secretary (1951), and with C.M.S. associations in Canada (1894-1923), New Zealand (1892-1927, 1936-1937), New South Wales (1893-1938), South Africa (1895-1923) and the West Indies (1897-1912), is also filed with the records of this department.

(c) *Finance Department.* The records embrace committee minutes from 1842 onwards, journals (1806), day books, cash books and ledgers. Papers relating to the Legal Section (minutes, 1885) are preserved with the records of this department.

(d) *Home Department.* The records, including minutes, reports, diaries, memoranda and correspondence, relate to the work of the Society within the British Isles, covering all aspects of publicity for and information about the Society. Other papers relate to deputations, recruiting, overseas visitors, partnerships, 'general wants', junior work, youth work, the study section, the Library, exhibitions and literature production. The period covered by these records is the 20th century, and most categories relate to a few years only.

(e) *Medical Department.* The minutes of various committees (Medical Committee, 1891) are assembled with a collection of reports and accounts relating to the Society's medical work. The correspondence with missions overseas, the earliest dating from 1910, is arranged by countries.

(f) *Woman Secretary's Department.* The minutes, correspondence and papers date from 1895.

2. *Overseas*

Minutes, correspondence and papers relating to the Society's operations in each mission area have been preserved.

(a) *Africa.* In addition to the general minutes (1880), the records relate to work in Kenya (from 1842), Mauritius (1856), Nigeria (1844), Sierra Leone (1823), Sudan (1905), Tanganyika (1900) and Uganda (1898).

(b) *Americas.* Correspondence and papers cover the Society's operations in Canada (Rupert's Land, 1821-1930, and British Columbia, 1857-1925) and the West Indies (1818-61).

(c) *Asia.* In addition to the general series regarding East Asia and West Asia, the categories of papers relate to Ceylon, Japan and to each of the numerous missions in India and China. The papers date from 1813 for Ceylon and India, with China from 1834 and Japan from 1875.

(d) *Australasia (New Zealand).* Papers cover the period 1819-1914.

(e) *Middle East.* The 'Mediterranean' records cover missionary work in Abyssinia (1830-41), Asia Minor (1818-80), Egypt (1826), the Greek islands (1815-80), Malta (1811-43) and Palestine (1849). Records of the work in Persia (from 1876) and Arabia (1898-1924) are also preserved.

3. *Auxiliaries, Other Societies and Unofficial Papers*

C.M.S. Associations and Unions in various parts of the United Kingdom kept their own minutes, many of which are now deposited in the archives. The C.M.S. collection also includes the records of the Church of England Zenana Missionary Society, founded 1880; the Eclectic Society of London, 1783-1814; the Female Education Society, 1834-99; and the Loochow Naval Mission, 1843-61. A number of individual missionaries' private papers are also deposited with the Society.

Availability

Applications should be addressed to the Archivist.

CHURCH OF ENGLAND CHILDREN'S SOCIETY
Old Town Hall Kennington Road London SE11 4QD

Founded in 1881 by Edward de Montjoie Rudolf as the Church of England Waifs and Strays Society, the organisation cares for children in need by means of adoption, foster homes and children's homes. The Society changed its name to the present form in 1946, and now complements the work of the local authorities in this field.

Papers

Many records of the Society have been preserved, not all of them in good order, and some of the records at present kept at the Society's headquarters in the Old Town Hall have been affected by flooding, general deterioration and the intrusions of mice. The headquarters were bombed during the war and flooding occurred during the subsequent fire-fighting. Many correspondence files remain, much of the correspondence relating to the administration of the children's homes in all parts of the country, often giving a picture of social standards at the turn of the century. The main records for the history of the Society are the annual reports from foundation, and the Society's journal, originally called *Our Waifs and Strays,* also dating from 1881. These records are preserved in good order at the Society's Conference Centre at Alveston Leys, near Stratford-upon-Avon, together with a large but miscellaneous collection of Branch Committee minute books, punishment books, diet books, matrons' logbooks, etc. Also at the Conference Centre are such items as Victorian collection boxes, appeals posters and notice boards, and a small collection of Victorian children's clothing and toys. Personal files (since 1881) on nearly 100,000 children who have been in the Society's care are preserved and form an important source for social historians, though the earliest records are scanty. The first 30,000 files are in the Greater London Record Office and the rest are still in the Society's offices. Among published material relating to the Society are an early history entitled *The First Forty Years*, written by Edward de Montjoie Rudolf; *Everybody's Children*, by Mildred de Montjoie Rudolf (Oxford, 1950); and *Thirteen Penny Stamps*, by John Stroud (1972); There are also many personal records of the founder of the Society, Edward de Montjoie Rudolf, mainly consisting of the diaries and scrapbooks which he maintained from boyhood until his death in 1933 and which are in the possession of his family.

Availability

Enquiries should be addressed to the Director.

CHURCH PASTORAL AID SOCIETY
Falcon Court 32 Fleet Street London EC4Y 1DB

Formed in 1836 by a committee under Lord Shaftesbury, the Society grants aid towards maintaining men and women to assist the incumbents of parishes. The C.P.A.S. has been of some influence in its control of Church of England patronage. These patronage responsibilities operate completely within the Church. The Society administers the Patronage Trusts of the Martyrs' Memorial and 'Church of England Trust, and of the Church Trust Fund.

Papers

Many records were destroyed by bombing in World War II. A complete set of fairly comprehensive annual reports from 1836, and a set of bound volumes of the journal *Church and People* from the first edition in 1889, have survived. Minute books forming an almost complete series have also been preserved. The Society also holds a collection of films and photographs dating from the 1920s and 1930s.

Availability

Although the minutes are not open to public inspection, the printed records may be seen by appointment with the Secretary.

CHURCH SOCIALIST LEAGUE

This was founded in 1906, developing as a result of discontent among Christian Socialists with the Guild of St. Matthew and the *Christian Social Union* (q.v.). Its platform was more clearly Socialist than any other Christian organisation of the period: 'The Church Socialist League consists of Church people who accept the principles of Socialism.' Its policy was sympathetic to Guild Socialism (see *National Guilds League*). After a series of splits, the League was dissolved in 1924.

Papers

No central collection of records relating to the League has been discovered. The most valuable single source is the journal, *Church Socialist*, published by the League from 1908-21. M. B. Reckitt was editor of this journal, 1914-19. He has retained a very substantial collection of printed material relating to the work of the League. This will be donated to the Library of the University of Sussex on Mr. Reckitt's death. A microfilm of certain of Mr. Reckitt's papers is available in Hull University Library. Also in Hull University Library are the papers of Conrad Noel, whose

Catholic Crusade was a breakaway from the League. For further details on these collections, and other relevant material, see *National Guilds League.*

The Community of the Resurrection, Mirfield, Yorks., was a centre of 'social sacramentalism' during this period and several of its members were prominent in the work of the League, particularly Fathers Samuel Healy and P. B. Bull. Reference should be made to the Library of the Community, which retains both printed and manuscript material. The records of the Community have now been deposited in the Borthwick Institute of Historical Research, York. One minute book (1911-16) of the 'London Over the Border' group is housed at the Stratford Reference Library of the London Borough of Newham.

Relevant material has been used in the following books: Peter d'A. Jones, *The Christian Socialist Revival, 1877-1914* (Princeton, 1968); M. B. Reckitt, *P. E. T. Widdrington* (1961).

CHURCH UNION
Faith House 7 Tufton Street London SW1P 3QN

The Church of England Protection Society was formed in 1859, and was renamed the English Church Union in 1860, when it incorporated several local Church societies. Its object was to defend and propagate High Church principles. In 1934 the English Church Union was united with the Anglo-Catholic Congress to form the Church Union.

Papers

The bulk of the Union's records have been deposited in Lambeth Palace Library. These consist of the surviving records of several constituent societies, as well as of the Union itself. They may be listed as follows:

(*a*) *Bristol Church Union.* Minutes of general meetings, 1848-67, and minutes of the Committee for the same period.

(*b*) *English Church Union.* 20 volumes of minutes of general meetings, 1866-1933; agenda and papers for Council meetings, formerly filed with minutes, for the period 1923-33; a case book of legal opinions, 1867-72; 10 volumes of minutes of the Legal Committee, 1868-1947; 5 volumes of minutes of miscellaneous committees, 1878-1933; Sustentation Fund Committee minutes, 1877-1927, together with a letter book of C. L. Wood, President of E.C.U., 1868-70; Educational Work Committee minutes, 1891-94; Press Committee minutes, 1891-94; Canon Law Committee minutes, 1891-98; and the minutes of the Finance Committee, 1906-33, and of several other specialist committees covering the 1920s and 1930s. In addition, correspondence and papers survive concerning the scheme for amalgamation of the E.C.U. and A.C.C. in 1932.

(*c*) *Catholic Union for Prayer.* Register of members, 1867-78.

(*d*) *Anglo-Catholic Congress.* Minutes of Council meetings, 1923-33; minutes of the Executive Committee, 1919-33; proceedings of the anniversary meetings, 1923-31; minutes of the Finance Committee, 1923-33; minutes of miscellaneous committees for the period 1921-52; five scrapbooks, 1924-39; and autograph registers of members, 1923-33.

(*e*) *Church Union.* Minutes of the Financial Committee, 1934-39; and minutes of the 'Committee on Report of Archbishops' Commission on the Relations of Church and State', 1936; of the Tewkesbury Convention Committee, 1937-38; the Women's Association Administrative Committee, 1937-39; and an analysis of parochial returns from English dioceses concerning the extent of Reservation of the Sacrament, 1949, together with returned questionnaires and analysis for a similar survey in 1954.

Enquiries as to the use of the above papers should be addressed to the Archivist, Lambeth Palace Library. In addition to the above papers, there are about six packing-cases and a number of parcels of assorted, uncatalogued papers concerning the Church Union at Pusey House, 61 St. Giles, Oxford. Enquiries should be directed to the Librarian, Pusey House.

CHURCH'S MINISTRY AMONG THE JEWS
Vincent House Vincent Square London SW1P 2PX

Founded in 1809 as the London Society for Promoting Christianity among the Jews, the society has undertaken Christian evangelisation among the Jewish people and reminds the Christian Church of its Jewish origins and its continuing obligations to the Jewish people.

Papers

A very full archive has been deposited in the Bodleian Library. The records comprise minute books of the General Committee (1808-90, 1893-1940) and sub-committees; and papers concerning the society's finances, its property, its staff, the general mission work of the society, mission work in England and in Israel.

Availability

Applications should be addressed to the Keeper of Western Manuscripts at the Bodleian Library.

CIVIL SERVICE UNION
15-21 Hatton Wall London EC1N 8JP

The Civil Service Union was founded on 22 October 1917, as the Minor Grades Association. In 1960 the Association amalgamated with the Civil Service Association of Minor Grades.

Papers

The Union records are preserved at the headquarters in London. The records are incomplete, but a proportion of useful material has survived. The minutes of the National Executive Council date from 1936, and membership records go back to October 1917. The reports of the N.E.C. from 1936 include the main information on wage agreements and negotiations. Copies of the *Journal* from 1943 are preserved, together with reports by Honorary Organisers from 1963 and also papers relating to legal cases from 1964.

Availability

The records are open to researchers and scholars by appointment with the General Secretary.

CLARION MOVEMENT

The *Clarion* newspaper was founded in 1891 by a group of radical Manchester journalists led by Robert Blatchford. Around this journal, committed to an ethical Socialism, a substantial movement developed, with particular strength in the working class of the Northern and newer urban centres, combining social and recreational as well as political activities. The movement developed a great impetus after the publication, and great success, of the penny edition of Blatchford's *Merrie England* in 1894. By the late 1890s Clarion Scouts, cycling groups (a National Clarion Cycling Club was founded in 1895), and a whole range of clubs and even cafés had developed, loosely grouped together as 'Clarionettes'. A Clarion Fellowship was established by Blatchford in 1901 to strengthen this movement and support the paper. Blatchford himself, and many of his Clarion supporters, played an important role in the formation both of the *Independent Labour Party* (q.v.) in 1893 and the British Socialist Party in 1911, but no independent political organisation developed around the *Clarion*. Blatchford's support for the war after 1914 split the movement, which by 1918 had lost its cohesion and drive. The *Clarion* itself continued publication until 1934, and a variety of 'Clarion' organisations still survives, but no longer with political significance.

Papers

By its nature the Clarion movement could have no single archive. The files of the *Clarion* itself are the best single source. Apart from those at the British Library, an incomplete file is retained at B.L.P.E.S., 1891-1934, with a complete file on microfilm covering the years up to 1915.

The best source for purely archival material is in the Archives Department, Manchester Central Library. The material here includes: records of the Clarion Newspaper Co. Ltd., 1891-95 (accounts, balance sheets, printing estimates, etc., together with the memorandum and articles of association, 1894); 4 volumes of letters from Robert Blatchford to his life-long collaborator, A. M. Thompson, 1885-1943; a collection of miscellaneous letters from Blatchford, 1909-43; letters to William Palmer from Blatchford and his wife, 1880-1936; minutes of the Manchester Clarion Club, 1913-21; a souvenir album of the Clarion Café, Manchester, presented to Blatchford in 1908; and a typescript by S. J. Berry, 'The Clarion Table: The Record of a Manchester Luncheon Group, written at the request of some of the members (1908-43)'.

Records relating to the post-1918 work of the Clarion Fellowship have been deposited in Nuffield College Library. These include: the National Clarion Fellowship Committee minute book, 1921-32; London Clarion Fellowship Committee minute book, 1922-26; and a manuscript volume entitled 'Essays and Addresses', by Arthur S. Hancock (1904).

Smaller items which could be mentioned include:
(1) Aberdeen Clarion Club minutes, 1899-1909, in Aberdeen University Library.
(2) Sheffield Clarion Ramblers, membership cards, handbooks, etc., in the Sheffield City Library.
(3) 'Clarion Rural Campaign, June-July 1933', a typescript of 12 pages in B.L.P.E.S.
(4) A few items are also deposited with the *National Labour Museum* (q.v.).

COBDEN CLUB

Founded in 1866, the Cobden Club aimed to encourage the growth and diffusion of those economic and political principles with which Cobden's name was associated. Its principal work was the advocacy of free trade, and funds were devoted to the printing and circulation of books, pamphlets and leaflets, and the organisation of meetings and lectures in support of free trade, peace, retrenchment and reform.

Papers

An assortment of records relating to the Cobden Club and the *Free Trade League* (q.v.) is deposited at Dunford House, Midhurst, Sussex. It is planned to move these papers in due course to the West Sussex Record Office. No detailed list of the papers has been made, but among the material there are minutes of the Cobden Club, 1866-*c.*1897, an autograph book signed at the inaugural dinner of the Club, lists of subscribers and subscriptions paid and a number of printed annual reports.

Availability

Enquiries should be addressed to the Archivist at the West Sussex Record Office.

COLLIERY OWNERS' ASSOCIATIONS

The National Coal Board is handing over the records of the industry for deposit in various local record offices. These records were formerly the property of the mining companies. The material often includes papers of the local coal owners' associations. Among the records already deposited are the following:

Derbyshire Coal Owners

Colliery records relating to the South Derbyshire coalfield are deposited at the Derbyshire Record Office. They comprise minutes of the South Derbyshire Colliery Owners' Association, 1915-46, and of its Joint District Board and Joint Disputes Board, 1912; signing-on book of the Church Gresley Colliery, 1921-53; an assortment of colliery maps and plans, 1872-1920.

Durham Coal Owners' Association

The papers at the Durham Record Office are principally the copies of minutes, memoranda, statistical information, etc., of the Association and related organisations sent out to members. They include minutes of the Colliery Owners' Mutual Protection Association and its Arbitration Committee, Mining Association annual reports, and monthly statistical reviews of the coal industry (incomplete series). There are also papers relating to the miners' strike (1926), the coal marketing scheme (1929) and miners' minimum wages (1929). The papers fill nine boxes and relate mainly to the period 1926-36. An assortment of other papers covers the Durham coal-mining industry in the 19th century, and there are three volumes of newspaper cuttings, 1892-1943.

Lancashire Coal Owners

At the Lancashire Record Office, Preston, the N.C.B. has deposited the minutes, accounts and correspondence of the South West Lancashire Coal Owners' Association, 1898-1955.

Leicestershire Colliery Owners' Association

A good collection of records is housed at the Leicester Museum. The minutes of numerous committees are available, e.g. minutes of the Commercial and Joint Meetings of Coal Owners, 1916-32, and its successor committee, 1932-48; the Joint Coal Production Board, 1940-42; the Conciliation Board, 1944-46; the Rescue Station Committee, 1914-46; the Reorganisation of Coal Mines Committee, 1931-46; Wages Board, 1937-44, etc. The other papers comprise reports and memoranda, insurance policies, accounts, maps and the records of the Central

Valuation Board in regard to nationalisation of the mines (1948). Among the files and printed material are numerous reports of the Secretary for Mines and H.M. Inspector of Mines; minutes and reports of the 1925 Royal Commission; the 1938 Royal Commission on Safety in Coal Mines, etc.; rules of the Leicestershire Coal Owners' Association, 1914; and papers relating to arbitrations, disputes and agreements. The collection amounts to some 70 items or volumes of material.

Monmouthshire and South Wales Coal Owners' Association

A substantial collection of records of the Association covering the whole period of its activities from 1873-1947 has been deposited in the National Library of Wales. These records include 21 volumes of general minute books, 1873-1947, covering annual meetings, special meetings, and meetings of Council, and also containing the early proceedings of the Finance Committee to 1888, and the Cardiff District Board to 1892.

There are six volumes of the proceedings of the Finance Committee, 1888-1944, and nine volumes of the Commercial Committee, 1919-47; nine volumes of the minutes of the Cardiff District Board, 1892-1947, fourteen volumes of the Newport District Board, 1874-1947, together with one volume of résumés of meetings, and sixteen volumes of the Swansea District Board, with two volumes of résumés. The records of other, more specialised, committees have also survived and include minutes of the Special Purposes Committee, 1927-47; the Joint Sliding Scale Committee, 1875-1902; the Joint Standing Disputes Committee, 1918-47; the Enginemen's Wages Committee, 1919-26; the Mines Act Committee, 1923-46; the Eight Hours Act Committee; and minutes of proceedings concerning Conciliation Boards, 1910-46. Other material includes a considerable amount of correspondence, notes, etc., on disputes, particularly in the 1890s; eleven volumes of disputes dealt with, 1890-1919; and tabulated information on disputes, 1903-19; résumés of decisions of Joint Standing Committees, in seventeen volumes, 1918-47; one volume on the cost of police protection during strikes, 1921; and various records of stoppages, arbitrations, coal industry reorganisations, surveys, etc., culminating in the records of the coal owners' compensation proceedings, 1946. In addition, there is a considerable amount of printed material, including 36 volumes of circulars, 1899-1946; official printed reports, 1874-1950; the *Coal Annual*, 1903-29, and various published works.

Availability

There is restricted access to these papers. Applications should be made in the first place to the Librarian, National Library of Wales.

Scottish Coal Owners' Association

The Association's papers are located at the Scottish Record Office. The collection, covering the years 1870-1947 is large and cannot easily be summarised. However, the papers can be grouped under certain headings and a few interesting items taken as examples:

(1) Administration, emergency measures and general papers: the 41 volumes include the minutes of the Scottish Coal Shipment Emergency Committee (1926), the Wages Advisory Committee (1944-46) and many other committees; papers relating to activities during the two world wars and the General Strike.

(2) Organisation prior to 1947: among the 17 volumes are papers relating to the 1925 Royal Commission on the Coal Industry, and the co-ordination of District Coal Marketing Associations.

(3)   Nationalisation and valuation: of the 44 volumes, most contain reports of the Valuation Committee on each coal-mining district in Britain.

(4)   Output, prices, exports, costs, transport, etc.: 49 volumes.

(5)   Wages and conditions of service: general papers in 50 volumes covering awards, agreements, disputes, housing, welfare and accidents.

(6)   Details of ascertainments of wages and costs (post-1921 settlement): 30 volumes.

(7)   Special wages investigations: papers relating to the pay of particular classes of workmen, six volumes.

(8)   Miscellaneous papers: 98 items. They include copies of agreements, public statements, petitions, etc.; papers of the Lanarkshire Coal Masters' Association (rules, reports, minutes, etc.); official papers of Royal Commission, 1925; etc.

Shropshire Colliery Owners' Association

Minute books and papers, 1946-52, are now in the Shropshire Record Office.

South Yorkshire Coal Owners

At Sheffield City Libraries the large N.C.B. collection includes some records of the South Yorkshire Coal Owners' Association. These comprise the deed of constitution, reports and accounts, and call sheets, 1884-1952, and minutes of meetings, 1937-54.

Staffordshire Coal Owners

Among the mass of N.C.B. material housed at the Staffordshire Record Office are minutes, files, etc., of the North Staffordshire Colliery Owners' Association, late 19th century onwards.

COMMON WEALTH

Founded from J. B. Priestley's 1941 Committee and the Forward March Movement in 1942 by Sir Richard Acland (Liberal M.P. for Barnstaple) during the wartime electoral truce, the party aimed to contest all by-elections on behalf of Labour or other 'progressive' candidates. The party won three seats for itself (1943-45) and in 1945 put up 23 candidates at the General Election. Membership of Common Wealth, however, was proscribed by the Labour Party in 1943, and the party's only success at the General Election was at Chelmsford where no Labour candidate stood. Common Wealth made its appeal during the war through its vigorous call for 'common ownership', 'vital democracy' and 'morality in politics', but failed to sustain its particular identity. Acland and other leaders eventually joined the Labour Party, and after 1945 the party contested no further parliamentary elections.

Papers

The records of Common Wealth have been deposited in the Library at the University of Sussex. The papers (c.1942-55) cover the political activities of the party, its central office, committees and local branches, and the related business of its founder, Acland, and one of its M.P.s, Hugh Lawson. The material includes correspondence, election leaflets, accounts, reports, printed pamphlets and books, and a fair selection of minutes, agenda, reports, etc., from special committees, and regions and local branches. The Acland and Lawson personal collection comprises correspondence, diaries, memoranda, press cuttings, leaflets, etc. The Library also holds the tape recordings, and related correspondence, collected by Dr. A. L. R. Calder for his thesis 'The Common Wealth Party 1942-45' (University of Sussex Ph.D.,1968). Interesting collections of papers, which include Common Wealth material, remain in private hands.

Availability

All enquiries should be addressed to the Librarian at the University of Sussex.

COMMONWEALTH INDUSTRIES ASSOCIATION
6-14 Dean Farrar Street London SW1H 0DX

The Empire Industries Association began operations in 1926 to promote the cause of Imperial economic co-operation and the protection of home industries. It had links with the old Tariff Reform League through its Chairman, Sir Henry Page Croft, and aimed to include or be associated with all the other organisations which were in anyway concerned with the development of safeguarding and Imperial preference. It maintained strong ties with the British Empire Producers' Association, the Federation of British Industries and the National Union of Manufacturers.

In 1947 it merged with the British Empire League (founded 1895); in 1958 it changed its name to the Commonwealth and Empire Industries Association, and in 1960 to the Commonwealth Industries Association. In 1965 the Commonwealth Fellowship and the Commonwealth Union of Trade merged with the Association and in 1967 the Commonwealth Industries Association became a company limited by guarantee. It has always enjoyed the backing of a strong Parliamentary Committee, and the present strength of this committee, which includes members of the two major parties, is 55.

Papers

There are minute books covering the whole period of the E.I.A./C.I.A.'s existence and the material relating to the inter-war period is of special political interest. There is unfortunately no general or personal correspondence relating to these organisations, but the minutes of the general meetings and the Parliamentary Committee provide an insight into the operation of one very important pressure group in British politics.

Minutes of the following meetings and committees are retained: general meetings, Council and Parliamentary Committee, 1926-35; Finance Committee meetings, 1926-39; Empire Development and Settlement Committee; Main Research Committee; Recruitment and Training Sub-committee (these largely cover the period 1933-36); Executive Committee, 1925-30, 1931-47; Parliamentary Committee meetings, 1945-47; Executive Committee meetings and joint meetings between E.I.A. and the British Empire League, 1947-55; Executive Committee meetings, 1956-67; Council meeting minutes, C.I.A. Ltd., 1967-73.

The Empire Industries Association and British Empire League annual reports, 1927-57, are available, together with the Commonwealth and Empire Industries Association annual reports, 1958-59; Commonwealth Industries Association annual reports, 1960-67; Commonwealth Industries Association Ltd., annual directors' reports, 1968-72; Empire Industries Association *Monthly Bulletin*, 1941-47; Empire Industries Association and British Empire League *Monthly Bulletin*, 1947-58; Commonwealth and Empire Industries Association *Monthly Bulletin*, 1948-60; Commonwealth Industries Association *Monthly Bulletin*, 1961-70; and the Commonwealth Industries Association journal *Britain and Overseas*, 1971 to date.

The Dean Farrar Street office also possesses a set of *Monthly Notes on Tariff Reform,* 1904-14, and a year's set of *The Tariff Reformer and Empire Monthly,* March 1917-February 1918.

Availability

Applications should be addressed to the Secretary.

COMMONWEALTH MIGRATION COUNCIL
6-14 Dean Farrar Street London SW1H 0DX

Formed in 1946, the Council aims to increase the flow of British migrants to the countries of the old Commonwealth.

Papers

Full records, minute books, reports, correspondence, etc., have been retained, together with copies of the Council's newsletter.

Availability

Applications should be addressed to the Director.

COMMONWEALTH PARLIAMENTARY ASSOCIATION
General Council 7 Old Palace Yard London SW1P 3JY

The Association, which was founded in 1911, has evolved with the Commonwealth. Starting as the Empire Parliamentary Association, administered by the U.K. branch, it changed its name in 1948 to the Commonwealth Parliamentary Association and the direction of its affairs came under the control of a General Council on which all branches were represented directly or indirectly. Management of the Association's affairs lies with the General Council, but each branch remains autonomous.

The C.P.A. is an association of Commonwealth parliamentarians who are united by community of interest, respect for the rule of law and the rights and freedoms of the individual citizen, and by pursuit of the positive ideals of parliamentary democracy. The Association exists to promote understanding and co-operation between Commonwealth parliamentarians and respect for the parliamentary institutions.

Papers

Records and publications prior to the formation of the Council are kept by the U.K. branch of the Association. Some papers were destroyed during the war, and the records have been pruned of ephemeral material. However, the surviving archive includes correspondence with the branches of the Association and with affiliated organisations, correspondence on, and all material produced for, the running of the Commonwealth and regional conferences, and correspondence on the day-to-day developments within the Commonwealth. Complete sets of all C.P.A. publications, both from the Council and the branches, are kept. These include *The Parliamentarian* (1920-); annual report and report of the general meeting (1911-, incomplete); constitutions, for various years; conference proceedings, assorted reports and papers; newsletters (1963-); annual reports and rules of the branches of the association; *Report on World Affairs* (1920-68).

The papers are readily available to bona fide researchers, who should write to the Secretary.

COMMONWEALTH PRODUCERS' ORGANISATION
25 Victoria Street London SW1H 0EX

Formed in 1916, the organisation exists to promote the interests of primary producers overseas and the development of reciprocal trade within the Commonwealth and Preference Area. Originally the British Empire Producers' Organisation, it is now involved in the Common Market debate, but takes no stance for or against the E.E.C.

Papers

The records at the association's offices consist of minutes since formation, various printed publications on matters of Commonwealth trade, a number of annual reports, and bound copies of the magazine which has appeared under various titles, including *Production, Empire Production and Export* and *Commonwealth Producer.*

Availability

Applications should be addressed to the Executive Director.

COMMUNIST PARTY OF GREAT BRITAIN
16 King Street London WC2

The party was founded in July 1920 as a fusion of various left-wing movements: the British Socialist Party, the larger part of the Socialist Labour Party, and individuals from the South Wales Socialist Society, the Shop Stewards' Movement, the Independent Labour Party and the National Guilds League.

Papers

Much the most useful material for the history of the party is to be found in pamphlets and periodicals. For a variety of reasons, archival material is extremely scarce, not least because of police activity during various periods of the party's history. Pamphlet material should be consulted either at the Marx Memorial Library or in such libraries as the British Library and the British Library of Political and Economic Science.

For archival material relating to the Communist Party, the Marx Memorial Library is again much the most useful source. Apart from an unpublished autobiography of Ellen Crawfurd (a suffragette and Communist) and a shelf of assorted cuttings, notes for books and photographs of Wal Hannington, the only archive material available at King Street consists of a few minute books for branches of the party. There are four minute books of the Dundee branch (1920-21, 1924-25, 1925-26, 1926-27), three for the Sheffield branch (1920-21, 1921-22, 1924) and a single minute book of the British Socialist Party for Manchester (Openshaw) for the period 1914-19.

Any application to use the material at King Street would have to be treated strictly on its merits in view of the very limited resources at present available.

It is believed that many individuals who have been actively involved in the work of the party have retained records. These have not been deposited in libraries and are not generally available. Six boxes of material, largely relating to the C.P.G.B., 1929-45, comprise the Ernest W. Darling Collection at the Hoover Institution, Stanford, California 94305. Some papers from the 1930s relating to Sean Murray of the Northern Ireland Communist Party are available at the Northern Ireland Public Record Office.

See also: *Socialist Labour Party; Marx Memorial Library; Social Democratic Federation; National Unemployed Workers' Movement; National Minority Movement.*

CONFEDERATION OF BRITISH INDUSTRY
21 Tothill Street London SW1

The Confederation was established in 1965 as the national representative of manufacturing industry. It resulted from the merger of three previously separate organisations: the Federation of British Industry (founded in 1916 to represent industrialists on all matters apart from industrial relations); the British Employers' Confederation (founded in 1919 as the National Confederation of Employers' Organisations, to represent the employers' interests on industrial relations); and the National Association of British Manufacturers (founded as the National Union of Manufacturers in 1915, to represent smaller manufacturers).

Papers

The Confederation has retained its records since its inception, but these are confidential. The records of the predecessor organisations of the C.B.I. are at present housed at the Confederation's offices, where they are being sorted and catalogued.

At present it is only possible to give a general description of these papers.

(*a*) *Federation of British Industries.* The records cover the whole period 1916-65 and include minutes of the Grand Council, standing and *ad hoc* committees; the papers of Presidents, Directors-General and Secretaries; a complete set of circulars distributed to members; sets of annual reports, publications, etc.; and the papers of the economic, overseas, technical, education and training, information and administration Directorates.

(*b*) *British Employers' Federation.* These records include: minutes of Council, standing and *ad hoc* committees; a complete set of circulars distributed to members; two large collections of miscellaneous files arranged by subject, the first containing pre-1958 material, the second containing post-1958 material; and papers relating to various associated bodies.

(*c*) *National Association of British Manufacturers.* The Association retained only a small collection of miscellaneous papers.

Availability

The above records are not at present available.

CONFEDERATION OF HEALTH SERVICE EMPLOYEES
Glen House High Street Banstead Surrey

The association was formed in 1910 as the National Asylum Workers' Union, which in 1935 changed its name to the Mental Hospitals and Institutional Workers' Union. In 1946 amalgamation was effected with the Hospital and Welfare Services Union, which was formed in 1943. This association had previously been called the Poor Law Officers' Union (1919) and the National Union of County Officers (1930). The present name was adopted in 1946.

Papers

Minute books of the M.H.I.W.U. and H.W.S.U. have been preserved. Unfortunately some of the latter have suffered deterioration. Neither correspondence nor press cuttings are retained indefinitely, but branch records are available. A history of the first twenty-one years of the M.H.I.W.U. has been published, together with a limited review printed in 1960. Copies of the Confederation's *Journal* from 1911 are also retained.

Availability

All records are housed at the head office, and researchers should apply for access in writing to the General Secretary.

CONFEDERATION OF SHIPBUILDING AND ENGINEERING UNIONS
140-2 Walworth Road London SE17

The Confederation was founded in 1890 and acts as a forum for the major shipbuilding and engineering unions.

Papers

A substantial collection of non-current papers, c. 1944-60s has been placed in the care of the Modern Records Centre, University of Warwick Library.

Availability

Further details concerning the extent and availability of these papers can be obtained from the archivist, Modern Records Centre.

CONFERENCE OF MISSIONARY SOCIETIES IN GREAT BRITAIN AND IRELAND
Edinburgh House 2 Eaton Gate London SW1

The Conference of British Missionary Societies was formed following the World Missionary Conference held in Edinburgh in 1910.

Papers

In addition to the minutes of the Standing Committee (1911-64) and its papers, the minutes of a number of special sub-committees have been preserved. These include minutes of the Medical Advisory Board (1916-64), the Home Base Committee (1917-55) and Home Council (1956-64), the United Council for Missionary Education (1907-52), the Youth Missionary Council (1939-55) and the Schools Committee (1946-65). Other series of papers relate to visual aids, the Christian Literature Council, work among Jews, and the International Missionary Council.

For the Overseas Departments, the archives are arranged according to geographical area. The series on Africa includes papers relating to education and literature, to work in particular countries, and there are minutes of regional committees. The series of papers covering Asia, the West Indies and the Middle East are similar in constitution. Earlier Africa and India material, deriving from the joint work of the International Missionary Council and the Conference of British Missionary Societies, is also in the custody of C.B.M.S.

The Conference also holds the records of the Association of Medical Officers of Missionary Societies (1904-35), the National Missionary Laymen's Movement (1910-54), the Church Assembly Missionary Council (1942-46) and others.

Availability

Researchers wishing to use the records should apply to the Archivist.

CONGO REFORM ASSOCIATION

Founded in 1904, the Association campaigned against misrule in the Congo.

Papers

Some records relating to the Association are included in the E. D. Morel Collection at the British Library of Political and Economic Science. Morel was Hon. Secretary of the Association, 1904-12. The papers comprise the following: letters written by Morel in his capacity as Secretary (apart from the letter books labelled C.R.A. there are relevant letters in other series); reports, memoranda, deputations, interviews with the Foreign Secretary, etc., and papers relating to the foundation, meetings, finance and winding-up of the Association; pamphlets issued by the C.R.A.; copies of periodicals edited by Morel, both the official organ of the Association, 1904-08, and the *African Mail* (formerly *West Africa* and *West African Mail*), 1901-15; an assortment of press cuttings, some of which relate to the C.R.A.

Other useful collections of private papers are the John Holt MSS. (in the possession of John Holt & Co., Liverpool) and the records of the *Baptist Missionary Society* (q.v.) and of the Aborigines' Protection Society (see under *Anti-Slavery Society*).

Availability

Researchers should apply to the Librarian at the B.L.P.E.S.

CONGREGATIONAL COUNCIL FOR WORLD MISSION
11 Carteret Street London SW1

The London Missionary Society was founded in 1795. In 1966 it amalgamated with the Commonwealth Missionary Society (Congregational) to become the Congregational Council for World Mission. Only the L.M.S. archives are described here.

Papers

The extensive records of the Society have been listed in detail. Board minutes (1795-1959) are available, together with the minutes of several committees, including the Consultative and Finance Committee (1895-1953), the Foreign Occasional Committee (1840-45, 1882-1955), the Home Occasional Committee (1841-1954), the Ladies' Committee (1875-1907) and the Committees on Literature (1866-1930), Medical Work (1909-55) and Ships (1864-1954). Home Department papers (1795-1935) and Candidates papers are also extant. The papers of the Overseas Department are sorted according to geographical area. For the 20th century, assorted minutes, papers, reports and journals are preserved relating to Central Africa, Madagascar, South Africa, Papua (New Guinea), the South Sea Islands, West Indies, China, India and Australia.

The records are to be deposited with the Librarian at the School of Oriental and African Studies, Malet Street, London WC1, to whom researchers should address applications to use the papers. In addition, a microfilm of the L.M.S. records is deposited in the University Library, University of California, Los Angeles.

CONSERVATIVE PARTY

The records of the Conservative Party are described under the following headings:

   I.   National

   II.   Regional

   III.   Constituencies

   IV.   Related Organisations

I. National

Introduction

A brief description of the organisation of the Conservative Party at national level is necessary in order to understand the nature and location of its records.

Central Office 32 Smith Square London SW1P 3HH

Founded in 1867, this is the administrative and political centre of the party. The record holdings of its Registry and the administrative departments will be examined below. Certain non-current records are retained at the 'warehouse' but these will be examined under the relevant administrative heading. A note on the Conservative Political Centre, the educational arm of the party, will be found under this heading.

National Union of Conservative and Unionist Associations
   (founded 1867)

This is a federation of constituency associations and organises the annual conference. Administratively separate from Central Office, it is also housed at 32 Smith Square, where its records are retained.

Conservative Research Department 24 Old Queen Street London SW1H 9HB

This was founded in 1929 and is responsible for political research, parliamentary briefs, assistance in drawing up policy statements, publications, etc. The party's reference and information Library is housed at Research Department. Certain of the Department's older records are housed at the Swinton Conservative College, near Ripon, Yorks.[1]

A survey of the records held in Conservative Central Office, Conservative Research Department and at Swinton Conservative College was conducted during 1971.[2] As a result of this survey it was decided to allow access in the first place to records up to 1951. Further information may be obtained by enquiry as follows:

Central Office: to the Organisation Department.
National Union: to the Secretary.

[1] For further details on these divisions, and their implications for the party's records, see G. D. M. Block, 'Conservative Party Archives', *Bulletin of the Association of Contemporary Historians,* no. 4, Summer 1972.

[2] By John Ramsden, Lecturer in History, Queen Mary College, London.

Conservative Research Department: to the Assistant Director (Information), Mr. G. D. M. Block. Researchers are advised to contact the latter with general enquiries. It should be noted that certain classes of records are confidential and access may be refused.

It was found that most of the records which were inspected were only ten to twenty years old. This is partly the result of a wartime fire and partly of a conscious policy whereby non-current papers were periodically destroyed.

The most important exception is the collection of material belonging to the National Union, much of which survives from 1867. The other prominent exceptions are the minute books of the Junior Imperial League from 1905, the minute books of the National Society of Conservative Agents from the 1890s, the minute books of the 1922 Committee from 1923, and several reports and memoranda on Central Office reorganisations from 1911. Taken together with the surviving literature and magazines, such as the *Conservative Agents' Journal,* the *Conservative Clubs' Gazette,* posters, election manifestoes and publicity leaflets, these sources give a very full picture of the party from about the time of World War I. There is less coverage of the years from the 1890s to 1918, and very little at all has survived for the first twenty years of Central Office's existence.

The failure to keep general correspondence is partly explained by lack of space at Smith Square and at the warehouse, where non-current papers are stored. It is probably also partially due to the habits of successive Party Chairmen: the collections of private papers belonging to Sir Arthur Steel-Maitland (at the Scottish Record Office) and Viscount Davidson (at the Beaverbrook Library) both include large quantities of their correspondence as Party Chairman. Some of their correspondence is naturally to be found in the collections of other prominent politicians with whom they were in close contact. For example, the papers of each Party Leader up to Churchill are now available to scholars, and include correspondence about the party organisation, and with the Party Chairman, the Principal Agent/General Director, and others. The A. J. Balfour papers are at the British Library and others are with the family at Whittingehame. Stanley Baldwin's papers are housed at Cambridge University Library, and the Bonar Law Collection is in the Beaverbrook Library.

Central Office

The Registry contains six General Files for correspondence, and also stores files for almost every Central Office department. The General Files now extant generally date from the late 1940s, though occasional files survive for the early 1940s.

The General Files are as follows:

(1) *Constituency Correspondence.* These contain one folder for each constituency, arranged in constituency number order. Literature orders for constituency associations are destroyed after one year, and the rest is weeded before transfer to storage boxes, about every three years.

The storage boxes contain miscellaneous correspondence about the general business of the constituency, selection of candidates, work of agents, electioneering, members, annual reports, etc. Perhaps the most interesting is the bulky special file kept on each by-election.

(2) *Area Correspondence.* One folder for each Area. These contain correspondence with Central Office agents, Area annual reports, some reports on local events, and details of Area meetings.

(3) *Outside Organisations Correspondence.* At least one folder per organisation, but more for allied groups like the National Society of Conservative Agents. They contain mainly correspondence *with* such bodies, but also some internal letters *about* them (e.g. bulky files on C.N.D. in the later 1950s).

(4) *Special Subject Files.* An alphabetical series of files on any subject which generates enough letters to justify a separate folder, e.g. 'Fascist Activities', 'Fetes and Bazaars', 'Flag Days'. The most interesting of these are probably the special series of files kept for each General Election campaign, and the files relating to party committees.

(5) *General Correspondence.* Used for all literature orders to others than constituency and Area associations, and for correspondence with the general public. In the earlier 1950s the storage boxes contain a wider range of correspondence by the Party Chairman and General Director. Some of the dates are misleading, because files seem to be removed for storage only when their subject is no longer current. Thus, some of the personal files of candidates and agents actually date from the 1930s.

(6) *Conservative Agents' Benevolent Association and Unionist Agents' Super-annuation Fund.* A few administrative records, but otherwise entirely personal files relating to the party's Benevolent and Superannuation Funds. The C.A.B.A. correspondence dates from 1942 and the U.A.S.F. from 1935.

Each report on party organisation produced between 1911 and 1952 has been retained together with some papers relating to the committees which produced the reports. A minute book of the 1948 (Maxwell Fyfe) Committee on party reorganisation survives, but this is very brief and gives little more than attendance lists and agenda.

A personnel card is kept for each employee of the party and for candidates and constituency officers. Some of these (but not all) survive from the 1920s, and give details of the careers of people who were employed by the party even before World War I. However, only the cards of the more important people of the period seem to have survived.

The following departmental records survive:

(a) Organisation Department

The Department obviously has a large scope and a variety of different records may be noted.

127 boxes of documents in the Registry store cover 55 groups of subject. The most interesting and important are:

Number	Subject	No. of box files
1 - 5	General Elections (1950-64)	20
8	Party Finance (1944-48)	1
11 - 13	Recruiting and Membership (1948-62)	4
14	Central Office Agents' Conferences (1945-69)	4
20	Common Market (1957-63)	1
26	Marginal Seats and Criticals (1953-70)	5
33	By-Elections (1960s)	1
42	Circulars to Central Office Agents (1945-70)	6
46	Party Conferences (1963-68)	1

The following groups may also be noted:

Industrial. The Trades Union National Advisory Committee minute books date from 1947. This Committee replaced the Labour Sub-committee of the National Union Executive, whose minute books are kept in the National Union Office. The minutes are very full, reporting discussions as well as their ultimate outcome, but tend to become more formal in the later 1950s. There are full reports of addresses by front-bench spokesmen, and of transactions by Area Trades Union Conferences. No correspondence of any age has been retained.

Local Government. A complete set of programmes and agenda of Local Government Conferences dates from 1947. A few verbatim reports are kept, but only for 1947, 1948 and the late 1960s. The programmes include the full texts of the papers presented to the Conference for discussion.

Local Government National Advisory Committee minutes are kept from 1944, consisting of typescripts in a loose-leaf folder. The Committee met about four times a year and discussed a wide variety of subjects connected with local government affairs, local finance, reform of local government, and local elections.

There were regular reports on local organisation and elections by the Local Government Officer, which are summarised in the minutes.

The minutes are very brief and formal, with the exception of special discussions on matters of party policy towards local government, e.g. disputes in 1947-8 about the desirability of using party labels in all local government elections.

Local government election results are only retained in detail for a few years. For Boroughs and U.D.C.s there are only 'state of the parties' and voting figures from 1964. Some earlier figures from 1953 survive in the Registry.

Sales and Supply. Stock ledgers are kept for all publications and other material (mainly stationery and publicity material) for the post-war years. One set of 16 loose-leaf ledgers covers the years 1953-68, and another set of three ledgers covers 1945-53. These consist of one page for each item, and give full details of supply, sales and stock, month by month. They also include supply and reprint costs. Six scrapbooks of literature have been kept; these aim to include one copy of every publication since 1945 in numerical order. Probably a few have been removed or lost, but almost everything has survived.

Overseas Bureau. Minute books of the Conservative Commonwealth and Overseas Council are kept, and are complete from the foundation of the Council in 1953. These are mainly for the Executive Committee, and the minutes kept give a very full account of addresses, business transacted and liaison with the Parliamentary Party.

Summary reports of the C.C.O.C. are presented to the Annual Business Meeting; for most years a copy is included in the minutes.

C.C.O.C. background papers also date from 1953, and a complete set is kept. There is a box file of each issue still available and calendars are periodically produced. There had been about 220 of these background papers by 1964.

Minute books of the Overseas Bureau Committee are kept, complete since 1949. These are very full reports on the activities of the Bureau, because each meeting includes a staff report on activity.

A card index has been kept since 1950 of the Bureau's contacts with foreign and Commonwealth students.

Some correspondence files dating from 1948-49 are kept in the Registry, but these are not complete. Only from *c.* 1958 are the subject files frequent.

(b) Accounts Department

The records include:

(1) *C.A.B.A. Journal* (complete from 1922). This gives details of income, investment and expenditure for the C.A.B.A. since its re-foundation in 1922. It lists all investments annually, other income only in summary form.

(2) *U.A.S.F. Journal* (complete from 1927). This gives a similar summary of all transactions relating to the investments of the pension fund, from its foundation in 1927.

(3) Record cards for all members of the U.A.S.F. have been kept from 1927: these record all contributions and all payments.

(4) Balance sheets for the C.A.B.A. and the U.A.S.F. are also kept, but the journals are a more complete source for the same information.

(5) Sales ledgers (1957-59). This is the last set of sales ledgers, after which the system was mechanised in 1959. The four ledgers have a page for each constituency or other buyer, and record all sales of literature.

(6) File on speakers. This is a file of miscellaneous memoranda, notes and letters, relating to the organisation and payment of professional speakers in the 1930s. This is in no way complete, but gives some coverage to a subject which has no other source material in Central Office.

(7) Purchasing ledgers (from 1946). These record all purchases — any item which passed through the Accounts Department; virtually all financial transactions except salaries. These are a complete set from 1946 to mechanisation in 1959.

(8) The accounts storeroom in the basement has:
    (i) summarised cash books, 1956-59 (2 vols.);
    (ii) speakers and missioners' expenses books (1929-64);
    (iii) Area Offices' expenses (1952-55);
    (iv) general cash books, 1952-64 (4 vols.);
    (v) payments to missioners, 1956-64.

(9) Record cards for Central and Area Office employees, complete set from 1947 to the present. These give names, jobs, addresses, etc.

(c) Central Board of Finance

The records include: minutes of C.B.F. meetings from 1946, full but factual. No correspondence is kept for more than three years at the most, but balance sheets have been kept from at least 1946. These records would be classed as confidential.

(d) Publicity Department

Very little material is retained. All back stocks of press releases were recently destroyed, but unfortunately without any master set being kept. The most complete set is at Research Department.

The following categories should be noted:

Press Cuttings. Thousands of boxes are kept at Central Office. There are a few which were opened in the 1940s and one or two which were opened in the 1930s. Most of them, however, date from after 1950 and cover a wide variety of topics. Earlier ones include personal boxes which are kept selectively: only cuttings of very important politicians are kept in large numbers, e.g. 87 boxes on Churchill, from 1919. Most long runs on major politicians (Baldwin, Bevin, Eden, etc.) date from the mid-1930s. Apparently complete sets of boxes on by-elections date from 1941, and many boxes on the Conservative Party from the 1940s. There are boxes on each General Election from 1945, but most other subject boxes start later. A large collection of press cuttings, formerly in the possession of the Conservative Party, is now deposited at B.L.P.E.S.

Publications. Only the following have been kept:
    (i) *Weekly News Letter,* from 1945 (later called *Weekly News*).
    (ii) *Monthly News Letter,* from 1949 (later *Monthly News*).
    (iii) *Notes on Current Politics,* from 1950.
    (iv) *Tory Challenge* (1947-53) and *Onward* (1953-57).

Broadcasting. Films of party broadcasts as follows: General Elections (from 1959), party political broadcasts (from 1953), Budget broadcasts (from 1956). There are also B.B.C. films of party conferences from 1955, scripts of all broadcasts from 1951, and a paper on pre-war political broadcasting, prepared by the B.B.C. Minutes of the All-Party Committee on Political Broadcasting exist from 1958.

Films. These were deposited in the National Film Archive, 81 Dean Street, London W1, and are available for viewing there with permission from Central Office. A further series was deposited at the N.F.A. by Mandson Films Ltd., who made them for Central Office:

(a) Series 'Britain under the National Government', made mainly in 1934-35, by the Conservative and Unionist Films Association. There is a wide variety of subjects, with some cartoons, and some films of speeches. Usually one reel, 35 mm. There is one, made in 1932, entitled *Impressions of Disraeli* (two reels).

(b) The films deposited by Mandson Films Ltd. were made by them for Conservative Central Office Productions, 1927-59. They include:
   (i) 1927, *Red Tape Farm* — about Lloyd George's 'interfering' land policy;
   (ii) 1930, *Socialist Car of State* — cartoon about MacDonald's Government;
   (iii) 1931, three films for the election, showing speeches by Baldwin and MacDonald;
   (iv) film of Neville Chamberlain, talking about foreign policy, 1938;
   (v) series of very short extracts from conference speeches, 1947-49;
   (vi) 1951, Churchill's speech in which he gave the pledge on housing;
   (vii) 1956, film of Eden's last public appearance as Prime Minister.
   (viii) 1958, *Macmillan, Man of the Moment,* long film showing his meetings with Menzies, Eisenhower, Nehru, etc.;
   (ix) 1958-59, Derick Heathcoat Amory as Chancellor.

The Registry has a few files from the Chief Publicity Officer from 1955, but most are more recent. It also has six minute books of the Advisory Committee on Publicity and Speakers, 1949-66.

(e) Conservative Political Centre

Very little material is retained in the C.P.C. Office; there is a list of all the C.P.C.'s publications since its foundation in 1945, together with file copies of each of them. *Objective*, a quarterly review, published from 1949 to 1958, is retained. Production ledgers since 1949 are still retained: these give the production and printing costs of all publications. A few photographs and blocks are also retained.

National Union

Minutes have been kept in different form for every party conference since the formation of the National Union in 1867.

1867-82: One volume of manuscript minutes of conference proceedings. The early ones are reported very fully, the later ones more formally. Some of these, but not all, include a list of delegates.

1883-95: One volume per conference, manuscript minutes. These are very full and most informative.

1896-1946: One volume per conference. These are much less informative, as they are in scrapbook form, with press cuttings and sections of the printed agenda instead of more informal manuscript notes. They do, however, have a typed list of the delegates attending. The exceptions are the special conferences of 1917 and 1930, for which there is a verbatim report in typescript. This was because the conferences of those years were special conferences to which the press was not invited.

from 1947: Full verbatim reports of each conference, as published and issued for general sale.

The only conferences for which minutes have not survived seem to be 1916 and 1943, both of which were special wartime conferences and not part of the general series. The other missing years (such as 1931 or 1938) were years when the conference was either suspended or postponed.

Two volumes contain the minutes of the Central Council from 1899-1945, and a series of loose-leaf files contains the more recent minutes.

The contents vary considerably at different times, but usually include lists of delegates attending, or at least the number attending. Reports to Council by the Executive Committee are sometimes included, and decisions or resolutions are recorded.

From the 1920s the Central Council became less concerned with administrative matters and became more of a political forum with a much enlarged membership. Thus, there are less matters of fact to record and more general political discussions and policy resolutions.

Reports of the Executive Committee to Central Council, from 1919-45, are contained in one volume. They are twice-yearly reports on organisational matters, and include a great deal of detailed information, such as circulation figures for pamphlets and posters, and numbers of meetings organised.

From 1923 these reports were printed for private circulation, and from 1938 were a handbook to the Central Council meeting where they were presented.

Annual reports, presented by Central Council to the conference, are bound in eight volumes, 1868-1939. Thereafter they are included in conference minutes. The later ones constitute a conference handbook and include more general information about fringe activities, etc. Up to 1907, the annual report also included a balance sheet.

Three large minute books of the Executive Committee cover the years 1897-1922, and eight loose-leaf files the years since 1922. There are also minutes of the Labour Sub-committee from 1917, and of the General Purposes Committee. All of these are very detailed in matters of organisation, but have a tendency to record only decisions, rather than discussions, in more general matters.

One-volume copy of National Union rules includes printed sets of rules as adopted in 1867, 1887, 1906, 1910, 1911, 1912, 1918, 1924, 1930 and 1938.

The Women's Conference reports are verbatim reports from shorthand notes made by a professional transcription service. They are not a complete set, and were discontinued in 1952, after which the only source would be press cuttings. There are three volumes before 1952:

1921-24 (2nd to 5th Conferences) - typescript
1924-28 (6th to 9th Conferences) - printed reports
1946-52 (19th to 25th Conferences) - typescript.

There are seven minute books of the Central Women's Advisory Committee covering the years from 1935. The material contained is varied: arrangements for conferences, discussions of policy, and addresses from M.P.s (summarised).

Two volumes contain all the minutes of the General Purposes Committee from 1936, and the main content is the arrangements for the Womens' Conferences: discussions of the agenda, speakers and resolutions, as well as administrative arrangements.

Three volumes of minutes of the Outside Organisations Sub-committee cover the years from 1944. This committee tended to have general discussions on a wide range of women's interests, as raised by correspondence. It also supervises relations with other women's bodies such as the W.V.S. or the National Council of Women.

Minutes of the Women's Charter Committee cover the years 1948-49.

Conservative Research Department and Swinton College

The library at 24 Old Queen Street is the party's working library, but is also to some extent the party's archival repository. The library has a good collection of *Hansard*, government publications, general printed books and pamphlets, and general reference works such as *Who's Who* or the *Dictionary of National Biography* for the use of the party in its work. The holdings of the library are all indexed or calendared. There are also indexes of some items known to exist elsewhere.

The major library holdings include the following: a virtually complete set of all the printed pamphlets and leaflets issued by the party back to 1868;[1] a set of the *Campaign Guide* and *Election Notes* issued for General Elections since 1885; a set of candidates' by-election addresses since 1922 (of which the earliest are kept in the warehouse); some individual addresses are lacking, but this is probably the most complete set in the country for the years covered; the *Ashridge Journal* (1930-48), a nearly complete bound set of this periodical which is not listed in B.U.C.O.P.; a bound set of *The Tory*[2] (1892-97), predecessor of the *Conservative Agents' Journal*; printed party conference reports since 1947; sets of *Notes on Current Politics* (since 1944), *Tory Challenge* (1947-53), *Home and Politics* (1920-30), *National Union Gleanings* (1893-1912) and all other traceable party periodicals.

Other material includes: bound General Election posters since 1929; many printed tracts and some typescript theses on the Conservative Party; some party reports (e.g. the Palmer Report on the party's youth movement); some sets of publications by parallel bodies, e.g. *Crossbow* (since 1957), *Tory Reform* pamphlets (1943-46) or *Solon* (1969-70).

Among very few holdings of manuscript materials are the formal minute book of the London Unionist M.P.s from 1906-19 and the diary of Sir Robert Sanders (Lord Bayford).[1] The latter is deposited on loan.

Office files and committee records come under the category of confidential documents and are sent from time to time to Swinton College, Yorks., when no longer required in London.

Research Department is the working department of a busy political party and many of the printed works it holds are also available in other libraries. But for documents which are not readily available elsewhere the Department tries to help scholars if it can. Owing to pressure from outside applicants it is made a condition that their work must be for a book, article or thesis which will eventually be available for other scholars to consult.

II. Regional

Material Held in Federation and Regional Offices

At present, Federation Offices exist at the following addresses:

East Midlands:	Church Street, Burbage, Hinckley, Leics.
Eastern:	Newmarket Road, Cambridge
Greater London:	32 Smith Square, London SW1P 3HH
North Western:	Woolton House, Byrom Street, Manchester
Northern Counties:	Woolton House, Portland Terrace, Newcastle-upon-Tyne
Scotland:	Atholl Crescent, Edinburgh
South Eastern:	32 Smith Square, London SW1P 3HH
Wales:	Faraday House, Fitzalan Place, Cardiff
West Midlands:	Milverton Terrace, Leamington

[1] These are due for publication.
[2] These are now available in microfilm.

Wessex:	The Priory, Brown Street, Salisbury
Western:	Magdalen Road, Exeter
Yorkshire:	Great George Street, Leeds

Information is available on the following areas:

1. *East Midlands*

Few records survive prior to 1939.

2. *Eastern*

A very useful set of records survives, although there is nothing prior to 1908. The records include minute books of the former Eastern Provincial Division and its successor from 1908-35 and from 1940 to date (the volume from 1935-40 has been lost). There is also a book of general accounts for the 1931-37 period, and a subscriptions list for 1939-49. Other records include minutes of the Women's Parliamentary Committee, 1920-28, and the Women's Advisory Committee, 1932-52 and 1960 to date. There are also accounts for this body from 1937-45. There is a useful minute book of the Agricultural Advisory Committee from 1950 to date.

3. *Greater London*

Records held at Conservative Central Office include the following groups:

(*a*) *London Municipal Society* (see also separate entry, pp. 156-7). The L.M.S. passed on their files to the Greater London Area in 1964, but most have been subsequently destroyed. A few boxes remain, which contain only Royal Commission Reports and other government publications relating to London local government.

A file of L.M.S. papers from the 1890s has survived, most of which concerns its evidence to a Royal Commission. There is also some miscellaneous election literature from 1939.

(*b*) *London Conservative Union:*

(1) Council and A.G.M. minutes survive from 1956. These consist of one large minute book and a loose-leaf file. Up to 1959 they tend to be very full and informative, after that they are more formal.

(2) General Purposes Committee and Executive Committee minutes date from 1954. These are contained in four minute books, with slight gaps and a few overlaps. There was a financial statement in detail presented to each G.P. Committee meeting. The reports also include full details of discussions on organisational matters, electioneering, local government matters, and relations with the L.M.S.

Executive Committee meetings also had a report from the Central Office Agent on the state of local organisation and a report from sub-committees (Women's, Y.C.s, etc.).

(3) Women's Advisory Committee minutes cover the years 1946-63.

Other than this, very little material has been kept because of the local government re-organisation of 1963 which invalidated most earlier items. There are, however, also some records of the London Constituencies Subscription Centre.

These include:

(*a*) Minutes of Management Committee from 1953, also some minutes of the Finance Committee and of some special meetings in 1952.

(*b*) Reports on money-raising and related financial matters.

(*c*) Lists of subscriptions to L.C.S.C. by constituency.

In addition, there is a variety of old minute books stored at the warehouse which include:

(a)   London Y.C. Council and Finance Committee, minute books, 1946-64. There are also some cash and account books for the same period.

(b)   London Young Britons, final minute book (1950s).

(c)   Home Counties: North Area minute books, 1932-63; these are very full and cover meetings of Council, all committees, and Y.C. Advisory Committee.

4. North Western

This collection is probably one of the fullest of any at regional level. Prior to the merger of the Lancashire and Cheshire Divisions of the National Union in 1925, the following material survives in the Federation Office:

(1)   Cheshire Division: minute books of the Council of the Cheshire Division, 1907-12, 1912-17, 1918-March 1925; also a bank pass book, Oct. 1914-June 1925.

(2)   Lancashire Division: cash books for the period 1907-22, 1923-25, minutes of the Finance Committee, 1907-24, and a cash book of the Labour Committee of the Lancashire Division, Sept. 1918-Dec. 1924.

After 1925 the following main items survive of the Lancashire and Cheshire Division:

(1)   Correspondence relating to the 1925 merger.

(2)   Executive Committee minute books.

(3)   Council minute books.

(4)   Area F. & G.P.s, M.B.s 1933-39.

(5)   A/c's, cash books for the periods, together with M.B.s of the Finance Committee.

(6)   Women's Advisory Committee, M.B.s.

There is, in addition, a considerable amount of material relating to the Junior Imperial League and similar organisations. The earliest records here are of the Lancashire and Cheshire Junior Unionist Association after 1910 right through its various successors to 1940. There are also minutes of the Manchester Junior Unionist Central Council, 1912-14, and some Lancashire Junior Imperial League records for the 1936-39 period.

5. Scotland

The two principal collections of 'central' Scottish records are housed in the Scottish Conservative Central Office at 11 Atholl Crescent, Edinburgh, and at the Glasgow and South-Western Regional Office at 72 Waterloo Street, Glasgow. They cover most of the history of the Scottish Party's national organisation since the formation of the National Union of Conservative Associations for Scotland on 24 Nov. 1882, and include a considerable amount of local material.

N.U.C.A.S. records consist of 16 bound volumes in Glasgow and two in Edinburgh. Three volumes of Council minutes cover the period 24 Nov. 1882-29 Mar. 1904. Other volumes contain detailed minutes of the Council's Leaflet Committee, 28 Feb. 1889-27 Oct. 1908; Literature Committee, 26 Mar. 1910-22 Nov. 1912; Registration Committee, 25 Mar. 1890-18 Oct. 1912. Printed rules, accounts and conference agenda from 1882 are also included. The entire history of the Eastern Division is covered in the Organisation Committee minutes (two vols.), 4 Jan. 1889-24 May 1893, and the Divisional Council minutes, (three vols.), 24 May 1893-27 Dec. 1912, which include printed reports; the Finance and Advice Committee minutes (11 Aug. 1882-[n.d.] 1912); and the Northern District C.A. minutes, vol.II (5 Sept. 1882-23 Feb. 1888). The Western Division is much less adequately covered. There are 'Special Fund' cashbooks of the Organisation Committee (11 Mar. 1889-11 Nov. 1891) and Divisional Council (Nov. 1906-Mar.

1910). There is an assortment of publications, including successive runs of the *Campaign Guide*, 1892-1918, at Edinburgh. Conservative negotiations for a merger with the Liberal Unionists are reported in detail in the minutes of the joint committee, 16 Feb. 1911-14 Jan. 1913.

Scottish Unionist Association collections of minutes, reports and publications are complete from the Central Council's first meeting on 24 Jan. 1913. A full collection of conference agenda (from 1913) is also stored at Glasgow. A very large amount of correspondence is collected at Edinburgh. Eastern Divisional Council minutes date from the original meeting of 29 Jan. 1913, and Western D.C. minutes from 5 Mar. 1913. Among a very large collection of material, both manuscript and printed, stored at Glasgow and Edinburgh, there are detailed financial accounts; Executive, Women's Advisory Committee and Junior Imperial League reports; papers and reports from many specialised groups; minutes of the Scottish agents' and organising secretaries' society; collections of tickets and posters; the late Sir Lewis Shedden's largely unpublished notes on Glasgow and West of Scotland political and social history and his published and manuscript articles on particular constituencies.

Scottish Conservative and Unionist Association records are equally comprehensive, from the change of title in 1965, including minutes of the Executive, Central Council and regional councils, together with a number of publications.

The Scottish Unionist Whip's Office and Office of the Chairman of the Party records are held at Edinburgh. They include a wide range of correspondence and publications, notably the correspondence of the former Political Secretary, Colonel Sir Patrick Blair, D.S.O., with constituencies and politicians.

Scottish Conservative Central Office records, held at Edinburgh, include a wide range of modern correspondence, press cuttings and publications.

Scottish Constitutional Committee minutes, 13 Sept. 1968-16 Mar. 1970, and correspondence are stored at the Scottish Central Office.

6. *South East Area*

A variety of useful records exists at Smith Square. These include:

(1) Council (from 1939). The records include: a box file containing, 1938-48, financial reports only; 1948-59, financial reports and annual printed reports; minutes of various special meetings, e.g. of Chairman and Agents, 1955, and a minute book reporting Council meetings, 1950 to present. This contains addresses by Ministers or M.P.s summarised; full reports of discussions on policy and organisation; summaries of annual reports and financial statements.

(2) Executive and F. & G.P. Committees (box file). Minutes of odd meetings in wartime; 1945-56, full minutes of F. & G.P. Committee (loose typescripts); 1945-53, full minutes of Executive Committee (loose typescripts). These contain general organisation matters relating to constituency affairs, local finance, membership, agents and local elections.

(3) Hon. Treasurer's Circulars (box file). Approximately monthly circulars sent out to constituency chairmen and treasurers. They give details of progress in fund-raising, constituency league tables, results of quotas, and comparisons with other Areas.

(4) New Towns and Housing Estates (box file). Literature, memoranda and correspondence relating to conferences on organisation in South Eastern New Towns, 1953 and 1957.

(5) Trade Union Committee minute book (1947-69). Agenda, minutes and reports of meetings survive and include reports from constituencies by organisers. Minutes tend to be formal, reporting decisions rather than discussions, except that they record discussions after a general address.

(6)   Education Committee minute book (1946-62). Minutes only, in a rather formal and brief form. Secretaries report on local political education work to each meeting, and the main other business is in co-operation with the National Advisory Committee on Political Education and the local C.P.C.s.

7. *West Midlands*

As with the North West and Scotland, records here are both extensive and detailed. The earliest material consists of a constituency records book of the Midland Union for the period 1885-1911. There are full minutes of the Council, Women's Organisation, Junior Imperial League and Labour Advisory Committee from 1886.

8. *Wessex*

No detailed information is available, but no records prior to 1928 have been uncovered.

9. *Yorkshire*

A useful collection survives, including minutes of the Council, Executive Committee and Finance Committee since 1886.

III.   Constituencies

The following list of records held in constituency offices has been compiled from returns sent to the project by local agents as a result of circulars distributed through Central Office. Since the survey was conducted in 1971 the redistribution of seats has altered the boundaries and names of various constituencies. The list should be regarded as an indication of the sort of material available, and the areas covered, rather than a definitive guide. Except where otherwise stated, records are retained by the association concerned.

Abingdon. M.B.s and ann. reps. Apr. 1910 to date.

Aldershot. M.B.s and ann. reps. Jan. 1934 to date. Press cuttings from 1948; local party journals from 1968; some correspondence dating back to 1945. Canvass returns, 1959, 1964, 1966. Also balance sheets and reports of Aldershot Conservative Club from 1931.

Angus North and Mearns. M.B.s June 1901 to date; ann. reps. from 1948. Some literature/correspondence from 1939 onwards.

*Ashfield.*M.B.s of former Broxtowe Women's Association from 1924.

Ashford. M.B.s 1886 to date.

Ayr. M.B.s 1898 to date. Press cuttings from 1922 onwards.

Ayrshire Central. M.B.s from formation in 1949 to present day; ann. reps. from 1950. Press cuttings from 1949.

Banbury. M.B.s from 1913. A constituency magazine, *Calling Quarterly*, from 1960.

Barking. M.B.s from 1954; ann. reps. from 1951.

Barkston Ash. M.B.s 1895-1933. Now deposited with Sheepscar Branch of Leeds City Library. Later M.B.s still with local association.

Barnet. M.B.s and ann. reps. since 1945. Local magazine, *Weekly Bulletin*, since 1949. Canvass returns, 1950 to date.

Barry. M.B.s and ann. reps. since 1951.

Basingstoke. M.B.s 1884 to date.

Bath. A very important collection deposited with the Archives and Record Office, Guildhall, Bath. The earliest items are minutes for the period Mar. 1857-Jan. 1877 and Feb. 1877-Dec. 1899. A full breakdown of material can be obtained from the Guildhall, Bath, or from the National Register of Archives.

Bedford. M.B.s and ann. reps. from 1930 to date. Literature/correspondence after 1960.

Bedfordshire South. M.B.s 1947 to date.

Belper. M.B.s 8 Nov. 1948 to date; ann. reps. 1950 to date (excluding 1962).

Bexley. M.B.s, ann. reps., membership records and financial statements, 1950 to date. Also certain key correspondence.

Billericay. M.B.s since formation of association in 1955.

Birkenhead. M.B.s 1922 to date; ann. reps. 1964 to date.

Birmingham Handsworth. M.B.s 1912 to date; ann. reps. 1914 to date. Press cuttings 1923 onwards (not continuous).

Blackburn. M.B.s 1961 to date.

Blackpool. A full collection of records, the earliest material dating from 1909, is now deposited in Lancashire Record office.

Bodmin. A useful collection of M.B.s etc., now deposited in Cornwall Record Office.

Bolton. M.B.s since 1898; ann. reps. since 1893. Also ledger and a/c books.

Bosworth. M.B.s since 1918. These, and other records, are now deposited in Leicestershire Record Office.

Bournemouth East and Christchurch. M.B.s from Nov. 1948 to date; ann. reps. over similar period.

Bradford (City). An important collection now deposited in Bradford Public Library. Exec. Comm. M.B.s (3): 1870-76, June 1876-Apr. 1886, Oct. 1937-Mar. 1940. General Council M.B.s, 1886-97, 1902-34. M.B.s of the Municipal Comm. (1887-1927) and Finance and Emergency Comm. minutes. M.B. of the Bradford Junior Conservative and Unionist Association, 1929-42.

Bradford Central. M.B.s (2): Feb. 1906-May 1925, Mar. 1926-Oct. 1949. M.B. of the West Ward, Oct. 1886-Mar. 1898. M.B. of the Women's Association, Mar. 1919-Nov. 1930. Deposited in Bradford Public Library.

Bradford East. M.B.s (3): Jan. 1887-Dec. 1905, Feb. 1906-Nov. 1921, Apr. 1926-Nov. 1934. M.B. of the Women's Association, Mar. 1937-Sept. 1951. M.B. of the South Ward, Jan. 1887-Jan. 1913. Deposited in Bradford Public Library.

Bradford South. M.B. Apr. 1919-Feb. 1930, deposited in Bradford Public Library.

Bradford West. M.B.s (2): Jan. 1887-Oct. 1906, Jan. 1907-Mar. 1924. Deposited in Bradford Public Library.

Brecon and Radnor. M.B.s of the former Breconshire Division, 1878-1918 (with gaps). No separate Radnorshire records survive prior to 1918.

Brentford and Chiswick. M.B.s and ann. reps. 1945 to date. Association yearbooks and magazines, 1948 to date. Correspondence from 1945. Canvass returns, 1938-39 and from 1953 to date.

Brierley Hill. All records of the old Kingswinford Division are believed to be lost.

Brighton Kemptown. Records date from 1961 only.

Bristol. M.B.s since 1904, badly charred as result of recent fire.

Brixton. M.B.s Jan. 1958 to date; ann. reps. 1959 to date.

Buckinghamshire South. M.B.s since 1948; ann. reps., books of press cuttings etc., for similar period.

Burton-on-Trent. M.B.s and ann. reps. 1950 to date.

Bute and North Ayrshire. M.B.s (and press cuttings) 1911 to date; ann. reps. from 1929.

Cannock. M.B. after 1930 of the Finance Comm.

Canterbury. Complete M.B.s and ann. reps. from 1946. A few earlier M.B.s back to 1900, but most destroyed by bombing in 1942.

Carlton. M.B.s and ann. reps. 1948 to date.

Carshalton. M.B.s from 1935; ann. reps. and some election correspondence from 1945.

Chelmsford. M.B.s and ann. reps. from 1924; some correspondence from 1933.

Chertsey. M.B.s since 1948; ann. reps. since 1954.

Chichester. A full and important collection of records, deposited in the West Sussex Record Office. The records, however, are not available for consultation except with the written permission of the Constituency Chairman. Three M.B.s of the division cover the periods May 1924-Dec. 1954. The minutes of the Women's Association exist from 1918-48. In addition, there are M.B.s of the Men's Conservative Association for the periods 1868-83, 1914-49 and 1949-55. More recent records are retained by the Association.

Chigwell and Ongar. M.B.s and ann. reps. after 1956.

Chippenham. M.B.s from 1900, but ann. reps. only from 1964. Election posters, leaflets, from 1935; press cuttings from 1945. A local journal, the *North West Wiltshire Critic*, exists for the period 1930-39. There are also some 19th-century propaganda plates and election posters, including one dated 1832.

Chorley. M.B.s and ann. reps. since 1945 deposited in the Lancashire Record Office.

Cirencester and Tewkesbury. M.B.s from formation, in Dec. 1917; ann. reps. from 1954. Some correspondence for the 1955 General Election.

Cities of London and Westminster. An important collection, now deposited in Westminster Public Library.

Clapham. A full and interesting collection, now deposited in the British Library of Political and Economic Science. M.B.s cover the periods Mar. 1889-Dec. 1903, 1902-09, 1918-25, 1930-34 and 1934-49. Press cuttings exist for the period 1932-37. There are also minutes of Clapham Park South Ward, 1907-36.

Clitheroe. A full set of records, now deposited in the Lancashire Record Office in Preston, including balance sheets from 1876, cash books from 1885 and complete minutes from 1909-47.

Cornwall North. A full set of records, now deposited in Cornwall Record Office.

Crosby. Minutes of the Association and its predecessors from 1901-63; also records of the Women's Association, 1922-56. Now deposited in Lancashire Record Office.

Croydon North East. M.B.s from 1955.

Dagenham. M.B.s and ann. reps. from 1947.

Darlington. M.B.s 1929 to date.

Dartford. M.B.s of the Association, and also of the Young Conservatives, from 1953.

Darwen. A very full collection with minutes complete from 1885, now deposited in Lancashire Record Office.

Denbigh. M.B.s from 1924; ann. reps. only from 1937.

Derbyshire South East. M.B.s and ann. reps. from 1945.

Derbyshire West. Minutes, 1890-1914, then only post-1945.

Doncaster. M.B.s from 1935. Press cuttings from 1961.

Dorking. M.B.s from 1950.

Dorset West. A very full and important collection, now deposited in the Dorset Record Office. These include M.B.s from 1913-58 for the Exec. Comm., and from 1919-45 for the Finance Comm. Minutes of Women's Association, 1928-40. M.B.s of Bridport Women's Branch, 1931-62. There are four volumes of minutes, 1888-1926, of the Bridport Conservative Club. There are also minutes of the Dorset Conservative Association, 1884-1907.

Durham North West. M.B.s from Sept. 1948.

Ealing South. M.B.s from 1950.

East Grinstead. M.B.s 1883-85 and 1906 to date; ann. reps. for similar period.

Eastleigh. M.B.s complete from foundation.

Eccles. Records now deposited with Lancashire Record Office.

Epping. M.B.s since 1945.

Epsom. M.B.s since 1918; ann. reps. since 1928.

Essex South East. M.B.s from inauguration, Feb. 1955.

Exeter. M.B.s and ann. reps. from 1953.

Falmouth and Camborne. M.B.s of the former Camborne Division, July 1919-49. M.B.s of new division, 1950 to date.

Farnham. M.B.s Jan. 1949 to date, with ann. reps. Also complete file of local journal *Common Sense*, 1949-68. Some correspondence also from 1949.

Fife West. A useful collection deposited in the Library of the University of St. Andrews. This consists of 29 boxes of papers covering the period 1948 to date.

Finchley. M.B.s 1912-24, 1929-34, 1934 to date; ann. reps. from 1960.

Flintshire West. Records now deposited in Flintshire Record Office.

Fulham. M.B.s from 1930 onwards.

Fylde North. M.B.s 1948 to date; ann. reps. 1950 to date.

Fylde South. M.B.s 1963 to date.

Glasgow. Some extremely early material survives. The earliest item is the M.B. of the Glasgow Conservative Operatives' Association covering the period Dec. 1836-May 1843. This is in the possession of Mr. Andrew Strang, O.B.E. There are full and continuous minutes of the Glasgow Conservative and Unionist Association (founded 25 Jan. 1869, as the Glasgow Working Men's Conservative Association).

Grantham. M.B.s from 1945; ann. reps. press cuttings and local journals from 1953.

Gravesend. Records for the period 1923-71 are now deposited in Kent Archives Office.

Grimsby. M.B.s from 1958.

Guildford. The original M.B. covering the period Feb. 1866-Aug. 1868, is deposited in Guildford Museum. M.B.s from 1906 to date are in the association offices. Ann. reps. exist from 1945 and press cuttings from 1926. There is some correspondence from 1945.

Haltemprice and Beverley. M.B.s Mar. 1955 to date. Much material destroyed in 1948.

Hammersmith. Minutes of Hammersmith Constitutional Association for the period 1886-1915 are deposited in Hammersmith Borough Library.

Hampstead. M.B.s 1888-1914, 1946 to date; some ann. reps. back to 1918.

Harborough. A very full and important set of records, now deposited in the Leicestershire Record Office. The earliest material, for the period 1867-91, includes minutes of the Central Comm. and the Finance Comm. together with ann. reps. There are minutes (1891-92) for the Joint Conservative and Liberal Unionist Comm. There are full minutes of a variety of committees from 1892 to 1963, with particularly full financial records.

Harrow East. M.B.s and ann. reps. 1946 to date.

Hartlepool. M.B.s of Exec. Comm., 1944-63. Also Finance Comm., 1957-64, and a variety of Young Conservative and branch records. All now deposited with Durham Record Office.

Harwich. A.G.M. minutes, 1912 to date. Exec. Comm. minutes, 1932-52 and 1961 to date. Minutes of National Liberal Exec. Comm., 1931-38. Press cuttings from 1906-19.

Hastings. M.B.s from 1859-1918 deposited in Hastings Public Museum.

Hemel Hempstead. M.B.s and ann. reps. from 1918.

Hereford. All pre-war records lost during World War II, although a M.B. of the Ledbury Branch Men's Association, for the period 1910-31, is in Herefordshire Record Office, together with minutes of the Brimfield branch (1886-1916) of the Herefordshire Conservative Union. There are also four volumes of minutes of the Hereford North Association for the period 1907-34, and three volumes of the Women's branch, 1922-48.

Hertford. M.B.s from 1906; ann. reps. from 1954 in the association office. Minutes of the Ware Unionist Association, 1898-1924, deposited in Hertfordshire Record Office.

Hertfordshire South West. M.B.s and ann. reps. since 1950.

Hitchin. M.B.s 1918-33, 1952 to date; ann. reps. 1952 to date.

Horncastle. M.B.s 1890 to date, but rather fragmented.

Huddersfield. An incomplete series of minutes, the oldest dating back to 1903. Condition very poor as a result of fire in 1966.

Ilford. M.B.s 1954 to date.

Ipswich. M.B.s and ann. reps. 1926 to date.

Isle of Ely. Full records of the Exec. Finance and G.P. Committees back to 1945.

Keighley. Records 1885-1939 in Sheepscar Branch, Leeds City Library.

Kensington North. Some surviving material, now in offices of South Kensington Conservative Association. (q.v.)

Kensington South. A considerable run of minutes back prior to 1914.

Kidderminster. M.B.s and ann. reps. from 1937.

Kincardine and West Aberdeenshire. M.B.s 1901-30 in University Library, King's College, Aberdeen.

Kingston-upon-Hull Conservative Federation. M.B.s dating back to 1947.

Kinross and West Perthshire. M.B.s, ann. reps. and some correspondence from 1917.

Kirkcaldy Burghs. A useful collection, deposited in the Library of the University of St. Andrews. In all, this collection amounts to 17 boxes of material, covering the period 1901 to date. There is also an additional box of material for the period 1901-39 relating to the Kirkcaldy Unionist Club.

Knutsford. M.B.s from 1885 to date.

Lancaster. Minutes of A.G.M., 1913 to date.

Leeds. M.B.s and ann. reps. from 1925 in the association offices. Nine volumes of cuttings for the period 1929-50 have been deposited in Leeds City Library.

Leek. Financial records, 1914-60, in Staffordshire Record Office.

Leicester North West. M.B.s and ann. reps. together with scrapbooks from 1937.

Lewes. M.B.s from June 1924; ann. reps. only from 1958.

Lewisham West. M.B.s from 1918 but not complete.

Lincoln. M.B.s 1918-30. There is also a M.B. of the Finance Comm., from 1906-16.

Louth. M.B.s 1944-57 now deposited in Lincolnshire Archives Office.

Maidstone. A full set of records, with minutes complete from 1885. Records now deposited in Kent Archives Office. There is even earlier material relating to elections in 1832, 1841 and 1885 which has also been deposited.

Mansfield. M.B.s from 1948.

Meriden. M.B.s from formation in 1955.

Middlesbrough. A useful set of records. M.B.s for the periods 1903-09, 1917-33, 1933-45 and 1946 to date.

Middleton and Prestwich. M.B.s from 1901-06. Fairly full records after 1928. All now deposited in Lancashire Record Office.

Monmouth. M.B.s and ann. reps. from 1919.

Nelson and Colne. M.B.s from Mar. 1946 to date.

Newark. M.B.s from Nov. 1892 to date. Balance sheets from 1932.

Newbury. A good collection of records, now deposited in Berkshire Record Office.

Newcastle-under-Lyme. Records prior to 1950 were destroyed by fire.

Newcastle West. M.B.s and ann. reps. from 1918.

Newport. A/Cs, 1888-91 deposited in Shropshire Record Office.

Norfolk Central. M.B.s 1948-72 in Norfolk Record Office.

Norfolk East. M.B.s 1934-47 in Norfolk Record Office.

Northampton. M.B.s and ann. reps. from 1925 are deposited in Northamptonshire Record Office.

Northants South. M.B.s from 1943; ann. reps. from 1947.

Northwich. Records prior to 1963 destroyed by office fire.

Norwich. M.B.s from 1904 to date.

Nottingham West. All pre-war records lost during 1939-45 period.

Nottingham South. M.B.s and a/c's 1935-69 in Nottinghamshire Record Office.

Oldham. M.B.s from 1945.

Oswestry. M.B. of former West Shropshire Conservative Association, 1907-14. M.B.s of Oswestry Division, 1918-38, and also of Women's Association over similar period. M.B.s of Hadnall Ward, 1923-64. Also a M.B., 1905-12, of the St. Martin's Lodge of the National Conservative League. For the 1901 by-election a volume of MSS., cuttings, etc., concerning Hon. George Ormsby-Gore's canditature still exists.

Oxford. A full set of records, with deposit promised to Oxford City Library.

Paddington North. An incomplete run of M.B.s and a/c's from 1906. Y.C. minutes from 1947.

Paddington South. M.B.s and ann. reps. since 1935.

Penistone. M.B.s 1928-30, 1945 to date; ann. reps. after 1953.

Peterborough. M.B.s from 1898 to date.

Petersfield. A large but unsorted collection with ann. reps. dating from 1909.

Plymouth Sutton. Association office bombed in 1941 destroying most records. M.B.s, ann. reps., and press cuttings, however, survive from 1938.

Poole. M.B.s and ann. reps. from 1908; a/c's from 1928 onwards.

Portsmouth South. M.B.s and ann. reps. from 1925. Eight volumes of M.B.s, 1924-68, of the Young Conservatives are in Portsmouth Record Office.

Reigate. A very full collection of records. These include minutes of the Reigate Conservative Registration Association from 1869-85 and its successor from 1885-1906. The inter-war period seems less well covered, although there are minutes of the Women's Advisory Committee from 1924-31. Press cuttings cover the periods 1906-10 and 1920 to date. A collection of mid-19th-century pamphlet material is deposited with the Borough Library.

Renfrewshire West. A good collection of pre-1914 material. This includes 20 letter-books for the period 1888-1911, three press cuttings books for the years 1890-1913, a minute book for 1899-1911, two ledgers covering the years 1886-90 and 1912-18. This is at present housed with Messrs. MacRobert Son & Hutcheson (Solicitors), Paisley.

Rochdale. Exec. Comm. minutes from 1937. A subscription book from 1936. Women's Association minutes from Nov. 1935.

Rochester and Chatham. M.B.s and ann. reps. from 1912.

Rother Valley. M.B.s from 1896.

Rushcliffe. Ann. reps. since 1902; M.B.s 1886-1961 in Nottinghamshire Record Office.

Rutland and Stamford. M.B.s dating from 1883 with gaps from 1918-23 and 1931-45; ann. reps. from 1929.

Rye and Bexhill. M.B.s from 1885, believed to be complete.

St. Albans. M.B.s from 1900.

St. Pancras North. A.G.M.s, 1926 to date; Exec. Cl., 1936 to date; F. & G.P. minutes, 1949 to date.

Sevenoaks. M.B.s Oct. 1918-40, 1946 to date; ann. reps. from 1946.

Sheffield Conservative Federation. Minutes of General Meetings since 1913; a cash book for the period 1913-19.

Sheffield Brightside. Exec. Comm. minutes 1910-28, a/c's from 1905. These records are at present in the office of Sheffield Conservative Federation (see above).

Sheffield Central. A few minutes prior to 1917, also at the Federation Office.

Sheffield Eccleshall. A variety of M.B.s from 1880s, some in the Federation Office.

Sheffield Heeley. M.B.s since inauguration in 1950 now deposited in Sheffield City Library.

Sheffield Hillsborough. M.B.s from Mar. 1948.

Sheffield Park. M.B.s since 1906; Women's Council since 1931; Y.C.s since 1947. There is also a M.B. of Sheffield Municipal Elections Comm., 1906-19.

Shrewsbury. No records earlier than 1933, when the Exec. Comm. minutes began. Women's Association minutes from similar date.

Skipton. M.B.s from *c.* 1900.

South Shields. M.B.s from 1952.

Southall. M.B.s from 1950.

Southgate. M.B.s from formation in 1948.

Southport. M.B.s from 1914. ann. reps. from 1887.

Sowerby. M.B.s and ann. reps. 1924 to date. Also minutes of the Primrose League Branch, 1887-1969. Constituency correspondence since 1949.

Stockton-on-Tees. An important collection of minutes, now deposited in Durham Record Office. The collection includes M.B.s of the Stockton Constitutional Organisation, the earliest dating from 1891. There are also minutes of the Women's Association (1923-38) and of the Unionist Labour Advisory Comm. (1925-34). There are also three volumes of press cuttings on local politics for the periods 1890-98, 1904-09 and 1910-23. There are minutes of the Junior Imperial League for 1923-24 (including a/c's) and 1937.

Stratford-on-Avon. M.B.s 1947 to date.

Surbiton. M.B.s 1955 to date.

Surrey East. M.B.s from 1937; ann. reps. from 1956.

Sutton Coldfield. M.B.s from 1945.

Swansea West. M.B.s from formation in Sept. 1948.

Swindon. M.B.s from 1950. Local journal, *Swindon Conservative Review*, from Aug. 1926 to July 1932.

Thirsk and Malton. M.B.s from 25 Nov. 1924.

Torquay. M.B.s continuous from 1885. Also copies of local journal, *Torbay Standard*, for the 1920s.

Torrington. M.B.s from 1949.

Truro. M.B.s since 1910; ann. reps., press cuttings since 1945.

Twickenham. M.B.s from 1945.

Tynemouth. M.B.s from Apr. 1949, together with ann. reps.

Uxbridge. Deposited now in Greater London Record Office (Middlesex Section).

Wakefield. Records exist of the former Rothwell Division from 1928-49 when it was amalgamated with Wakefield. M.B.s and ann. reps. 1949 to date.

Walsall North. M.B.s 1955 to date.

Wanstead and Woodford. M.B.s 1945 to date.

Warwick and Leamington. M.B.s 1885 to date.

Watford. M.B.s, together with all correspondence, since 1949.

Wells. A useful collection. M.B.s and ann. reps. 1924 to date; a/c's from 1936.

West Bromwich. No records prior to 1947.

Westminster St. George's. See under Cities of London and Westminster.

Westminster Abbey. See under Cities of London and Westminster.

Weston-super-Mare. Despite a serious fire in the association office in Nov. 1967, an interesting collection of records still survives. This includes a/c's for the 1911-38 period, press cuttings since 1934 and Exec. Comm. minutes from 1944. Minutes of the Junior Imperial League for the years 1925-31 also exist.

Whitehaven. F. & G.P. minutes from 1932.

Wirral. A very full set of minutes, dating from the formation of the association in Feb. 1885. Ann. reps. cover a similar period. Press cuttings from Sept. 1936.

Woking. M.B.s 1949 to date.

Wokingham. M.B.s 1948 to date.

Wolverhampton East. M.B. of the former division 1918-30, now in the possession of Dr. G. Jones, Department of Government, L.S.E.

Wolverhampton West. M.B.s of this division, 1908 to early 1950s, together with press cuttings books in the possession of Dr. G. Jones, Department of Government, L.S.E.

Wood Green. Records now deposited in Greater London Record Office (Middlesex Section).

Woolwich West. A full set of records, some 31 volumes in all. The earliest constituency material is Exec. Comm. minutes from 1912. A full variety of minutes cover the inter-war period.

Worcester. Another useful set of records. The earliest item is a M.B. of the Worcester District of the National Conservative League from 1888-1914. The minutes of the Exec. Comm. of the association cover the period 1931-48. There are minutes for the Women's Organisation (1929-49) and the Junior Unionist Association (1909-32). There is an association subscription register for the period 1935-43.

Worcestershire East. Records deposited in Birmingham City Library include Exec. Comm. minutes, 1897-1915, Divisional Comm. minutes, 1885-1915, Liberal Unionist Association, 1905-15, Unionist Association Finance and Advisory Comm., 1916-18.

Worthing. M.B.s and ann. reps. 1948 to date.

Wrexham. M.B.s from Dec. 1913.

IV. Related Organisations

Active Backbenchers' Committee

Formed in 1932 by a group of Conservative backbenchers, the Committee aimed to scrutinise and criticise legislation, with a view to eliminating objectionable features thereof. The group went out of existence about 1960.

Papers

The records are at present in the possession of the former Secretary, W. van Straubenzee, M.P. No details on extent are known.

Availability

Enquiries should be addressed to Mr. van Straubenzee.

Association of Conservative Teachers
32 Smith Square London SW1P 3HH

Formed in 1925 by C. W. Crook, M.P. a former President of the National Union of Teachers, the Association was succeeded in 1966 by the National Advisory Committee on Education.

Papers

Very little material on education is retained at Conservative Central Office, because of reorganisation within the Department in the mid-1960s. Apart from the Association of Conservative Teachers, the Department embraces the work of the Conservative Graduates' Association and the *Federation of Conservative Students* (q.v.). Minutes of these committees for the post-war years, and in some cases back to 1930, are kept in the Registry.

Correspondence is retained for a few years only, but copies of the journals (e.g. *Right Angle*, 1948-53, *Conservative Teacher*, 1953-63, and *Focus on Education*, 1965-72) are kept in the Research Department Library.

Conservative Private Members' Committee ('1922 Committee')

This is an organisation of the entire backbench membership of the Conservative Party in the House of Commons. It is a forum for the discussion of Conservative opinion in the House; it is not authorised to formulate policy.

Papers

Older minutes of the Committee have been retained at Conservative Central Office, 32 Smith Square, London SW1P 3HH:

Volume 1:	1923-28
Volume 2:	1928-34
Volume 3:	1934-38
Volume 4:	1938-43
Volume 5:	1943-49

This latter volume is apparently missing. The more recent minutes from 1949 are in the care of the present Secretary. All these minutes are apparently brief, with the earliest books as the most informative. Even then, they record business done and not usually the nature of the discussions.

Availability

These records are not available for research purposes.

1922 Committee records were used in the recent history of the Committee: Philip Goodhart, *The 1922: The story of the Conservative Backbenchers' Parliamentary Committee* (1973).

Federation of Conservative Students
32 Smith Square London SW1P 3HH

Founded in May 1930 as the Federation of University Conservative and Unionist Associations, the Federation took its present name in 1967. The F.C.S. aims to encourage the formation and maintenance of active student Conservative associations in all institutions of higher education; to provide assistance and information to such associations; to express the students' viewpoint to the Conservative party; to recruit active and able party members; to provide a common platform for political discussion; and to speak as a representative body of Conservative students.

Papers

Committee minutes for the post-war years, and in some cases dating from 1930, are preserved at the Conservative Central Office, 32 Smith Square.

Availability

Applications should be addressed to the Director.

Junior Imperial and Constitutional League

The League was founded in 1906 to organise youth in support of the Conservative and Unionist cause. As a result of the Fraser Report (1938) and the Palmer Report (1943) the League was replaced in 1946 by the Young Conservative movement.

Records in Conservative Central Office include: a complete set of minute books (six volumes), 1905-44, which relate to the Council, A.G.M.s, Executive Committee, Finance Committee, Publication Committee; 1928 J.I.L. Central Council meeting documents; annual reports, 1922-39, though this is an incomplete set; two files of miscellaneous notes, correspondence, etc., relating to Youth Organisation, 1937-47: these mainly concern the work of the Fraser Committee (1937) and the Palmer Committee (1943), together with financial statements, cheques, wartime pamphlets and memoranda; a very full and informative folder of press cuttings on the J.I.L., 1932-46; minute book of Telbridge J.I.L. branch, 1935-36; the Hendon Division J.I.L. Council rules, 1931; N.E. Derbyshire, Unstone branch documents; Chesterfield branch documents, *c.* 1927. The League published the following journals, which survive: *Junior Imperial League Gazette* (1920-25), *The Imp* (1925-36), *Torchbearer* (1937-39).

Young Britons

This was founded in 1925 to teach the principles of the Conservative faith to members in the age group 6-14 years.

Papers

A small collection of archive material of the Young Britons is housed in the Registry Store at Conservative Central Office. This consists of a few miscellaneous bundles of correspondence and minute books, some dating back to the 1930s but the majority going no further back than the 1950s.

Young Conservative Organisation

The organisation was founded in 1946, and is the successor body of the Junior Imperial League.

Papers

The records at Conservative Central Office include: minute books of the National Advisory Committee from 1946 (three volumes): these are brief and formal rather than informative; and certain general correspondence for the late 1940s. Copies of the Y.C.s' journals (*Advance*, 1946-53, *Rightway*, 1954-58, *Impact*, 1964-68, *Tomorrow*, 1970-) are retained at Conservative Research Department.

CONSTITUTIONAL PARTY

Although the 'party' as such had no central organisation, it fielded candidates in the 1924 General Election in constituencies where local Conservative and Liberal parties joined forces, and where individual Liberal candidates received Conservative support against Socialism.

Papers

The private collections of individual Constitutional Party candidates must be consulted. Among these the most important are the Winston Churchill papers, eventually to be deposited at Churchill College, Cambridge. The papers of Captain C. E. Loseby are with the family in Guernsey.

CONSUMERS' COUNCIL

The Council was established in January 1918 as a consultative body by the former Food Controller, Lord Rhondda, and his successor, J. R. Clynes. Its aim was to enlist the co-operation of the organised working classes and the co-operative movement in the work of the Ministry of Food in attempting to control the distribution and prices of essential foodstuffs. Representatives were drawn from the Parliamentary Committee of the Co-operative Congress, the Parliamentary Committee of the T.U.C., the War Emergency Workers' National Committee, and the Standing Joint Committee of Industrial Women's Organisations. In addition there were three representatives of 'unorganised consumers'. The Council survived as an active body to the end of 1920.

Papers

It seems that the main body of Consumers' Council material has not survived among the public records. However, eight boxes of papers, relating to the activities of the Council, survive in the Labour Party's archive at Transport House and an indexed list has been produced by the staff of the Royal Commission on Historical Manuscripts. This may be consulted at the National Register of Archives and at Transport House. These were the papers of Dr. Marion Phillips, Chief Woman Officer of the Labour Party, as the representative of the Standing Joint Committee of Industrial Women's Organisations on the Council, and in view of the absence of any other surviving records they are of particular importance. The material in Transport House comprises her files of circulated papers, with other correspondence relating to the subjects dealt with by the Council. The largest group of papers relates to National Kitchens and contains a considerable amount of detail on local efforts to provide mass-catering at low prices. Other subjects covered include jam, meat and bacon, milk and dried milk supplies, potatoes and sugar; the largest of these files is that on milk and has particular reference to quality control and the arguments for and against the direct supply of milk from farmers to retailers.

Availability

On application in writing to the Librarian, the Labour Party, Transport House.

CO-OPERATIVE MOVEMENT

There is no central collection of co-operative records. The closest approximation is the Library of the *Co-operative Union*, which has a very valuable accumulation of documents, journals and pamphlets (see pp. 76-77). The Co-operative College, Stanford Hall, East Leake, Loughborough, Leics, also has a useful collection of journals. The *Bishopsgate Institute* has two relevant collections, the G. J. Holyoake papers and the George Howell MSS. Reference should also be made to the Plunkett Foundation for Co-operative Studies, 31 St. Giles, Oxford.

The 'Register of Co-operative Historical Records' at the Co-operative Union is the best guide to the great deal of material available. The societies listed below have retained useful collections of their own. For convenience, the organisations are listed in alphabetical order:

Co-operative Party
158 Buckingham Palace Road London SW1W 9VB

Papers

The bulk of Co-operative Party records has been destroyed: first of all during World War II, and secondly during the party's move from its premises in Victoria

Street to its present address in the early 1960s. At this time much correspondence, which would now be regarded as invaluable, was destroyed. Apart from current material, therefore, the surviving records largely comprise minutes and published material such as magazines and pamphlets.

The Co-operative Party minutes include bound volumes from 1917-50. From 1950 they have been issued with other minutes of the Co-operative Union in annual volumes, and copies of these from 1925-71 are in the party's Library (with the volume for 1945 missing). Minutes of the Co-operative Party's Parliamentary Group date from 1945. The party also has copies of its annual conference reports and proceedings from 1920-65. Since 1965 the annual report has continued to be issued, but the conference report has contained notes on decisions taken rather than full minutes. Co-operative Union Congress reports, 1903 to date, are also kept in the Library.

Copies of the party's *Monthly Letter* are retained from 1945 to 1965. In that year it was replaced by a bi-monthly broadsheet, *Platform,* which has, since 1970, been incorporated in *Co-operative News.* Other journals, such as the Co-operative Union's *Co-operative Review,* from 1828 to 1905, are similarly retained.

Another source for the history of the party is copies of its pamphlets, also in the Library. These include policy documents dating from 1918, and copies of the *Britain Reborn* series of the 1930s.

Of the current records the most useful are files of speakers' notes, issued since 1964, although there are copies of similar notes for the 1920s.

Very little information was received from local branches of the Co-operative Party. However, minutes of the Birmingham and District Co-operative Party have been microfilmed by Birmingham Central Reference Library. These date from 1918. See also *Labour Party: Constituency Records.*

Availability

Applications should be made to the Secretary of the Co-operative Party.

Co-operative Party Scottish Committee
95 Morrison Street Glasgow G5 8LR

Formed in December 1917 as the Scottish Parliamentary Representation Committee, it adopted its present title in September 1920.

Papers

These include minute books dating back to 1917.

Availability

Apply to the Secretary.

Co-operative Production Federation Ltd.
42 Western Road Leicester LE3 0GL

The Federation was founded in 1882 to link together some 15 Co-operative productive societies that had developed under Owenite and Christian Socialist influence. Its objects were to promote unity of action among its members, and to assist its members by finding capital, markets, etc. The Federation has similar functions today. The societies themselves operate on a co-partnership and profit-sharing basis, and are engaged chiefly in the clothing, footwear manufacture and printing trades.

Papers

The records of the Federation have been deposited in Hull University Library: Minutes of the following committees survive: the Federation, 1896-1961, the Federation Propaganda Committee, 1915-19, the Co-operative Co-partnership Propaganda Committee, 1918-60, Footwear Commodity Committee, 1943-62, the Co-operative Production Federation Footwear Ltd., Management Committee and Advisory Sub-committee, 1946-54, the Lancashire and Yorkshire Centre of the Labour Association for the Promotion of Co-operative Production, 1897-99, and the Stanton Memorial Scholarship Committee, 1918-48. Other records include a volume of press cuttings relating to the 70th Co-operative Congress, 1938, with copies of newspapers reporting the death of J. J. Worley, who presided at the Congress, 1944; two volumes of press cuttings relating to the Co-operative Production Federation, 1961-68; a visitors' book, 1947-52; a cash book 1895-99; and a ledger, 1918-20.

Availability

Applications should be made to the Librarian, Hull University Library.

Co-operative Union Ltd.
Holyoake House Hanover Street Manchester M60 0AS

The Co-operative Union is the national federation of the consumer co-operative societies in the British Isles. It was established after the Co-operative Congress of 1869 when a Central Board for co-operatives was set up. This became the Co-operative Union in 1889. The Co-operative Congress is the annual meeting of the Union. The Union provides advisory services and acts as a co-ordinating body to the co-operative movement.

Papers

The Co-operative Union Library has a very important collection of records relating to the history of the co-operative movement. The minutes of the Central Committee of the Union have been retained since 1897, as have annual Co-operative Congress reports since 1869. The Library has a very full collection of co-operative journals, including the movement's official journal, the *Co-operative News* (1971 to date), the *Scottish Co-operator* (1908, 1920, 1946 to date), the *Co-operative Review* (1926 to date), the *Year Book of Agricultural Co-operation* (1927 to date), the *Co-operative Magazine and Monthly Herald* (1827), *The Co-operator* (later *The Anti-Vaccinator*) (1860-71), the *Co-operative Union Quarterly Review* (1914-19), the *Co-operative Union News Service* (1928-51), *The Wheatsheaf* (later *Co-operative Home Magazine*) (1897-1964). This is a selection of a large variety of journals available which are supplemented by a comprehensive collection of jubilee and centenary histories of co-operative retail societies, and a wide range of pamphlets, leaflets and occasional publications covering all aspects of co-operative activities, issues and problems.

Three 'Special Collections' in the care of the Library are invaluable for tracing the development of the co-operative movement: the Robert Owen correspondence from 1820 onwards (some 3,000 letters); the G. J. Holyoake correspondence, 1835-1903 (4,000 letters); and the Edward Owen Greening correspondence (some 11,000 documents, as yet unclassified).

In addition to these records, the Co-operative Union Librarian has compiled a 'Register of Co-operative Historical Records', comprised of some 250 replies to questionnaires to all members of the Co-operative Union. This is a definitive guide to records of the co-operative movement at local level.

The minutes of the Union are not generally available. Each application will be treated on its merits. For other material, enquiries should be made to the Librarian of the Co-operative Union.

Co-operative Union: Scottish Section
95 Morrison Street Glasgow G5 8LR

Papers

Minutes are comprehensive from 1945, but some are available for an earlier period. Scottish annual reports have been retained from 1905.

Availability

Apply to the Secretary.

Co-operative Women's Guild
342 Hoe Street Walthamstow London E17

The Guild was founded in 1883 as the Women's League for the Spread of Co-operation. It then became the Women's Co-operative Guild, a title it retained until the present one was adopted in 1963. The Guild's importance in co-operative activities lay in its organisation of women and its breaking of the male monopoly of co-operative organisation in its early days. Its obvious form of activities was on consumer questions, but under the General Secretaryship of Miss Margaret Llewelyn Davies (1889-1921) it involved itself in wider questions of women's emancipation, including the problems of housing, health insurance, employment of young persons, divorce law reform, anti-sweating campaigns, and in encouraging women to join trade unions. In 1921 an International Women's Co-operative Guild was established, and this survived as an independent organisation until 1963, when it became a department of the *International Co-operative Alliance* (q.v.).

Papers

A substantial series of records of the Co-operative Women's Guild survives in deposited collections at the British Library of Political and Economic Science, and at Hull University Library.

1. *At B.L.P.E.S.*

This collection, presented to the Library by Miss Lillian Harris, Margaret Llewelyn Davies's lifelong friend and companion, consists of eleven volumes and appears to represent records accumulated by Miss Davies. The collection illustrates the aims and activities of the Guild during roughly the period 1890-1944, and reveals also the personal influence of Miss Davies and Miss Harris in encouraging the spread of co-operation among working-class women. Volume 1 consists of manuscript, typed and printed material covering the activities of the Guild, 1890-1944; Volumes 2-5 are concerned with a propaganda campaign organised by the Coronation Street branch of the Sunderland Co-operative Society, 1902-04, and include three scrapbooks, including letters, printed material and photographs; Volume 6 has records of the Sheffield enquiry, 1902, and the promotion of People's Stores in Bristol, 1905-06; Volume 7 contains photographs and prints of a visit to Belgian co-operators in 1906; Volume 8 consists of press cuttings and correspondence connected with the retirement of Miss Davies and Miss Harris from the Guild, Oct. 1921; Volume 9 is a testimonial presented to Miss Davies at this time; Volume 10 includes drafts of a speech by Miss Davies in June 1933, and material relating to the appearance of a new banner, 1933; and Volume 11 is a photograph album, covering the years 1903-38.

2. *At Hull University Library*

This is a more substantial collection, formerly in the possession of the Guild itself and at present entirely unsorted and uncatalogued, and packed in a number of boxes and trunks. The bulk of the records appears to date back no earlier than the 1920s, and includes records of the Guild itself and of the International Women's Co-operative Guild. At this stage any description must necessarily be regarded as provisional, and what follows is therefore only a rough guide to the contents of this collection. Further details may be obtained from Hull University Library.

(a) *The Guild*. There appears to be a full set of formal records, including minutes of the Central (from 1963 Executive) Committee and copies of its circulars, 1917-18; minutes of the joint meetings of the Central Committee and Sectional Secretaries, 1938-65; a complete file of annual reports; minutes and certain correspondence of the Guild Convalescent Fund, 1908-42; Guild accounts dating from the 1940s, and branch correspondence dating from the reorganisation of the filing system in 1954. A tin trunk contains a small collection of material from a former President of the London Guild which appears to have been used in the updating of the history of the Guild. This contains: a minute book of the Battersea Women's Socialist Circle, 1908-10; a Citizenship Sub-committee minute book for 1912, and a large collection of *Monthly Bulletins* for the 1930s and 1940s; and a manuscript draft of the history. As far as can be ascertained, apart from a 'Guild Miscellaneous' file for the 1920s, other records of the Guild are of more recent provenance and include files on Congresses, papers on training courses, notes relating to various Commissions of Enquiry into the work of the Guild, speakers' notes, a schedule analysis relating to branch activities from the 1950s, policy statements of the same period, papers relating to the appointment of General Secretaries, papers relating to the 'Caravan of Peace', 1958, and the Guild Development Year, 1965-66. It is possible that earlier material survives, but this will only become apparent in a more systematic examination.

(b) *International Women's Guild*. It appears that the formal records of the International Guild are now in Austria, but a number of records are housed with the Guild's own records. Again a description at this stage must be impressionistic. The collection, however, contains the following: a box of typescripts, photographs and obituary notes relating to Mrs. E. Freundlich, 1948; papers relating to the Campaign for World Government, 1950s; circular letters dating from 1939; reports in German, French and English; a file of papers relating to the Liaison Committee on the Status of Women, 1943; conference papers from the 1940s; papers on various committees relating to the participation of youth and the household economy; and a box containing 20 or 30 files, again relating to the general work of the International Guild.

International Co-operative Alliance
11 Upper Grosvenor Street London W1X 9PA

The Alliance was founded by the International Co-operative Congress held in London in 1895, and is a world-wide confederation of co-operative organisations of all types. The Alliance acts as a forum for exchange of information, promotes mutual trading and financial relations between co-operative organisations, and generally represents the co-operative movement internationally. It is one of the oldest of existing international voluntary bodies. The Secretariat is located in London but regional offices have been established in New Delhi and Tanzania. A history of the Alliance has been published: William Pascoe Watkins, *The International Co-operative Alliance* (1970).

Papers

A large collection of papers has been retained at the offices of the Alliance, covering much of its history. The bulk of the material has been filed in a very large number of parcels: a rough index to this is extant. However, over the years many of these have been disposed of, through reasons of space, and the index is not an exact guide to what survives. The bulk of the parcels contains correspondence, memoranda, research papers, and past copies of journals published by the I.C.A. The Alliance has retained copies of its various publications. These include copies of the *Review of International Co-operation* (from 1908-28 known as *International Co-operative Bulletin*), a bi-monthly in English, French, German and Spanish; *Co-operative News Service*, a monthly in English; *Agricultural Co-operative Bulletin;* and *Consumer Affairs Bulletin.* Copies of now defunct journals, e.g. *Cartel* (1950-64), are also retained.

The Alliance has retained full runs of its formal records, including the Congress reports (nos. 2, 3, 4 of which are in French), minutes and papers of the Central and Executive Committees and records of various specialist auxiliary committees.

Availability

Each request will be considered on its merits. Enquiries should be directed to the Administrative Secretary.

League of Co-operators

The League was founded as the National Co-operative Men's Guild in 1911 to provide a forum for men co-operators to discuss co-operative matters and problems. In 1962 it opened its ranks to women and adopted the title League of Co-operators. In 1967 the League amalgamated with the National Guild of Co-operators.

Papers

No records were passed on to the National Guild. They are believed to be in private hands, but to date have not been traced.

London Co-operative Society: Political Committee
116 Notting Hill Gate London W11 2BR

The L.C.S. was founded in 1920 as an amalgamation of earlier societies. Its Political Committee was established in 1921 as a Co-operative Representational Council. Today it is active in all the areas served by the Society: an area north of the Thames stretching from Southend in the east to the Chilterns in the west. It is affiliated to the Co-operative Party, and to every Constituency Labour Party in its area; to the Eastern and Southern and to the Greater London Regional Councils.

Papers

The Political Committee has retained many of its records dating back to 1921. The most important of these are a complete run of minute books from 1921 to the present. Similarly a full run of financial records survives. Little correspondence apart from essential current material is maintained. The Political Committee has over the years produced many leaflets, pamphlets and broadsheets; many of these have been retained. Quarterly reports of the Committee are published in the L.C.S.'s *Members Report.*

Availability

There is no general access. Enquiries should be directed to the Secretary of the Political Committee.

National Guild of Co-operators
30 Oak Road Manchester M20 9DA

The Guild was founded in 1926 and provides a meeting-ground for all men and women interested in the working and development of the co-operative movement. It aims 'to uphold and spread knowledge of co-operative principles, to extend the application of these principles to social affairs, to aid in all ways and at all times the establishment of the Co-operative Commonwealth'. In 1967 the League of Co-operators amalgamated with the Guild.

Papers

The Guild retains its records, which include minute books, 1942-55, 1962 to date; annual reports, 1930 to date; Guild leaflets and posters; correspondence has not been retained.

Availability

The records are available for research purposes: applications should be made to the Librarian, National Guild of Co-operators.

Royal Arsenal Co-operative Society Ltd.: Political Purposes Committee
147 Powis Street, London SE18

The Society was founded as the Royal Arsenal Supply Association in 1868 and was registered under its present name in 1873. Today it is the largest co-operative grouping in South London. Its Political Purposes Committee was first established in 1921 and today is active in some 40 constituencies in South London and the Home Counties. Through this committee the R.A.C.S. is affiliated to the Labour Party, locally, regionally and nationally, being the only co-operative society directly linked with the party in this way. The Committee is also affiliated to the Co-operative Party.

Papers

These are retained in the office of the Political Secretary. Seven minute books of the Political Purposes Committee provide a summary of the Society's political work from 1922 to the present. Other records are sparse, however. A considerable amount of material was destroyed, through lack of space, in the late 1950s. Other records are very recent, e.g. account books go back no further than 1960 and correspondence dates back for some two years only. Information about the Committee's work can be found in the R.A.C.S.'s quarterly reports, and the annual report and statement of accounts, copies of which date back to 1921. The bulletin of the Society, known as *Comradeship* until 1948 and *Home News* from 1948-65, now *News of the R.A.C.S.*, also has regular notes on the political work of the Society.

Availability

On prior application in writing to the Political Secretary, Royal Arsenal Co-operative Society.

Scottish Co-operative Women's Guild
95 Morrison Street Glasgow G5 8LR

The first branch was formed under the auspices of Kinning Park Co-operative Society in 1890. The national organisation was formed in 1892.

These are retained in the Guild's offices and include minutes and reports dating back to 1892. Correspondence is of a more recent date.

Availability

Applications should be made to the General Secretary.

Woodcraft Folk
13 Ritherdon Road London SW17

The Woodcraft movement developed in the early years of this century to stress, among the younger generation, the benefits of a more 'natural life', with an emphasis on courage, cleanliness, physical and moral fitness, and community spirit, but without the nationalistic emphasis of the Boy Scouts. The movement gave rise to the Order of Woodcraft Chivalry in 1916, and the Kibbo Kift Kindred in 1920. The Woodcraft Folk developed out of the latter, and was more working-class in emphasis, close to the co-operative movement. The Woodcraft Folk (Federation of Co-operative Woodcraft Fellowships) was established at the end of 1925. Its programme has remained substantially the same since then: 'The Woodcraft Folk is a movement for all children who can benefit physically and mentally from its activities.' The Folk is an auxiliary organisation of the Co-operative Union.

Papers

Records at the Folk's headquarters are incomplete, as a result of several moves prior to 1938, and subsequent clearances of material through shortage of space. However, a large collection of material, which has been carefully amassed since 1928, is in the care of the Folk's President, Mr. Basil Rawson, 14 Strelley Avenue, Sheffield S8 0BG.

These include cyclostyled copies of all minutes of the National Folk Council and the National Folk Education Committee, together with auxiliary material; copies of broadsheets and newsletters; annual financial statements; annual delegate conference agenda and results; documentation of all national and many district and group camps; complete documentation of international contacts, including conference and international camp reports and printed matter; similar documentation relating to the Folk's involvement with the co-operative movement, the national and local Youth Service, UNESCO, UNICEF, aid for UNRRA, developing countries, etc. Also in Mr. Rawson's care are copies of published material such as annual reports, leaflets, monthly magazines, books; cyclostyled publications including monthly magazines, reports, leaders' training manuals; and thousands of photographs and slides of local and international activities. These records are catalogued and indexed.

Many of these records are, of course, duplicated in the London office.

Availability

Apply to the General Secretary.

COUNCIL FOR THE PROTECTION OF RURAL ENGLAND
4 Hobart Place London SW1W 0HY

The Council was founded in 1926 and brought into association a number of organisations already interested in protecting the English countryside, together with interested individuals. Today the Council, which substituted 'Protection' for 'Preservation' in its title in 1969, has some fifty constituent bodies and nearly two hundred affiliated bodies, but a great deal of its strength now derives from a number of county branches, county committees and district branches.

The Council's aims may be stated as follows: to protect the beauty of the English countryside; to act as a centre for obtaining and giving advice and information on matters affecting the protection of rural scenery; and to rouse public opinion to an understanding of the importance of this work and the need to promote it.

Papers

A large collection of records dating back to 1926 survives at the offices of C.P.R.E. These include both formal records, such as a complete run of minutes of the Executive Council, and a great deal of correspondence and papers relating to the variety of the Council's activities. All these records are carefully card-indexed and cross-referenced so that particular activities, such as cases dealt with by the Council, can be easily traced. A number of records has been transferred to microfilm: these particularly concern branch matters, and tend to be records relating to less obviously important matters. It is likely that more records will eventually be microfilmed. The bulk of the Council's records consist of: correspondence with branches, constituent and affiliated bodies, and other interested bodies, with M.P.s and government departments, etc.; submissions to Parliament, research work relating to this, etc.; work relating to campaigns, etc.

There is a considerable amount of material relating to branches and local groupings, including correspondence and occasional reports. However, relations between these and the national Council vary — many have a large degree of autonomy and they can be contacted separately.

Annual reports run from 1926, and during the early years the Council also produced a monthly report sent to each member. This has now been replaced by a bi-monthly bulletin. Copies of these are retained by the Council. Copies of pamphlets published by the Council, of increasing number in recent years, have also been retained.

The Council's papers, in fact, provide an excellent insight into the work of a pressure group: on the one hand, relations with and response to grass-roots work; and on the other hand, the records of a high-level national pressure group, working closely with prominent individuals and organisations. In addition to these central records, the Lancashire Record Office has the minutes of the Lancashire branch of the Council from 1933-63.

Availability

Applications must be made in writing to the Secretary of the Council.

COUNCIL FOR THE PROTECTION OF RURAL WALES
Meifod Montgomeryshire

Papers

The older records, up to about 1950, have been deposited in the National Library of Wales. They consist of the minutes of the General Committee, 1928-33; of the Executive Committee, 1928-35; and of the A.G.M., 1929-34; annual reports from 1928-50 with interruptions; Executive Committee correspondence with members from the 1920s to 1950; a one-volume record of members, 1934-50, box files containing names of subscribers, 1934-38; various financial records; and assorted files on the management of the Snowdonia National Trust, 1936, and dealings with the Welsh Nationalist Party, 1935 and 1948. Other general papers include miscellaneous correspondence, drafts of pamphlets, literature on exhibitions, etc. Other material is concerned largely with particular aspects of the Council's work. A considerable amount of material is concerned with particular cases, which the Council worked on, arranged by counties. These date from the 1920s. A good deal of material also survives for special concerns of the Council: offensive advertisements, 1928-39; roads and bridges; flora, etc.

Availability

Applications should be made to the Librarian, National Library of Wales.

COUNCIL OF ACTION

The Council was established at a joint conference of representatives of the Parliamentary Committee of the T.U.C., the National Executive of the Labour Party, and the Parliamentary Labour Party, on 9 August 1920. The immediate background was the *Jolly Roger* incident of May 1920, when dockers in the Port of London refused to load a cargo of arms bound for Poland. This was in the international context of the attempt at the end of April by General Pilsudski to restore 'Greater Poland' at the expense of Bolshevik Russia. Consequently, a special Labour conference on 13 August 1920 empowered the Council of Action 'to use all the resources at the disposal of Labour to prevent the British nation from being plunged into war, and by all the means open to them to restore peace to the world'. The Council had an existence of less than a year, and the achievement of its immediate aim, and the resultant divergence between the National Council and local Councils of Action over the next steps, led to the dissipation of its energies by the beginning of 1921.

Papers

The joint Secretaries of the Council were F. Bramley, H.S. Lindsay and J.S. Middleton, the Labour Party Assistant Secretary. It was through the latter that the records now form part of the Labour Party archive at Transport House, where they have been listed by members of the staff of the Royal Commission on Historical Manuscripts. An indexed list is available and may be consulted at the National Register of Archives or at Transport House. The records comprise: administrative records, some minutes of the National Council and of various meetings; internal and official correspondence; foreign correspondence and papers; correspondence with local Councils and reports of local meetings; various memoranda; papers on munitions; papers relating to a visit to Paris by W. Adamson and H. Gosling; a box of unsorted press cuttings; papers relating to printing work, including advertisements, circulars, etc. These records form a valuable accumulation, illustrating in over 1,000 pieces of correspondence from local organisations the growing split between the strictly limited aims of the National Council, and the local Councils and mass meetings. The latter attempted to extend the scope of the Council to include campaigns against government policy in Ireland, and on wage and living standards and trade with the Soviet Union. The National Council stuck to a constitutional position and sought to direct the local Councils into orthodox channels. As a result, the correspondence declines from January 1921 and ceases in April. This correspondence, however, is the most important group in the collection. The relatively small group of foreign correspondence suggests that, although the immediate occasion of the formation of the Council was the international situation, it is as a phenomenon in British politics that its significance must be seen.

Availability

On application in writing to the Librarian of the Labour Party.

COUNCIL OF CHRISTIANS AND JEWS
41 Cadogan Gardens London SW3 2TD

Formed originally in 1941, the Council's founder members included Archbishop William Temple and the Chief Rabbi, Dr. J. H. Hertz. The Council brings together the Christian and Jewish communities in Britain in a common effort to fight the evils of prejudice, intolerance, and discrimination between people of different religions, races and colours and to work for the betterment of human relations, based on mutual respect, understanding and goodwill. The Council's pioneering work in the fields of inter-faith education and ecumenical relations includes the arrangement of lectures, conferences, study groups and publications. Local branches have been formed, work is undertaken in conjunction with other organisations, and the Council is a member of the International Consultative Committee for organisations for Christian–Jewish relations.

Papers

The records have been preserved in the Council's offices. They include a complete set of the minutes of the A.G.Ms., the Executive Committee, a number of sub-committees and working parties, and the standing conference of local councils. A large selection of correspondence survives. This covers a wide variety of subject-matter and includes letters to and from many eminent public figures. Also available are annual reports, copies of the Council's quarterly magazine *Common Ground* (from *c.*1946), the bi-monthly newsletter (from the mid-1960s) and publications such as the Waley-Cohen Memorial Lectures.

Availability

The records are as yet unsorted and not generally available. Enquiries should be addressed to the General Secretary.

COUNCIL OF FOREIGN BONDHOLDERS
68 Queen Street London EC4N 1SL

The Council was formed in 1868 and incorporated in 1873 under licence from the Board of Trade and reconstituted in 1898 by special Act of Parliament, its principal object being to protect the interests of holders of bonds issued in the United Kingdom on behalf of overseas governments, states and municipalities. It seeks to prevent or settle any default which may occur, and to safeguard generally the interests of bondholders.

Papers

The Council has a fairly extensive archive which includes a complete set of its annual reports and minute books.

All correspondence since 1939 and in some cases earlier correspondence has been retained. Press cutting books from 1939 with cuttings from the British and foreign press are held, and 477 volumes covering 1851-1939 are deposited with the Guildhall Library (in London).

Availability

Researchers are advised by the Council to consult in the first instance the annual reports which reproduce public announcements made by the Council and details of all debt settlements. Complete sets of the annual reports are available in the British Library, the Guildhall Library, London University Library and the Bodleian Library, Oxford.

Correspondence files and minute books are not generally available, but access may be given in particular cases on proper notice.

COUNTRY LANDOWNERS ASSOCIATION
7 Swallow Street London W1R 8EN

The Association was founded in 1908 with the close involvement of, among others, Walter Long, M.P., the Earl of Onslow and Charles Bathurst, later Viscount Bledisloe. It adopted its present name in 1949, having previously been known as the Central Land Association (1908-18) and the Central Landowners Association (1918-49).

The Association's object is to protect and promote the interests of the owners of agricultural and other rural land.

Papers

The records of the Association have been deposited with the Institute of Agricultural History, Reading University. Enquiries should be addressed to the Librarian at the Institute.

DAVID DAVIES MEMORIAL INSTITUTE OF INTERNATIONAL STUDIES
Thorney House 34 Smith Square London SW1P 3HF

Established in 1952 as a successor to the *New Commonwealth Society* (q.v.) founded by Lord Davies of Llandinam, the organisation aims to advance and promote the development of the science of international relations in the political, economic, legal, social, educational and related fields. The Institute carries on research and generally promotes the study of and the dissemination of material concerning international relations.

Papers

Records of the Institute are kept in the office at Smith Square. For the history of the Institute itself these are full.

Availability

Enquiries should be addressed to the Institute's Secretary.

'DIE-HARDS'

Those Unionist members of the two Houses of Parliament who in 1910 stood out in determined resistance to the Parliament Bill were known as 'die-hards' or 'ditchers'. A committee of this group was formed in July 1910, with Lord Halsbury as Chairman and F. E. Smith and Lord Willoughby de Broke as joint Secretaries.

Papers

No records of the 'die-hard' movement as such have been found. The Halsbury papers at the British Library contain material relating to the 1911 crisis, and certain minutes and papers of the 'Halsbury Club' are included in the Selborne papers at the Bodleian Library. The papers of Lord Willoughby de Broke were deposited in 1973 in the House of Lords Record Office. Several other collections of papers should be mentioned. These include: the Birkenhead papers with the family, the Carson collection at the Northern Ireland Public Record Office, the Salisbury archive at Hatfield House, and the W. S. Blunt papers at the British Library.

Availability

In each case, application should be addressed to the appropriate Archivist, Librarian or owner of the papers.

DIVORCE LAW REFORM UNION
39 Clabon Mews London SW1

Founded in 1906, the Union was incorporated as a company, limited by guarantee, in 1914. In 1946 the Marriage Law Reform Society was formed. This amalgamated with the D.L.R.U. in the early 1960s.

Papers

Only the more recent records are retained. No papers of the D.L.R.U. previous to 1939 appear to have survived, and only miscellaneous records of the M.L.R.S. are available. However, recent minute books, the bulletin *Just Cause* and correspondence remain in the offices.

Availability

Enquiries should be addressed to the Secretary.

ECONOMIC LEAGUE
24 Buckingham Palace Mansions Buckingham Palace Road London SW1W 0SR

Founded in 1919, the League aims 'to preserve personal freedom and free enterprise and actively to oppose all subversive forces, whatever their origin or inspiration, that seek to undermine the security of Britain in general, and of British industry in particular'.

Papers

The records of the Economic League during the 1920s and 1930s have been destroyed as a result of various moves of offices. The entry on the *Radical Right* should be consulted.

EIGHTY CLUB

Founded in 1880, shortly before the General Election of that year, the Club worked to promote Liberal education and to stimulate Liberal organisation. H. H. Asquith was the first Secretary of the Club, and Lloyd George was sometime President. The Club continued to exist into the 20th century.

Papers

Few records survive. Researchers should examine the papers of the 4th Earl Grey (one of the founder members) at the University of Durham Library; the Lloyd George papers at the Beaverbrook Library; the Asquith papers at the Bodleian Library; and the papers of William M. Crook (one-time Club Secretary), also now deposited at the Bodleian. The papers of Oscar Browning, including correspondence regarding the Eighty Club, are with the Historical Manuscripts Commission and are the property of Hastings Public Library. The late E. Gordon Godfrey, the last surviving officer of the Club, left no papers relating to the Eighty Club.

ELECTORAL REFORM SOCIETY OF GREAT BRITAIN AND IRELAND
6 Chancel Street London SE1 0UX

Founded in 1884 as the Proportional Representation Society, the association aims to promote the use of the single transferable vote form of proportional representation, especially in the United Kingdom, in parliamentary and local government elections. In 1959 the present name was adopted.

Papers

A very full set of records has been preserved. These include a complete run of minute books, a great deal of uncatalogued correspondence (with members of the Society, and on elections and other matters), reports, submissions to Parliament, press cuttings and pamphlet material. Other material on proportional representation is included in the papers of the 4th Lord Grey, one of the Society's founders. These papers are at the University of Durham.

Availability

Some of the Society's records are in the personal care of the Secretary, and others are in the Society's office. The House of Lords Record Office has microfilms of certain of the more important material. Enquiries should be addressed to the Secretary.

ELECTRICAL CONTRACTORS' ASSOCIATION
55 Catherine Place London SW1E 6ET

Founded originally in 1904, the Association now incorporates the National Electrical Contractors' Trading Association Ltd., and the National Federated Electrical Association. The organisation looks after the interests of electrical contractors generally, representing them on the industry's councils and committees and dealing with commercial, legal and parliamentary matters, with industrial and labour relations and with courses of craft and management training.

Papers

Most of the records have not been preserved. However, minutes of the Council dating from formation have been kept. The minute books of E.C.A., N.E.C.T.A. and N.F.E.A., are very full. They are mainly industrial relations and commercial matter, but some are concerned with political pressure-group activities.

Availability

These records are not generally available.

ELECTRICAL ELECTRONIC TELECOMMUNICATIONS UNION/PLUMBING TRADE UNION

Hayes Court West Common Road Bromley Kent BR2 7AU

The Electrical Trades Union was formed in 1890, as a result of the amalgamation of the Amalgamated Society of Telegraph and Telephone Construction Men (Manchester) and the Union of Electrical Operatives (London). Amalgamation was effected in 1917 with the Electrical Winders' Society and in 1934 with the National Union of Lift and Crane Workers. In 1968 the E.T.U. amalgamated with the Plumbing Trades Union and the union's present name was adopted. The United Operative Plumbers' Association of Great Britain and Ireland was formed in 1865, from thirteen local plumbers' societies. The name was changed in 1911 to the United Operative Plumbers' and Domestic Engineers' Association, and in 1931 to the Plumbers', Glaziers' and Domestic Engineers' Union. In 1946, after reorganisation, the name P.T.U. was adopted. Amalgamation was effected in 1921 with the United Operative Plumbers' Association of Scotland.

1. Plumbing Trades Union

A substantial archive exists. The main series of papers comprise the following: minutes and rules, 1849-76, 1880-91; N.E.C. minutes, 1876 to date; District Committee (North Wales) minutes, 1921-30; quarterly returns, 1867-1909; monthly, quarterly and annual reports, 1910-28; annual reports, 1929 to date. Reports: delegate meetings, 1919, 1923-46; biennial conference, 1948 to date; Rules Revision Committee, 1951 to date; P.T.U. (journal), 1947 to date; National Joint Council for the Plumbing Industry, minutes, 1915-21; circulars to members, 1919 to date. Correspondence on legal opinion relating to rules, disputes, demarcation, benefits, 1912-15, 1921.

In addition there are copies of the rules for various years and lists of members in quarterly returns and annual reports (1867-1930). Papers relating to wage negotiations include material from 1896 and the 1941-42 dispute, and also copies of local agreements, demarcation rules, working rules, etc., from 1900. A copy of Sidney Webb's notes of the U.O.P.A. (c.1900) is available, together with emblems and papers of the Apprenticeship Council (1920 to date), etc. Branch records include material from London, Brighton, Colwyn Bay, Kirkcaldy, Liverpool and Torquay.

Certain records of earlier plumbers' associations have also survived:

Manchester Society of Operative Plumbers and Glaziers, minutes, rules, cash books and membership records, c.1837-72;

East London Society of Operative Plumbers, minutes, etc., c.1871-89;

United Operative Plumbers' Association of Scotland, minutes, 1898-1920, annual reports, 1885-98, rules and amalgamation papers;

Scottish Operative Plumbers' Protective and Benefit Federal Union, members (Edinburgh branch), 1865-92;

National Operative Plumbers' and Kindred Trades Union, later National Plumbers' Society, a few papers.

A further assortment of local records is housed at the National Library of Scotland. The Scottish records include papers of the Edinburgh Lodge, Operative Plumbers' Association of Great Britain and Ireland, 1872-91, the Executive Council of the Scottish Operative Plumbers' Protective and Benefit Federal Union, 1891-93, along with the Edinburgh branch records, 1891-1908, and the Edinburgh branch, United Operative Plumbers' Association of Scotland, 1887-98.

2. *Electrical Trades Union*

Only the records of the E.T.U. are preserved: papers of the earlier and incorporated associations have not survived. The main series comprise: E.C. minutes, 1890 to date; assorted minutes, A.S.T.T.C.M. (Manchester), 1889-94, 1909-16; annual report and balance sheet, 1890 to date; reports of Rules Revision Conferences, 1898 to date, Policy Conferences, 1947 (1st) to date, Youth Conferences, 1949-56; journals, 1905 to date; rules and membership, records from 1896 and 1889 respectively. Papers relating to wage negotiations and agreements are complete from 1919, with in addition minutes of the National Railway Electrical Council, National Joint Industrial Councils for the Electrical Contracting and Supply Industries, National Joint Trade Union Craftsmen's Iron and Steel Committee (from 1947) and the National Joint Council for Civil Air Transport (from 1948). Of branch records, only the London Central branch minute book, 1897-98, is available. The official history of the E.T.U. was published in 1952.

Full records of Edinburgh Central branch of the E.T.U., 1926-60, are at the National Library of Scotland.

Availability

Enquiries should be addressed to the General Secretary.

ELECTRICAL POWER ENGINEERS' ASSOCIATION
Station House Fox Lane North Chertsey Surrey

The Association was formed in 1912 and has had a continuous existence since then.

Papers

The records at the Association's headquarters have not yet been catalogued or sorted. Detailed lists cannot therefore be given. Minute books date from the Association's foundation, as do the rules and individual membership records. Copies of reports, however, go back only about twenty years, and correspondence is only retained for ten years. Papers relating to wage agreements and negotiations, from 1920, are available; also there is much material on legal cases. Copies of the journal from 1918 (with a few gaps) and some printed histories in article form, together with a small assortment of press cuttings, make up the collection.

Availability

Applications should be addressed to the Editor at the Association's head office.

EMPIRE CRUSADE

Launched in December 1929 to promote the cause of Empire Free Trade, the Empire Crusade was Lord Beaverbrook's one venture into independent political leadership. The Crusade was not merely a newspaper campaign; it raised money, enlisted supporters, set up local committees, conducted mass meetings, and finally ran candidates at by-elections. Beaverbrook provided the drive and organisational resources, and through him a substantial Fund was raised. Until March 1931 the Crusade put up a firm challenge to the Conservative leadership, but with no real enthusiasm for Imperial preference and 'food taxes' either in Britain or the Dominions, and with Beaverbrook's side-step into support for the *Agricultural*

Party (q.v.), the Crusade foundered amid the financial crisis later in 1931. Echoes of the Crusade continued in later years, but Beaverbrook no longer campaigned with intensity.

Papers

There are 42 boxes of Empire Crusade material among Lord Beaverbrook's papers at the Beaverbrook Library. These include 120 files of correspondence, 1929-31, four files on possible candidates and agents, and other files of press cuttings interspersed with correspondence, office material including financial statements, subscription lists, invitations to speak, and campaign organisation papers. There are also some farmers' letters and a file on a speakers' course. The Baldwin MSS. at Cambridge University Library should also be consulted. Only a very few papers of C. A. McCurdy, Trustee for the Empire Crusade Fund, have been found. The material at Westminster Central Library relating to the St. George's Division by-election (March 1931) is of particular interest.

Availability

Applications should be addressed to the Director of the Beaverbrook Library.

EMPLOYERS' PARLIAMENTARY COUNCIL

The Council was created in 1898 as an offshoot of the Free Labour Protection Association, a strike-breaking body founded by a number of prominent employers in the previous year. The Council's object was to oppose 'the movement towards state socialism . . . and the influence of the T.U.C. in Parliament'. In the next few years the Council ceased to function, but over the next twenty years the full-time officials of various employers' organisations met informally to discuss, among other things, legislation affecting labour matters.

Papers

A small collection of letters, pamphlets, broadsheets, etc., relating to the Council is at present in the care of Dr. H. F. Gospel at St. John's College, Cambridge.

For the later, more informal meetings, a record may be found in a minute book in the care of the *Engineering Employers' Federation* (q.v.), entitled 'Private Meetings of Secretaries of Employers' Organisations 1898-1916'.

ENGINEERING EMPLOYERS' FEDERATION
Broadway House Tothill Street London SW1

Founded in 1896, the Federation aims to promote and protect the interests of federated associations and their member firms; to provide and maintain, by national negotiation with trade unions, an agreed code of wages and working conditions; to assist in the avoidance and settlement of disputes; to provide statistical and other information and advice on labour problems to its constituents; to make any necessary representations in respect of proposed or existing legislation or of government policy affecting the industry; to encourage and advise on training and safety matters, and on the efficient use of resources; to give members of associations such pecuniary, legal or other assistance as may be considered beneficial to the Federation as a whole.

The Federation is managed by a General Council of *ex officio* members and elected representatives, and executive action is taken by the Council through the

Management Board of *ex officio* members, members appointed by the General Council and co-opted members. The Council comprises 115 members and the Board 95.

Papers

The main records are in the form of Executive Committee (now Management Board) minutes, which have been preserved since 1896; general letters to firms from 1896 and to federated associations since 1900; National and Central Conference reports from 1897; district wage settlements from 1897-1952; statistical summaries of average hours and earnings of certain classes of manual workers, employed in federated firms, from 1914. Between 1898 and 1915 a Parliamentary Committee's proceedings were minuted until its activities were taken over by an Emergency Committee (now Policy Committee). Other preserved records include files on membership, cash books and subscription registers, indexed correspondence on issues raised, on microfilm from 1896-1960 and in original to date, and decisions books on national agreements. The E.E.F. also has a collection of law reports from about 1850, Board of Trade/Ministry of Labour *Gazettes* from *c.* 1900, *Hansard* reports from 1920, and copies of all National Arbitration Tribunal and Industrial Disputes Tribunal awards, extensive Industrial Court awards, and considerable detail of fluctuations in wage rates in other industries.

Availability

Access to confidential records and the copyright therein is strictly reserved. Applications for access to non-confidential records are considered on their merits.

Local Associations

The records of associations in the Federation are their own responsibility as the associations are autonomous. Record keeping varies; sometimes little or nothing has survived, as at Liverpool where the records were destroyed by bombing. The following collections may be mentioned:

Coventry and District Engineering Employers' Association

A number of records survives, dating back to the formation of the Association in December 1907. A number of records was destroyed in World War II, but the following survive:

1. Minutes of the Association Management Board going back to 1915. These are detailed accounts of the issues raised by member firms and of the policy decisions made. The minutes include information relating to wage claims in the district, industrial disputes, trade union activities and earnings levels in member firms.
2. Minutes of the Association A.G.M.s.
3. Various circular letters issued to member firms concerning, e.g., the engineering industry lock-out of 1922.
4. Documents relating to the Coventry District Toolroom Agreement of 1941. The documents include notes on all conferences held in the procedure relating to the conclusion and interpretation of the 1941 agreement.

Within categories 2 and 3, the coverage is incomplete due to the destruction which occurred during World War II. However, the documents provide a considerable amount of information on industrial relations within the Coventry engineering industry, bearing in mind that the majority of engineering companies in the district have always belonged to the Association.

Northern Ireland E.E.A.

Minute books and other relevant records going back over one hundred years to formation in 1866 are available.

Preston District E.E.A.

Minute books from the time of foundation in 1893 have survived, together with more recent records of negotiations, etc. The Association considers its records to be confidential.

Scottish E.E.A.

The Association holds minute books dating from the end of the last century and other selected material.

Sheffield E.E.A.

Unfortunately the records were destroyed by enemy action in 1940. However, bound volumes of local conference notes dating back to 1913 have survived. These notes record the negotiations on wages and working conditions which took place at district level in the local engineering and special steel industry in Sheffield. These records are retained in the Association's offices.

West Midlands E.E.A.

All records older than ten years or so were destroyed through lack of space in the Association's offices. Current policy is to microfilm records of possible future value older than five years.

ENGLISH-SPEAKING UNION OF THE COMMONWEALTH
Dartmouth House 37 Charles Street Berkeley Square London W1X 8AB

Founded originally in 1918, the Union obtained a Royal Charter in 1957. The organisation aims to promote mutual trust and friendship between the peoples of the British Commonwealth and the United States of America.

Papers

Reports on the work of the organisation are published annually for members. Minutes of the meetings of the Governing Body and other committees are kept, but they remain private and confidential.

Availability

Apart from the published materials, the records are closed.

EUGENICS SOCIETY
69 Eccleston Square London SW1V 1PJ

The Society was founded in 1907 as the Eugenics Education Society. The present title was adopted in 1926. The word 'eugenics' had been coined by Sir Francis Galton, and he became the Hon. President of the Society in 1908. Today the Society defines its aims as follows:

to study hereditary and environmental aspects of human qualities, to formulate and support proposals for improving these qualities and enabling them to develop to their full potential in the individual, to foster a responsible attitude to parenthood, to promote relevant research and to facilitate communication between those interested.

Papers

The Society has retained a substantial collection of records. These include minutes of the Council, 1907 to date; Executive Committee, 1933 to date; and General Purposes Committee, 1928-30; Propaganda Committee, 1935-40; Education Committee, 1936; Finance Committee, 1932-62; Honorary Officers Meeting, 1927-32; Research Committee, 1923-31; Statistics Sub-committee, 1928-30; Birth Control Investigation Committee, 1928-32; Homes in Canada Committee, 1940; Problem Families Committee, 1947-56; Ad Hoc Committee, 1944-54; Voluntary Sterilisation Committee, 1963. Annual reports run from 1908 to date, and there is a substantial collection of unsorted correspondence, though this does not appear to date back earlier than 1920.

A large collection of press cutting albums, dating back to 1907, provides an important guide to the activities of the Society: they are organised chronologically and by subject. Subjects covered include population, genetics, genes, heredity, psychology, national health, birth rate, birth control, sterilisation, etc. The Society has retained a run of its journal, *Eugenics Review*, 1908-68. This was replaced in 1968 by the *Journal of Bio-social Science*, which is published by the autonomous Galton Foundation; and by a quarterly *Bulletin* published by the Society.

The Library of the Eugenics Society contains a very useful collection of books and pamphlets covering the major topics in the eugenics and associated fields. Reference should also be made to the papers of Sir Francis Galton, deposited in University College Library, London, and in the Wellcome Institute of the History of Medicine.

Availability

There is no general access to these papers. Each application will be considered on its merits. Enquiries should be directed to the General Secretary of the Society.

EUROPEAN MOVEMENT: BRITISH COUNCIL
Europe House 1A Whitehall Place London SW1

Set up in July 1948, as the United Kingdom Council of the European Movement under the chairmanship of the Liberal peer Lord Layton, to co-ordinate the activities of British organisations, or British sections of international organisations, working for the cause of European unity. The broad span of its objectives allowed for support from members of all political parties: both Clement (later Lord) Attlee, M.P., and the Rt. Hon. Sir Winston Churchill, M.P., were Presidents; the Rt. Hon. Julian Amery, M.P., and Victor Gollancz were Vice-Presidents.

That broad span of objectives has contributed, too, to the survival of the European Movement as the most central co-ordinating agency of British initiatives towards European unity.

Papers

Among the papers which have been preserved are a full set of Executive Committee minutes from 1948; Management Committee minutes, 1961-65; accounts and minutes of A.G.M.s, 1955-66; copies of the journal *Into Europe*, 1967-70 (with gaps), and an assortment of particular papers and pamphlet material.

Availability

Enquiries should be addressed to the Director of the European Movement.

EVANGELICAL ALLIANCE
19 Draycott Place London SW3 2SJ

The society aims to express the essential unity of all Christian believers in joint action.

Papers

Only printed materials are available. The main records are annual reports from 1900 and annual volumes of *Evangelical Christendom,* which was the Alliance's journal until the 1950s when it was superseded by *Crusade.* Some of the reports are not held at the British Library.

Availability

Applications should be addressed to the General Secretary.

FABIAN COLONIAL BUREAU

The Fabian Colonial Bureau was formed in October 1940 as a special department of the Fabian Society, with Rita Hinden as Secretary. It became an important organ for research, information and policy proposals, particularly during the period of Labour government, 1945-51. During the later part of the 1950s, with the growth of the colonial independence movement, its influence waned somewhat and in 1963, to avoid overlapping of interest, the Bureau merged with the Fabian International Bureau.

Papers

The records of the Bureau covering the whole period of its independent existence have been deposited at Rhodes House Library, Oxford. The collection consists of a large correspondence, committee papers, files on various countries, and publications, sorted into some 180 boxes. Two boxes consist of files presented by Arthur Creech Jones, who with Rita Hinden was responsible for the establishment of the Bureau. These consist of correspondence, memoranda, etc., arranged territorially and by subject, e.g. material on New Zealand dates back to 1929, on India to 1931, while there is material on 'Foreign Trade and Economic Policy', 'Mandates', 'Colonial Policy', etc., dating back to the mid-1930s.

Thirteen boxes of 'Home Correspondence' consisting of files arranged alphabetically cover the period 1943-66. These should be seen with other groups of correspondence, including the correspondence of Creech Jones with the Bureau, 1954-64, 1 box, and the correspondence received at F.C.B. by Hilda Selwyn-Clarke, 1959-62, 1 box. Correspondence with M.P.s (10 boxes, containing some 45 files) reveals the extent and variety of the work of the Bureau. Also in this group is a list of M.P.s with special interest in colonial affairs, and correspondence with some of them (1950-60) and Parliamentary Books containing records of questions on colonial matters and a card index of M.P.s, 1951-55. Another grouping of correspondence is that with the Colonial Office and other Ministries, 1942-53, particularly important between 1945-51.

Another grouping of papers concerns what is generically termed 'Colonial Policy and Development'. This covers the period 1936-60, and includes papers concerning the Labour Party Advisory Committee on Imperial Questions, correspondence with the Labour Party and Trades Union Congress, material of the Committee of Ex-Ministers, 1951-52, questionnaires, correspondence, notes and printed papers relating to the Colonial Development Corporation.

There is also a substantial collection of conference and committee papers for the whole history of the Bureau.

However, the bulk of the manuscript material, filling some two-thirds of the boxes, consists of correspondence with, and papers about, colonial and other overseas territories with which the Bureau was concerned. Although the material in this category sometimes duplicates that in others, territorial files are a very important source for the development of the Bureau's attitudes.

In addition to these, Rhodes House Library has five boxes of newspaper cuttings, 1940-65, concerning colonial affairs, and photographs 'of historic interest', 1943-49, together with a collection of F.C.B. publications, including material about the Bureau's journal *Empire*, later *Venture*.

Additional material connected with the work of the Bureau occurs in two other collections in Rhodes House Library: the papers of Arthur Creech Jones and of C.W.W. Greenidge.

Availability

Applications should be made to the Librarian, Rhodes House.

FABIAN SOCIETY
11 Dartmouth Street London SW1

Founded in 1884 as a Socialist society, the Fabian Society has played a central role in left-wing politics since then. Among its early leaders were Graham Wallas, G. B. Shaw, Sidney and Beatrice Webb. *Fabian Essays in Socialism* in 1889, edited by Shaw, displayed what became the distinctive Fabian emphasis on gradualism. During the 1890s the characteristic policy was one of 'permeating' the major parties with Socialist ideas, but in the years just before and during World War I the Society drew closer to the Labour Party. The Society has been affiliated to the Labour Party from its inception in 1900, and most leaders of the party have at one time or another been members of the Society. During the early 1930s the New Fabian Research Bureau was founded by G. D. H. and Margaret Cole and others, and in 1939 this amalgamated with the older society, retaining the traditional name. The 'self-denying ordinance' adopted at that time precludes the Society from adopting a collective position on major issues. Today the Society sponsors and publishes individual research on matters of political and social importance.

Papers

The older records of the Society have been deposited in the Library of Nuffield College, Oxford. The material includes minutes, correspondence, various manuscripts, etc., and forms a valuable archive covering all phases of the Society's history. This description follows the lists of the records available at Nuffield College. Minute books include those of the Executive Committee from 1885; Fabian Society meetings from 1884; sub-committees, 1899-1912, 1916-34; the *New Fabian Research Bureau* (q.v.), 1931-38; the Publishing Committee, 1893-1938; the Organising and Propaganda Committee, 1907-16; The Finance Committee, 1907-38; Fabian Nursery, 1910-25; Fabian Summer Schools, 1907-46; Fabian Women's Group, 1908-30; together with Fabian Summer School logbooks, a visitors' book, etc.; lists of members and associates of the Fabian Nursery, and committee attendance books.

Correspondence is very full and includes 'letters from celebrities', filed alphabetically; correspondence from Sidney Webb, 1891-1939; correspondence from Beatrice Webb, 1893-1912, 1928-41; and papers on the H. G. Wells controversy, c. 1907; correspondence from G. B. Shaw, 1891-1950. A further recent deposit of Fabian Society papers at Nuffield College supplements the above, and includes committee papers and correspondence up to the 1960s.

Other records include lists of members from 1890; material on local societies, including records of St. Pancras and Central Group, East London Group, and Kensington and District Group; material relating to the Fabian Nursery, Summer Schools, Women's Group and the London School of Economics; various manuscripts including a 'Draft Report on Fabian Policy' by R. C. K. Ensor, and 'Report on the Progress of Socialism in England during the two years ending July 1893', a typed copy corrected by Shaw and Webb; various proofs of Fabian publications; *New Statesman* supplements, 1913-17, together with papers concerning the Poor Law Commission and the Conference of Professional and Manual Workers, 1938; various accounts and correspondence relating to the sale of manuscripts, letters, etc., and publishing agreements and correspondence; records relating to the *Society for Socialist Inquiry and Propaganda* and the *New Fabian Research Bureau* (q.v.); official notices issued by the Society, 1886-1939; 'Various documents of historical interest', consisting of press cuttings, occasional correspondence, syllabuses, manifestoes, etc.; and photographs and blocks of various personalities active in the Socialist movement. Other material dating from the 1930s includes correspondence relating to tracts and other publications; and miscellaneous files relating to Fabian activity in the 1950s.

A collection of local Fabian Society material is available at B.L.P.E.S. This contains handbills, newspaper cuttings, etc., relating to local activities, c. 1890-1912. B.L.P.E.S. has, of course, a great deal of material concerning the activities of the Fabians and the Society. The Passfield papers are an invaluable source, but the Library also holds the papers of Graham Wallas, diaries of G. B. Shaw, and a manuscript of E. R. Pease's *History of the Fabian Society*, with marginal notes by Shaw.

Certain other records have been deposited, e.g. records of the Cambridge University Fabian Society are available at Cambridge University Library, and records of the Edinburgh Fabian Society, 1909-60, may be seen at the National Library of Scotland. Certain papers of the Cardiff Fabian Society are deposited with Glamorgan Record Office. The Sheffield Central Library possesses minutes of Sheffield Fabian Society. The unpublished autobiography of F. W. Galton is at B.L.P.E.S.

Availability

All these records are available on application to the relevant librarians. There are certain conditions relating to the use of the Passfield papers.

FAMILY PLANNING ASSOCIATION
27-35 Mortimer Street London W1N 8BQ

During the 1920s the *Malthusian League* (q.v.) had sponsored the establishment of the Walworth Women's Advisory Clinic and the North Kensington Women's Welfare Centre to provide information and facilities for birth control. At the same time Dr. Marie Stopes was developing her campaign with the same end. In 1930 the National Birth Control Council was established to co-ordinate these activities. In 1931 this became the National Birth Control Association, and in 1939 the Family Planning Association. The Association's aims are to provide information and education on family planning and responsible sexual relationships, including consultation and advice on birth-control methods, sub-fertility and psychosexual problems. One of the major achievements of the Association has been the establishment of Family Planning Clinics throughout the country and the acceptance of family planning as part of the National Health Service.

Papers

The Family Planning Association has retained an extensive archive, which is at present being sorted and listed by the Association's own archivist. The records include the minutes and papers of the North Kensington Centre and the Walworth Clinic from the 1920s, as well as a very comprehensive collection of papers relating to the administration and activities of the Association from 1930. Minutes of the Executive Committee and its sub-committees cover the whole period, and a recent appeal by the Association for records of local clinics has brought a wide response, e.g. records of the Liverpool Clinic from 1931, and of the Birkenhead Clinic from 1934, are now with the main collection in London. The collection is being listed under the following class headings: Administration; Annual General Meetings, Annual Reports and Branch Conferences; Ancillary Services; Branches and Federations; Committees and Councils; Conferences; Contraceptive Testing; Government Departments; Hospital Boards; International Planned Parenthood Federation; Local Authorities; Money Raising Organisations with Related Functions; Officers, Patrons and Supporters; Parliament; Publications and Publishers; Publicity; Royal Commissions; Training. All these groups contain correspondence, memoranda, etc., which provide a full guide to the history of the Family Planning Association and to the birth control movement generally. The Association retains copies of its journal, *Family Planning*, from 1952, and a run of its house journal, *Quarterly Letter*, and its successor, *F.P.A. News*.

Availability

Enquiries should be addressed to the Archivist.

FAMILY WELFARE ASSOCIATION
501-505 Kingsland Road Dalston London E8 4AA

Formed in 1869 as the Charity Organisation Society, the present name was adopted in 1946. The Association aims to preserve and protect the good health (in particular the mental health) of families, individuals and groups within the community. The work of the Association includes provision of a casework service, the promotion of education and research, the creation and administration of charitable trust funds, and the establishment, support or assistance of charitable centres for giving advice and guidance. The Association publishes annually the *Guide to the Social Services* and the *Charities Digest*.

Papers

The contents of the old C.O.S. Library are now housed on permanent loan with the Goldsmiths Library at Senate House, London University. A complete set of the C.O.S. and F.W.A. regular periodicals is similarly lodged with the National Institute for Social Work Training. The balance of the 'archive' material, comprising a cross-section of casework records, minute books and annual reports, is lodged with the G.L.C. at County Hall. A diary of Sir Charles Stewart Loch, Secretary to the Council of the London C.O.S., 1875-1914, is also deposited in the Goldsmiths Library.

The papers at the Greater London Record Office have been listed and arranged by the origin of their deposit, i.e. the central office and the several area offices. The main series of Council minutes is complete from 1869-1950, and there is a very wide assortment of committee minutes mostly of the mid-20th century. Other papers include agenda for various committees, reports of Council and of separate district committees bound in annual volumes, 1871-1961 (1958-59 missing), newspaper cuttings and other printed material, case cards and case papers. In addition there is a large quantity of local area material.

Availability

A sixty-year rule applies to all the material at County Hall except for that which is published, e.g. annual reports.

FAWCETT LIBRARY
27 Wilfred Street London SW1E 6PR

The Fawcett Library, founded in 1926 by what is now the Fawcett Society, is the main repository for records relating to the women's suffrage movement.

The Library has a unique collection of both manuscript and printed material relating to various aspects of the women's movement. The printed material includes a large collection of pamphlets on feminist issues, books, particularly biographies by and about women, as well as complete runs of various journals, and a large number of volumes and drawers of press cuttings on the women's movement generally, dating from 1926.

Manuscript material includes records of various suffrage organisations. These include: the National Union of Women's Suffrage Societies; the predecessors of the Fawcett Society; the Women's Freedom League; the Women's Tax Resistance League; and various smaller groups. These collections are described in detail under the heading *Women's Suffrage Societies.* (q.v.)

In addition to these records, the Library has collections of both personal papers and the records of various societies. The former include: a multi-volume collection of autograph letters, the core of which is formed by the correspondence of Dame Millicent Fawcett, but also including letters of Elizabeth Garrett Anderson; Louisa Hubbard; Dr. Elsie Inglis; other Fawcett papers include Dame Millicent's notes for speeches and her Boer War concentration camp inquiry diary; also preserved are papers of Eleanor Rathbone, including correspondence regarding the granting of the franchise to Indian women; the letters of Josephine Butler; certain papers of Alice Williams, Teresa Billington Grieg, Philippa Strachey, and diaries of a journey to Australia by Edith How-Martyn.

Society records include those of the various *Women's Emigration Societies* (q.v.), from 1862-1969; the *Josephine Butler Society* (q.v.); the *British Vigilance Association* (q.v.); the Nationality of Women Committee, consisting of two boxes of material; Equal Pay Committee, Equal Rights International, consisting of various papers; the *National Women's Citizens Association* (q.v.); the Association of Post Office Women Clerks; the Council of Women Civil Servants and the National Association of Women Civil Servants; the Consultative Committee of Women's Organisations; the *British Federation of Business and Professional Women* (q.v.); and the Scottish Women's Hospitals, London Committee correspondence.

Availability

Enquiries should be directed to the Librarian. Membership may be necessary.

FEDERAL UNION
13 Chester Square London SW1

Formed in 1938, the organisation aims for a regional Federal Union to include Great Britain, as an intermediary step towards full world government. The Research Institute of the Union, under the chairmanship of Sir William Beveridge, set out to explore the technical difficulties and, since these were considerable, it grew into a semi-autonomous body. The Federal Trust for Education and Research (12A Maddox Street, London W1) was set up after World War II as a separate entity whose trustees are appointed by the Federal Union.

Papers

Archival material includes annual reports, minutes and organisational memoranda, e.g. statements of aims (1939), draft constitution as agreed by National Council (Dec. 1939) and amended constitutions, statement of policy (30 Mar. 1940), reports of foreign section (1940), report on research and information departments (1940).

A large number of pamphlets has been produced, together with the journals, *Federal Union News* (1939-44), *Federal News* (1944-55) and *World Affairs* (1955-63). Annual reports and duplicated papers and articles of the Federal Trust for Education and Research have been retained.

Availability

Enquiries should be addressed to the Secretary of the Union.

FEDERATION OF CIVIL ENGINEERING CONTRACTORS
Romney House Tufton Street London SW1P 3DU

The Federation was founded in 1919 from 35 contracting firms under the chairmanship of Lord Cowdray.

Papers

The Federation's files are regarded as confidential and are not available to researchers.

FELLOWSHIP OF RECONCILIATION
9 Coombe Road New Malden Surrey

The Fellowship was founded in late 1914 as a direct response to the situation created by the outbreak of World War I. It is an inter-denominational Christian pacifist body which seeks to contribute to reconciliation between peoples and the abandonment of violence.

Papers

Records of the Fellowship of Reconciliation have been deposited at B.L.P.E.S. The earliest records relating to the foundation of the Fellowship do not appear to have survived, but signed minutes for the General and Executive Committees exist from 1915 onwards, and minutes of a number of other committees also survive. These include a Conscription Committee, 1916-19; an International Committee, 1915-21; the Political Group, 1917-18; a Propaganda Committee, 1915-18; the Literature Committee; the Magazine Management Committee; and the Social Service Committee, 1915-21. Other records in this collection include a press cutting album for World War I; a small group of deposited papers derived from F. T. Hatton Bradley of Leigh-on-Sea concerning his conscientious objection and imprisonment, 1917; a minute book of the Christian Pacifist Forestry and Land Units, 1940-46; and the minutes of a committee for the management of The Mount conference centre, Haverhill, 1953-57.

The London Union of the Fellowship has also retained many of its records.

Certain records relating to the Fellowship in Wales can be found in the George M. Ll. Davies Collection, National Library of Wales. These include reports, letters, bulletins and memoranda, cyclostyled and typewritten, 1916-47.

Records of the International Fellowship of Reconciliation are at the Siegmund-Schultze Archiv., Soest, West Germany.

The journal of the Fellowship is *Reconciliation Quarterly*, formerly known as *Christian Pacifist* and *Reconciliation*.

Availability

Access to the records is granted on application to the respective libraries.

FINANCE HOUSES ASSOCIATION
14 Queen Anne's Gate London SW1H 9AA

Founded in 1945, the Association aims (*a*) to encourage, promote and protect the interests of members in the exercise of their business; (*b*) to represent members in their relationship with government departments, local and other public authorities, trade associations, the press, etc., and to treat members' interests in regard to actual or proposed legislation; and (*c*) to foster good relations between members and the public generally.

Papers

Records are preserved at the Association's offices, but they are not generally available to researchers. Enquiries should be addressed to the Secretary.

FINANCIAL REFORM ASSOCIATION

Founded in 1848, the Association advocated 'economical government, just taxation and perfect freedom of trade'. It was active at least up to World War I.

Papers

No records of the Association have been located, although some material may exist in the private papers of members. The F.R.A. published a number of tracts and books, together with its *Almanack and Year Book* and the journal *Financial Reformer*.

FIRE BRIGADES UNION
59 Fulham High Street London SW6

Founded in 1913 as the Firemen's Trade Union, the organisation's first General Secretary was Jim Bradley. In 1918 the name was changed to its present form.

All records previous to *c.* 1948 were destroyed during the last war. An official history of the union has appeared: F.M. Radford's *Fetch the Engine* (1951). Further enquiries should be addressed to the General Secretary.

FOOD MANUFACTURERS' FEDERATION
1-2 Castle Lane Buckingham Gate London SW1E 6DN

Formed in 1913 as the Confectionery and Preserved Food Manufacturers' Federation, the organisation adopted its present name in 1917. The Federation now embraces a large number of affiliated associations.

Papers

The records are housed at the Federation's offices. They include Executive Committee minute books from 1913 to the present day, and minute books of various sections (dealing with specific foods or groups of foods) and affiliates. Annual reports and statistics from 1966 and copies of the journal from 1914 are also preserved.

Availability

Whilst some of the recent minute books remain confidential, the records may be seen by appointment with the Librarian.

FREE CHURCH FEDERAL COUNCIL OF ENGLAND AND WALES
27 Tavistock Square London WC1H 9HH

Formed in 1940 by the amalgamation of the National Council of Evangelical Free Churches (1896) and the Federal Council of the Evangelical Free Churches of England (1919). Also incorporated in the organisation is the National Free Church Women's Council. The F.C.F.C. represents the interests of twelve English and Welsh denominations, including the Baptist Union, the Methodist Church and the United Reformed Church. The Council enables the Free Churches to act together in matters affecting the responsibilities and rights of the Federated Churches.

Papers

Various records associated with the work of the Council are retained. Most important is the assortment of minute books of the Council and several committees (General Purposes, Finance, Executive, Education, etc.). A list of these minute books and other documents is available and can be seen on application to the General Secretary. Annual reports from foundation are a second most valuable source, and the monthly journal *Free Church Chronicle* should be consulted. Other documents preserved relate to the Federal Council, local Councils and the London Free Church Council.

Many records relevant to the history of the Free Churches have been deposited in the Greater London Record Office. The records of the *Liberation Society* (q.v.) and the *National Education Association* (q.v.) are of particular interest. Other material includes deposits made by the Congregational and Methodist churches and the F.C.F.C. itself. These records are described in an article, Alison C. Reeve, 'Free Church Records and the G.L.R.O.', *Free Church Chronicle*, Dec. 1973.

Other important collections are preserved at Dr. Williams's Library, Gordon Square, London WC1 and at Friends House Library. A published history of the F.C.F.C., E. K. M. Jordan, *Free Church Unity* (1950) is useful.

The records at the F.C.F.C. offices may be seen by appointment at the discretion of the General Secretary. For the G.L.R.O. collections, enquiries should be addressed to the Archivist.

FREE TRADE LEAGUE
177 Vauxhall Bridge Road London SW1

Formed as the Free Trade Union in 1903, the organisation aimed to promote freedom in the widest sense in all matters connected with business and commerce, to safeguard the free import of food and raw materials, to maintain the general principle that taxation should be imposed for revenue purposes only, and to resist the policy of protection as certain to complicate relations with the Empire states.

Papers

Certain records, as yet unsorted, relating to the Free Trade League and the *Cobden Club* (q.v.) are housed at Dunford House, Midhurst, Sussex, and are to be deposited in due course with the West Sussex Record Office. No details as to the extent and nature of the F.T.L. papers are available. Naturally, researchers should also examine the private papers of prominent free traders. An interesting set of papers has been retained by Mr. S. W. Alexander, current President of the F.T.L., at 44 Speed House Barbican London EC2.

Availability

Enquiries should be addressed to the Archivist at the West Sussex Record Office, and to the Secretary of the F.T.L.

FRIENDS OF EUROPE

Formed in 1933, the Friends aimed to provide accurate information about National-Socialist Germany for use throughout the English-speaking world; to contribute to the defeat of aggressive Nazism; to oppose the domination of Europe by any one power; and to work for a united Europe, based on respect for law and the rights of small nations.

Papers

The Rennie Smith collection at the Bodleian Library, Oxford, includes material relating to the Friends of Europe. Smith was a Labour M.P. (Penistone) from 1924-31, and Secretary of the organisation from 1933. Among the papers are letters to Lord Tyrrell of Avon, in response to the 'Friends of Europe' Rennie Smith Fund, 1940, and a copy of a letter by Smith concerning Friends' work in the United States. The rest of the collection comprises diaries, correspondence, photographs, notebooks and manuscript articles, many of which are relevant to Friends of Europe. The Friends published a mass of material during the 1930s.

Availability

Enquiries should be addressed to the Keeper of Western MSS. at the Bodleian Library.

GENERAL FEDERATION OF TRADE UNIONS
Central House Upper Woburn Place London WC1

Following a T.U.C. recommendation, the G.F.T.U. was established at Manchester in January 1899 by a group of unions seeking mutual financial support. The Federation was merely a committee controlling a fund, and it secured the adhesion of 44 unions, representing a quarter of Congress membership. The G.F.T.U. promotes industrial peace and conciliation in disputes, and administers a fund for mutual assistance and support. It continues to provide many services and dispute benefit to affiliated societies.

Papers

All records which survive are contained in bound annuals from 1899 to date, in the Library at Central House. These annuals include details of proceedings at meetings and conferences (including international gatherings), some minutes and correspondence, quarterly and annual reports, balance sheets and articles. The journal *Federation News* is also valuable. Some unprinted minutes of meetings are retained by the General Secretary, but most unpublished documents have been destroyed.

Availability

The Library may be used by appointment with the General Secretary.

GLASGOW CITIZENS' UNION and GLASGOW RATEPAYERS' FEDERATION

The Ratepayers' Federation was formed c. 1899 to protect members' interests and to watch over the policies of Glasgow City Corporation. The Citizens' Union was a contemporaneous anti-Socialist organisation.

Papers

Certain records are housed with Messrs. Bird, Son and Semple (writers), 223 Hope Street, Glasgow C2. These comprise a Ratepayers' Federation minute book of directors, 1903-22, together with a cash book, 1936-66, prints and circulars, c.1900-12, pamphlets and newspaper cuttings, 1927-30, 1930-37. For the Glasgow Citizens' Union, the following survive: out letter book from 71A West Nile Street, Glasgow, 1899-1902, minute book, 1898-1903, a volume of bound pamphlets 'Citizens' Union Reports', a variety of printed items, and other pamphlets published by the *Anti-Socialist Union* (q.v.) and on municipal reform. See also *National Union of Ratepayers' Associations* and *London Municipal Society*.

Availability

All enquiries should be addressed to the Secretary, National Register of Archives (Scotland).

GOLD STANDARD DEFENCE ASSOCIATION

The Association was founded in 1895 by B. W. Currie (1827-96), an opponent of bi-metallism.

Papers

A collection of papers, 1895-1901 survives in the care of Glyn Mills & Co., 67 Lombard Street, London EC3. This includes correspondence, lists of subscribers, pamphlets, etc.

Availability

Enquiries should be directed to Glyn Mills & Co.

GUARDIAN
192 Gray's Inn Road London WC1

Founded in 1821 as the *Manchester Guardian,* the newspaper changed its name to its present form in 1959.

Papers

The main archives of the *Guardian,* the *Manchester Evening News* and their parent company — the Manchester Guardian and Evening News Ltd. — have been deposited with the Manchester University Library. The archives include commercial records and correspondence, accounts, minutes of meetings and editorial records, together with bound volumes of both newspapers and of the former *Evening Chronicle.* Of the *Guardian* paper, the bulk of the material is of a business and financial character, but with a large assortment of letters to and from outside contacts, members of the staff and contributors. Few of these letters date from the period before C. P. Scott's editorship (1872-1929). The collection also includes 73 reporters' diaries (1868-1944), 42 newspaper cuttings books and 19 boxes of 'foreign correspondence' (1912-39). Other material remains stored at the *Guardian* premises in Broughton Lane, Manchester. This archive contains several interesting series. Although mostly business records, the collection includes the Reuter and Press Association correspondence of J. R. Scott and L. P. Scott (1939-59 approx.). Also included in the archive are personal files of J. R. Scott and the private correspondence of L. P. Scott (1947-58 approx.). Other series cover news services (since World War II), personnel files, pensions, the London printing project (1957-60) and negotiations with *The Times* (q.v.). A large part of the C. P. Scott papers, including some correspondence and all his interview notes with leading politicians, is deposited at the British Library. However, other correspondence, notes, memorabilia and typescript of 'political diaries' (1911-28) are housed in Manchester University Library. Further correspondence of C. P. Scott is deposited at Balliol College, Oxford, and at Manchester Central Library. The papers of W. Crozier, Editor of the *Manchester Guardian* from 1932-44, are with the Beaverbrook Library and with the family.

HEADMASTERS' CONFERENCE
29 Gordon Square London WC1

Founded in 1869 by a group of eminent headmasters meeting over dinner, the association now has 205 members representing the major independent and direct-grant secondary schools in the British Isles and some 50 schools overseas. The Conference protects members' interests and provides a vehicle for discussion of general educational principles and problems which affect such schools as are in close connection not only with the Universities of Oxford and Cambridge but with the whole field of higher academic studies.

Papers

The Conference records its proceedings in printed committee bulletins and the report of its A.G.M. These are consolidated annually and distributed to members and associate members only. Records available in the Library go back to 1869. The bulletins incorporate the main conference minutes, but the original minute books and other manuscript material are not generally available. Many papers have been destroyed through shortage of space, and what remains is unsorted and stored in bundles in the office basement. More recent papers, including files on particular subjects, have been preserved. A history was published in 1969: *The Origins of the Headmasters' Conference*, by Dr. Alicia Percival.

Availability

Bona fide researchers may see the records by arrangement with the Secretary.

HEALTH VISITORS' ASSOCIATION
36 Eccleston Square London SW1

The Association was established in 1896, as the Women Sanitary Inspectors' Association, but was not registered as a trade union until 1918. The words 'and Health Visitors' were added to the name in 1915; it was changed in 1929 to Women Public Health Officers' Association, and in 1962 to its present form.

Papers

These are housed in the offices of the Association and include: minutes of the Executive Committee, 1902-15, 1926 to date; of the annual meeting, 1928 to date; annual reports, 1906-13; handbooks and reports, 1913-16; handbook, 1917-18, 1919, 1920 (no reports issued); handbook and reports, 1921-38; annual reports, 1939 to date. In addition, there are copies of *Women Health Officers* from 1947 to date.

Availability

Students should contact the General Secretary of the Association to make an appointment.

HIRE PURCHASE TRADE ASSOCIATION
3 Berners Street London W1E 4JZ

Founded in 1891, the Association aims to protect the interests of persons trading on fair and equitable terms upon hire-purchase and credit-sale systems.

Papers

Nearly all the records previous to 1939 were destroyed by bombing during World War II. One or two old documents and some pre-war minute books (for the years 1893-1934) have survived, together with more recent records.

Availability

Enquiries should be addressed to the General Secretary.

HOWARD LEAGUE FOR PENAL REFORM
125 Kennington Park Road London SE11 4JP

The Howard Association was founded in 1866 and amalgamated with the Penal Reform League in 1921, when it adopted its present title. The League aims to promote a climate of opinion in which improved penal methods will flourish, and to do this it supplies information to interested parties, provides speakers, and is building up a specialised library and information service.

Papers

Certain records are retained in the office of the Howard League. These are not extensive: hardly any correspondence, for example, has survived. There is, however, an unbroken run of minute books from 1927 to date, which forms the most important record of the League's activities. Annual reports date back to 1921, as do copies of the *Howard Journal*. The League also has an assortment of pamphlets dating from the 1920s and 1930s. The University of Warwick Library purchased a selection of the League's library in 1966. This contained a small manuscript collection consisting of a group of notebooks and press cuttings. This collection is now in the Modern Records Centre of the University of Warwick Library.

Availability

On prior application in writing to the Director, Howard League for Penal Reform, and to the Archivist, Modern Records Centre, University of Warwick Library.

IMPERIAL ALLIANCE FOR THE DEFENCE OF SUNDAYS

The Alliance grew out of the Archbishop of Canterbury's Advisory Committee on Sunday Observance, established in 1905. The work of the Committee led to the recognition of the need for a new pressure group to arouse public opinion on the need to preserve the Lord's Day, and this was set up in 1907. Until 1917 it was closely connected with the Sunday Lay Movement (founded earlier, in 1901) and in 1924 amalgamated with the Central Sunday Closing Association (founded in 1866). It joined with the *Lord's Day Observance Society* (q.v.) in 1965.

Papers

The records of the Alliance are held in the offices of the Lord's Day Observance Society. They consist of minutes of the Archbishop's Advisory Committee, 1905-07, recounting the eventual attempts to establish a national movement, and minute books of the Alliance's Executive Committee covering the period 1908-11 (including a report of the inaugural meeting), 1912-16, 1917-22, 1950-65. The latter volume contains various typescript notes, including a brief history of the Alliance by William Peck. There is also a 'Diary of Record of Special Incidents' for 1909-10, including MS. notes, press cuttings, notices and leaflets.

The collection also contains certain records of societies with which the Alliance united:

(*a*) *Central Sunday Closing Association*. Minute books, 1866-68, 1885-87, 1892-97, 1908-10, 1913-17, 1917-24; annual reports, 1866-79.

(*b*) *Sunday Lay Movement*. One book containing notes of preliminary meetings and committee meetings, 1901-05, and a minute book, 1906-11.

Availability

As for Lord's Day Observance Society.

IMPERIAL AND COMMONWEALTH AFFAIRS: The Records of Selected Societies and Organisations in Britain.

Many relevant pressure groups and institutions are dealt with in the main alphabetical sequence.[1] Notes on other archives are given below, and students seeking further information may be helped by the Colonial Records Project at Rhodes House Library, Oxford; the Librarian at the Institute of Commonwealth Studies, University of London; and the Librarian at the Royal Commonwealth Society. A. R. Hewitt's *Guide to Resources for Commonwealth Studies in London, Oxford & Cambridge* appeared in 1957.

Association of Commonwealth Universities
36 Gordon Square London WC1H 0PF

The organisation was founded in 1913 as the Universities Bureau of the British Empire. Records have been retained, and enquiries should be addressed to the Secretary-General.

British Commonwealth Ex-Services League
49 Pall Mall London SW1Y 5JG

The League was founded in 1921 (as the British Empire Service League) by Field Marshal Earl Haig and Field Marshal Smuts to link together the ex-service organisations of the Commonwealth.

Records which are retained include a full report of the founding conference in Cape Town (1921); biennial and triennial reports of the Empire and Commonwealth Councils; Minute books; and copies of the magazine *Empire and Commonwealth* (1925-1960). Enquiries should be addressed to the Secretary-General.

British Empire League

Founded in 1895 by Sir John Lubbock (1st Lord Avebury) and others, the League aimed to secure the permanent unity of the Empire. Apart from published records, the Avebury Collection at the British Library (Add. Mss. 49638-49681) may be useful.

Ceylon Association in London
2/3 Crosby Square London EC3A 6AA

Founded in 1888 for 'the protection and furtherance of the general interests of Ceylon', the Association maintains a large library of books and records. Most of these have been catalogued up to the end of 1964 as an Appendix to the Association's Annual Report for that year. Enquiries should be addressed to the Secretary.

---

[1]

Anti-Slavery Society	English Speaking Union
British Association of Malaysia and Singapore	Fabian Colonial Bureau
British Commonwealth Peace Federation	Indian Affairs
British Commonwealth Union	Joint Africa Board
Canning House	Liberation
China Association	Missionary Societies
Commonwealth Industries Association	Round Table
Commonwealth Migration Council	Royal African Society
Commonwealth Parliamentary Association	Royal Commonwealth Society
Commonwealth Producers' Association	Tariff Reform League
Congo Reform Association	West India Association
Empire Crusade	Women's Emigration Societies

Colonial Civil Servants Association

The papers covering the years 1947-61 are deposited at Rhodes House, Oxford. No detailed catalogue has been compiled. However, the records comprise the constitution, minutes of conferences, circulars, bulletins and correspondence. In all there are 22 files. Enquiries should be addressed to the Librarian.

Commonwealth Press Union
Studio House Hen and Chickens Court 184 Fleet Street London EC4A 2DU

Founded as the Empire Press Union in 1909, the organisation seeks to protect the interests of member journalists. Records comprise minute books, conference papers and books, and assorted miscellaneous papers, such as Annual Reports. Enquiries should be addressed to the Secretary.

Imperial Commercial Association

Founded in 1918 by Lord Inchcape, the Association aimed to develop and expand British trade and to preserve the rights of the trader against aggression. No records of the Association have been located, and only a few papers remain with the present Lord Inchcape.

Imperial Federation League

Active only in the late nineteenth century, the League was founded by those who believed that a central administration representing the whole Empire was necessary. No formal archive is known to exist, but the published records and copies of the journal (1886-93) are available, for example at Rhodes House, Oxford. H. O. Arnold-Forster was onetime Secretary of the League, and his papers are at the British Library (Add. MSS. 50275-50357).

Imperial South African Association

Pamphlets and annual reports (1897-8) are available at the Royal Commonwealth Society, with other published records at the British Library and at Rhodes House, Oxford. The papers of Geoffrey Drage at Christ Church, Oxford, include relevant material.

International African Institute
210 High Holborn London WC1V 7BW

Founded in 1926 as the International Institute of Languages, the Organisation is not tied to the Commonwealth and is an international, independent and non-political organisation for the study of African people, their language and culture. The Institute's Library has been transferred to the University of Manchester. Records include minutes, copies of the Institute's publications and periodicals.

League for the Exchange of Commonwealth Teachers
Ord Marshall House 124 Belgrave Road London SW1V 2BL

The League was founded as the League of the Empire in 1901 (later becoming the League of the British Commonwealth and Empire). Its objects are to promote friendly and educational intercourse between the different countries of the Commonwealth through the Scheme for the Interchange of Teachers.

The League has retained many of its records, and enquiries should be addressed to the Executive Secretary. Published records of the League of the Empire are available at Rhodes House and other major libraries.

Royal Overseas League
Overseas House Park Place St James's Street London SW1

Founded in 1910 by Sir Evelyn Wrench, the League is essentially a non-political association of Commonwealth citizens and its aim is to promote friendship and understanding between the peoples of the Commonwealth and to maintain its traditions by individual service. Records exist, including Council Minute Books, Annual Reports, copies of the magazine *Overseas*, pamphlets and printed matter. The minutes remain confidential, but individual enquiries concerning the records will be considered on their merits by the Director General.

Victoria League for Commonwealth Friendship
38 Chesham Place London SW1X 8HA

Formed in London in 1901 at the request of the Guild of Loyal Women in South Africa, the Victoria League is an association independent of party politics founded 'to promote a closer union between the different parts of the British Empire by the interchange of information and hospitality, and by co-operation in any practical scheme tending to foster friendly understanding and good friendship within the Empire'. Whilst the provision of hospitality to Commonwealth visitors, migrants and servicemen has been the main field of work, the League has promoted valuable education programmes and the dissemination of information and literature regarding the British Dominions. Wartime work was of tremendous value, with the League running clubs and welfare facilities for overseas servicemen.

Branches have been active in the United Kingdom and many Commonwealth countries.

The records of the Victoria League have been retained. Minute books cover the Central Executive Committee and the Central Council, the Hospitality Committee, the Education Committee, etc. Correspondence is not kept, except for some files relating to property and legal matters. Annual reports from 1901 have been published, and copies of the journal *Hands Across the Sea* (now defunct) are available. Publicity material, circulars and pamphlets have survived, and a short history, *Seventy Years of Service 1901-1971*, appeared in 1971. Most of the records may be seen by arrangement with the Secretary of the Victoria League.

INDEPENDENT LABOUR PARTY
197 Kings Cross Road London WC1

The Independent Labour Party was founded in 1893, and was affiliated to the Labour Representation Committee in 1900. The I.L.P. retained its affiliation to the Labour Party until 1932, while holding its own conferences and developing its own policies. In 1932, after growing differences between the Labour Party and the I.L.P., the latter disaffiliated. Since then the party has retained an independent existence.

Papers
1. *National Records.*

The I.L.P. archive was listed and catalogued in Bristol with the aid of a grant from the Social Science Research Council. At the time of writing it was not possible to provide a full description of these records, and enquiries for further information should be directed to the Hon. Sec., I.L.P.

The offices of the I.L.P. were hit by enemy action during World War II, and many records were destroyed. The core of the present I.L.P. archive is provided by the papers of Francis Johnson, a former Secretary of the party. The collection contains an extremely important series of documents, letters and pamphlets, and includes a wide range of letters from such figures as Keir Hardie, William Morris, H. M. Hyndman, J. R. MacDonald, as well as numerous foreign personalities active in the Labour and Socialist movements.

The material in the archive is extremely informative, both for the early campaigns of the party (for example, there is an extensive collection, by constituencies, of the correspondence concerning early I.L.P. election campaigns) and on the development of the social and political policies of the party. It also contains valuable correspondence of prominent leaders of the I.L.P., including twenty years of letters of J. Keir Hardie to his agent in Merthyr, and most of J. Bruce Glasier's correspondence to his family, particularly while Chairman of the I.L.P. Access to these papers was restricted while they were being listed and catalogued.

A number of records of the National Administrative Council of the I.L.P. are deposited in B.L.P.E.S. These include three volumes of signed minutes: from the first meeting of the N.A.C. to 1895, 1896-97, 1897-99; two volumes of mimeographed reports from head office, containing circulars, letters, financial statements, resolutions, for the years 1898-99, 1921-22; and a volume containing summaries of new and lapsed branches and membership, 1918-21.

Other collections of private papers are extremely useful for the early history of the I.L.P. Particularly important is the J. R. MacDonald Collection. This collection is eventually to be deposited at the Public Record Office.

2. *Local and Regional Records.*

The following is a selection of records deposited in libraries:

Aberdare. Records in Glamorgan Record Office.

City of London. Three M.B.s, 1908-16; 11 volumes of correspondence files, 1909-16, including general correspondence, agenda, financial statements, circulars, etc.; duplicated material, 1913-22, including leaflets, extracts from Hansards, reports, etc.; and an account book, 1914-16. These records have been deposited in B.L.P.E.S.

Clifton and Swinton. M.B.s, 1919-21, are housed in Swinton Library.

Dowlais. Records deposited in University College, Swansea.

East Ham. Records in B.L.P.E.S.

Gillingham. The following records are deposited in B.L.P.E.S.: three M.B.s, 1920-22, 1926-28, 1928-31.

Halifax. A MS. history of Halifax I.L.P. by John Lister is contained in the Alf Mattison Collection, Brotherton Library, University of Leeds.

London and S.E. Counties. No. 6 Divisional Council: M.B.s, 1909-16, correspondence files, 1912-15, and divisional conference agenda, 1910-21, deposited in B.L.P.E.S.

Manchester Central. M.B.s, 1902-12, in Manchester Public Library.

North London and District Federation. Correspondence files, 1909-12, in B.L.P.E.S., including agenda, reports and financial statements, press cuttings, circulars, etc.

Nottingham. A M.B., 1927-31, is deposited in Nottingham University Library.

Sheffield Attercliffe. M.B.s, 1918-23, in Sheffield Public Library.

Sheffield Brightside. Records in Sheffield Public Library.

Wallasey. M.B., 1894-1900 in *National Labour Museum* (q.v.).

Warrington. Records in Warrington Municipal Library.

Watford. M.B.s, 1904-10, correspondence files, 1905-10, in B.L.P.E.S.

3. *Scottish I.L.P. Branch Records.*

Arbroath. M.B.s, 1908-18, 1920-39, have been deposited in Arbroath Library.

Ayrshire North. (Saltcoats branch). Records are deposited in the North Ayrshire Museum.

Edinburgh Central. A M.B. of the branch from formation in 1892-94 is in the possession of Mr. Tom Oswald, M.P. Other records are in the National Library of Scotland.

Glasgow I.L.P. Federation. A useful collection of records is deposited in the Mitchell Library, Glasgow. These include Executive Council minutes, 1917-33, certain branch and committee minutes, and financial records.

INDIAN AFFAIRS: SOCIETIES AND ORGANISATIONS IN BRITAIN, 1900-47

Only a selection of relevant organisations are described below, and it is important to note that details have not been given for non-political pressure groups such as the India Society (cultural) or the Manchester Chamber of Commerce (q.v.).

It is most convenient to classify the groups by their aims, though the traditional 'left-right' analysis is not very satisfactory in a constantly varying political situation. It is helpful to use contemporary British government policy as a yardstick. Thus, three groups [4, 10 and 13] may be termed 'diehard' in that they firmly believed British government policy to be 'going too far and too fast' towards eventual Indian independence.

The most important of all the organisations was the British Committee of the Indian National Congress, which, until the so-called 'Moderate/Extremist' nationalists split in the years 1918-21, could claim to be the spokesman for the whole spectrum of Indian nationalist opinion. In 1921 Congress adopted Gandhi's constitution which specified *swaraj* [self-government] as its aim and simultaneously dropped its commitment to strictly constitutional agitation. This marked not only the end of the Congress organisation in Great Britain [2] but the breaking of all ties with the constitutionalist nationalist, notably the Indian Liberals [7] and the followers of Mrs Annie Besant [3, 5, 6 and 8]. The Indian National Congress was not represented in Britain until Krishna Menon broke away from the Commonwealth of India League [8] to form the India League [9] which supported the policies of Nehru.

It was not until the 1930s that the question of India's future became a really important question in British politics. Thus, there were a proliferation of new pressure groups, of which the main ones only are listed below. Two organisations [11 and 12] tended to be favourable to Nationalist aspirations whilst the Union of Britain and India [14] was a Government sponsored body defending the government's policy on India against the Churchillite India Defence League [13] and the Indian Empire Society [10].

The major repository for archival collections on India is the India Office Library which houses the private collections of most of the Viceroys, Secretaries of State and important provincial Governors; see Stanley C. Sutton: *A guide to the India Office Library* (H.M.S.O., 1967).

A very large number of the private papers of Indian civil servants, Indian Army Officers, etc., have been collected at the Centre of South Asian Studies at Cambridge; see Mary Thatcher (ed.): *Cambridge South Asia Archive* (Cambridge, 1973).

For other collections in the British Isles, see M. D. Wainwright and Noel Matthews: *A guide to Western Manuscripts and Documents in the British Isles relating to South and South East Asia* (Oxford, 1965).

[1] Royal Society for India, Pakistan and Ceylon

The organisation incorporates the East India Association, founded in 1866. The E.I.A. aimed for the independent and disinterested advocacy and promotion, by all legitimate means of the public interest and welfare of the inhabitants of India generally. Major office holders included 2nd Baron Lamington, Chairman of the Council, 1908-22, and President, 1922-40; Lord Pentland, Chairman 1922-5; and Sir Louis Dane, Chairman 1925-32. Many wealthy Indian princes acted as benefactors. The Association was active in making political representations during the nineteenth century and again in the 1930s, but the organisation eschewed party politics. The periodical *Journal of the East India Association* appeared 1867-1942, and then continued under the name *Asiatic Review*. An official history, *Four Score*, (ed. Sir John Cumming), was published in 1947. The records of the Association are available at the India Office Library (Hand List EUR/F147). The papers include: Minute Books, 1873-1963; Financial Papers, *c.* 1865-1963; Membership correspondence, 1929-49; Correspondence and General Papers, 1876-1958. Also within this collection are the papers of the India Society (formed in 1910 for the appreciation of Indian art and literature) and of the National Indian Association (founded in 1870 to further the educational and social progress of India).

[2] British Committee of the Indian National Congress

Formed in 1889 and formally constituted as a component part of the Indian National Congress in 1908, the Committee after 1918 was rent by the divisions in Indian politics between the moderate and extreme nationalists. Under the new Congress constitution of 1920, the British Committee was abolished. Office holders included Sir William Wedderburn, Bt. (1838-1918), President 1889 and 1910, and one time Chairman of the Indian Parliamentary Committee at Westminster. The printed journal was *India* (1890-1920) and *Hind* (1921-2), and unpublished records are available in the Nehru Memorial Library, Teen Murti House, New Delhi, India.

[3] Indian Home Rule League: British Auxiliary

Active from 1916 to 1920, the League had George Lansbury as President and John Scurr as its Honorary Secretary, and worked closely with the British Labour movement. However, by 1920 Lansbury and others found their positions in the Labour Party clashing with the constitutionalist, royalist, anti-Congress Party line of Annie Besant, the League's initiator. The Lansbury papers are available at B.L.P.E.S., and Annie Besant's extensive correspondence and papers are housed at the headquarters of the Theosophical Society, Adyar, Madras, India.

[4] Indo-British Association

Founded in 1917 to counteract the Home Rule Movement in India, the Association was active up to *c.* 1922 and aimed for the 'safeguarding of the interests of the Indian peoples, which at present are absolutely inseparable from the continuance of British Rule'. The Association published over twenty pamphlets, and worked in circularising business interests. No relevant archives have been located as yet: the Sydenham collection at the British Library is disappointing in this respect. Further details are available in M. K. Hassan: *Indian Politics and the British Right 1914-22* (London Ph.D., 1963).

[5] Britain and India Association

Mainly a Theosophist organisation, the Association was founded in 1919 and was active in the early 1920s, lecturing to various organisations in Britain and organising political conferences on Indian affairs. The Association looked to the day 'when Britain and India will stand side by side, united and as equals in the great commonwealth of nations'. Relevant papers may be found amongst the Besant Collection at Adyar, and the Association's journal *Britain and India* (from 1920) is available.

[6] Parliamentary Committee on India

Formed in 1919 and later known as the British Committee on Indian Affairs (to 1928), the organisation embraced Theosophists, Trade Unionists and several Labour politicians (see [3] above). The periodical *United India* appeared weekly, 1919 to 1921. Again the Besant papers and the Lansbury papers are of value. The papers of the secretary, John Scurr, M.P., have not yet been located.

[7] Indian Reform Committee

This was formed in 1920 as a British organisation in support of the Indian Moderate or Liberal Party. No archival sources are known to have survived.

[8] Commonwealth of India League

Working to attain Dominion status for India, this Group was formed in 1923 and succeeded the Indian Home Rule League: British Auxiliary. Whilst mainly a Theosophist organisation, the executive members included V. K. Krishna Menon, Major Graham Pole (Labour M.P., 1929-31) and Peter Freeman, M.P. V. K. Krishna Menon has retained some material (see below), and some papers of Major Graham Pole are available at the University of York library.

[9] India League

Formed in 1930 by Krishna Menon to fight for India's independence, the League has survived to the present day. The Honorary General Secretary may be contacted at Wheatsheaf House, 4 Carmelite Street, London EC4. A good collection of records has been retained. Persons wishing to see the League papers should apply to the Honorary President, V. K. Krishna Menon, Teen Murti Marg, New Delhi, India.

[10] Indian Empire Society

Formed in 1930 to ensure the retention of India within the Empire, the Society's secretary was Sir Louis Stuart. His papers at the Bodleian Library, Oxford, include an assortment of I.E.S. correspondence, 1930-48, including correspondence with Lord Sydenham (1931-3); Miscellaneous typescript material, press cuttings and other printed matter is also available in the Stuart collection.

[11] India Conciliation Group

Formed in 1931, the group was a Quaker organisation active up to 1950.
The papers of the Secretary, Agatha M. Harrison, are deposited at Friends House Library. The material includes twelve boxes of India Conciliation Group material, covering correspondence, subject files, circulars and printed matter. Correspondents include Gandhi, V. K. Krishna Menon, Lord Irwin, Eleanor Rathbone and Stafford Cripps.

[12] Friends of India:

No papers have been located, but the journal *India Bulletin* (1932-4) is available.

[13] India Defence League

Formed in March 1933 to oppose the Government's proposals for Indian constitutional reforms, the League enjoyed the support of numerous eminent British politicians and public figures. No formal archive is known, but the private papers of members are often of value. Vice-Presidents include Winston Churchill, Rudyard Kipling, Lord Lloyd and Sir Henry Page Croft. The Churchill papers are to go to Churchill College, Cambridge, where the rich collection of Croft papers and the papers of Lord Lloyd of Dolobran are already available. Much printed material may be found within the private papers of Sir John Perronet Thompson at the India Office Library [Handlist EUR/F. 137].

[14] Union of Britain and India

Active in 1934 and 1935, the organisation was an officially blessed counter movement to the India Defence League and the Indian Empire Society. The U.B.I. generally supported the Government's White Paper on Indian constitutional reforms. The *U.B.I. London Weekly* appeared 1934-5, and several files of private U.B.I. correspondence can be found in the Sir John Perronet Thompson collection at the India Office Library. [Handlist EUR/F. 137.]

INDUSTRIAL PARTICIPATION ASSOCIATION
25-28 Buckingham Gate London SW1

Founded in 1884 as the Labour Association for Promoting Co-operative Production based on the Co-partnership of Workers, the organisation was later known as the Labour Co-partnership Association (1902) and the Industrial Co-partnership Association (1927). The present name was adopted in 1972. It provides a forum for the exchange of ideas and experience, and acts as a centre of information and advice, on all aspects of participation, involvement and motivation in work. Through research, conferences and publications, the Association promotes the best human relations practices in industry.

Papers

The records are preserved at the Association's offices. A full set of minute books dates from 1884. Miscellaneous papers include, for example, notices of meetings. Apart from back correspondence, at least two copies of every original paper are kept. The most comprehensive record of the Association's activities is provided in copies of the Association's journal, which has appeared as a monthly and later as a quarterly from 1894.

Availability

Applications should be addressed to the Director.

INDUSTRIAL SOCIETY
Robert Hyde House 48 Bryanston Square London W1H 8AH

Established as the Boys' Welfare Association in 1918 by Sir (then the Rev.) Robert Hyde, the organisation became the Industrial Welfare Society in 1919 and took its present name in 1965. Today the Society exists to promote the fullest involvement of people in their work to increase the effectiveness and profitability of the organisation and the satisfaction of the individual. Its endeavours are undertaken through concentrating on leadership, management—union relations, communication and involvement, terms and conditions of employment, and the development of young employees. Earlier campaigning work included improved physical working conditions and pension schemes, holidays with pay and the establishment of personnel departments. The Society has over 12,000 member organisations representing both management and the trade unions.

114

Papers

A good collection of records is housed at the Society's headquarters. Full series of minute books from 1918 cover proceedings of the A.G.M.s Council, the Executive Committee and the Finance Committee. Other minute books of committees include the following volumes: Central Committee of Industrial Welfare Supervisors' Associations, 1925-31; Campaign Committee, 1928-30; I.W.S. Birmingham and District Advisory Committee, 1921-22; Medical Advisory Committee, 1951-60. Annual reports date from 1919 and provide balance sheets and details of members. Correspondence is not usually preserved, but one interesting file of paper relates to the 'Duke of Edinburgh's Conference', 1954. An original ledger kept by Robert Hyde and a volume of early press cuttings are available. Other material includes papers relating to various prominent members of the Society. *The Industrial Society* by Elizabeth Sidney was published in 1968. The Society's monthly magazine is probably the oldest in Britain, and one of the oldest in the world, on the subject of people and their work. Established in 1918 as the *Boys' Welfare Journal*, it became the *Journal of Industrial Welfare* in 1920, *Industrial Welfare* in 1922 and *Industrial Society* in 1965.

Availability

Applications should be addressed to the Secretary.

INLAND REVENUE STAFF FEDERATION
7-9 St George's Square London SW1

The Inland Revenue Staff Federation was formed on 28 May 1938, and now incorporates the Association of Officers of Taxes, the National Association of Taxes Assessing and Collecting Services, and the Valuation Office Clerical Association.

Papers

The extensive records, which include those of the earlier associations, go back in some cases to the 1920s. Up to 1970, rules were recorded and registered with the Registry of Friendly Societies and only current membership records are kept by the Federation.

Minutes of the Executive Committee date from formation. The annual delegates conference is reported annually in the Federation's journal, *Taxes*, published monthly from September 1912. Bound volumes are kept by the Federation. Odd copies of the progress report (a popularised version of the annual report) from 1949 are available. Miscellaneous correspondence, covering a wide field but dealing mainly with personal cases, has been preserved. Details of wage agreements, negotiations, etc., can be followed in the records of arbitration cases and the Arbitration Tribunal, which date from 1925, and the equal pay records from 1951. The records of negotiations concerning amalgamations include correspondence dating from 1922. The Federation also holds copies of all stencilled memoranda issued to the Executive Committee, members of sub-committees and advisory committees, branch secretaries and office secretaries, dating back to about 1936. Branch records are not available at the headquarters.

Availability

Researchers may consult the records at the Federation offices by prior arrangement with the General Secretary.

INSTITUTE OF AGRICULTURAL HISTORY AND MUSEUM OF ENGLISH RURAL LIFE
University of Reading Whiteknights Reading Berks RE6 2AG

The Museum of English Rural Life was established by the University of Reading in 1951 with the aim of conserving the material culture of the English countryside and of collecting together records of past methods and practices. It was eventually decided that the Museum should concentrate on the more limited field of the development of agricultural science and technology and in order to bring together in one organisation the necessary resources for the study of agricultural history an Institute of Agricultural History was established in 1968 at the University of Reading. This institute has three main areas of activity: (1) it co-ordinates teaching and research in the subject; (2) it contains a documentation unit which is responsible within the Institute for compiling classified, subject indexes of reference to printed sources on agricultural history, for publishing bibliographies on specialised topics and for listing archival sources in other record repositories; (3) the Institute has subsumed the Museum of English Rural Life which continues to collect and conserve artefactual and archival material in support of the Institute, and which carries on a programme of exhibitions and other services for the general public. The Museum holds an object collection of agricultural machines and implements, crafts tools and domestic equipment.

More recently the Museum has been concerned to build up archival holdings relevant to its subject interest in agricultural history and technology. The principal specialist collections are

(1)   A photographic collection of approximately 168,000 prints and 200,000 negatives, from *c.* 1850. This includes the photograph libraries of *Farmer's Weekly* and *Farmer and Stockbreeder.*

(2)   A trade record collection derived from the industries servicing agriculture, and particularly from farm machinery makers and dealers. Some 1900 firms are represented, from large-scale manufacturers, such as David Brown Tractor Sales Ltd, Marshall-Fowler Ltd, and Ransomes, Sims and Jefferies Ltd, to small local concerns. Records include business, technical and publicity material, from the late eighteenth century to the present day. Some collections in other repositories have been photocopied. The archive is being catalogued and indexed with the aid of a grant from the Social Science Research Council.

(3)   A collection relating to the agricultural co-operative movement in England in the nineteenth century and twentieth century. The archives of thirty agricultural cooperatives have been acquired or photocopied, including businesses registered both as friendly societies and companies. The earliest cooperative represented is the Aspatria Agricultural Society (1870). The principal archives of the Plunkett Foundation, the Land Settlement Association (q.v.), the market section of the National Federation of Women's Institutes (q.v.) and some branch societies have also been microfilmed.

(4)   A collection relating to agricultural unionism in England. The Country Landowners Association (q.v.) and the National Union of Agricultural and Allied Workers (q.v.) have deposited their national administrative, business, legal and social history records from 1906 and 1907 respectively.

(5)   A collection relating to agricultural organisations and societies. The chief holdings are the archives of the Old Board of Agriculture (1793-1822) and the Royal Agricultural Society of England after 1838 (q.v.).

(6)   A farm record collection. Some 900 holdings are represented, from the seventeenth century. Record categories include accounts, field books,

diaries, and agreements. A number of holdings in other repositories have been microfilmed. The collection has been catalogued by the University Archivist and is located in the University Library.

Enquiries relating to records except farm records should be directed to the Keeper, Museum of English Rural Life, University of Reading. Farm record enquiries should be directed to the Archivist, the Library, University of Reading.

INSTITUTE OF DIRECTORS
10 Belgrave Square London SW1X 8PW

Founded in 1903, the Institute received its Royal Charter in 1906. It aims to raise the standards and status of directors and promotes the interests of free enterprise, and provides information and other services to directors of all types of company.

Papers

Most of the records in the Institute offices date only from 1949, when the Institute was revivified. From that date, annual reports and accounts, membership registers, bound copies of the journal *The Director*, and records of annual conferences are retained. Press cuttings from 1954 and copies of the journal for 1922 are also available.

Availability

Enquiries should be addressed to the Librarian and Research Officer.

INSTITUTE OF JOURNALISTS
2-4 Tudor Street London EC4Y 0AB

The Institute of Journalists was founded as the National Association of Journalists in 1884 and changed its name c. 1889. It aimed to promote, by all reasonable means, the interests of journalists and journalism.

Papers

The Institute has its minute books dating back almost to its inception, and also records of its membership back to c. 1893. Various regional organisations of the I.O.J. have also retained their district minutes back to their date of inauguration. The I.O.J. does not keep any but current correspondence, but has kept copies of its publications. Its own journal was called *Proceedings* until 1912, when it became the *Journal*. In addition to its own publications, it has copies of the magazine, the *Journalist*, from 1891.

Availability

Written application to the Secretary is necessary. The minutes are not usually made available, and the researcher is referred to the appropriate issue of either *Proceedings* or the *Journal* where they are summarised.

INTERNATIONAL INSTITUTE OF SOCIAL HISTORY
Herengracht 262-266 Amsterdam Netherlands

The Institute was founded in 1935 under the inspiration of Dr. N. W. Posthumus, Professor of Social and Economic History at Amsterdam University, and with necessary funds provided by an insurance company associated with the Dutch Labour movement. The Institute's prime concern since its foundation has been with the history of the Labour and Socialist movements. The core of the Institute's collections is the vast assemblage of original papers and publications of Marx and Engels and their followers. The first collection acquired consisted of material that belonged to the Jewish Social Democratic Party 'Bund'. This was followed by the Marx—Engels archives, including various manuscripts, excerpts, documents, correspondence, etc.; the archives of the Russian periodical *Vpered!* (1873-77); and a large collection of manuscripts, pamphlets, periodicals and books concerning anarchism collected by the Austrian historian, Max Nettlau (1865-1944). This collection includes records of William Morris's Socialist League, 1885-90, and papers of Bakunin. Voluminous papers of Karl Kautsky, interpreter of Marx and ideologue of the Second International, are also housed in the Institute. Around these collections a vast archive of, among others, French, Italian, Spanish, Dutch and British papers has developed.

The archives are organised within departments. Examples are: Africa, Asia, Australia; Anarchism; Central Europe; Eastern Europe; England and North America; France, Italy and Israel; Iconography; International Organisations; Netherlands, Belgium, Luxembourg.

It would be impossible to give a comprehensive list of the rich archive collections at the Institute. What follows is therefore a selection. It is divided for convenience into three sections. The first section lists briefly the more important of the archives relating to personalities and movements chiefly active outside Britain. Many of these collections, however, contain correspondence relating to Britain, e.g. the Scheu papers. The second section lists the more important of the international organisations in which various British movements played a part. The final section, dealing with the archives relating directly to British history, is in more detail than the previous two.

1. *Foreign Archives*

Adler, V.: part-archive — correspondence and manuscripts.
Akselrod, P. B.: archives, 1880-1928.
Bakunin, K.: part-archive.
Bebel, A.: part-archive — correspondence, manuscripts, notes, excerpts.
Bernstein, E.: archives — collection of correspondence and manuscripts.
Commune de Paris: collection of correspondence and documents.
Cooper, Th.: collection of correspondence, 1847-57.
Dukhoberg: part-archive — correspondence, 1898-99.
German Socialists: a collection including letters from various correspondents, such as Kugelmann, Karl Liebknecht, Luxemburg.
Goldman, Emma: an archive including correspondence, notes, documents.
Guesde, J.: correspondence and manuscripts.
Herzen, A.I.: correspondence, etc.
Humbert-Droz: xerox copies of correspondence.
Jung, H. F.: archives, 1862-88.
Kautsky, K.: correspondence and documents.
Korsch, K.: part-archive.
Kropotkin, P.: correspondence, manuscripts and documents.
Landauer, G.: archives.
Liebknecht, Wilhelm: archives.
Malatesta, E.: correspondence.
Ponstein, B.: correspondence, press cuttings.
Scheu: correspondence, etc.
Smirnov, V. M.: correspondence, 1870-1900.

Trotsky, L. D.: correspondence, manuscripts, 1917-22.
Wedemeyer, J.: part-archive.

Institutional archives in this section include those of the Dutch Labour Party and records relating to the Spanish Civil War.

2. *International Archives*

Asian Socialist Conference, 1952-62.
Centr'aide Ouvrière Internationale, 1951-60.
International Anarchist Congress, London, 1881.
International Confederation of Free Trade Unions, 1949-67.
International Federation of Industrial Organisations and General Workers' Unions, 1923-64.
International Federation of Lithographers, Printers and Similar Trades, 1896-1949.
International Federation of Trade Unions, 1914-45.
International Graphical Federation, 1949-60.
International Labour Organisation, 1919-68.
International Metalworkers' Federation, 1951-67.
International Organisation of Industrial Employers, 1920-40.
International Union of Socialist Youth Organisations, 1907-15.
International Union of Students, 1946-70.
International Working Men's Association, minutes of the General Council, 1864-72.
Labour and Socialist International archives, 1923-45.
Miners' International Federation, 1890-1968.
Second International, 1921-23.
Socialist International, 1945-67.
Socialist Youth International, 1923-46.
Socialist Parties of the European Community and the Socialist Faction of the European Parliament, 1954-70.
Socialist Group of the Consultative Assembly of the Council of Europe, 1957-61.

The papers donated by Prof. J. Braunthal also provide an invaluable source on relations between the Socialist parties, particularly in the inter-war years.

3. *British Archives*

Among the records in this section are the following personal collections: certain correspondence of Robert Owen, with notes for speeches, reprints of articles, etc., and minutes of organisations with which Owen was involved: the Central Board of the Association of All Classes of All Nations, 1838-40, the Directors of the National Community Friendly Society, 1838-43, and the Directors of the Rational Society; certain correspondence of and relating to Ernest Jones, 1840-69; 3 manuscripts of lectures by William Morris; 38 letters from various correspondents to Robert Murray, 1896-1943, including 5 from Keir Hardie; a manuscript of H. N. Brailsford's book *The Levellers;* correspondence of G. D. H. Cole, chiefly with publishers, 1913-35, but including some personal correspondence, 1954-57, correspondence about the World Socialist Movement, 1955-57, and a number of typescripts of books and articles; correspondence, 1910-50, of H. J. Laski, including letters from G. B. Shaw, Graham Wallas, Beatrice and Sidney Webb, H. G. Wells, together with manuscripts of books, articles and lectures; a small group of correspondence of J. S. Middleton; and the E. Sylvia Pankhurst Collection, consisting of letters, manuscripts, typescripts, etc. (for details, see pp. 284-5).

Papers of societies include the archives of the *Socialist League* (q.v.), 1884-90, consisting of reports, minutes, manifestoes, correspondence, etc.; balance sheets and accounts, 1881-82, of the Homerton Social Democratic Club; reports of the proceedings of the 3rd and 4th Annual Congresses of Trades Societies and Trades

Councils, 1871-72; records of the Workers' Socialist Federation (in E. Sylvia Pankhurst Collection); and records up to the end of 1916 of the *National Council for Civil Liberties* (q.v.). Other groups of records which should be mentioned include parliamentary broadsheets, 1831-32, and strike bulletins for the 1926 General Strike, including papers collected by Raymond Postgate and J. P. M. Millar. The Postgate Collection also contains reports and correspondence in answer to questionnaires about the Strike.

INTERNATIONAL PEACE SOCIETY
Fellowship House 3 Browning Street London SE17

The Society for the Promotion of Permanent and Universal Peace, generally known as the Peace Society, was founded in 1816. The first impulse to its formation came from the *Society of Friends* (q.v.) and it was an avowedly religious, but non-sectarian, movement. It stressed the importance of international arbitration and was prominent in the convening of International Peace Congresses. The old Peace Society was split by disagreements over World War I, and the International Peace Society, founded in 1916, took over many of its functions.

Papers

A collection of minute books, interspersed with a small amount of correspondence, is in the care of the International Peace Society. Details are not available. Access to these records is not generally granted.

The papers of Henry Richard, M.P. (1812-88), Secretary of the Peace Society, 1848-88, are deposited in the National Library of Wales. Papers of the Doncaster Auxiliary of the Peace Society, 1845-51, are contained in the Clark papers at Doncaster Museum. Two minute books (1844-57) and annual reports (1858-59) of the Peace Society Margate Auxiliary are retained at Friends House Library, which is also rich in printed pacifist literature.

The Peace Society's organ during the 19th century was the *Herald of Peace* (founded 1821), and later the *Olive Leaf* (1903-15).

Annual reports were published, 1821-1902.

IRON AND STEEL TRADES CONFEDERATION
Swinton House 324 Gray's Inn Road London WC1

The Confederation was formed in 1917 to facilitate the amalgamation of unions operating in the iron and steel industry. The amalgamated unions affiliated to the Confederation, keeping their separate identity. At the same time, a central organisation, the British Iron, Steel and Kindred Trades Association (BISAKTA), was set up, to which members of the unions constituting the Confederation gradually transferred. New members joined BISAKTA. For practical purposes, the Confederation and BISAKTA are the same organisation, but the Confederation could still accept the affiliation of other unions.

Three unions affiliated to the Confederation on its formation: the British Steel Smelters, Mill, Iron, Tinplate and Kindred Trades Association, the Associated Iron and Steel Workers of Great Britain, and the National Steel Workers' Association Engineering and Labour League. The Amalgamated Society of Steel and Iron Workers affiliated in 1920, and the Tin and Sheet Millmen's Association in 1921.

These are retained at the head office of the Confederation.

(1) Minutes and reports and complete records of the activities of the Confederation cover the period from 1917 to date. Copies of the journal survive from 1917 to date, and of the Confederation's journal, *Man and Metal*, from 1923 to date.

(2) *British Iron, Steel and Kindred Trades Association.* Full records, including minutes and reports, run from 1917 to date.

(3) *British Steel Smelters, Iron, Tinplate and Kindred Trades Association* (established 1886 as the British Steel Smelters' Association). Minutes cover the period 1886-92, 1910-18, and bound reports, containing the journal, reports of conference, details of membership, finance, etc., are continuous from 1886-1917. Minutes of the Benefit Society survive for 1911-13.

(4) *Associated Iron and Steel Workers of Great Britain* (formerly Amalgamated Malleable Ironworkers, established 1862). Minutes of the Executive Council run from 1887-1914. The *Ironworkers' Journal* (1869-1916) also contains the minutes of the Executive, together with the minutes of the Midland Iron and Steel Wages Board and the Board of Conciliation and Arbitration for the Manufactured Iron and Steel Trade of the North of England, etc. Correspondence survives concerning the Neath dispute, May-August 1900.

(5) *National Steel Workers' Association Engineering and Labour League.* (established 1888). Minutes of the annual meeting for 1908 are extant, as are quarterly reports for March, September and December 1900, and September 1903.

(6) *Amalgamated Society of Steel and Iron Workers* (established 1888 as the Associated Society of Millmen). A typescript history, written by O. Coyle (1925), survives.

(7) *Associated Society of Millmen* Executive Council minutes date from 1888-93.

(8) *Tin and Sheet Millmen's Association* (established 1898). Rules for 1906 and the amalgamation agreement of 1922 have been retained.

(9) *National Amalgamated Society of Enginemen, Cranemen, Boilermen, Firemen and Electrical Workers* (established 1891, amalgamated with British Steel Smelters' Association, 1912). The following records survive: the General Secretary's first annual report, 1891; report and statement of accounts, 1905, 1906, 1911 and 1912; and the General Secretary's notes, 7 May 1908.

(10) *Iron and Steel Trades Federation* (1912-16). There are minutes of meetings, 1914-16.

Availability

By previous application in writing to the Research Department.

Note

Certain records are currently in the process of being transferred to the Modern Records Centre, University of Warwick Library.

ITALIAN REFUGEES RELIEF COMMITTEE

Formed in 1927, the organisation aimed to help opponents of Fascism who were refugees from Italy.

Papers

Correspondence and papers are deposited at Reading University Library and comprise records of the London and Paris Committees, 1927-30. The main series are correspondence, together with reports of the London and Paris Committees, 1927-28, balance sheets, accounts, 1927-30, receipts, lists of subscribers' addresses, circulars, printed ephemera and newspaper cuttings. A supplementary set of similar papers 1920-49, at present with the University Italian Department, is to be integrated into the main collection. The additional material includes correspondence, cuttings and pamphlets relating to Italian politics.

Availability

Applications should be addressed to the Librarian at the University of Reading.

JEWISH ORGANISATIONS IN BRITAIN

Many societies and organisations relating to the interests of the Jewish community in Britain have been active during the twentieth century, and no detailed survey of the records of these bodies has been attempted by this project. However, two major organisations are treated in this book: *Board of Deputies of British Jews* and *Zionist Federation of Great Britain* (q.q.v.). The text also describes records of the *Church's Ministry among the Jews* and the *Council of Christians and Jews* (q.q.v.).

The following note points to some of the other bodies active in British public life, and indicates the main centres for the collection of Jewish archives and for research in this field.

The Anglo-Jewish Association, Woburn House, Upper Woburn Place, London WC1, was founded in 1871 and is the most important of the organisations not covered in this survey. It has worked to promote the social, moral and intellectual progress of the Jews, and has been active in the field of Jewish colonisation. Enquiries should be addressed to the Secretary.

The *Jewish Year Book* gives details of the numerous Anglo-Jewish societies and institutions, foreign assistance organisations and international bodies, many of which remain in existence and have an address in Britain. Apart from specifically Zionist groups such as the British Israel World Federation, the Jewish Dominion of Palestine League and the Federation of Women Zionists of Great Britain and Ireland, the range of organisations includes bodies concerned with the social welfare of the Jewish community in Britain, e.g. the Association of Jewish Youth, the Jewish Welfare Board, the Trades Advisory Council of the Board of Deputies, the Association of Jewish Ex-Servicemen and Women and the Association of Jewish Refugees in Great Britain.

Information and guidance may be given by the Jewish Historical Society of England (established in 1893) at 33 Seymour Place, London W1, and at the Mocatta Library, University College, London WC1, which itself acts as a repository for Jewish archives. Other important centres exist at the Parkes Library, University of Southampton; Manchester Central Library; the Jewish Museum and the Jewish Memorial Council at Woburn House; the Middle East Centre at St Antony's College, Oxford; the Jewish National and Hebrew University Library, Jerusalem, and the Central Zionist Archives, P.O.Box 92, Jerusalem. Naturally, much relevant material is available at the Public Record Office in London and in the Israel State Archives. Among other useful addresses are: Institute of Jewish Affairs, 13 Jacob's Well Mews, London W1; World Jewish Congress, 55 New Cavendish Street, London W1; and the Jewish Chronicle Library, 25 Furnival Street, London EC4.

In 1973 a project under the auspices of the British Academy, in conjunction with the Israel Academy, began a survey of records relating to the British Mandate in Palestine and the foundation of the State of Israel. It is hoped that the findings of this project, including information on the records of many of the Jewish organisations in Britain, will in due course be made available. Enquiries should in the meantime be addressed to Dr C. P. Cook, c/o Anglo-Palestine Archives Project, British Academy, Burlington House, Piccadilly, London W1V 0NS.

JOINT AFRICA BOARD
25 Victoria Street London SW1H 0EX

Formed in 1923 as the Joint East African Board, the organisation changed its name in 1949 to embrace Central Africa and in 1965 adopted the present name. The Board aims to provide a channel of unofficial communication between the authorities and individuals in the U.K. and Central and Southern Africa, for the promotion of British agricultural, industrial and commercial interests.

Papers

The records at the Board's offices consist of minutes, annual reports, published and unpublished memoranda on various subjects of interest to East, Central and Southern Africa, together with correspondence.

Availability

Enquiries should be addressed to the Secretary.

'JOINT FOUR'
Gordon House 29 Gordon Square London WC1

Formed in 1919, the Joint Executive Committee of the Associations of Headmasters, Head Mistresses, Assistant Masters and Assistant Mistresses acts to co-ordinate views on all matters of educational and professional policy which are the common concern of the constituent Associations. The Joint Four represents the views of the Associations in dealings with government departments, other national organisations of teachers and with the national organisations of Local Education Authorities. In addition to its wide involvement in all matters affecting secondary education in this country, the Joint Four has co-operated fully in the work of the international teachers' organisations, the International Federation of Secondary Teachers and the World Confederation of Organisations of the Teaching Profession.

Papers

The Joint Four has copies of annual reports going back to the 1920s, and also minutes of meetings going back over the same period.

Availability

Application to see the records should be made to the Secretary.

Headmasters' Association
29 Gordon Square London WC1

Founded in 1891 and incorporated three years later as the Incorporated Association of Headmasters, the Association has grown from a group of headmasters representing the ancient grammar schools, and now has over 1,800 members, embracing both the independent and maintained sectors of secondary education in England, Wales and Northern Ireland. A separate association exists for Scotland. The H.M.A. exists to safeguard the interests of members, their character and status, and the educational principles in which they believe.

The main records are included in the H.M.A. *Review,* published usually three times a year from the 1890s. The series includes Council minutes for the early years, and then summaries of Council proceedings, membership statistics and analyses, notes for the advice and information of members, and articles. Unfortunately the original records have not been systematically preserved, and those which do survive at the H.M.A. offices are in a state of disarray. Minutes of the Council and the Executive Committee, and the proceedings of the 18 H.M.A. divisions, were filed away, but it is not known if they survive.

Availability

Applications should be addressed to the General Secretary.

Association of Head Mistresses
29 Gordon Square London WC1

Founded in 1874 by Frances Mary Buss as the Association of Head Mistresses in Endowed and Proprietary Schools, the Association now represents head mistresses in all types of recognised secondary schools in both the independent and maintained sectors. The Association aims to promote the cause of education generally, to consider all measures in Parliament or elsewhere affecting the profession, and to support and protect the status and interests of women engaged in secondary education.

Papers

A well-organised archive is housed at the Association's offices. The main series of Executive Committee minutes go back to 1874, and the proceedings of the annual conference also date from the Association's early days. Sub-committee minutes cover such subjects as careers, finance, examinations, salaries and pensions, boarding schools and international affairs. Annual reports go back to the Association's incorporation in 1896 and some from before that date, with lists of members and occasional papers which are published in bound volumes. These papers include conference speeches, articles on educational matters, and some E.C. minutes. Relatively little early correspondence has been preserved, but some interesting pieces survive. Recently a press cuttings book has been kept. The Association treasures two photograph albums, one of members attending the 1890 conference and the other of past Presidents of the Association. Other papers relating to the work of F. M. Buss are housed at the North London Collegiate School. The records were used by Jan Milburn for her London Ph.D. (1969), 'The Secondary Schoolmistress: A Study of her Professional Views and their Significance in the Educational Developments of the Period 1895-1914'.

Availability

Applications should be addressed to the Secretary.

Assistant Masters Association
29 Gordon Square London WC1

The Incorporated Association of Assistant Masters in Secondary Schools, popularly known as the A.M.A., was founded in 1891 and incorporated ten years later. The Association was formed to fight the evils of low status, insecurity of tenure, abysmal salaries and the absence of a pension scheme. The subsequent history of the A.M.A. relates mainly to these matters. The association continues to promote the cause of education generally and to protect and further the interests and status of members.

Papers

An extensive archive is housed at the Association's headquarters. Unfortunately a large proportion of the original documentation is unsorted and stored away in the office basement. It is not possible to give details of this collection. The main proceedings of the A.M.A., however, are recorded in printed series: the monthly journal dates back almost to foundation and contains records of Council debates, chairman's addresses, etc. The annual reports include records of various sub-committees on accounts, legal funds, benevolent funds, and the Joint Scholastic Agency, an A.M.A.-sponsored recruiting agency active until the 1950s. The early annual reports are especially full. Until about 1955 a year-book was produced, containing annual reports, Burnham reports, membership and teaching statistics, etc. These date from the 1920s. Of the manuscript materials, the most important series are the full unedited records of annual Councils and the minute books of the Executive Committee, and sub-committees on educational problems, legal matters, organisation and publicity, and parliamentary affairs. The mass of unsorted material includes transcripts of debates, typescripts of articles, and financial papers and correspondence. A personal file on each member of the A.M.A. is preserved, and the Association operates an information bureau, making available to members reports on teaching conditions in schools. Most of these reports are recent.

Availability

The personal files, and most of the original documents, are not open to researchers. But the printed material, and in some cases the minute books, are available. Applications should be addressed to the General Secretary.

Association of Assistant Mistresses
Gordon House 29 Gordon Square London WC1

Formed in 1884 as the Association of Assistant Mistresses in Public Secondary Schools, the organisation was widened in 1922 to embrace all secondary schools. The Association seeks to promote the cause of education generally, and to protect and improve the status and professional interests of teachers.

Papers

Most of the records were destroyed in 1940, when the Association's offices suffered some damage. All that survives from the period 1884-1940 is a set of annual reports which includes a considerable amount of material about the Association. Since 1940, minutes of metings, publications, etc., have been retained.

Availability

From time to time access to the material is granted to those scholars who make written application to the Secretary.

JOSEPHINE BUTLER SOCIETY

The Association for Moral and Social Hygiene was established in 1915 as a result of the amalgamation of the Ladies' National Association for the Abolition of State Regulation of Vice and for the Promotion of Social Purity (founded 1869) with the British Branch of the International Federation for the Abolition of State Regulation of Vice. The title of Josephine Butler Society was adopted in 1953.

These have been deposited in the Library of the *Fawcett Society* (q.v.), together with a collection of letters of Josephine Butler herself. There is a considerable bulk of material which has at the time of writing not been sorted or listed in detail. It includes records of the predecessor organisations and of the Association for Moral and Social Hygiene. The records of the Ladies' National Association have been briefly listed, and include seven volumes of minutes of the Executive Committee, 1875-1915; a Special Sub-committee minute book, 1912-15; a minute book of the London Branch Committee, 1883-86, and of the London Council, 1887-95.

Certain records of the National Association for the Repeal of the Contagious Diseases Act (1869-86) are also in the Fawcett Library.

Availability

Applications should be made to the Librarian, the Fawcett Library.

KNIGHTS OF ST. COLUMBA
54 Berkeley Street Glasgow C3

Formed in Glasgow in 1919, the Knights of St. Columba is now the strongest body of Roman Catholic men in the British Isles. The Knights sought to secure for their people the material benefits of which they were deprived through the national or religious prejudices of those days. The society continues to promote Catholic interests, the spiritual and material welfare of members and their dependants, and to co-operate with non-Catholic organisations in being of service to the community generally, both at home and overseas.

Papers

Minute books and other original documentation does exist but remains confidential to the Order. A history of the Order by W. J. Loughrey and J. Walsh was published in 1969.

Availability

The records are not open to inspection, but information on past or current activities can be obtained by enquiry from the head office at Glasgow.

LABOUR CHURCH MOVEMENT

The movement was started by John Trevor, a former Unitarian minister who believed that in a spiritually exhausted age the Labour movement provided the focus for a non-sectarian replacement of organised religion. The first Labour Church was established in Manchester in 1891, and during the early 1890s scores of such churches were established, particularly in the Midlands and North of England. A Labour Church Union was established in 1893. During the late 1890s the movement declined. Trevor left the Union in 1898, and by the eve of World War I the movement had all but disappeared.

Papers

Few records appear to have survived. The most substantial collection is that relating to Birmingham Labour Church, deposited in Birmingham Public Library. Certain records of the Stockport Church, including a syllabus of winter lectures, 1908-15, are in Stockport Public Library.

The *Labour Prophet,* founded in 1892, is a valuable source. This ceased publication in 1898. Its successor, *Labour Record,* ceased publication in 1902.

See also: *Clarion Movement; Independent Labour Party; Socialist Fellowship.*

LABOUR PARTY

Labour Party records are described in the following sections:

I. National Organisation

II. Regional

III. Constituency Parties and Trade Councils

I. National Organisation

Introductory Note

The records of the Labour Party are at present housed at the headquarters of the party, at Transport House, Smith Square, London SW1. In May 1971 the Labour Party National Executive Committee decided to open the archives for research purposes, subject only to a 15-year rule. Prior to this decision, in February 1967, two members of the staff of the Royal Commission on Historical Manuscripts had begun the long task of a detailed listing of the records held at Transport House. The following report on the archives of the Labour Party was made possible through the work done by the Commission's staff, and it is arranged in accordance with their own cataloguing operation. The Commission's staff concluded their work *in situ* in September 1973, at which time some two-thirds of the party's archives and deposited manuscripts had been listed. Copies of the lists may be consulted at the National Register of Archives (as N.R.A. 12,415), at the Labour Party, and at the national libraries. The work of listing and cataloguing the remaining material is now being undertaken by the party's own staff.

To a large extent, the surviving records of the Labour Party fall conveniently into coherent administrative or chronological groups. Where possible, they have been catalogued on this basis, with a self-contained list and index being prepared for each group. Each of these groups has been identified by code letters (e.g. L.R.C. for Labour Representation Committee, W.N.C. for War Emergency Workers' National Committee). In addition to the main central archive of the L.R.C. and the Labour Party, certain other archive groups exist in the Labour Party's custody at Transport House. These fall into three categories:

(i)   The records of those organisations, such as the W.N.C. and the Council of Action, which were closely connected with the Labour Party, and whose records are housed in Transport House by the coincidence of common personnel (e.g. J. S. Middleton, Assistant Secretary of the Labour Party, was Secretary of the W.N.C.).

(ii) Papers of those such as Dr. Marion Phillips and Arthur Henderson, who were intimately connected with the Labour Party organisation, some of whose records were therefore found in the Labour Party offices.

(iii) A number of small groups of personal papers, such as those of Henry Vincent, the Chartist leader, which are housed in Transport House through purchase or deposit.

Researchers wishing to use the Labour Party archive should approach the Librarian of the Labour Party at Transport House. A fee of £2 per month per individual is charged for use of the archive.

The basic archives of the Party can be divided into the following main categories:

1. *National Executive and Finance Committee Minutes, 1900–*

These, obviously of fundamental importance, have not been catalogued, but are available for research purposes subject to the usual 15-year rule. There are indices at the beginning of each volume.

2. *Labour Representation Committee, 1900-06*

Except for the N.E.C. minutes and any parliamentary correspondence that may have survived in the papers of the Parliamentary Labour Party, the H.M.C. list of the Labour Representation Committee records, together with a projected addendum list of correspondence which has recently come to light, represents the bulk of the remaining archive of this period in the party's history.

The L.R.C. was formed in February 1900 and changed its name at the annual conference in February 1906 following on the L.R.C.'s success in the General Election of that year. The archive which has survived consists of a series of 31 box files of general secretarial and administrative correspondence, each box containing approximately 400 letters and papers; three volumes of copy out-letters, with a time-span from September 1902 to January 1904; two volumes of agenda for the Executive and other committees and conferences and drafts of minutes, 1900–06; a box of signed copies of the L.R.C. and L.P. Constitutions, returned by intending parliamentary candidates, 1902–11; and a large file of press cuttings referring to events in May-July 1904.

Reflecting the comparative lack of parliamentary influence and the small number of Labour M.P.s, the general correspondence of the L.R.C. is concerned with the forging of a viable national organisation for the winning of elections. A National Agent was not appointed until after the 1906 election, and it was only at this point that the affairs of the local parties became the predominant feature of the correspondence. The main participants are therefore the national secretaries and local representatives of the trade unions which supported the Labour cause. Another element in the correspondence is that concerned with the central organisation of the party, office administration, committee meetings and the like. There is every little in these files relating either to parliamentary tactics or the formation of party policy, except when these had to be explained to local organisations.

During this period of the party's history the files of general correspondence were arranged in chronological order rather than subject order. Each box was used until it was full, when another was begun. Once the L.R.C. was properly established, the life-span of one of these boxes was little more than a single month. Within each box there were alphabetical divisions and letters were filed in these sections according to the name or the organisation or writer of the letter. There was no further ordering beyond the initial letter of the alphabet; filing was therefore somewhat imprecise. A single series of correspondence with an individual may be spread over a number of boxes, although there are examples of cumulation of past letters and their placement in the 'terminal' file; and there are many letters misfiled, either because the secretary chose varying initials to represent the organisation, or because the letter was filed on one occasion under the name of the trade union and on another under the name of the secretary. In the L.R.C. list, little extensive reorganisation has been undertaken. It is intended that the index should supply the necessary continuity and grouping.

Each item in the archive has been given an individual number, preceded by a box number and a group code. Thus, LRC 8/247 indicates that the document is in the L.R.C. correspondence box 8. Where necessary, too, each item has been individually described in the list. This practice is inevitable, given the organisation of the archive on a chronological rather than topical basis. An appendix describing 178 documents, 1900-06, abstracted from the main L.R.C. series, is available as LRC/App.

3. *Labour Party: General Correspondence, 1906-07*

Although the change of the party's name occurred in 1906, so that the period 1900-06 provides a convenient time-span for a listing operation, the really significant change for the archivist occurred in 1907. The change in 1907 was from box files, with alphabetically divided interiors, to filing cabinets housing individual files, giving rise to a subject rather than a mainly chronological/alphabetical filing sequence.

The records of the party for 1906-07 are filed under the old system and are thus logically a continuation of the L.R.C. series. They include approximately 8,000 in-letters and copy out-letters (L.P./G.C. 1906-07).

The disadvantage of the post-1907 system for the archivist is that he can no longer be certain that what he has in terms of files is a complete sequence. There is, however, an advantage for listing, in that subject files can more easily be described as a unit, with a summary of the subjects, followed by a list of correspondents. Records after late 1907 have been listed in subject volumes.

4. *Labour Party Subject Files, Volume I*

Approximately 30 file boxes of Labour Party papers subsequent to the change in filing methods have been classified and listed in detail under subject headings and classified as 'Subject Volume I'. Most of these contain pre-World War I material, but a significant group relates to the post-war attempts to unionise the police, to ex-Inspector John Syme and the National Union of Police and Prison Officers. The method of dealing with the party's post-1907 records is to assign a classification to each subject dealt with in a file (e.g. CAN, candidates; UNE, unemployment), followed by a two-figure group for the year with which the main contents of the box commence, with sub-numbering for the boxes if more than one are, or seem likely to be, found. This system makes it possible to assimilate into the sequence of listed files any material discovered or deposited as work progresses, and obviates the need to sort the contents of the strong-room in detail before any listing is begun.

The subjects and years of this post-1907 correspondence dealt with are: affiliation, 1906-08, 1910-13; campaigns, 1913; candidates, 1906-14 (2 boxes); conferences, 1913, 1918; Dublin disturbances, 1913; elections, 1908-09; Henderson, 1908-15; International Socialist Bureau, 1908-09, and 1911-14; Joint Board, 1908-19 (2 boxes); J. Ramsay MacDonald, 1908, 1909 (mainly correspondence about his Leicester constituency, parliamentary affairs and L.P. office matters, handed over to the L.P. office for reply); Miners' Federation of Great Britain, 1910-14; Police, 1919, 1920, 1924, 1925; Scottish Advisory Council, 1914-22; Ben Tillett, 1908-14 (papers concerning the relations of the Dock, Wharf, Riverside and General Workers' Union with the Labour Party); and unemployment, 1908-10. The series LPL comprises material relating to the local politics and constituency affairs of a single town or district. The date taken as the identifying one for each box in the post-1907 series is the earliest one from which the main sequence of correspondence runs; there may also be included a small group of earlier material incidental to the main series, which itself may extend over several years.

5. *Labour Party Subject Files, Volume II*

Volume II consists principally of material transferred to the strong-room in three transfer cases, having apparently been sorted and annotated by Rose Davy, one-time personal assistance to Morgan Phillips. It consists of 42 files, most of which are wholly or in part original archive groups. This volume also describes a box of material on the Joint Labour delegation to Hungary in 1920.

Subjects covered include: agriculture, 1930-42; Edward Carpenter's 80th birthday, 1924; papers on the capital levy, 1922; material on conscientious objection, 1940; the Communist Party, 1921; *Daily Herald*, 1924, 1938; discipline, 1934, 1938, 1940; early closing, 1918, 1930; anti-Fascist activity, 1933-37; Arthur Greenwood's removal from office, 1942; socialisation of medicine, 1930, 1934; L. Haden Guest; the joint delegation to Hungary, 1920; press controversy with the I.L.P., 1932; mines; E.D. Morel; *1944 Association* (q.v.) (Morgan Phillips's file as a member, together with notices and minutes, and reports on meetings, 1956-59, also a few personal letters, list of members, bank statement and cashed cheques, 1953); Labour newspaper, 1906-10; parliamentary files, 1919-34, 1956-61; pensions, 1935, 1937; propaganda, 1913, 1918, 1940; rents, 1920-30; reparations, 1929; Russia, 1918-20, 1921, 1935-43; seamen, 1918, 1922-29, 1935; shipping industry, 1934; Socialist League, 1935-37; trade unions, 1918-42, 1950-51; women's suffrage, 1912-15 (including correspondence with a number of suffrage organisations).

6. *Labour Party Subject Files, Volume III*

Volume III deals principally with a number of large groups of papers relating to inter-war topics.

These include affiliation payments, 1917-19; *Daily Herald*, 1919-30; domestic service, 1923-31; a questionnaire on Fascist activity, 1934; infant welfare/baby clinics, 1913; Harold Laski correspondence and drafts, 1938-50; Liquor Traffic Special Sub-committee, 1922-23; National Labour Memorial of Freedom and Peace, 1917-21; Labour Party offices, 1924-29; distress and relief, 1914, 1917; Rent Restrictions Act Committee, Dr. Marion Phillips's papers, 1930-31; union funds, 1922-23; *Women's Labour League* (q.v.), 1908-15.

7. *War Emergency Workers' National Committee* (q.v.)

8. *Council of Action* (q.v.)

9. *Labour and Socialist International* (ref. LSI/1-)

The records of the Labour Party's relations with the International from *c.* 1917 to its reconstitution in the late 1940s are listed. This group consists of about 30 boxes containing correspondence, conference papers, memoranda, etc., which give a detailed picture of the vicissitudes of the organisation. Matters covered include the Inter-Allied Socialist Parties Conference in London, 1918; papers concerning the International Labour and Socialist Conference at Berne in 1919, including the texts of speeches, the Lucerne conference of late August 1919, and Geneva, 1920; relations with the Vienna Union (International Working Union of Socialist Parties, conferences at Hamburg, 1923, Marseilles, 1929, Brussels, 1929, Vienna, 1931); United Front moves in the early 1930s; attitudes to Spain in the 1930s; the Spanish Civil War; contacts with Socialists in exile in London in World War II; and moves towards the re-formation of the L.S.I. In addition to these papers detailing the party's relations with the International, at least one minute book of the British Section of the International survives for the period 1905-18.

10. *Other Material*

(a) *Finance Department.* The records of the Finance Department form probably the largest single group of the remaining archive. These records, contained in a considerable number of volumes, are generally of a conventional ledger kind.

(b) *International Department.* This group includes the agenda, minutes and reports of the Advisory Committees on International and Imperial Affairs, of which Leonard Woolf was secretary, and the Sub-committee of the N.E.C. on International Affairs. There is also a considerable amount of overseas correspondence (at least 21 boxes, 1920s to 1940s) and files on arrangements for British Commonwealth Labour Conferences during the inter-war period. It is a substantial group, which can be supplemented by material filed in the J. S. Middleton papers (see below: LP/JSM(Int.)).

(c) *'J. S. Middleton papers'*. This is a large group of papers which were in the possession of J. S. Middleton, long-time Assistant Secretary and later General Secretary of the Labour Party. The group consists of 31 boxes: 16 General (LP/JSM), 13 International (LP/JSM Int.) and 2 Research Department Conference decisions since 1918 (LP/JSM (Res.)). The files are in alphabetical order within each box. It would seem that, apart from a small amount of personal material, including a box of picture postcards from Labour notables, the 'Middleton papers' are effectively extensions of the main Labour Party files. The 16 boxes of General papers have been listed in detail.

(d) *Miscellaneous*. The rest of the archive provides no obvious, distinct subject heading and only a general indication of the extent of the records can be given. Nevertheless, there is a considerable amount of material of importance. On a different level, three boxes of Spanish children's drawings of the Civil War period, apparently the response to aid organised by the International Solidarity Fund, give a moving insight into reactions to the war. Other records of a more conventional kind include a box on Transport House, and a box on the Organisation Sub-Committee of 1932, together with general administrative papers, and range from material concerning the Baby Hospital built in memory of Mary Middleton and Margaret MacDonald, 1930s and 1940s, to other material including five boxes of written and printed evidence for the Distressed Areas Commission, 1936-37; two boxes of correspondence concerning magistrates; six boxes of results and analyses of local government elections, 1940s and 1950s; minutes of the Reconstruction Sub-Committee, 1941-44; three boxes of correspondence, etc., on the Labour Party delegation to China, 1954; three boxes of Morgan Phillips office papers. General files in the strong-room for the post-war period are unsorted, but include local and general election files, conference arrangements files and material on branches. More recent records must be assumed to remain, *pro tem*, in the originating departments. In addition to these, a group of papers survive which concern the party's relationships with outside bodies, though the links were usually very close. Among these can be counted the records of the party's relationship with the National Council of Labour; certain papers relating to the *Women's Labour League* (q.v.), one box of which appears to relate to the Labour Party's side, another to be records of the League itself, including letters to branches and petty cash books (*c.* 1907-15); certain records of the *1944 Committee* (q.v.), an organisation of businessmen sympathetic to Labour, which again seem to be a mixture of Labour Party records and signed minutes (1944-48) of the Committee itself. Another valuable small group is made up of the financial records of the *Daily Citizen*, 1912-15. A volume of signed minutes, 1916-17, of the Standing Joint Committee of Industrial Women's Organisations should also be noted.

11. *Various Deposits and Purchases*

(a) *Robert Applegarth*. A small collection consisting of 38 items, largely personalia.

(b) *Henry Barker* (1858-1940), builder and Labour activist: papers including material relating to the Labour Union.

(c) *Arthur Henderson* (1863-1935). The Henderson papers are a very miscellaneous collection relating to Arthur Henderson and his son W.W. Henderson, later 1st Baron Henderson. The material dates from 1916, and includes a few papers about Henderson's work in the War Cabinet and a considerable number of Cabinet circulars, confidential prints and memoranda. The more valuable items concern his

131

work with the League of Nations as President of the Disarmament Conference from 1933. There are also papers relating to the office of Chief Industrial Commissioner, 1916-17; correspondence about his visit to Russia in 1917; some material about the General Strike and industrial conciliation; and papers relating to his term as Foreign Secretary, 1929-30, with special reference to the appointment of ambassadors. The material connected with W. W. Henderson is more sparse and stems from his service in the Press and International Departments of the L.P. Perhaps the most interesting item is a copy of notes by Hugh Dalton of his activities at the beginning of the 1939-45 war, including comments on the Jewish problem and the foundation of the Ministry of Information.

(d) *Bronterre O'Brien* (Chartist leader). Some ten letters from and related material.

(e) *Marion Phillips* (1881-1932). Chief Woman Officer of the Labour Party and M.P.; Sunderland C.L.P. files, 1929-31.

(f) *Dr. Marion Phillips's* papers as a member of the *Consumers' Council* (q.v.).

(g) *Henry Vincent* (Chartist leader). Correspondence with John Minikin (c. 70 letters) together with other items, including copies of the *Vindicator*.

(h) *Frederick Pickles papers.* These consist of personal correspondence and items relating to Socialist politics in the 1880s and 1890s. Correspondents include William Morris, Eleanor Marx, J. Bruce Glasier, J. Keir Hardie, etc.

12. *Transport House Library*

The Labour Party Library at Transport House has a valuable collection of some 8,000 books, 500,000 pamphlets, runs of now defunct periodicals and some 443 current periodicals. The Library has a most useful collection of press cuttings dating from 1918 and covering a large variety of topics. Categories for 1918-45, apart from Politics and Political Parties, are now with the Manchester University Library, but the party has retained all press cuttings since 1945 and the Politics and Political Parties groups since 1918.

In addition, the Library has a collection of photographs, party posters, etc.

Annual reports of the Labour Party, 1900-60, are on microfilm in the Library. It should be noted that annual reports and official journals of other organisations closely linked to the Party may also be found in this Library.

The Library is primarily to serve members of the party and its research staff. More general access may be granted subject to prior appointment. Enquiries should be directed to the Librarian.

13. *'Infancy of the Labour Party'*

A useful collection at B.L.P.E.S., with the above title, includes minutes, letters and other papers collected by Edward Pease, 27 Feb. 1900-5 Dec. 1912, with one paper of 18 Aug. 1918. A microfilm of certain meetings of the Parliamentary Labour Party, post-1945, has also been deposited at B.L.P.E.S.

Enquiries regarding these records should be directed to the Librarian, B.L.P.E.S.

II. Regional

Addresses

Greater London: Herbert Morrison House, 195-7 Walworth Road, London SE17
East Midlands: 542 Woodborough Road, Mapperley, Nottingham
West Midlands: Rooms 13-15, Swan Buildings, 113 Edmund Street, Birmingham
Northern: 31 Acorn Road, Newcastle-upon-Tyne
Yorkshire: 13 Queen Square, Leeds

Lancashire and
   Cheshire: 40-42 Frederick Road, Salford
Southern: Ruxley Towers, Claygate, Esher
South Western: 67-69 Queens Road, Bristol
Eastern: 33 Lower Brook Street, Ipswich
Wales: 42 Charles Street, Cardiff
Scotland: 8 Royal Crescent, Glasgow

Information is available on the following regions:

Greater London

Records date from the foundation of the London Labour Party in 1919 and cover the whole history of the party, and its successor, the Greater London Regional Council. They include minutes of the Executive Committee from 1919, annual reports from 1939, reports and papers of the L.C.C. Policy Committee, 1939-65, and of the G.L.C. Labour Group after 1965. In addition to these formal records, there are various files covering the activities of the London Party, both in terms of policies, e.g. housing, transport and education, and party politics. The latter includes a great deal of material on election activities, particularly for the 1950s, and relationships with the borough parties. Three files relate to the work of Herbert Morrison, and include papers and press cuttings of the 1930s and 1940s. The collection also includes runs of the *Labour Party Circular* (after 1918 *Labour Chronicle*) from 1915-24, of *London News*, 1939-64, and *Hit Back* since that date.

Much of the material, particularly for the later period, is unsorted.

East Midlands

Minutes and reports of the Council have been retained since its foundation in 1942. Some recent subject files and copies of the organiser's reports are in the Modern Records Centre, University of Warwick.

West Midlands

Young Socialists' minutes and copy reports to National Organiser are deposited in the Modern Records Centre, University of Warwick Library.

Yorkshire

No records of historical value have been retained.

South Western

No relevant papers have been retained.

Eastern

Certain papers are in the care of Stanley Newens, M.P.

In addition to these regional records, records relating to the Welsh and Scottish parties survive.

Wales

Records are deposited at the National Library of Wales and at Coleg Harlech. For all research on the Labour Party in Wales, the Library of University College Swansea should be consulted.

M.B.s 1935 to date, annual reports from 1918, and various pamphlets from 1945 are retained at the party offices. A microfilm is available at the National Library of Scotland. This contains minutes of the Scottish Workers' Parliamentary Elections Committee, 1900-02; the Scottish Workers' Representation Committee, 1903-07; and the Labour Party (Scottish Section), 1907-09.

III. Constituency Parties and Trades Councils

For convenience, this list contains information on Trades Councils (T.C.s) and Trades and Labour Councils (T.L.C.s) as well as constituency Labour Parties (C.L.P.s). The latter information was obtained from replies to a circular distributed by the Labour Party. The information concerning Trades Councils was obtained from a circular to individual councils. The list should not be taken as definitive. Except where otherwise indicated, the records are retained in the local offices.

Aberdare T.C. An MS autobiography of Edmund Stonelake, former Secretary of the council, is deposited in the Library of University College, Swansea.

Aberdeen City L.P. Records from 1947-59 are deposited in the University Library, King's College, Aberdeen.

Aberdeen South C.L.P. M.B.s date from 1958.

Aberdeen T.C. M.B.s 1876-1955 (with gaps for the period 1939-52) are housed in the University Library, Aberdeen; ann. reps. 1890-1904 (with the years 1892, 1898, 1899 missing) are deposited in the B.L.P.E.S.

Aberystwyth and District T.C. M.B.s and ann. reps. 1943 to date. A useful brief history of the Trades Council was compiled by a former Secretary, C. H. Evans, and a copy is kept with the other records.

Abingdon and District T.L.C. M.B.s 1953 to date; ann. reps. 1954 to date.

Altrincham, Sale and District T.C. M.B.s 1950 to date; ann. reps. 1953 to date. Some correspondence has been kept since 1963, together with statements of accounts etc.

Ammanford, Llandybie and District T.L.C. M.B.s 1917-25, 1937 to date; ann. reps. 1917, 1937 to date. Also surviving are account statements, 1917, 1934 to date, some old correspondence, and membership figures, together with a collection of press cuttings.

Angus South C.L.P. M.B.s from 1948; M.B.s of Carnoustie local party, 1944-65.

Arundel, Bognor Regis and District T.C. M.B.s 1953 to date.

Ashton-under-Lyne, Stalybridge, Dukinfield and District T.C. A useful collection deposited in Ashton Library. It includes M.B.s 1920-29, 1936-39, 1949-55; ann. reps. 1902; a/c's for period 1906-62; and a small amount of correspondence from 1920.

Ayrshire South T.L.C. M.B.s 1926 to date; ann. reps. 1924-52.

Bacup, Rawtenstall and Ramsbottom T.C. Until 1968 these formed three separate councils. Records of Bacup and Ramsbottom before that date are missing. However, a full set of M.B.s for Rawtenstall from 1906 to date survives, together with a summary history of the work of the council from 1952.

Banbury and District T.C. M.B.s 1947 to date; ann. reps. 1948 to date. Constituency records are in Oxfordshire Record Office.

Bannshire C.L.P. M.B.s 1924 to date; several letter books of correspondence for the 1950s; election addresses dating back to 1955.

Bangor L.P. Records in University College, Bangor.

Barking C.L.P. M.B.s 1933-46.

Baron's Court C.L.P. Records in the Labour Party archives at Transport House.

Barry T.C. Records in University College, Swansea.

Bath T.C. M.B.s and ann. reps. 1891 to date.

Bedford C.L.P. A useful collection dating back to the 1920s has been deposited in B.L.P.E.S.

Bedwellty C.L.P. M.B.s 1918-55.

Belfast T.L.C. Minutes for 1899 only in Northern Ireland P.R.O.

Belper C.L.P. M.B.s 1941 to date; ann. reps. 1938, 1945 to date; correspondence from 1956; election literature including press cuttings from 1945.

Bermondsey T.L.C. M.B.s and ann. reps. from 1945.

Berwick C.L.P. M.B.s 1938-49, are deposited in Northumberland Record Office.

Bexley Borough T.C. M.B.s date back to 1947, as do a certain amount of correspondence and a/c's; ann. reps. date back to 1969; copies of a monthly news-sheet from 1967 also survive.

Birmingham L.P. A useful collection with M.B.s dating back to 1933 (with breaks), ann. reps. and correspondence from 1945, and a certain amount of election literature for the 1950s.

Birmingham T.L.C. Records from 1866-1956 have been deposited in the Reference Library, Birmingham Public Libraries.

Birmingham Selly Oak C.L.P. M.B.s 1936-40 and minutes from 1964-70 are deposited in the Modern Records Centre, University of Warwick.

Bishop Auckland C.L.P. M.B.s date back to 1959 and ann. reps. to 1957. Very little else survives before 1958.

Blandford and District T.C. M.B.s from 1946 to date.

Bolton T.C. M.B.s and ann. reps. from *c.* 1910.

Bournemouth and Christchurch T.L.C. All records for the period 1890-1948, including M.B.s, ann. reps., correspondence, etc., are kept at Poole Public Library. Records since 1948 are with the Secretary.

Bradford City L.P. M.B.s 1958 to date; ann. reps. 1961 to date; election literature from *c.* 1960.

Brideford and District T.C. M.B.s only from 1966.

Bridgwater and District T.C. M.B.s 1923-32, 1946 to date; ann. reps. 1948 to date; also kept are certain records of delegates and secretaries dating back some years.

Bridlington and District T.C. M.B.s 1962 to date; ann. reps. since 1966.

Brierley Hill T.C. Amalgamated with Dudley T.C. in 1966. Records up to that date in Dudley Borough Libraries.

Brighouse T.C. M.B.s 1914-26; ledger book, 1905 to date.

Brighton Kemptown C.L.P. M.B.s, ann. reps., correspondence and election material since the formation of the party in 1957.

Bristol T.C. Records deposited in Bristol Archives Office.

Brixton L.P. Records of 1948-70 deposited in Labour Party archive, Transport House.

Bromley T.C. Full records since 1967.

Burnley T.L.C. Records in Burnley Public Library.

Bury T.C. A fire in 1952 destroyed most records prior to that date, with the exception of an accounts book, 1941-70, and T.U.C. circulars dating back to 1943. Post-1952 records include: M.B.s 1952 to date; ann. reps. 1963 to date; correspondence and records of attendance since 1961.

Buxton and District T.L.C. M.B.s 1945 to date.

Caernarvonshire L.P. M.B.s of Labour Council, 1912-27, and three memoranda books have been deposited in the National Library of Wales.

Caerphilly C.L.P. Records in University College, Swansea.

Cambridge and District T.L.C. M.B.s from 1945.

Cambridge City L.P. Records date back to 1913 and include (up to 1951) the papers of the Trades Council.

Canterbury C.L.P. Records, 1927-37, deposited in Kent Archives Office.

Canterbury and District T.C. M.B.s 1912 to date.

Cardiff T.C. M.B.s 1940 to date, but ann. reps. and other material date back only to 1968. Constituency material is in University College Swansea.

Carlisle C.L.P. M.B.s 1936-43 deposited in the Record Office, Carlisle.

Carlisle and District T.C. M.B.s date back to the formation of the Council as a separate entity in 1929; ann. reps. date back to 1950.

Castleford T.L.C. Ann. rep. for 1899 in Transport House Library.

Chatham T.L.C. M.B.s 1918-21, 1921-23, have been deposited in Marx Memorial Library.

Chepstow L.P. M.B.s 1932-52, in Monmouthshire Record Office.

Chigwell and Ongar C.L.P. M.B.s 1955-64.

Colne Valley C.L.P. A very good collection which includes M.B.s from 1891; ann. reps. from 1918; correspondence and election literature dating back to 1907; copies of rules and constitutions from 1891; and photographs of parliamentary candidates from 1895 onwards.

Consett and District T.C. M.B.s from 1945.

Conway C.L.P. M.B.s and ann. reps. only from 1958.

Coventry L.P. Records, to early 1960s, are in the care of University of Warwick Library. This deposit also includes records, 1940s to 1960s, of the Trades Council.

Darlington T.C. M.B.s 1913-19, 1944-51, 1953-64, 1964 to date, together with ann. reps. and a broken set of a/c's and membership figures for the same years.

Daventry and District T.C. Records, including M.B.s, ann. reps., press cuttings, etc., date only from 1964.

Deal and District T.C. M.B.s from 1937; ann. reps. from 1954; a/c's from 1946; monthly newsletters from 1954.

Deptford C.L.P. M.B.s and ann. reps. from 1951.

Derby L.P. M.B.s 1924-65; cash books, correspondence, etc., deposited in Derby Public Library.

Derbyshire South C.L.P. M.B.s from 1945.

Dereham and District T.C. M.B.s from 1950.

Dewsbury and District T.C. Records from 1917 are housed at Dewsbury Public Library.

Doncaster. Records of the Borough and Divisional L.P., 1914-48, in Cusworth Hall Museum, Doncaster.

Dorchester T.C. M.B.s from 1956 to date, and ann. reps. from 1964.

Dublin T.C. Seven volumes of records of the council, 1893-1932, are housed in the National Library of Ireland.

Dunfermline T.C. Report and balance sheet, 1895-96, in Dunfermline Public Library.

Ealing T.C. M.B.s and ann. reps. from 1947; correspondence from 1957.

East Grinstead T.C. Records only from 1968.

Edinburgh T.C. Records of the Edinburgh and Leith Workers' Municipal Committee, 1899-1903, are deposited in the National Library of Scotland.

Edinburgh North C.L.P. M.B.s from 1954.

Epping C.L.P. Records with Stan Newens M.P., include minutes, 1929-35, of the old Woodford Division, M.B.s and correspondence since 1945 of the present constituency.

Epsom and Ewell C.L.P. M.B.s from 1937.

Exmouth T.C. All old records were lost in floods.

Exmouth L.P. M.B.s and ann. reps. 1942 to date; detailed agenda from 1954; monthly notices to members and records of urban district elections, also dating from 1954.

Eye C.L.P. Records from 1950s only.

Faversham C.L.P. M.B.s 1918 to date; ann. reps. 1945 to date. Miscellaneous other material dating back to 1920s.

Finchley C.L.P. M.B.s from 1949, plus some general correspondence.

Fleetwood and District T.C. Material dating back to early 1960s only.

Flint and District T.C. M.B.s from 1962.

Galashiels District T.C. M.B.s 1920-40.

Galloway L.P. M.B.s from 1957.

Glasgow T.C. A comprehensive archive is housed in the Mitchell Library, Glasgow. It includes M.B.s 1884-1960 (with gaps 1889-1900, 1904-10, 1927-28); ann. reps. 1886 to date; and correspondence with the Scottish T.U.C. during the General Strike of 1926, together with the 1926 Glasgow Central Co-ordinating Committee minutes.

Glasgow City L.P. M.B.s 1937 to date. A few earlier items are held by the Mitchell Library, Glasgow.

Glasgow Craigton C.L.P. M.B.s and ann. reps. 1955-70.

Glasgow Maryhill C.L.P. M.B.s *c.* 1915 in possession of W. Hannan, M.P.

Glasgow Woodside C.L.P. M.B.s 1960 to date.

Goole C.L.P. M.B.s and ann. reps. from 1950.

Gorton T.L.C. All records believed lost.

Greenwich L.P. Records of the period *c.* 1927-58 are now deposited in the Library of the Labour Party, TransportHouse. These include M.B.s from 1928, ann. reps. from 1933, together with a/c books for the early 1920s.

Greenwich T.L.C. M.B.s and ann. reps. 1953 to date. Some old correspondence and press cuttings from 1964. Photocopies are to be deposited in the Borough Archives.

Halifax T.L.C. M.B.s 1907-12, 1921-26, 1927-33, 1950-56; a/c and membership details, 1907-26.

Hamilton C.L.P. M.B.s and ann. reps. date back to the formation of the party in 1918; in addition, varied correspondence dating back to 1946 is retained.

Haringey L.P. Certain recent records in the party's office. Papers of Don McIlwain, former Labour leader, to be found at Bruce Castle Library, Tottenham.

Harlow and District T.C. M.B.s 1957 to date.

Harrow Central C.L.P. M.B.s 1920 to date, plus a few press cuttings, 1920-33, 1966 to date.

Haslingden T.L.C. M.B.s 1904 to date; correspondence from 1958 together with 'written documents of achievements and issues dealt with by the Trades Council'.

Hastings and District T.L.C. M.B. for 1932.

Heanor Local L.P. M.B.s 1918-25 in Derbyshire Record Office.

Hertfordshire Labour Federation. M.B.s 1932-59 have been deposited in the Hertfordshire Record Office with a 20-year restriction on access.

Heston and Isleworth C.L.P. M.B.s from 1930; ann. reps. from 1945. A certain amount of General Strike literature and various other, unspecified, old documents.

Holborn and St. Pancras South C.L.P. No records before 1948. M.B.s 1948 to date in the Archives of the Labour Party.

Home Counties Federation of Trades Councils. M.B.s 1927-37 in possession of Secretary, Luton T.C.

Honiton C.L.P. The older records have been lost.

Hornchurch C.L.P. The records are deposited at regular intervals in the Greater London Record Office. They include minutes of the General Management Committee of Hornchurch Central Party, 1942-45, and of the C.L.P. from that date, together with M.B.s on the Town Ward local party from 1940 and of St. Andrews Ward, 1958-63.

Horsham and District T.C. No records more than three years old are retained.

Huddersfield Labour and Socialist Election Committee. M.B. 1909-18 and letter book 1911-19 have been deposited in Huddersfield Public Library.

Huddersfield and Kirkburton Central L.P. M.B.s and ann. reps. from formation of party in 1918 to date; copies of the monthly *Huddersfield Citizen*, 1926-65; copies of early pamphlets from 1900s. Election addresses and leaflets from 1903.

Huddersfield and District T.L.C. M.B.s 1898-1917, 1934-58; ann. reps. 1915-61; letter book 1905-13; a/c's Treasurer's reports, 1906-18. These records have been deposited in Huddersfield Public Library.

Hull T.C. M.B.s, a/c's, correspondence, posters, 1930-63, have been deposited in Hull Public Library.

Huntingdon and District T.C. M.B.s since the foundation of the council in 1943.

Ilkeston C.L.P. Records to be deposited in Derbyshire Record Office.

Ilkeston, Heanor and Eastwood T.C. M.B.s and ann. reps. from 1949, together with some correspondence.

Inverness Burgh L.P. M.B.s from 1947.

Ipswich C.L.P. Forward, the Ipswich Labour monthly, No. 1 (October 1938) to No. 11 (Sept. 1939), has been deposited in Ipswich Public Library. A considerable amount of material relating to the Ipswich Labour movement is contained in the Ratcliffe Collection at the Ipswich and East Suffolk Record Office.

Jarrow L.P. Records going back to 1923, and including papers concerning the Jarrow March, are deposited in Durham Record Office.

Keighley T.C. M.B.s 1942 to date; ann. reps. 1946 to date.

Kensington South C.L.P. M.B.s since 1949.

Kent Trades and Labour Federation. A number of early M.B.s are deposited in Marx Memorial Library.

Kidderminster and District T.L.C. M.B.s 1930 to date.

Lambeth T.C. M.B.s and ann. reps. from 1966 only.

Lancashire Federation of Trades Councils. A large amount of material with Secretary of Manchester and Salford T.C.

Leeds T.C. M.B.s 1882-1940, plus a broken run of ann. reps. for the same period are deposited in Leeds City Library.

Leeds South East C.L.P. M.B.s from 1947.

Leicester L.P. Very little survives.

Leominster and District T.C. M.B.s and ann. reps. 1956 to date.

Lewes and District T.C. M.B.s 1948 to date; ann. reps. 1961 to date.

Lincoln C.L.P. M.B.s 1918-35.

Liverpool T.C. M.B.s 1878 to date; ann. reps. from 1888. The M.B.s to 1929, together with various other items of interest, have been deposited in Liverpool Central Library.

Liverpool Wavertree C.L.P. M.B.s 1956 to date; no complete run of ann. reps. survives, and correspondence is generally kept for only twelve weeks.

Llanelli C.L.P. M.B.s to date are retained in office. Some records are retained in Carmarthenshire Record Office.

London. North London Socialist Club minutes, 1896-99, Brotherhood Church minutes, 1926-33, and miscellaneous papers are deposited in Islington Public Library.

London T.C. The records of the Trades Council are held in the T.U.C. Library. These include M.B.s 1860-1953; ann. reps. from 1873; press cuttings, 1885-86, 1930-47; minutes of the Central Workers' Committee on Unemployment, 1905-7; account books, 1860-74.

Loughborough and District T.L.C. M.B.s 1870-1970; ann. reps. 1920-70.

Louth C.L.P. M.B.s 1953 to date. The local parties also have certain M.B.s from 1950.

Lowestoft and District T.L.C. M.B.s, ann. reps. and correspondence from 1950; press cuttings and a/c's from 1935; in addition, a financial ledger and attendance book dating back to formation of council in 1913 survives.

Lowestoft C.L.P. M.B.s 1925 to date; M.B.s of local party from 1938. In addition, there are various files of correspondence and a collection of post-war election addresses. These are probably to be deposited in Transport House.

Luton and District T.L.C. M.B.s 1927-43, 1966 to date; ann. reps. and press cuttings from 1966.

Maldon C.L.P. M.B.s and other records of the General Management Committee from 1947, and of the annual meetings from 1925. Material collected for the fiftieth anniversary celebrations of the party in 1968 have been deposited in Transport House.

Manchester and Salford T.C. M.B.s 1944 to date; ann. reps. 1931 to date.

Manchester Blackley C.L.P. An incomplete run of minutes from 1950; other material dates only from the early 1960s.

Market Harborough and District T.L.C. M.B.s from 1949.

Merton and Morden C.L.P. A useful collection including M.B.s from 1936 has been deposited in B.L.P.E.S.

Midland Counties Trades Federation. Original records believed destroyed, but see under *Walsall District T.C.*, (p. 141).

Minehead and District T.C. No records appear to have survived.

Montrose Burgh Labour Representative Committee. Arbroath branch M.B. 1910-14 deposited in Arbroath Library.

Morpeth C.L.P. M.B.s from 1920, plus a selection of other material.

Nantyglo and Blaina T.L.C. M.B.s and ann. reps. from 1962 only.

Neath C.L.P. Records have been deposited in Library of University College, Swansea.

Nelson and Colne C.L.P. M.B.s and ann. reps. from 1919; correspondence, election literature and press cuttings from the 1920s.

Newcastle-under-Lyme C.L.P. Possible deposit of older records in Staffordshire Record Office; M.B.s 1946 to date, plus sundry other items.

Newport T.C. M.B.s from 1934.

Northampton L.P. M.B.s 1924 to date, plus a selection of other records from 1947.

Norwich Labour Party and Industrial Council. M.B.s from 1932; ann. reps. from 1924. M.B.s, 1898-1909, of the Executive Committee of the Norwich T.C. are deposited in Norfolk and Norwich Record Office.

Nottingham South L.P. M.B.s and papers, 1919-38, are deposited in Nottingham City Library, as are records of the Broxtowe L.P., 1917-45. Other material from 1966 only.

Oldham and District T.L.C. 32nd ann. rep. for 1899 is deposited in the Library of Transport House.

Oxford and District T.C. A very good collection which consists of M.B.s continuous from 1898 to date; a sporadic list of ann. reps. from the early 1900s; a large, if unsystematic, collection of press cuttings dating back to the 1890s. These have now been deposited in Ruskin College, Oxford.

Paddington South. M.B. 1896-1902 in B.L.P.E.S.

Paisley Labour Representation Committee. M.B. 1909-11.

Paisley L.P. M.B.s from 1947, but all other records were destroyed in 1969.

Peebles-shire and Selkirk T.C. M.B.s 1920-40, 1950-58, 1958-60, 1962-64, 1965-66. These have been deposited in the Chambers Institution, Peebles Library.

Peebles and South Midlothian C.L.P. M.B.s 1919-26 in National Library of Scotland.

Penarth Trades Union Council. No records before 1960.

Peterborough Trades Union Council. M.B.s. 1909 to date; ann. reps. 1943 to date. In addition there is a large collection of press cuttings.

Peterborough L.P. M.B.s from 1918 to present; ann. reps. from 1961. The earlier material is on permanent loan with Peterborough Central Library.

Peterlee and District T.C. Records only from foundation of council in 1964.

Plymouth Central L.P. No records appear to have survived.

Pontypridd T.C. and L.P. Records deposited in Pontypridd Public Library.

Port Talbot and District T.C. No records prior to 1964.

Preston T.C. Records to be deposited in Preston Library.

Renfrewshire West C.L.P. M.B.s from 1946.

Retford and District T.C. M.B.s 1911 to date, occasional ann. reps. from same period and a collection of old correspondence and account statements.

Rhondda: Mid Rhondda T.C. M.B. 1909-22 in National Library of Wales.

Rhyl and District T.C. M.B.s from 1943; ann. reps. from 1961.

Ross-shire L.P. M.B.s from 1953.

Roxburgh, Selkirk and Peebles C.L.P. Papers, 1925-55, in National Library of Scotland.

Rugby L.P. Minutes and correspondence, 1940s to 1960s are deposited in the Modern Records Centre, University of Warwick Library.

Ruislip-Northwood C.L.P. M.B.s and other records since the inauguration of the C.L.P. in 1948; in addition, the party has records dating back to 1935 when the area was part of the Uxbridge constituency.

Rutland and Stamford C.L.P. M.B.s from 1945.

Ryde and East Wight T.L.C. M.B.s and ann. reps. 1955 to date.

Rye and District T.C. M.B.s 1953 to date.

Saffron Walden C.L.P. Minutes of the constituency party have been destroyed. Minutes of the local party, however, date back to 1920.

St. Albans T.C. M.B.s 1914 to date; ann. reps. 1935 to date; account statements 1945-71. Other papers are of more recent date.

Salford City L.P. M.B.s 1920-61 in possession of E. Frow; part of the *Manchester Working Class Movement Library* (q.v.).

Sheffield T.L.C. M.B.s 1900 to date; ann. reps. 1892 to date; certain correspondence from 1920s. Sheffield Central Library have on loan certain items belonging to the council.

Sheffield City L.P. M.B.s and ann. reps. 1900 to date.

Sheffield Brightside (L.P.) Political Council. Records in Sheffield Public Library.

Sheffield Hallam C.L.P. M.B.s 1933-64 deposited in Sheffield Public Library.

Sittingbourne and District T.C. M.B.s 1918-25, 1955-67; ann. reps. from 1961; accounts from 1938.

Skipton C.L.P. M.B.s from inter-war years.

Southall C.L.P. M.B.s ann. reps. and correspondence, 1930s to date; election literature from 1945.

Southall T.L.C. M.B.s 1938 to date.

Southend Joint Labour and Socialist Election Committee. M.B.s for 1914, deposited in Marx Memorial Library.

Stafford C.L.P. M.B.s 1933-54 in Staffordshire Record Office.

Stirling and District T.L.C. M.B.s 1907-26, 1945-51; membership book 1942-49. These have been deposited in the Stirling Burgh Library.

Stirling C.L.P. Records, 1951-58; Women's Section, 1948-54; Stirling Local Labour Party. 1951-60. These are deposited in Stirling Burgh Library.

Stoke-on-Trent North C.L.P. No inter-war records survive.

Stowmarket and District T.L.C. M.B.s 1941-56.

Stratford-upon-Avon C.L.P. M.B.s of the constituency party prior to 1960 have been lost. Records of the local party survive, however: M.B.s 1937-51, membership list and cash book 1919-46 (records are deposited in Warwickshire Record Office).

Suffolk Federation of Trades Councils and Labour Representation Committee. M.B.s 1918-27 deposited in Ipswich and East Suffolk Record Office.

Swansea L.P. Swansea Labour News, Nos. 1-247 (Sept. 1921-June 1926).

Tamworth and District T.C. M.B. 1914-17 in Staffordshire Record Office.

Thirsk and Malton C.L.P. Records, 1946 to date and numerous press cuttings.

Todmorden T.L.C. All Trades Council reports are held in the offices of the *Todmorden News and Advertiser*, Fielden Square, Todmorden, Lancs. Other material is kept in the Weavers' Institute, Burnley Road, Todmorden, Lancs.

Tonbridge T.C. M.B.s and ann. reps. from 1964 only; accounts and membership figures date back to 1912.

Torquay L.P. M.B.s and ann. reps. 1925 to date.

Torrington C.L.P. Records from 1958 only.

Totton and District T.C. M.B.s and ann. reps. 1945 to date, together with a large amount of old correspondence.

Truro T.C. M.B.s from 1959.

Vauxhall C.L.P. A full set of records deposited in B.L.P.E.S.

Wakefield T.C. M.B.s 1891-1949, 1955 to date.

Walsall and District T.C. Minutes are in Whiston deposit in Walsall Central Library. This also includes copies of minutes of Midlands Federation of Trades Councils.

Walsall South C.L.P. Records from 1965 only.

Wansbeck C.L.P. M.B.s 1917-50 in Northumberland Record Office.

Watford and District T.C. M.B.s 1925-31, 1941-50; ann. reps. from 1950.

Wednesbury and District T.C. M.B.s 1914 to date. The older M.B.s are deposited in Wednesbury Public Library.

Wellingborough C.L.P. Minutes of the Finance and Executive Committee, and General Management Committee, 1925-30, 1936-45, 1947-60. Finance and Executive Committee minutes, 1961-68. General Management Committee minutes, 1961-67.

Welwyn Garden City and District T.C. No records.

West Bromwich T.C. No records survive.

West Lothian T.C. M.B.s 1940 to date.

Wisbech and District T.C. Records, 1946 to date.

Wolverhampton C.L.P. Contact via Dr G. Jones, L.S.E.: M.B.s 1907-48.

Wolverhampton Central C.L.P. Contact via Dr G. Jones, L.S.E.: M.B.s 1948-50.

Woolwich C.L.P. M.B.s and ann. reps. 1903 to date; various but unclassified correspondence, together with a good collection of press cuttings.

Worcester L.P. M.B.s Women's Society, 1927-30; St. John's Ward, 1929-45; St. Martin's Ward, 1925-33.

Wycombe Trades Union Council. Correspondence from 1930.

Yeovil C.L.P. M.B.s 1914 to date. Possible deposit in Somerset Record Office.

Yeovil and District T.C. M.B.s 1907-17, 1948-70.

York C.L.P. M.B.s 1900 to date (with gaps); ann. reps. from 1961.

York and District T.C. M.B.s 1956 to date; ann. reps. from 1890 in yearbook form duplicated for 1960s. These records are deposited in the York City Library.

LABOUR RESEARCH DEPARTMENT
78 Blackfriars Road London SE1 8HF

The Fabian Research Department was founded in 1912, developing out of the Control of Industry Committee founded by Beatrice and Sidney Webb, under the aegis of the Fabian Society. In 1916 the Department became a separate organisation with individual membership, and shortly afterwards invited trade unions and other labour bodies to affiliate to it. In 1918 it changed its name to the Labour Research Department. The continuing functions of the Department are to carry out research into problems of importance to the Labour movement, to supply information to its affiliated organisations, which by 1973 numbered 1,600, and to issue publications.

Papers

The Department has retained records dating back to its foundation, although many of the most valuable documents, including a large amount of original material collected during the General Strike of 1926, were destroyed during World War II. Minutes of the Executive meetings are complete, and minutes of other committees also survive. A full set of annual reports is also extant. A small collection of miscellaneous manuscripts survives but no further details on these are available.

The L.R.D. has retained copies of some 300 pamphlets which it has published since 1916, together with copies of its books. The pamphlets are at present being microfilmed. The Department also holds a complete set of its journal, *Labour Research*, dating from July 1917.

Relevant material may also be found in the Passfield papers at the British Library of Political and Economic Science. This consists of manuscript, typescript and printed material, 1912-29.

Availability

Enquiries about the L.R.D.'s records should be directed to the Secretary. Permission to use the Passfield papers must be obtained from the Librarian, B.L.P.E.S.

LAND SETTLEMENT ASSOCIATION LTD.
43 Cromwell Road London SW7 2EE

Formed in 1934, the Association aimed originally to discover whether unemployed industrial workers could be successfully redeployed as self-supporting smallholders. The Association worked in co-operation with Government departments and officials, particularly the Commission for Special Areas, and with voluntary organisations, in purchasing land. From 1947 it has acted as the agent of the Ministry of Agriculture for the administration of smallholding estates which are its property. Since the beginning of World War II the Association has worked for the general development of smallholdings, rather than on the redeployment of industrial workers. Various services in marketing are provided on a co-operative basis.

Papers

The Association has retained very full records, including minutes, annual reports and many of its publications. The annual reports are being microfilmed by Reading University for its Institute of Agricultural History. Other publications may be consulted at the British Library.

A large assortment of papers of the Welsh Land Settlement Society Ltd., including estate plans and other records dating from the early 1930s, has been deposited in the Glamorgan Record Office.

The published records are open to inspection. Bona fide scholars engaged in serious historical research may be given access to other papers. Enquiries should be addressed to the Information Officer. For those in the Glamorgan Record Office, application should be made to the Archivist.

LAW SOCIETY
113 Chancery Lane London WC2

The Society was founded in 1825 as the Law Institution. Its name has been altered by successive Charters, but its aims have remained the same. These are to promote professional improvement among solicitors and to facilitate the acquisition of legal knowledge.

Papers

Extensive records relating to the Society have been retained in its headquarters. The principal categories of records include the proceedings of the Council of the Society and of its standing committees since its foundation. Proceedings of the general meetings of the Society have also been retained, although these are for the most part published in the *Law Society's Gazette* (a complete file of the *Gazette* exists in the Society's Library). The proceedings of the Disciplinary Committee (as constituted under the Solicitors Acts) are also extant. A very large collection of archives (much now on microfilm) concerns the personal records of all solicitors from 1907 onwards (personal records prior to this date are now housed at the Public Record Office).

Availability

Certain material, such as the individual personal records of solicitors, is of a private and confidential nature for the more recent period. Except for this confidential material, bona fide applications to consult other records will normally be assessed on their merit on application to the Secretary. Other organisations, such as the Law Society of Scotland, the Institute of Legal Executives and the many autonomous local organisations (such as the Birmingham Law Society and Bristol Law Society), may also possess relevant archive material.

LEAGUE FOR DEMOCRACY IN GREECE
26 Goodge Street London W1

Founded in 1945, the League has enjoyed the support of, among others, Sir Compton Mackenzie, Lord Soper (President), and the Labour M.P.s Benn Levy and Seymour Cocks. The League's campaigns are mainly concerned to secure the release of political prisoners, the banning of torture, illegal arrests and military tribunals, and the restoration of democratic freedom and justice in Greece.

Papers

A valuable archive has been built up in the League's offices. The records include Executive Committee minutes and reports, abour 13 boxes of circulars issued to members since 1945, 60 boxes of cuttings from the British, American and European press, a substantial amount of printed pamphlet material, and photographs.

Most of the papers are accessible to all those interested. For the Executive Committee minutes and reports, however, each application is judged on its merits. Enquiries should be addressed to the Secretary. Other material is available with the Greek News Agency, 309 Kentish Town Road, London NW5.

LEAGUE OF COLOURED PEOPLES

Founded in 1931, the League was the first conscious and deliberate attempt to form a multi-racial organisation in Britain, led by blacks but with white members, to state the cause of the black man against injustice, to improve relations between the races, and to protect and promote the social, educational, economic and political interests of its members and of black people generally. The League was dissolved in 1951.

Papers

The records of the League have not been located. However, published material is available at the British Library and the Marx Memorial Library, etc. This includes annual reports and copies of the *Newsletter,* and of the journal *The Keys* (1933-39). An article by Roderick J. MacDonald, 'Dr. Harold Arundel Moody and the League of Coloured Peoples, 1931-47: A Retrospective View', appeared in the Jan. 1973 edition of the journal *Race.* Kenneth Little in his book *Negroes in Britain* (1948) makes extensive use of the League's records, which now appear to have been mislaid.

LEAGUE OF NATIONS UNION

Founded in 1918 to promote the formation of a World League of Free Peoples for the securing of international justice, mutual defence amd permanent peace, the Union was a British organisation, incorporating the previous League of Nations Society and the League of Free Nations Association. During the inter-war years the Union worked to promote the aims and objects of the League of Nations and to secure the wholehearted acceptance by the British people of the League as 'the guardian of international right, the organ of international co-operation, the final arbiter in international differences, and the supreme instrument for removing injustices which may threaten the peace of the world'. The main effort of the Union was therefore broadly educational, providing published material, speakers and organised courses.

Papers

The extensive records — essentially minute books — have been deposited in the British Library of Political and Economic Science. No detailed catalogue is available as yet, but the papers fall into five sections:

(*a*)   General Council, minutes, 1919-43.
(*b*)   Executive Committee, minutes of the League of Free Nations Association, June-Nov. 1918; and minutes of the Union, Nov. 1918-May 1946.
(*c*)   Administrative and Financial Committees and sub-committees, assorted minutes and papers.
(*d*)   Miscellaneous special committees: 76 items, covering such subjects as 'appeals', China and the Far East (1932-34), Christian organisations, economics, educational organisation, International Labour Office

(1940-41); international policy, limitation of armaments, mandates, minorities, penal reform, refugees, Research Department, revision of the Covenant.

(e) Other records. These include papers relating to the British Universities League of Nations Society (1926-36), the Geneva Institute of International Relations (1925-38) and the London International Assembly.

Other branch records are located elsewhere. An extensive collection of records of the Welsh National Council has been deposited in the National Library of Wales. These include the signed minutes of the Council, 1923-45; minutes of the Executive Committee, 1922-56, the Finance Committee, 1922-55, the Advisory Education Committee, 1922-51, the North Wales Committee, 1927-38, and of the Campaign Committee, 1946; a ledger, 1925-46, and cash books, 1925-37; and a series of general and branch files of correspondence and miscellaneous material.

Another relevant group consists of papers in the Lord Davies of Llandinam Collection, also at the National Library of Wales. These have not yet been catalogued, but consist largely of correspondence, arrangements for speakers, publicity, etc., stemming out of Lord Davies's work for the Welsh Council, as President and Chairman.

The Gwilym Davies Collection in the National Library also contains relevant records: files of correspondence, press cuttings, notes and pamphlets, 1920s and 1930s.

Some papers of the Green Lane branch, 1931-44, are available at the Coventry City Record Office.

Availability

For the main archive, applications should be addressed to the Librarian at B.L.P.E.S. As regards the National Library of Wales, enquiries should be directed to the Librarian. There is no general access to the Lord Davies Collection.

LEFT BOOK CLUB

The Club was launched in May 1936 by the publisher, Victor Gollancz, with the aid of H. J. Laski and John Strachey. The Club published a regular series of books, of left-wing appeal, chiefly on international affairs, and through their wide readership, and the activities of local groups, the Left Book Club exercised a widespread influence. The German-Soviet Pact of 1939 weakened the Club, and during World War II its influence diminished. It was wound up in 1948.

Papers

No Left Book Club archive has survived. Victor Gollancz Ltd., the publishers, has basic correspondence and papers concerning contracts for books published by the Club, but these are the usual records of a publishing house and of no political importance. Victor Gollancz himself, on the testimony of his daughter, retained only a few family papers, which are not regarded as of historical significance.

The chief source for the activities of the Club would be copies of its journal *Left News*.

Correspondence of H. J. Laski has been deposited in Hull University Library.

Papers of John Strachey are in the care of his widow, but are not at present available. It is believed, however, that the collection contains correspondence on the Left Book Club. This was used in Hugh Thomas, *John Strachey* (1973).

LIBERAL AND RADICAL CANDIDATES' ASSOCIATION

The Association was founded in 1924, and membership was open to Liberals who were candidates at the General Election of 1923 or subsequent elections, or who were prospective candidates. The Association was divided into educational policy groups, who, met periodically to discuss questions of importance to the party. It also organised nationwide campaigns and arranged speakers for these from among its membership. Sir Herbert Samuel was Chairman, and Sir Francis Acland Vice-Chairman, of the Association.

Papers

No records of the Association as such have been located. Some relevant material may survive in the usual collections of private papers of prominent Liberals.

LIBERAL INTERNATIONAL (BRITISH GROUP)
1 Whitehall Place London SW1

Formed in 1947, the Liberal International is the British section of the World Liberal Union, a body co-ordinating the activities of Liberal parties, providing information on international affairs for Liberal parties and promoting the acceptance of Liberalism throughout the world.

Papers

For the British group, the only historical records are minutes of the Executive and general meetings, back to 1949. The Liberal International as a whole has similar records and reports of international Liberal meetings since foundation of the organisation.

Availability

Sets of records are in London, and can be seen by arrangement with the Organiser of the British Group and the International Secretary-General.

LIBERAL LEAGUE

Founded on 24 February 1902, at a meeting of Liberal Imperialists in Lord Rosebery's London house, the League included among its members Sir Edward Grey, Asquith, Sidney Webb, R. W. Perks and R. B. Haldane. The League aimed to bring together for common action supporters of Rosebery's Chesterfield Policy for reform of the Liberal Party along the lines of 'efficiency'. The League constituted the organisation of the Liberal Imperialist Group and soon incorporated the existing Liberal Imperialist Council. Beneath the umbrella of 'sane Imperialism', the League gathered together landowners, collectivists and Nonconformists. After the formation of the Liberal Government in 1905 the League became a negative, critical force which, after Rosebery's resignation, was eventually dissolved in May 1910.

Papers

Records of the Liberal League are included in the Rosebery papers at the National Library of Scotland. The two volumes cover the years 1901-10. Among the many other collections of private papers which should be consulted are the Asquith MSS. at the Bodleian Library, the Haldane papers at the National Library of Scotland, and the Herbert Gladstone papers at the British Library. In the years

1902-05 the League published nearly 200 pamphlets, most of which are held in the British Library of Political and Economic Science.

Availability

Applications should be addressed to the appropriate Librarian.

LIBERAL PARTY
7 Exchange Court Strand London WC2

The records of the Liberal Party are described here in three sections:

I. National.

II. Regional.

III. Constituencies.

I. National

Partly because of the frequency with which the party has moved headquarters, and partly as a result of the divisions within the party after 1916, the central records that survive are extremely sparse. A few surviving records of the national organisation of the party may be consulted at the Library of the *National Liberal Club* (q.v.). The only central records in this institution prior to the inter-war period are the minutes of the Liberal Central Association, 1874-1914. These are in four volumes and cover the periods 1874-83, 1883-96, 1896-1911, 1911-14. This last minute book is only partly filled, which suggests that no formal records were recorded thereafter. If they were, the records have apparently been lost.

For the inter-war period, the position as regards records is similarly bleak. Two minute books of the Liberal Council survive, recording Executive Committee meetings, January 1927-June 1939. An unsorted collection of records of the Women's National Liberal Federation is also deposited with these in the National Liberal Club.

Annual reports and proceedings of the National Liberal Federation may be consulted at the British Library. These date from 1879-1936, when the Federation amalgamated with the Liberal Party Organisation. The 47th Annual Report is missing.

Records held by the Liberal Party Organisation appear to be of current relevance only. In the absence of a major central archive, the papers of prominent Liberal leaders are indispensable.

The Asquith papers at the Bodleian Library and the Lloyd George papers at the Beaverbrook Library are very important. The Asquith papers contain much relevant correspondence and eight boxes on the post-war Liberal Party including much material on General Election finance and organisation.

The Lloyd George papers are of obvious importance for the Lloyd George Liberal Party (Coalition Liberal Party). No other central archive survives which records the history of this group, which reunited with the official Liberal Party as a result of the 1923 Tariff Election.

The Herbert Gladstone papers at the British Library are useful for the organisation of the party in the 1900s and the 1920s. The papers of Sir Donald Maclean at the Bodleian Library supplement those of Herbert Gladstone for the 1920s. These papers include notes on the organisation of the Asquith Liberals, 1918-19, meetings with Lloyd George, 1918-24, notes on Liberal reunion, 1924, and papers relating to General Elections. The papers of Sir Archibald Sinclair,

Viscount Thurso, are deposited in the Library of Churchill College, Cambridge. These include boxes on Liberal organisation, 1931-39, six boxes on the Scottish Liberal Organisation, 1931-39, and a file of correspondence, 1935-36, with the Duke of Montrose on closer relations with the Scottish Nationalists. These papers are not available while cataloguing is in progress. In addition, the papers of W. M. Eagar, Secretary of both the Liberal Land Inquiry and the Liberal Industrial Inquiry are available at the *Reform Club* (q.v.).

Several related organisations possess useful records, in particular the *Society of Certificated and Associated Liberal Agents* (q.v.).

See also *National Liberal Party*.

II. Regional

At regional level the historian of the Liberal Party is better served. Although there are still depressing areas where records have been destroyed or lost (as in the case of the London Liberal Party), the following collections exist:

Eastern Counties Liberal Federation

A useful collection, although not catalogued, exists in the Federation offices. It is best for the 1918-30 period, but very sparse thereafter.

Home Counties Liberal Federation

A very small amount of material is deposited in the Library, National Liberal Club. This includes annual reports from May 1924 to December 1945, together with one set of rules for 1908 and an amended list of rules for 1933. The papers of W. Crook, now deposited in the Bodleian Library, Oxford, are very informative for this area in the 1920s.

Leeds Liberal Federation

The records of the Federation have been deposited in the Sheepscar Library, Leeds. Permission to quote from the material is needed. The collection is made up of the following material: minutes of General Council, 1 vol., 1912-39; minutes of Executive Committee, 2 vols., 1894-1924 and 1925-57; minutes of Cabinet Committee, 2 vols., 1897-1919 and 1919-36; minutes of Finance Committee, 1912-36.

Leicester Liberal Federation

The records of the Federation have been deposited in Leicester Museum. They cover the period 1853-1923. The collection includes minute books of the Executive Committee, General Purposes, Election, Finance and School Board Election Committees, 1876-1923, and annual reports, 1908-12.

Manchester Liberal Federation

A very useful set of records exists in the Federation office. There is an incomplete run of minute books from 1879 to date; the gaps are mainly for the 1920s. There are also minute books of the Finance Committee for 1910-39, and of the Municipal Joint Committee for 1926-36. In addition there are minute books of the Liberal and Progressive Group on the Manchester City Council, 1910-26, and of the Manchester Municipal Progressive Association, 1910-15.

Midland Liberal Federation

The records of the former Midland Liberal Federation have been deposited in the University of Birmingham Library. They constitute one of the best regional collections of Liberal material. The collection includes minute books from 1894-1935 (6 vols.). There are useful press cuttings on the 1950 and 1951 elections, together with correspondence, etc., for 1959 and for the Small Heath by-election of 1961. There are cash books for 1894-95 and for the 1947-58 period. There is a file of correspondence with Liberal Clubs in the region (1950-56) and correspondence with Young Liberals (1950-54). The records of the West Midlands Women's Liberal Federation for the period 1948-61 have also been deposited.

North West Liberal Federation
Records are retained in the Federation's offices.

Western Counties Liberal Federation
Records are believed to be in the care of the present secretary.

Yorkshire Liberal Federation
The records of the Federation have been deposited in the Sheepscar Library, Leeds. They consist of four volumes of minutes for the period 1902-64.

In addition to these regional records there are also the records of the Scottish Liberal Federation, the Welsh Liberals and the Ulster Liberal Party.

Scottish Liberal Federation
Records are deposited in Edinburgh University Library, as are the records of the Scottish Women's Liberal Federation. Records of the Scottish Liberal Club are retained by the Club, 109 Princes Street, Edinburgh EH2 3AG.

Liberal Party of Wales
Various records are deposited in the National Library of Wales, including material relating to the North Wales Liberal Federation.

Ulster Liberal Party
Certain recent material is deposited in the Northern Ireland Public Record Office.

III. Constituencies

A survey of constituency records, conducted with the aid of the Liberal Party Organisation, was undertaken in 1971. Compared with both the Conservative and Labour parties, the number of old constituency records that can still be located is very small. Except where otherwise stated, records are retained in the association's offices.

Aberdeen. Records have been deposited in the University Library, King's College, Aberdeen. These include M.B.s 1909-22.
Aberdeenshire West and Kincardineshire. M.B.s from 1945.
Aberystwyth. M.B.s of the Women's Liberal Association 1894-98 are deposited in the National Library of Wales.
Altrincham and Sale. M.B.s and ann. reps. 1916 to date are deposited in Cheshire Record Office.
Banbury. Material relating to the elections of 1886 and 1892 is in Oxfordshire Record Office.
Birmingham. The following records survive: M.B.s of the Executive, 1876-84; Management Committee, 1883-89; General Committee, 1898-1915; Management Committee, 1912-25; Liberal Club General Committee, 1933-38.
Bradford. Records survive for the period prior to 1914.
Bridlington. M.B.s 1951 to date.

Bristol West. M.B.s 1928 to date; ann. rep. 1944 to date; a/c's from 1930.

Burnley. A letter book 1877-87 is deposited in Burnley Public Library.

Caernarvonshire. Correspondence 1924-36 is deposited in the National Library of Wales.

Cambridge and County. M.B.s of the Women's Liberal Association are deposited in Cambridgeshire and Isle of Ely Record Office.

Cambridge University Liberal Club. Correspondence and papers 1950-60 in Cambridge University Library. Other records are in the Fitzwilliam Library, Cambridge. An earlier M.B. 1880-96 is in the Edwin Montagu Collection at Trinity College, Cambridge.

Cardiff Junior Liberal Association. M.B. 1886-95 in Cardiff Central Library.

Chester. M.B.s 1879-1964 deposited in Chester City Record Office.

Chorley. M.B.s from May 1934 to date.

Clapham. M.B.s 1957-70 are now deposited in the Minet Library, London SE5. The collection includes correspondence from 1950 to date.

Conway. M.B.s from Oct.1948.

Coventry. M.B.s of the Coventry Municipal Committee 1885-1929 are deposited in the Coventry City Record Office.

Daventry. One surviving M.B. covers 1926; nothing else pre-war has been uncovered.

Derbyshire West. M.B.s 1918-35.

Dewsbury. No papers appear to have survived.

East Grinstead. Nov. 1956 to date.

Esher. M.B.s of Executive Committee 1953 to date.

Flintshire. Records from 1919 to 1939 are deposited in Flintshire Record Office.

Great Yarmouth. M.B.s 1952 to date. Earlier records lost when former Liberal Club closed in 1951.

Harborough. One of the finest sets of records in the country. Continuous and full minutes from 1891. In possession of E. Rushworth, 16 Main Street, Kirby Muxloe, Leicester.

Hastings. M.B.s, with occasional gaps, since 1949.

Hereford. M.B.s of Executive Committee and A.G.M.s 1923-33; also of the 1929 Campaign Committee in possession of J. M. Whitmarsh, Bicknor, Fiddler's Green, Townhope, Herefordshire.

Hertfordshire East. M.B.s 1948 to present.

Heywood and Royton. A useful collection with material prior to 1948 relating to the former Royton Division. M.B.s 1949-57, 1961 to date; ann. reps. 1936-40, 1947-70; account books 1945 to date; press cuttings re local elections 1934-38. Some fairly routine correspondence from W. Gorman (Liberal M.P. for Royton 1923-24) to his agent, 1923-27.

Ilford North. M.B.s 1945 to date.

Leicester South East. M.B.s from Mar 1949, a/c's 1948 to date; also a cash book of the Spinney Hill Ward 1898-1968. In possession of R. C. Neale, 23 Hollington Road, Leicester.

Leicester North West. M.B.s June 1945 to date.

Lincoln. Minutes, etc., are deposited in Lincolnshire Archives Office.

Llandwynda Liberal Association. Records in National Library of Wales.

Manchester Exchange. M.B.s 1927-48 in the office of the Manchester Liberal Federation, 53 Spring Gardens, Manchester.

Merioneth. One of the most useful constituency collections, deposited in Merioneth Record Office. A full set of minutes from 1898-1955, together with files re registration, 1909, 1910, 1914. There is also an M.B. of the Welsh Land, Commercial and Labour League, 1898-1908, which became the Arthog Liberal Association. There are minutes for the Arthog Liberal Society 1912-37.

Newcastle-under-Lyme. Accounts from 1948, M.B.s from 1958.

Oldham. M.B.s 1950 to date.

Penrith and the Border. A useful collection with M.B.s from 1885 to date, including some leaflets and correspondence.

Richmond. M.B.s 1946-52, 1956 to date.

Sheffield. Correspondence 1876-1905 in Sheffield Central Library.

Shrewsbury. All pre-war M.B.s were destroyed in the early 1950s.

Sudbury and Woodbridge. The surviving records of the association are held by Alderman Aubrey Herbert in the Library, Chilton Hall, near Sudbury, Suffolk.

Thurrock. M.B.s since 1947.

Tonbridge. M.B.s from 1950.

Walthamstow West. M.B.s 1888 to date; ann. reps. 1888-1903; party newspaper May-Oct. 1925. Some correspondence after 1920s.

Worcestershire North Liberal Council. Executive minutes 1903-17 in Worcestershire Record Office.

Yeovil. An M.B. for the period 1890-94 for the former South Somerset Liberal Association; minutes of Yeovil Association Oct. 1937-Jan. 1951; also minutes of Crewkerne Liberal Club Trustees 1885-1900, minutes of Martock Branch, National League of Young Liberals, 1925-39.

LIBERAL UNIONIST PARTY

This developed from the group of Liberals who broke away from the Liberal Party in 1886 over the question of Home Rule for Ireland. Joseph Chamberlain and Lord Hartington (later 8th Duke of Devonshire) were its leading members. From the 1890s it worked closely with the Conservative Party. In May 1912 it formally became part of the Conservative and Unionist Party.

Papers

At present, no central archive of Liberal Unionist records is known to exist. The workings of the Liberal Unionist Association and of the L.U. Council are, however, recorded in the major collections of personal papers. The Joseph Chamberlain papers at Birmingham University Library and the papers of the 8th Duke of Devonshire at Chatsworth House, Derbyshire, are most useful. Other papers worth mentioning are those of the 2nd Earl Selborne (Party Manager, 1887-92) in the Bodleian Library, Austen Chamberlain at Birmingham, Leonard Courtney in the B.L.P.E.S., and Arthur Elliott in the National Library of Scotland. Of the Liberal Unionist archives at regional level, a particularly good set exists for Scotland. There the Liberal Unionist Association 'central' minutes are complete (from 1886) and reasonably detailed, including Executive and committee minutes, annual printed reports, accounts and newspaper cuttings. Four bound volumes cover the Western Division (10 May 1886-3 Mar. 1913) and two relate to the Eastern and Northern Division (10 Nov. 1886-5 Dec. 1912). All are stored in the Glasgow offices of the Conservative Party. The minute book of the West Birmingham L.U.A. at Smethwick Public Library covers *c.* 1886-1912, but is not as informative as the Scottish records. At the National Library of Wales there is a collection of letters, 1887-90, of Henry Tobit Evans, mainly relating to Liberal Unionist affairs. Other private papers which should be noted include those of Lord Heneage at Lincolnshire Archives Office, Henry Brooke Taylor at Derbyshire Record Office, and Henry Bagshaw at Sheffield Public Library. Official L.U. publications, besides a series of over 300 propaganda pamphlets, include *The Liberal Unionist* newspaper (1887-92) and *Memoranda* (1893-1912), available at the British Library.

LIBERATION
313/315 Caledonian Road London N1

Formed in 1954 as the Movement for Colonial Freedom, the organisation adopted its present name in 1970. M.C.F. has pioneered campaigning work in Britain for the right of all peoples to full independence and the principle of international mutual aid. Liberation continues to press for the application of the Four Freedoms and the Declaration of Human Rights to all peoples, and the abolition of imperialism and neo-colonialism.

Papers

Unfortunately the early M.C.F. records have been lost, probably due to the organisation's various changes of premises. Some early papers however may exist in the private collection of Lord (Fenner) Brockway, the Movement's President. The bulk of the records at the present offices go back to about 1965 only, and comprise in the main printed material, annual reports, pamphlets and circulars, with a considerable amount of correspondence and subject files. Copies of the journal *Liberation*, formerly *Colonial Freedom News*, are also kept.

Availability

All materials may be seen by arrangement with the General Secretary.

LIBERATION SOCIETY

The full title of the Society, which was founded in 1844, was the Society for the Liberation of Religion from State Patronage and Control. It aimed for the abrogation of all laws and usages which confer privilege, or inflict disability, on religious or ecclesiastical grounds; the discontinuance of all payments from public fund, and of all compulsory exaction, for religious purposes; and the disestablishment of the state churches in England, Wales and Scotland.

Papers

Records covering the period 1850-1957 have been deposited at the Greater London Record Office. They include minutes, lists, agenda, correspondence, accounts, posters and cuttings.

Availability

Enquiries should be addressed to the Archivist at County Hall.

LIBERTY AND PROPERTY DEFENCE LEAGUE

Formed in 1882 by Lord Elcho (later Lord Wemyss), Herbert Spencer and others, the League aimed to uphold the principle of liberty and guard the rights of labour and property of all kinds against undue interference by the state, and to encourage self-help against state intervention. During its lifetime up to c. 1933 the League spawned other associations, such as the Employers' Parliamentary Council, the Free Labour Protection Association (1898) and the Middle Class Defence League (1906). Over 200 industrial pressure groups federated with it by 1900.

Papers

The League published unofficial journals, *Jus* (1887-88) and *Liberty Review* (1893-1909), and issued annual reports, 1882-1921, and over a hundred pamphlets.

These are available at the British Library and B.L.P.E.S. The papers of the 11th Lord Wemyss are preserved at Gosford Castle, East Lothian, in the custody of the present Earl. The political papers are arranged in a series of chronological portfolios holding correspondence, pamphlets, speeches, etc. They include material relating to the Liberty and Property Defence League.

Availability

A catalogue is available at the National Register of Archives (Scotland). Enquiries regarding access to the papers should be addressed to the Registrar.

LICENSED VICTUALLERS' CENTRAL PROTECTION SOCIETY OF LONDON LTD

Linburn House 340 Kilburn High Road London NW6

The Society was founded in 1833 and incorporated under its present title in 1893. Since 1892 the Society's London Central Board has been the central organisation for a number of affiliated societies of licensed victuallers in Greater London and adjoining counties. The Board gives advice, guidance and assistance to its affiliated societies and their individual members, and uses its influence in Parliament and other bodies to protect the licensed trade. Whilst directly protecting the interests of retailers, the Society also co-operates with the wholesale side to protect the interest of the trade as a whole.

Papers

The records of the Society are kept at its headquarters in Kilburn. They include a full run of minute books, dating back to the Society's foundation in 1833, and cover the activities of the governing body and of the various committees, including the Parliamentary, Publicity, Finance and Legal Committees. These are the most valuable sources for the history of the Society. In addition, there are reports dating back to 1833. Until 1892 these are often no more than lists of members. Thereafter the annual report is fuller, covering the various activities of the Society.

A large collection of other material, including scrapbooks containing manuscript material, was destroyed during the summer of 1972 owing to pressure on space when the Society moved its offices. These would have been a valuable supplement to the minutes and reports. Correspondence is generally not kept beyond ten years.

The Society retains certain publications relating to its activities, e.g. copies of its journal, *Licensing World*, for the 1940s, and editions of the *Official Annual*, containing statistical information, dating from 1892.

Availability

The records may be consulted by prior application in writing to the Secretary of the Society.

LINK

The organisation was founded in 1937 by Admiral Sir Barry Domville and E. C. Carroll, a former editor of the British Legion newspaper; the Link was organised to propagandise against war with Germany. Carroll had been editing the *Anglo-German Review* which was thereafter utilised by the Link. Domville was already on the Council of the *Anglo-German Fellowship* (q.v.) but felt there was a need for co-ordination and an organisation to enlist popular support.

No records of the organisation are known to survive. However, the Domville diaries, deposited at the National Maritime Museum, Greenwich, may contain valuable material.

Availability

Enquiries should be made to the Custodian of Manuscripts, National Maritime Museum.

LLOYD GEORGE 'COUNCIL OF ACTION FOR PEACE AND RECONSTRUCTION'

Anxious to bring about a British 'New Deal' and to establish a power base through which to influence the next General Election, Lloyd George launched his Council of Action in July 1935. In his speeches he advocated a National Development Board, public control of the Bank of England and a small inner Cabinet as in the 1916-22 government. Financed by the Lloyd George Liberal Fund, the Council's policies included a five-year armistice, a five-year non-aggression pact, reduced tariffs, abolition of quotas, and sanctions against Italy. Although early meetings were supported by several eminent Conservative politicians and representatives of the Free Churches, enthusiasm for the Council of Action was not sustained and the organisation had little influence on the 1935 election. In later years the Council continued to be a vehicle for Lloyd George's policies, particularly in the sphere of foreign affairs. In late 1939 the Council was active with regard to the possibilities of a negotiated peace with Hitler.

Papers

The surviving records are included in the Lloyd George MSS. at the Beaverbrook Library. A section of the catalogue, under the heading 'New Deal and Council of Action', gives details of correspondence and papers 1934-39, correspondence with T. F. Tweed, miscellaneous papers and press cuttings.

Availability

Applicants should write to the Director of the Beaverbrook Library.

LOCAL GOVERNMENT ASSOCIATIONS

Introductory Note

The extensive reorganisation of local government in Britain has meant that the organisations contacted by the survey were no longer in existence after April 1974. The future structure of local government organisations was not, at the time of writing, finally resolved. Consequently, students should regard the information given below as only a mere indication of the extent and nature of records which existed.

Association of Municipal Corporations

Formed in 1873, the Association aimed to watch over and protect the interests, rights and privileges of municipal corporations, as they might be affected by public Bill legislation or by private Bill legislation of general application to boroughs; and to take action in relation to other subjects in which municipal corporations generally might be interested.

Extensive records are retained covering the work of the Association during its existence, including minute books, reports, etc. Many of the correspondence files contain material of an ephemeral character and need 'weeding out'.

County Councils Association

The Association was formed in 1890 after the passing of the Local Government Act in 1888. The organisation liaised between the government and the county councils. Its finance was initially provided for in the County Councils Association (Expenses) Act, which enabled county councils to pay an annual fee for the Association's maintenance. Later on this was supplanted by the Local Government Act, 1948.

Papers

A substantial archive exists. It includes:

Minutes and annual reports. All the minutes and annual reports from 1890 to the present are available, with the exception of those for 1904-07 which are missing. The minutes act as a cross-reference index to the appropriate correspondence files. Most of the more important correspondence, in full or in summary form, is published in these documents, which are bound in annual volumes with the *County Councils Gazette*.

Correspondence. Theoretically most of the correspondence dates from 1890, although much is missing for the early years. Files are by subject, and the number of files on each subject depends on the weight of correspondence involved. All the files are indexed. Files are searched periodically and routine material destroyed. In general most of the important material has been kept.

Reports. Part of the function of the C.C.A. was to produce evidence on various government measures and reports concerning local government. These reports are all kept, and generally published by the Association.

Rural District Councils Association

The Association was founded in 1895 to afford an opportunity to rural district councils to give expression to their opinions, press their merits on governments of the day and generally have a watching brief over laws which affected R.D.C.s.

Papers

The Association has retained a complete set of reports of A.G.M.s and conferences dating back to 1901, and of minutes of the Executive Council, including reports of all its committees. There is a full run of the Association's monthly journal, *District Councils Review*, dating back to 1895.

Urban District Councils Association

The Association was founded in 1894 to further the interests, rights and privileges of urban district councils, especially with regard to public and private Bill legislation and government orders and regulations.

Papers

Formal records, such as minutes since 1894, have been retained together with various other records, at present unsorted.

LONDON GROUP ON AFRICAN AFFAIRS

The London Group on African Affairs was formed in August 1930, to assist the inter-racial work of the several Joint Councils of Europeans and Africans established in various parts of Africa. Its purpose was to keep in touch with actual conditions prevailing in all parts of Africa, to undertake investigations, to inform public opinion and to press for reforms and improvements where necessary in the interests of equity and progress. The Chairman was John P. Fletcher and the Hon. Secretary was Frederick Livie-Noble.

After the outbreak of war in 1939 the Group as such came to an end; but its work was continued and expanded by the *Fabian Colonial Bureau*, (q.v.) formed in 1940, whose papers are also kept in Rhodes House Library.

Papers

A full collection of records of the organisation has been deposited, via the Oxford Colonial Records Project, in Rhodes House, Oxford.

The papers, contained in five boxes, cover the period 1925-42. The main contents of the first box, in addition to material relating to the 'Ballinger Appeal', are concerned chiefly with the problems of the South African Protectorates and their relation with the Union.

The second box contains the L.G.A.A. minute book for 1930-39. Other files in this box deal with proposals for closer union between the Rhodesias and Nyasaland, South African native policy and the South African Institute of Race Relations.

The first file of box 3 is concerned with East African affairs: forced labour in Kenya, the Kakamega goldfields, the question of closer union in East Africa, and the Report of the Kenya Land Commission. In file 2 are papers about Liberia and the League of Nations, to whom the Liberian Government had appealed for financial aid, and the conflict between Liberian and American interests. The third file holds papers of the Consultative Committee on African Affairs, of which Livie-Noble was a member; it was formed in 1936 at the suggestion of Sir John Harris, Secretary of the Anti-Slavery and Aborigines' Protection Society.

Another aspect of the Group's work is represented in box 4 — help for Africans in England. The five files contain correspondence with numbers of Africans working or studying here and with people and organisations prepared to assist them, papers of the African Students' Committee, and papers relating to a delegation from the Gold Coast Aborigines' Rights Protection Society.

Box 5 contains much material relating to the *Abyssinian Refugees Relief Fund* (q.v.).

Availability

Application should be made to the Librarian, Rhodes House, Oxford.

LONDON MUNICIPAL SOCIETY

The Society was formed in 1894 as a front organisation for the Conservative Party in London local government politics. Its initial aims were to win control of the London County Council and to secure a decentralisation of power from it to new municipalities. The Society fought local elections first as the Moderate and later as the Municipal Reform Party, and it was closely associated with the ratepayers' movement. An independent *National Union of Ratepayers' Associations* (q.v.) was formed in 1938. The L.M.S. was dissolved in 1963.

Papers

A number of records survives in the Guildhall Library. There are three volumes of Executive Committee minutes, 1894-1963; two volumes of L.M.S. Council minutes, 1894-1963; two volumes of A.G.M. minutes, 1894-1963; and a large assortment of printed material, pamphlets, leaflets and some typescript notes. This collection includes election notes for speakers, other election literature, statistical memoranda, newspaper cuttings (1895-1943), a monthly review of municipal work and progress (1904-*c.* 1920), copies of the journals *Ratepayer* (1921-48) and *The Londoner* (1948-63).

Availability

Enquiries should be addressed to the Librarian at the Guildhall Library.

LONDON POSITIVIST SOCIETY

The Positivist Society of London was founded in 1867 to propagate positivist social principles. It sponsored regular public meetings and publications and its influence is now continued through the Auguste Comte Memorial Lectures held at the London School of Economics.

Papers

A collection of records of the London Positivist Society and the English Positivist Committee are deposited in B.L.P.E.S. The papers include a volume of reports of meetings of the Society, 1878-91; an Attendance Book, 1892-1923; a 'Register of Sacraments'; and volumes of minutes of meetings of the English Positivist Committee, 1883-1956; a volume of minutes of the Guild of Young Positivists, 1910-22; a Cash Book, 1917-50; a Ledger, 1928-38; and a Petty Cash Book, 1934-51; and box files of papers and correspondence covering the period 1916 to the 1950s. Amongst the correspondence is a small group of letters from Frederick Harrison relating to the Society's work. This supplements the collection of Frederick Harrison Papers, also deposited in B.L.P.E.S. This collection consists of letters to Harrison, with his letters to Morley, Beesly and Bridges, some literary manuscripts and press cuttings, 1850-1922.

The London Positivist Society's collection of leaflets, reports, books, etc. and a run of the journal, the *Positivist Review* (later known as the *Humanist*) are also now in the care of B.L.P.E.S.

Availability

Enquiries should be directed to the Librarian, B.L.P.E.S.

LONDON REFORM UNION

Formed about 1892, the organisation mainly included members of the Liberal Party. Campaigning to improve the municipal government of London, the administration of its public affairs, and the collective organisation of its civic life, the London Reform Union was closely associated with the Liberal Party and the Progressive Party in London local government elections. It continued to exist until after World War I.

Papers

A number of printed records is retained at the B.L.P.E.S. These include annual reports, 1892-1918; speeches; 'proceedings', 1892; the report (and assorted papers) of a Special Committee on the Reform of London Government, 1907; and numerous books, pamphlets and leaflets on local government, politics and elections. Also at B.L.P.E.S. is the unpublished autobiography of F. W. Galton, Secretary of L.R.U. 1898-1918. The papers of W. H. (Lord) Dickinson are deposited at the Greater London Record Office, and a good collection of Progressive Party literature is housed at the Guildhall Library.

Availability

Applications should be addressed to the Librarian at B.L.P.E.S., and the Archivist at G.L.R.O.

LORD'S DAY OBSERVANCE SOCIETY
55 Fleet Street London EC4Y 1LQ

The Society was founded in 1831, by Joseph Wilson and his cousin the Rev. (later Bishop) Daniel Wilson. It has been in continuous existence since then and is today the sole surviving society of a powerful movement to preserve the Sabbath. It united with the Working Men's Lord's Day Rest Association, 1920, the Lord's Day Observance Association of Scotland, 1953, and the Imperial Alliance for the Defence of Sunday, 1965.

Its aims are:
(a) to maintain the sanctity of the Lord's Day;
(b) to educate public opinion and promote the observance of the Lord's Day for worship, by means of publications and meetings;
(c) to oppose any such changes in legislation which would cause further commercialisation of Sunday and the spread of Sunday labour;
(d) to conduct missions for the purpose of reaching children for Sunday school and teaching them the proper observance and meaning of the Lord's Day.

Papers

These consist of minutes, reports and journals dating back to the inception of the Society in 1831. Some of the records were destroyed during World War II by enemy action, but the gap is fairly well bridged by some duplicate records. Thus, the break in the run of annual reports is covered by minutes for the same period. Eleven minute books of Executive Committee meetings cover the period 1831-1929. There is one volume missing, 1929-35, and two volumes cover the period 1935 to date. These latter two are not available for research purposes. In addition there is a minute book of the Worthing Branch of the L.D.O.S., 1929-41; two minute books of the joint committee of the Society and the Working Men's Lord's Day Rest Association which established the Young People's Union for Lord's Day Observance, 1915-17, 1917-20; and one minute book of the Finance Committee, 1926-32.

There are bound volumes of annual reports for the 1832-75 and 1926-51 periods. Thereafter, reports were incorporated in the Society's magazine. There is a run of the *Magazine* from its foundation in 1843 to 1877, and 1926 to date. Since 1952 it has been known as *Joy and Light*. Correspondence is not generally kept beyond three or four years.

In addition to these, the records of the following societies with which the L.D.C.S. has united survive in its offices:

(1) *Brighton, Hove and District Rest Day Association.* Two minute books cover the period 1917-31, 1931-36.

(2) *Imperial Alliance for the Defence of Sunday* (q.v.).

(3) *Scottish Associations.* There is one minute book of the Glasgow Working Men's and West of Scotland Sabbath Protection Association, 1896-1911, with printed annual reports, 1851-81; and a minute book of the Scottish Sabbath Protection Association, 1911-33.

(4) *Working Men's Lord's Day Rest Association.* Six volumes of handwritten minute books of the Executive Committee cover the period 1857-1920. The occasional letter survives in these volumes. Printed annual reports run from 1858-80.

Availability

Records may be seen by previous arrangement with the General Secretary. No extracts from the papers may be published without the written consent of the General Secretary.

MAGISTRATES' ASSOCIATION
28 Fitzroy Square London W1P 6DD

The Association was founded in October 1920 with the object of educating and instructing Magistrates in the Law, the administration of justice and the best methods of preventing crime.

Papers

A full set of minutes of the Council and Executive Committee (from 1921) is retained at the headquarters of the Association. Minutes of a variety of sub-committees (e.g. Licensing, Juvenile Courts, Mental Health) are extant since 1945; No correspondence, other than current material, is retained; summaries of evidence to Royal Commissions, etc. are included in the Annual Reports of the Association. These exist from 1940 onwards in the Association's headquarters. No branches existed prior to 1950; however, there are now over fifty of these and any extant branch records would still be with the branch concerned.

Availability

Access is normally granted to 'bona fide' research workers, but very recent material may be treated as confidential.

MALTHUSIAN LEAGUE

The League was founded in 1877 with the object of promoting the understanding of Malthusian doctrine and its bearing on social problems, i.e. the necessity of restricting births in order to eliminate poverty, social unrest and wars. The League was the founder member of the International Federation of Neo-Malthusians and Birth Control Leagues.

Papers

The chief source of information for the activities of the League is its journal. This was published as *The Malthusian* (1879-1921, 1949-52) and as *New Generation* (1922-49). Annual reports were also published.

Papers of C. V. Drysdale (1873-1961), Secretary of the League and editor of its journal 1907-16, and later President of the League, are deposited in B.L.P.E.S.

The collection does not include formal records of the League. It largely consists of notes, drafts, etc., for Drysdale's published works on the Malthusian doctrine.

Availability

Enquiries concerning the Drysdale papers should be directed to the Librarian, B.L.P.E.S. Copies of *The Malthusian* and annual reports are also available in this library, as well as in the British Library.

See also *Eugenics Society; Family Planning Association; Marie Stopes Memorial Centre*.

MANCHESTER WORKING CLASS MOVEMENT LIBRARY
111 King's Road Old Trafford Manchester M16

Founded by Ed and Ruth Frow, this private institution houses material relating to the working-class movement.

Papers

The archive holdings of the Library consist at present of the following main collections:

(1) The papers of C.T.C. Giles, a former President of the National Union of Teachers. These form a very useful collection.

(2) The minutes of the Amalgamated Union of Building Trade Workers (Manchester District Committee) from Oct. 1930, consisting of some 28 volumes.

(3) The minutes of Salford City Labour Party from Apr. 1920 to the end of 1961.

(4) The papers of Marie Philibert, including much material on the Teachers for Peace movement.

(5) George Mearns papers, the records of an Oldham foundry worker active in the *National Council of Labour Colleges* (q.v.).

Availability

Enquiries should be addressed to Mr. Frow.

MARIE STOPES MEMORIAL CENTRE
108 Whitfield Street London W1

The Society and Clinic for Constructive Birth Control was founded in 1921 by Dr. Marie Stopes to campaign for a comprehensive birth-control service. A birth-control clinic was established as The Mother's Clinic. This changed its name in 1960 to the Marie Stopes Memorial Clinic, and in 1968 to the Marie Stopes Memorial Centre. This aims to offer a birth-control service to men and women, and to pioneer research into new methods and services.

Papers

The chief source for the activities of the Society and Clinic is the Marie Stopes Collection, deposited at the British Library. At the time of writing these have been roughly arranged, and no additional MSS. numbers have been assigned to them.

The Centre itself retains the first minute book of the Society together with other miscellaneous records. Many of the older case records, particularly for the 1920s, have been destroyed through lack of space. Recent case histories are of course confidential. The Centre retains copies of *Birth Control News* (1921-46).

The records are made available on application to the British Library and the Marie Stopes Memorial Centre.

MARINE SOCIETY
5 Clark's Place London EC2

A philanthropical society founded by Jonas Hanway in 1756, the organisation aims to assist boys to go to sea, either with advice or by grants.

Papers

The records are deposited at the National Maritime Museum, Greenwich. They cover business proceedings, and include minutes, agenda, letter books, and a register of persons helped by the society, 1756-*c*. 1949. The collection does not include any original correspondence.

Availability

Application should be addressed to the Custodian of Manuscripts.

MARX MEMORIAL LIBRARY
Marx House 37A Clerkenwell Green London EC1

The Library was founded in 1933 as a working-class library for the study of social science. It contains one of the richest collections in Britain of material of every sort connected with the working-class movement. Though it specialises in Marxist literature, its holdings include an important collection of printed ephemera relating to radical and Socialist history. From time to time books and papers of persons active in left-wing and radical movements have been acquired by the Library, so that it now holds a significant archival collection.

Papers

The records held by the Library may be described as follows:
(*a*) Material relating to national and international movements and organisations:
  (1) *International Working Men's Association (1st International)*. Minutes (printed), 5 vols., 1864-72.
  (2) *International Working Men's Association*. General rules, 1871.
  (3) *First of May Committee*. Minutes, 1900-10, 1922, 1925.
  (4) *War Emergency Workers' National Committee*. Minutes, 1914-18.
  (5) *People's Convention* (1940-41). A package of material (contents unspecified).
  (6) *National Unemployed Workers' Movement*. In a cabinet of Hannington's papers a considerable amount of material exists connected with the N.U.W.M. Among the items are:
    (i) The agenda and conference reports of the N.U.W.M. for 1923, 1924, 1929, 1931 and 1939.
    (ii) A few minutes, but mainly reports of the National Administrative Council (N.A.C.) of the N.U.W.M.
    (iii) Assorted local publications of N.U.W.M. area and branch organisations. In nearly all cases, only odd issues were ever published.
    (iv) An important collection (11 files) of letters and documents formerly belonging to W. Gallacher, concerning unemployment benefit cases which he raised in the Commons.
    (v) Printed bulletins of the Unemployment Research and Advice Bureau.

(7) *National Minority Movement.* Much pamphlet material, together with the reports of the annual conferences from Aug. 1924 to Aug. 1929.

(8) *'The Middle East Committee'.* Notes and press cuttings deposited by R. Page Arnot, 1954-58.

(9) *Social Democratic Federation.* Annual conference reports, 1894-1910.

(10) *British Socialist Party.* Annual conference reports, 1912-20.

(11) *Communist Party.* Annual conference reports, 1920 to date.

(12) *Independent Labour Party.* Annual conference reports, 1908-12, 1914, 1916-30, 1932.

(13) Annual conference reports of the Labour Party, Trades Union Congress, etc.

(*b*) Papers relating to local groups and branches of Socialist and radical movements:

(1) *Chatham Trades Council.* Minutes, 1918-21, 1921-23.

(2) *International Working Men's Association.* Minutes of London Branch, 1917-21.

(3) *Southend Socialist Sunday School.* Minutes, 1902-15.

(4) *Southend Joint Labour and Socialist Election Committee.* Minute book for 1914.

(5) *Rhondda District, South Wales Miners' Federation.* Annual reports, 1913-14, 1916-20, 1922-23.

(6) *Leicester Society for the Promotion of Peace.* Minute books for 1901 and 1913.

(7) *Social Democratic Federation.* London County Council Election Committee minute book, 1907.

(8) *Kent Trades and Labour Federation.* Unspecified number of minute books.

(9) *Medway Joint Labour Council.* Minute book, 1936-40.

(10) *Leyton Shop Stewards' Committee.* Minute book, 1944-45.

(11) *Social Democratic Federation.* Hackney and Kingsland Branch, minute books, 1903-06.

(12) *British Socialist Party.* North West Ham Branch, minute book, June 1917-Jan. 1919.

(*c*) Personal papers. Among the items are:

(1) James Connolly papers. An important collection but by no means complete.

(2) Maud Brown papers. This collection consists of an envelope of photographs, together with much pamphlet material, but no archival source material.

(3) A letter from Eleanor Marx regarding a Socialist meeting in the Midlands.

(4) Last letter of the German Communist, Edgar André (photocopy).

(5) Letter from Mrs. Adelaide Knight, suffragette, in Holloway Prison, to her husband, 1906 (photocopy).

(6) Manuscript of article by H. M. Hyndman, 'Socialism, Trade Unionism and Political Action' (1900). The original is in the Institute of Marxism-Leninism, Moscow. The article is printed with a commentary in the *Quarterly Bulletin*, No. 40, of the Marx Memorial Library, 1966. (photocopies).

(7) Friedrich Engels: microfilm of articles of apprenticeship, deed of partnership and of dissolution. (Originals are said to be with a Manchester firm of solicitors.)

In addition, the Library possesses duplicated news-sheets issued by strike committees and local councils of action during the General Strike (1926) and a few printed French Resistance papers.

Scholars wishing to use the collection should apply to the Librarian.

MASS-OBSERVATION

Mass-Observation (M.-O.) was founded in 1937 by Tom Harrisson, Charles Madge and Humphrey Jennings. Their aim was to give 'a true picture of Britain in the late 1930s' since they felt that the media did not adequately reflect prevailing public feelings. The operation formed two distinct parts: one part concentrated upon a study of 'Worktown' and was carried out by paid professional staff over a period of years. 'Worktown' was based mainly on Bolton, but was also a conglomerate of other Lancashire towns. The other part of the operation covered the whole of Britain, and panels of 'observers' were recruited to report upon themselves through directives issued by M.-O. The information sought ranged from buying and drinking habits to rumours current at any given time. The two parts of the operation were separate but co-ordinated in order to provide a detailed documentary account, both objective and subjective, of British life as it was then lived. After the outbreak of World War II the 'observers' were asked to keep diaries rather than to rely on directives sent from M.-O. These were kept throughout the war and subsequently returned to M.-O., some as late as 1967. Additionally, the M.-O. panel carried out in-depth studies of constituencies where by-elections were held. Client work played a large part in financing M.-O., particularly after the outbreak of war, when one of the major clients was the Ministry of Information who commissioned M.-O. to carry out surveys on air-raids, official propaganda of all sorts, civilian morale and other matters of public concern. M.-O. ceased this kind of work in 1949 and has full documentation covering private opinion and attitudes during the period 1937-49.

Mass-Observation still exists, but as a commercial market research company, Mass Observation (U.K.) Ltd.

Papers

The M.-O. archive is now the property of Tom Harrisson and is on loan to the University of Sussex. It covers the years 1937-49. Approximately 80 per cent of the archive has survived in good condition; this breaks down into three categories:

(i)   *The reports from observers.* These are in some 1,000 boxes, each of which is slowly being catalogued. Each box will contain a detailed description of its contents with cross-referencing. A master index is being established which will give the topic covered, the box number, file letter, section number, e.g. 1/A/2, which enables the information to be easily retrieved.

(ii) *The war diaries.* These run from 1944 to 1967 (the last date on which a diary was returned). They are at present uncatalogued but arranged by diarist and date with a card index.

(iii) *Client and other work.* These form 2-3 per cent of the whole collection and are contained in 4 x 4-drawer filing cabinets. They are typewritten reports, prepared mainly for clients. They are arranged by date, and each file is numbered. There is a complete index to this section of the archive, much of which refers to World War II on the home front.

In addition to the M.-O. archive there are the papers of Mrs. Mary Adams (Director of Home Intelligence, 1939-41, at the Ministry of Information). There are approximately eleven file boxes which are arranged but have yet to be indexed in detail. This particular collection is useful to M.-O. since it provides an insight into the M.O.I. use of M.-O. and related research.

Access is at present granted on written application to Tom Harrisson, D.S.O., O.B.E. (c/o the University Library, University of Sussex), but owing to difficulties of space, control of the archive and the friable nature of much of the material, the M.-O. archive is not yet readily available, although it is hoped that a Leverhulme grant for four years will help this position.

METHODIST MISSIONARY SOCIETY
25 Marylebone Road London NW1
The Methodist Missionary Society was founded in 1786 and has been active in all parts of the world up to the present day.

Papers

The substantial archives at the Society's headquarters have been carefully catalogued.

1. *Home Affairs*
Minute books of the General Committee date from 1798 to 1964, with certain gaps covered by a series of 'rough' minute books. A number of special committees, for example those relating to finance, home organisation, temperance and social welfare, medical mission, and women's work, kept their own minute books, of which a large proportion have been preserved. The papers relating to candidates do not extend beyond 1910, and the main series of correspondence is mostly 19th century. More recent records are found with the Home Organisation papers, including material relating to annual meetings (1906-67), conferences (1912-71) and young people's organisations.

2. *Overseas Affairs*
The collection of papers is divided according to geographical area. The series are by no means complete or up to date, but there is a fair amount of material relating to the 20th century. Two general categories relating to Central Africa and West Africa are supplemented by series of papers on Gambia, Gold Coast, Kenya, Nigeria, Rhodesia, Sierra Leone, South Africa and Zambia. The papers include correspondence, area sub-committee minutes, synod minutes, biographical papers, maps and plans. The American series relates to British Guiana, British Honduras, Canada and the United States (19th century), the Dominican Republic, Haiti, Panama and the West Indies. The large Asian collection covers Burma, Ceylon, China and Hong Kong, and India. Further series record the Society's work in Australia, New Zealand and the South Sea Islands during the 19th century. Papers relating to European countries and the Middle East are also preserved.

3. *Auxiliaries, Other Societies and Unofficial Papers*
This collection covers minutes of District Auxiliaries in Britain, the papers of local societies (19th century) and the records of former branches of the Methodist Church, including the United Methodists and the Primitive Methodists.

Availability

The records may be used by researchers on written application to the Society's Archivist.

MILITARY COMMENTATORS' CIRCLE

c/o 27 Sispara Gardens London SW18 1LG

Formed originally during World War II, the group was revived by Captain Eugene Hinterhoff in 1953.

Papers

A number of files (1953-70) in the B. H. Liddell Hart Collection relates to the Military Commentators' Circle. There are seven files of correspondence, mainly about the administration and affairs of the group. Although lists of speakers (mainly from abroad) are retained, no records of talks or discussions were kept. The minute books, with committee notes, records of A.G.M.s, elections and resignations, remain with the Secretary.

Availability

The Liddell Hart papers are not yet open, but they are eventually to be housed at King's College, London. Enquiries should be addressed to the Archivist, Centre for Military Archives, King's College, and to the Secretary of the group.

MODERN RECORDS CENTRE

University of Warwick Library Coventry CV4 7AL

The Modern Records Centre was established in the Library of Warwick University in October 1973, with the aid of a grant from the Leverhulme Trust. The aim of the Centre is to ensure the preservation and collection of primary sources for British political, social and industrial history, and it has already secured the deposit of a variety of collections of importance to students of twentieth century history. Many of these are mentioned in the text of this book. As the Centre is so recently established, it is not possible to provide a comprehensive list of archives deposited there. However, the Modern Records Centre issues a quarterly *Information Bulletin* (No. 1, April 1974) and this lists recent acquisitions. Enquiries should be directed to the Archivist, Modern Records Centre.

MUSICIANS' UNION

29 Catherine Place Buckingham Gate London SW1

The union was established in Manchester in 1893, as the Amalgamated Musicians' Union. In 1921 amalgamation was effected with the National Union of Professional Orchestral Musicians, and the name was changed to the present form. There had been previous organisations, for example the Manchester Musical Artistes' Protective Association, 1874-76, and the Birmingham Orchestral Association, 1874-78.

Papers

A good collection of records is preserved at the union's headquarters. A complete run of Executive Committee and sub-committee minutes from July 1921 to date is introduced by the minutes of a joint meeting on 1 July 1921 of the Executives of the Amalgamated Musicians' Union and the National Orchestral Union. Minutes of the A.M.U. Executive Committee (1894-1921) have also been preserved. Complete records of membership date from about 1930, and rule books go back to 1894. Reports and journals include: monthly report and journal, Jan. 1895-July 1921; monthly report of the Musicians' Union from Aug. 1921;

Musicians' Union reports and journal; Executive Committee reports to biennial conferences, 1945 to date; *The Musician*, 'Voice of the Musicians' Union', from July 1950 to date.

Certain Scottish branch records have also survived. The Glasgow branch, formed in about 1895, has Minutes of branch meetings (1902-1907, 1915 to date) and committee meetings (1918 to date). Minutes of the Scottish District Council for the years 1904 (foundation meeting) to date are also available.

Minutes (1874-76) of the Manchester branch of the Musical Artistes' Protection Association have been deposited with the Musicians' Union records.

The history of the union has been written up in a Calendar and Diary of References, published in 1917, and in 'The Story of the Amalgamated Musicians' Union', four articles by E. S. Teale, reprinted from the *Musicians' Journal*, 1929-30.

Availability

Persons wishing to see the records should apply to the General Secretary of the union.

NATIONAL ALLOTMENTS AND GARDENS SOCIETY LTD.
22 High Street Flitwick Beds. MK45 1DT

The Society was founded in 1930 as an amalgamation of the National Union of Allotment Holders Ltd. and the Agricultural Organisation Society. It is the recognised central body of organised allotment-holders and leisure gardeners in England and Wales and has some 1,700 societies and over 230 local authorities affiliated to it. The main aims of the National Society are the formation of allotment and gardening associations, safeguarding of their interests through improved legislation, and advising and assisting generally on all problems which face the amateur gardener today. The primary object of the Society is to try and ensure that allotments and gardens are made available to all those who require them and to instil a better understanding of the fact that gardening is a recreation for the mind and body as well as a source of economic wealth to the nation.

Papers

The Society has not retained its old records. The best source for the history of the Society is the collection of pamphlets, of a publicity and propaganda nature, published by the Society. These may be consulted at the office of the Society, but will also be available at the British Library.

NATIONAL AND LOCAL GOVERNMENT OFFICERS ASSOCIATION
NALGO House 8 Harewood Row London NW1

The Association was formed in 1905, and amalgamated in 1930 with the National Association of Poor Law Officers and in 1963 with the British Gas Staff Association. The union now has almost half a million members.

Papers

Many records of the Association, which had been used by Alec Spoor in his book *White Collar Union: Sixty Years of NALGO* (1967) were apparently destroyed in late 1973. The surviving records, including minutes of the National Executive Council, the Finance and General Purposes Committee, and the Service

Conditions and Organisation Committee, are now in the care of the Modern Records Centre, University of Warwick Library. Signed minutes of the British Gas Staff Association, 1946-63, and the National Poor Law Officers' Association, 1896-1930, are also in the care of the Modern Records Centre.

Availability

Applications should be made to the Archivist, Modern Records Centre, University of Warwick Library.

NATIONAL ASSOCIATION FOR MATERNAL AND CHILD WELFARE
Tavistock House North Tavistock Square London WC1H 9JG

The Association developed from the Infant Welfare Movement which began at the end of the nineteenth century as a result of widespread concern at the high rate of infant mortality. A Child Welfare Centre was established in St Helens in 1899. The first London centre, at Battersea, was opened in 1902, and by 1910 there were 100 such centres operating in the United Kingdom. In 1911 the Association of Infant, Welfare and Maternity Centres was formed to assist these centres, and in 1912 the National Association for the Prevention of Infant Mortality and for the Welfare of Infancy was established to co-ordinate the activities of the various organisations working in the same field. In 1938 the above-mentioned associations amalgamated to form the National Association of Maternity and Child Welfare Centres and for the Prevention of Infant Mortality. This name was later changed to the National Association for Maternal and Child Welfare. From its foundation the Association was closely involved with the National League for Physical Education and Improvement (founded in 1905, and known from 1918 to its dissolution in 1928 as the National League for Health, Maternity and Child Welfare), which acted as a link between many voluntary national organisations concerned with safeguarding motherhood and the health of the young.

Papers

The National Association has retained many of its records at its offices. These include minutes of the National Conferences on Infant Mortality, 1906-12, which were in effect the predecessors of the present Association; minutes of Executive and other committees of the National Association, 1912 to date; minutes of the Association of Infant Welfare and Maternity Centres; bound copies of Annual Conference Reports, 1924 to the present; and copies of Annual Reports from 1914. Copies of the Annual Survey, 1966-70, also survive.

Availability

All enquiries concerning these records should be directed to the General Secretary.

See also: *National Society of Children's Nurseries.*

NATIONAL ASSOCIATION OF COLLIERY OVERMEN, DEPUTIES AND SHOTFIRERS
29-31 Euston Road London NW1

The General Federation of Firemen's Examiners and Deputies Associations of Great Britain was formed in 1910 as an amalgamation of various area associations. It adopted its present title in 1947.

167

Papers

Certain records, including annual reports, correspondence, agreement records, 1910 to date, are retained at the offices of the Association.

Availability

These records are available on prior application to the General Secretary.

NATIONAL ASSOCIATION OF PROPERTY OWNERS
14-16 Bressenden Place London SW1E 5DG

The Association was founded in late 1969 as an amalgamation of the National Federation of Property Owners and Ratepayers (founded 1888), the Property Owners' Protection Association (founded 1903) and the Association of Land and Property Owners (founded in 1939 as the Association of London Property Owners, which changed its name on amalgamation with the Land Union in 1953).

Papers

The surviving records of all the constituent bodies are now in the care of the National Association of Property Owners, whose own records since 1969 begin a new series.

1. *National Federation of Property Owners and Ratepayers*

The records of the Federation were transferred to Bressenden Place on amalgamation. They consist largely of a number of parcels, containing committee minute books and papers. The main series, of Administrative and Finance Committee minutes, run from 1902-69, and these are supplemented by minutes of various sub-committees. Also surviving are reports of conferences, bound in volumes, from 1894-1926, and annual and half-yearly reports, similarly bound, from 1888-1928. From 1928 the main source for the Federation's history is the run of its journal, *Property Gazette*, known as *Property* from 1949-68, when it amalgamated with the *Property Owners' Journal*.

2. *Property Owners' Protection Association*

The main available source for this Association is the run of its journal, the *Property Owners' Journal*, from 1903-69.

3. *Association of Land and Property Owners*

This is a useful collection with a complete run of Council minutes from 1940 to its last meeting on 8 Dec. 1969, and a number of parcels of A.G.M. papers for the same period. Other records include: a variety of cash books; council attendance book for the 1950s; various papers on the formation of ALPO, on amalgamation; a variety of administrative material, etc. There is a run of ALPO's journal, known as *Current Record*, 1946-50, thereafter as the *Real Estate Journal* (incorporating the *Land Union Journal*).

4. *Land Union*

The Union was founded in 1910 as a response to the Lloyd George land policies. It amalgamated with ALPO in mid-1953. Two minute books have been retained with the ALPO records.

Availability

Applications regarding all the above records should be made to the Director, National Association of Property Owners.

NATIONAL ASSOCIATION OF SCHOOLMASTERS
Swan Court Waterhouse Street Hemel Hempstead Herts

The Association was formed in 1919 and is now the second largest teachers' union.

Papers

It is understood that many earlier records were destroyed by enemy action in the Second World War. The bulk of surviving records to 1961 has been deposited in the Modern Records Centre, University of Warwick. They include minute books of 3 local associations, Leicester (1920-26) Newcastle-on-Tyne (1921-26) and London (1919-38), as well as the Finance and General Purposes Committee of the National Association (1923-5), conference reports and proceedings and bound volumes of the Association's journal from 1921. A collection of press-cuttings and specimens of all propaganda and educational pamphlets had been kept and was included in the deposit. Only a limited amount of correspondence was available, but there is documentation covering legal and quasi-legal cases such as the Sunderland school meals case, the McCarthy Report on the Durham Dispute, the Wood Report on the Teesside Dispute and some salary disputes resolved in court. Most of the Burnham reports regarding salary negotiations are also available.

Availability

Applications should be made to the Archivist, Modern Records Centre, University of Warwick.

NATIONAL CAMPAIGN FOR THE ABOLITION OF CAPITAL PUNISHMENT
2 Amen Court London EC4

The National Campaign was launched in 1955. It was the successor to a series of organisations campaigning to abolish the death penalty, dating back to the early 19th century. From 1822 until the 1860s the Society for the Abolition of Capital Punishment pursued the campaign, and a society with the same name campaigned from 1902 until World War I. The National Council for the Abolition of the Death Penalty was established in 1925, and this was the chief campaigning body until 1948. Thereafter the work of the Council was continued by the sub-committee on the Death Penalty of the *Howard League for Penal Reform* (q.v.). One of the predecessor organisations of the League, the Howard Association, had advocated the abolition of the death penalty since its foundation in 1866.

Papers

The National Campaign for the Abolition of Capital Punishment has retained a file of minutes dating back to 1955, together with correspondence and press cuttings from 1957. Enquiries regarding these papers should be made in writing to the Chairman of the Campaign.

Papers of the Rt. Hon. Lord Gardiner, former Chairman of the National Campaign for the Abolition of Capital Punishment, are deposited in the British Library (Add. MSS. 56,455-56,463). These concern his involvement in various activities relating to the abolition of the death penalty, 1946-69, and consist of nine volumes of correspondence.

No large corpus of records relating to previous organisations appears to survive. Reference should be made to the records of the Howard League for Penal Reform.

The National Council for the Abolition of the Death Penalty published the following: annual reports, 1926-48; *News of the Campaign*, 1929-31; and *The Penal Reformer*, published quarterly by the Howard League and the National Council, 1934-39.

NATIONAL CHAMBER OF TRADE
Enterprise House Henley-on-Thames Oxon. RG9 1TV

This was founded in 1897 to promote and protect the interests of the retail trade.

Papers

The National Chamber of Trade has retained many of its records covering much of its history. These are unsorted and at the time of writing were in store. No further information is available.

Availability

These records are not presently available. Enquiries should be directed to the General Secretary.

No comprehensive survey of the records of local Chambers of Trade was undertaken, but the following information may be of use:

Bradford. Minutes date back to the Chamber's inauguration in 1903, and bound volumes of the journal date from 1904.
Leeds. Secretaryship is exercised by Leeds Chamber of Commerce: they have records of the Chamber of Trade dating back only to 1941.
Manchester. Minute books date back to 1941.
Sheffield. Minutes date from its formation in 1963.

NATIONAL CHRISTIAN EDUCATION COUNCIL
Robert Denholm House Nutfield Redhill Surrey

The National Sunday School Union was founded in 1803 as a response to the Sunday School movement started some twenty years earlier by Robert Raikes. It adopted its present title in 1966. It is an inter-denominational body, which aims: 'to win children and young people for the service of God through the saving knowledge of God's Holy Word and the saving power of the Lord Jesus Christ'. Its function is now, as it has been throughout its history, to promote education in Christian principles, and to this purpose the N.C.E.C. offers its affiliates in many thousands of churches and Sunday schools a training in the techniques of religious education as well as financial aid, and acts as a publisher of literature on Christian education. The International Bible Reading Association is an integral part of the N.C.E.C.

Papers

Although certain records were destroyed during World War II, papers dating back to the early years of the Sunday School movement are retained in Robert Denholm House. The bulk of these consists of minute books. The earliest covers the period 1802-14 and records one of the first attempts at a local Sunday School society, at 'Kingsland, Newington and adjacent villages'. There is also a minute book of the Sunday School Union, 1810-14, and this period is also covered in another volume, 1810-17. The main run of the minutes of the governing body of the Union, known variously as Committee, Council and Assembly, extend from 1822 to date, in 27 volumes. These form the fullest record of the Sunday School Union's activities, and include reports from various subsidiary committees, including the executive board of Management, the Business and other committees. The minutes of these various committees are also retained separately in parcels, many of which date back to the 1920s. The Council Business Papers are retained in volumes from 1884-1910, and from 1940 to the present.

Other minutes include those of the Ladies' Committee for the early part of the 20th century, and for the I.B.R.A. and Missionary Committee from 1892, as well as occasional minute books for other committees. Also surviving are the following which relate to national activities: a volume of copies of in-letters, 1837-43, a correspondence book for 1895, and a volume of copies of out-letters, 1907-08; a report of deputations for c. 1845; a commonplace book of notes, 1828-44; a volume of the names of members of the Council, 1901-60; a record of the Joint Conference of the N.S.S.U. Board of Management and the Executive of the Council of Christian Education, 1935; an account book of the School Buildings Loan Fund, 1913-48; and visitors' books for the various buildings of the N.S.S.U. There is an almost complete set of annual reports from 1837 to the present. The run of the Union's journal, *Sunday School Chronicle*, 1878-1966, is also a useful source. This has been replaced recently by a 'house journal', *Link*, which acts as an organ of communication between the various groups of N.C.E.C.

In addition to these records of the central organisation, various records of auxiliary and local Sunday School Unions are deposited at Robert Denholm House. The largest collection are the records of the West London Auxiliary Union and consist of a series of minute books. The earliest of the original books is a damaged volume for 1825-27. What appears to be a copy volume made in the 1890s covers the years 1814-20. Another volume covers the period 1841-48, and there is an almost complete run of minutes from 1869-1958. A secretary's 'private minute book' is useful for 1896-1912. The annual reports of this Auxiliary date from 1814 and there is an incomplete run up to 1952.

Certain South London Auxiliary minute books and attendance books also survive, and these date back to 1851, covering the middle decades of the 19th century. Similarly, the North London Auxiliary's records date back to 1845 and appear to extend to the 1920s. Local Sunday School Unions' records include those of the Sydenham and Forest Hill branch for the 1870s, Southend, Spalding (2 books, 1928-63) and St. John's Wood, 1903-10.

In addition to these manuscript sources, Robert Denholm House has a useful collection of printed works concerning the Sunday School movement, many published by the N.S.S.U. Many of these, such as the *Graded School Quarterlies*, are very useful in tracing the development of teaching methods.

The Robert Raikes Historical Society, whose Secretary, Mr. Bentley, is an Executive Officer of the N.C.E.C., is also based at Robert Denholm House. This Society has as its concern the preservation of records of the Sunday School movement and has supplemented the N.C.E.C. records with an interesting small collection of papers, pamphlets, books, etc., on Sunday Schools.

A brief history of the N.S.S.U. has been written by Cecil Northcott: *For Britain's Children* (N.S.S.U., 1954).

Availability

Access is given on prior application being made to the N.C.E.C.

NATIONAL COMMITTEE FOR THE PREVENTION OF DESTITUTION

This was established in 1909 as the National Committee for the Break-up of the Poor Law, to promote reforms on the lines of those advocated in the Minority Report of the Poor Law Commission. Beatrice Webb was throughout the chief inspiration of the Committee's work. By 1912 it was clear that its primary aims had failed, but it continued its activities until the outbreak of World War I.

Papers

The best sources for the history of the Committee can be found at B.L.P.E.S. The records there include: manuscript minutes of the Committee's Finance and General Purposes Sub-committee, 1909-12, and of the Meetings and Membership Sub-committee, 1909-12; a series of lecture notes for use by Committee speakers; a series of leaflets describing the work of the Committee, 1910; and copies of the Committee's journal, *The Crusade*. The Committee also published reports of proceedings of the National Conference on the Prevention of Destitution, 1911, and copies of these are also at B.L.P.E.S. The Passfield papers, also in this library, are a further source. The Beatrice Webb diaries are particularly useful. Relevant material may also be found in the Fabian Society papers at Nuffield College, Oxford.

Availability

Application should be made to the Librarian, B.L.P.E.S; or, in the case of the Fabian Society material, to the Librarian, Nuffield College, Oxford.

NATIONAL COUNCIL FOR CIVIL LIBERTIES
186 King's Cross Road London WC1

The Council was founded in 1934. It works to promote the rights of the individual, to oppose racial, political, religious or other forms of discrimination and abuses of power.

Papers

Records of the Council are held by Hull University Library. These form a very important collection containing both administrative and case records. A microfilm of N.C.C.L. minute books covers the years 1944-63; annual reports run from 1938-39, 1946-47, 1947-48, 1948-49, 1959-60. Later reports were published in *Civil Liberty*. The Library has a full run of *Civil Liberty* from April 1937. A series described as 'Archives' dates from 1934-52, and contains correspondence relating to the formation and running of the N.C.C.L.; general correspondence; duplicated circulars issued by the Council; notes on deputations; pamphlet material; material on Fascist activities in the 1930s; 'minutes of Proceedings of an Inquiry into Disturbances in Thurloe Square', July 1936; papers on fund-raising activities and the financial situation of the Council; material on wartime activities; correspondence regarding the foundation of branches; committee papers; papers relating to national and international Conferences, etc.; and papers relating to the formation of policy. A large number of files relates to the activities of 'local groups', and covers the period from 1937.

The main series of files relate to the actual civil liberties work of the N.C.C.L. and the topics covered include: bail, 1936-38; police activities, 1934-38; conscientious objection, 1939-51; 'wartime' activities, 1939-45; democratic rights for the Armed Forces; problems involved in the hiring of halls, and policy towards the police; police activities generally, 1934-60; foreign and colonial matters, 1935-56; rights of women, children and young persons; conscription; 'International Organisations and the United Nations'; elections, 1935-50; merchant seamen, 1942-48; rights of council house tenants, 1948-57, and rent tribunals, 1953-54; capital punishment; race legislation; deportation; aliens legislation; 'Political Discrimination', 1934-60; libel and legal cases from 1935; 'Films and Censorship', 1934-60; freedom of speech and assembly, from 1939; 'The Law', 1937 onwards; mental health; discrimination in employment; drugs; 'freedom of travel'; 'Security', 1947-58. Some 60 files relate to Fascist activities and anti-Semitism, 1939 to the 1960s, and these include material on Fascist activity in the East End of London in the 1930s, anti-Fascist demonstrations, 1937-38, and campaigns to counter anti-Semitic activities from the 1930s onwards. A considerable number of files relates to foreign and Commonwealth affairs, and these chiefly date from the 1940s. 'United Kingdom' and 'Ireland' files contain considerable information on Scottish and Welsh nationalism, the situation in Northern Ireland, the activities of the Irish Republican Army, etc. Other files contain records of court cases, and material relating to the administration of justice.

This collection, in other words, provides a valuable insight into the work of the Council, and the development of civil liberties at home and abroad.

Availability

Enquiries concerning this collection should be directed to the Librarian, Hull University Library.

Note

A small collection of material relating to an earlier National Council for Civil Liberties, active during World War I, was deposited by the late Raymond Postgate at the International Institute of Social History, Herengracht 262-266, Amsterdam-C. It consists of the carbon copy of a typescript with reports about tribunals (short case histories of conscientious objectors, reports about the behaviour of the tribunals, the attitudes of military and non-military members); a dissertation about civil liberties under the Defence of the Realm Act, 1914-16; and about industrial conscription; reports about the treatment of conscientious objectors, etc. Some cyclostyled material of the N.C.C.L. is also available.

The collection can be consulted on request to the International Institute of Social History.

NATIONAL COUNCIL OF LABOUR

This was established in 1921 as a National Joint Council linking the Labour Party and the Trades Union Congress. In 1942 the Co-operative Party joined the Council, which then adopted its present form.

Papers

Minutes, correspondence, agenda and other documents can be found at the *Trades Union Congress* archive (q.v.). The archive of the Labour Party at Transport House similarly has relevant papers.

Availability

As for Labour Party and T.U.C.

NATIONAL COUNCIL OF LABOUR COLLEGES

The National Council of Labour Colleges was established in 1921 as the culmination of a movement for 'independent working-class education'. An important step in this movement had been the foundation in 1908 of the Plebs' League (1908-27) which played an important part in the strike of Ruskin College students in 1909, and the consequent foundation of the Central Labour College, first at Oxford, and later based in London. The Council continued the work of this residential college (closed in 1929), and co-ordinated the movement's increasing local activities. The N.C.L.C. survived without the aid of state grants, and came frequently into conflict with the *Workers' Educational Association* (q.v.). The N.C.L.C.'s educational work was merged with the Education Department of the *Trades Union Congress* (q.v.) in 1964. An N.C.L.C. Publishing Society was established in 1929.

Papers

Records of the National Council of Labour Colleges, including material relating to the Plebs' League and the Central Labour College, have been deposited in the National Library of Scotland. For this reason, descriptions of these groups of papers appear under a single heading. They comprise some 100 boxes of manuscript material. A set of Plebs' League and N.C.L.C. pamphlets and books, and an almost complete set of *Plebs*, have also been deposited, in the Department of Printed Books.

The following description of the archive follows the lines of the inventory drawn up by the National Library, which follows as far as possible the original filing. Some 35 boxes contain the 'main files'. These include correspondence and papers of the Plebs' League, 1919-29, and of the Central Labour College from the Ruskin College strike to 1929; a variety of correspondence on courses with individuals and organisations; papers on organisation and finance, and correspondence of the Scottish Labour College, 1919-67; correspondence and papers of the N.C.L.C. from 1920; and papers relating to relations with outside bodies such as the Labour Party, the T.U.C., the W.E.A., the Communist Party, various international bodies, etc. Other papers in this series concern general problems of adult education, the history of the Labour College movement, press files containing correspondence with the press and cuttings from the 1920s, and boxes of material — for example, manuscript and typescript drafts — on publications.

The minutes of the Executive Council and annual conferences cover the history of the N.C.L.C.

Quarterly and annual reports to the Executive of the N.C.L.C. on the work of the Postal Courses Department run from 1923-64, minutes of the Central Labour College house meetings cover the period 1910-15, minutes of the Manchester Plebs' League Council run from 1918-20, minutes of the Scottish National Committee run from 1923, and there is a substantial collection of minutes of various divisions and colleges, and of the N.C.L.C. Publishing Society.

Other boxes and files contain a collection of lectures and notes for courses from the 1920s; material on the various educational schemes originated by the N.C.L.C., including postal courses, class work, etc.; miscellaneous circulars on organisation of tutorial work from 1923; statistics on tutorial classes for the same period; and correspondence with and papers relating to the regions of N.C.L.C. The National Library is also receiving bound copies of general circulars which were sent out to all the Labour Colleges and organisers, and also bound copies of the organiser's circulars.

Availability

The records are not generally available pending the appearance of a history of the N.C.L.C. by J. P. M. Millar and Dr. J. Lowe. Enquiries should be directed to the National Library of Scotland.

NATIONAL COUNCIL OF SOCIAL SERVICE
26 Bedford Square London WC1B 3HU

The Council was founded in 1919 to promote and organise co-operation in all aspects of voluntary social work. Although it obtains financial aid from the government, it still relies largely on voluntary support. It pioneered the Citizens' Advice Bureau service, rural community councils, Councils of Social Service and community associations, through which it works on a local basis. Nationally, some 160 voluntary organisations are members of the Council, which sponsors among others the National Council for Voluntary Youth Services, the Women's Group on Public Welfare, the National Association of Women's Clubs, the Churches and Religious Bodies Consultative Group and the Standing Conferences for Local History.

Papers

The Council has retained a full collection of records, dating back to its inception. These include formal records, such as minutes of the Executive Committee and the various sub-committees, and papers relating to the various activities of the Council. These latter records are retained in the Council's Registry and are filed alphabetically by function or activity, e.g. 'Appeals', 'Broadcasting', 'Finance', 'Health', 'Immigrants'. The largest grouping of records are those marked 'Village Halls', which consist of a large amount of papers and correspondence relating to local activities. Full records relating to the following important topics are retained: the British National Conference on Social Work; the International Conference on Social Work; the Councils of Social Service, including records of the London C.S.S.s; the Women's Group on Public Welfare, Women's Clubs, etc. In short, records relating to the various aspects of the Council's work throughout its history have been retained and are an important source for examining the development of the voluntary social services.

The Council issues annual reports, copies of which have been retained, and publishes various pamphlets and journals, viz. a *Newsletter* and *Social Service Quarterly Journal.*

Availability

It is not possible to provide general access to the Council's records, but particular requests may be sent to the Administrator for consideration.

NATIONAL COUNCIL OF WOMEN OF GREAT BRITAIN
36 Lower Sloane Street London SW1W 8BP

The National Council of Women acts as a co-ordinating body for a number of women's organisations. Its origins were in the 1870s, with the foundations of Ladies' Associations for the Care of Friendless Girls. From 1888 these Associations held conferences, where papers on various topics relating to the women's movement were delivered. At the same time, Unions of Women Workers were being formed. From 1892 the conferences and related activities were co-ordinated by a Central Conference Committee, and Central Conference Council of the National Union of Women Workers was established in 1894. In 1895 this became the National Union of Women Workers of Great Britain and Ireland and in 1918 the National Council of Women of Great Britain and Ireland. In 1929 it adopted the present form of its title. From 1897 the organisation has formed the British section of the International Council of Women.

Papers

The National Council of Women has retained many of its records, though the bulk of these appears to consist of printed material. A manuscript minute book, describing the origins of the Central Conference Committee, and including reports of executive meetings, 1892-1900, survives. Other early minute books have not been traced, and recent minutes are regarded as confidential. Correspondence is not generally retained, though a small collection of the more interesting letters does survive. However, the activities of the Council can be traced in the printed reports, of which the Council retains a full collection.

These include reports of the Central Conference of Women Workers from 1888, which include transcripts of papers delivered; handbooks and reports of the National Union of Women Workers, which include reports of business meetings, etc.; and reports of international conferences from 1888. Two useful collections published in book form are Mrs. Mary Wright Sewell (ed.), *Report of Council Transactions, 1899-1904*, in two volumes; and *Transactions of the International Congress of Women, 1899*, edited by the Countess of Aberdeen.

The Council retains bound volumes of its journals: *An Occasional Paper* (1908-20), *N.C.W. News* (1921-31), *Women in Council* (1931-72), *Council* (from 1972).

Availability

Enquiries should be directed to the General Secretary.

NATIONAL EDUCATION ASSOCIATION

Founded in 1889, the Association had its roots in the *Liberation Society* (q.v.) and enjoyed strong Nonconformist and Liberal Party support. It aimed to promote a system of free, popularly-controlled, non-sectarian education.

Papers

Records of the Association, 1889-1959, have been deposited at the Greater London Record Office. These include minutes of the Association to 1959, and a large quantity of pamphlets and books on educational matters, particularly on religious education, for the first half of the 20th century, but chiefly for the 1930s and 1940s. The W. J. Rowland Collection at Dr. Williams' Library includes correspondence, press cuttings and leaflets relating to the N.E.A. These papers and other N.E.A. materials are detailed by Arnold P. Derrington in 'The National Education Association of Great Britain, 1889-1959: A Short Account and Bibliography', *History of Education Society Bulletin*, No. 11, Spring 1973.

Availability

Enquiries should be addressed to the Archivist at the Greater London Record Office, and for the Rowland papers to the Librarian at Dr. Williams' Library.

NATIONAL FARMERS' UNION OF ENGLAND AND WALES
25-31 Knightsbridge London SW1

The union was founded in 1908, with the aim of promoting and protecting the interests of those engaged in agriculture and horticulture.

Papers

Records retained include Council minutes since 1908, minutes of the Executive Committee, 1909-19, and of the General Purposes Committee from 1919 onwards. Published material with the union includes copies of the yearbook, 1910 to date; N.F.U. *Broadsheet*, 1921-47; the *N.F.U. Record*, 1922-47; and *British Farmer* from 1948. The archival records of the Union are now deposited in the Institute of Agricultural History (q.v.).

Availability

Application should be made to the Institute of Agricultural History.

NATIONAL FARMERS' UNION OF SCOTLAND
17 Grosvenor Crescent Edinburgh EH12 5EN

Papers

Minute books survive from 1913, and annual reports date from 1919. Copies of the *Farming Leader* are also retained.

Availability

Applications should be made to the Organiser and Publicity Officer.

NATIONAL FEDERATION OF BUILDING TRADES EMPLOYERS
82 New Cavendish Street London W1M 8AD

The Federation, founded in 1878, is the central organisation of employers in the building trade dealing with all commercial and industrial aspects.

Papers

The Federation has copies of its minutes and annual reports since its inception. More ephemeral papers are destroyed after ten years. Copies of the Federation's journal, the *National Builder*, run from 1921.

Availability

Applications should be made to the Secretary. Facilities for research, however, are severely limited and access is not guaranteed.

NATIONAL FEDERATION OF OLD AGE PENSIONS ASSOCIATIONS
91 Preston New Road Blackburn Lancs.

The Federation developed from a number of old-age pensions associations which grew up, particularly in the Lancashire and London areas, in the late 1930s. The Federation itself was established in 1940, and has as its aim the advancement of the conditions of old-age pensioners.

Records survive in the Federation's offices, and include minutes, annual conference reports and certain correspondence. There is a complete run of the Federation's journal, *Pensioners' Voice*, since 1940.

Availability

Applications should be made to the General Secretary.

NATIONAL FEDERATION OF WOMEN'S INSTITUTES
39 Eccleston Street London SW1

The first Women's Institute was founded in Ontario, Canada, in 1897. The first W.I. in the United Kingdom was founded in Anglesey in 1915. The National Federation was established in 1917 with some 137 Women's Institutes as members. Today the figure is over 9,000.

The main purpose of the Women's Institute is to improve and develop conditions of rural life; to provide for the fuller education of countrywomen in citizenship, in public questions both national and international, in music, drama and other cultural subjects, also to secure instruction and training in all branches of agriculture, handicrafts, domestic science, health and social welfare; to promote international understanding among countrywomen; to provide a centre for social intercourse and activities; and to develop co-operative enterprise.

Papers

The National Federation has retained many of its records dating back to 1917. These include minutes and papers of the Executive Committee and sub-committees, verbatim reports of A.G.M.s and complete copies of the annual reports. Files on most of the 9,000 institutes are retained. It is hoped that these may be transferred to microfilm in the future. The work of the Federation is, in fact, fully documented. These records are retained in the Registry of the Federation's headquarters. The Press Office has a collection of agency press cuttings (though most of these appear to be recent), as well as copies of official press releases.

Each of the administrative departments publishes pamphlets and leaflets on its particular theme, e.g. crafts, public affairs, speech and drama, music. Records of these are on file since 1948. The journal of the Federation is *Home and Country*. This is an independent publication, based at 11A King's Road, London SW3 and copies of the journal since its inception in 1919 are retained there. The headquarters also has copies dating back to the 1920s. The Federation circulates a newsletter, *N.F.W.I. News,* and the sub-committee bulletin. These are distributed to area officials and replace earlier circulars, copies of which have been retained.

Every W.I. is affiliated not only to the National Federation but also to a County or Island Federation with its own administrative structure. These area organisations retain their own records.

Availability

Enquiries should be directed in writing in the first place to the Press and Public Relations Officer.

NATIONAL GRAPHICAL ASSOCIATION
Graphic House 63-67 Bromham Road Bedford

The Association was founded in 1964 by the previously independent Typographical Association and the London Typographical Society and amalgamated with the Association of Correctors of the Press, the National Society of Electro-typers and Stereotypers, the National Union of Press Telegraphists and the Association of Litho Printers.

Papers

Most surviving records of the Association, its predecessor organisations and the amalgamated societies have been deposited in the Modern Records Centre, University of Warwick. The records of the former London Typographical Society are particularly full. The Society was formed in 1848, as the London Society of Compositors. There had, however, been earlier organisations dating from 1801. In 1955 the Society amalgamated with the Printing Machine Managers' Trade Society, and the name was changed to London Typographical Society.

The records include: minute books of the London Society of Compositors dating from 1906, with one book for 1861-62. Committee minutes include Emigration (1853-57) and Political (1909-16). Agenda books cover the years 1915-47. Other important records are quarterly reports, annual reports and trade reports, all dating from 1848, with gaps. Details of membership, rules, wage negotiations and agreements, amalgamation schemes and legal cases are all recorded.

Also housed with these papers are the surviving records of several other organisations. These include:

London General Society of Compositors, 1826-34;

London Union of Compositors, 1834-45;

London Society of Compositors (Branch of National Typographical Association), 1845-48;

National Typographical Association, 1845-c. 1848;

Society of London Daily Newspaper Compositors, to 1853, when amalgamation was effected with the L.S.C.;

Printing Machine Managers' Trade Society, 1839-1955. This last collection covers minutes of Council and committees, annual reports and balance sheets (1882-1950), agenda books and rules.

The records of the National Society of Electrotypers and Stereotypers have been deposited in Cambridge University Library. These include: minutes of the Executive Sub-committee, 1912-63, and the National Council, 1912-63.

Availability

Applications should be made to the Archivist, Modern Records Centre, University of Warwick and to Cambridge University Library.

NATIONAL GUILDS LEAGUE

The League was founded in April 1915 to propagate the ideas of Guild Socialism, particularly among trade unionists. The ideas of Guild Socialism had been developed since 1912 in the columns of A. R. Orage's journal *New Age*, and by S. G. Hobson, and were expanded by a group of radical intellectuals, including G. D. H. Cole, in a series of books and pamphlets. Essentially the League advocated workers' control of industry, through a series of national Guilds, developing out of trade unions organised on industrial lines. These guilds would organise industry in association with the state, though after 1920 this was amended to read 'in association with other democratic functional organisations within the community'. The Russian Revolution and its aftermath split the movement, which increasingly relied on 'propaganda by experiment', i.e. producer guilds attempting to compete with private enterprise in a variety of trades. Building Guilds were established and a National Building Guild was set up in 1921. A National Guilds Council was set up to link these producer guilds, trade unions and the League. In 1923 this absorbed the League, but was itself wound up soon afterwards.

Papers

The columns of *New Age* are an invaluable source for the early development of Guild ideas. A considerable amount of material relating to the League itself has been deposited in two major libraries: Nuffield College Library, Oxford, and Hull University Library.

1. *Nuffield College*

Six boxes of papers and correspondence accumulated by J. P. Bedford cover the work of the League, the National Guilds Council, guilds in special localities and industries and topics of special interest to guild members. This collection includes minute books of the League (4 vols.), the Council (1 vol.), the N.G.L. London Group (5 vols.), and the N.G.L. Glasgow and District Group (1 vol.). A small note book with entries in G. D. H. Cole's handwriting relates to conferences of the League, 1920-24. The G. D. H. Cole papers at Nuffield College include correspondence and press cuttings, which are also relevant, as are various items in the collection of Cole's articles. The Library also has copies of the League's annual reports, 1916-22; the League's journal *The Guildsman*, 1916-21, known as *The Guild Socialist*, 1921-23, and *New Standards*, 1923-24; and copies of pamphlets and leaflets published by the League and by individual guilds, particularly in the agricultural and building industries.

2. *Hull University Library*

Several collections, largely on microfilm, relate to the work of participants in the Guild movement.

(a) *A. J. Penty.* Penty's book *The Restoration of the Guild System* (1906) was a forerunner of many Guild Socialist ideas. Records relating to his work include material on the N.G.L., miscellaneous correspondence, a collection of press cuttings, obituary letters and notices, and certain other miscellaneous material.

(b) *M. B. Reckitt.* Reckitt was a prominent member of the League. Records on microfilm include material on National Guilds, the Building Guilds and the Industrial Parliament Scheme; the National Building Guild and Guild of Builders (London) Ltd., 1922-23; the Furnishing Guild, Engineering Guild and Guild of Clothiers; certain material on the New Town Trust Ltd., the New Town Agricultural Guild Ltd., and Workers' Control League.

(c) *Malcolm Sparkes.* Sparkes was a Quaker businessman who played an important role in the work of the Building Guilds. His wife compiled a biographical memoir, 'Malcolm Sparkes — Constructive Pacifist' and a microfilm copy of this, together with various other items, is deposited in the Library.

(d) *F. W. Dalley.* Material on microfilm in this collection includes: correspondence with G. D. H. Cole, A. R. Orage, S. G. Hobson, H. B. Brougham and W. Laud; papers on the N.G.L., including annual reports, 1916-19; minutes of the first Annual Meeting, 1916, and minutes of the National Guild Council, 1924-25; a variety of papers on the producer guilds and notes on various League activities; and material relating to later campaigns and organisations for workers' control, such as the Workers' Control League.

(e) *Conrad Noel.* The Rev. Conrad Noel, Vicar of Thaxted, was active from its inception in the N.G.L. His papers, deposited in the Library, include a variety of files relating to his religious work, notebooks, typescripts of books and articles, and volumes of press cuttings. Few of these appear to relate directly to the N.G.L.

Availability

All these records are available on application to the relevant Librarians.

NATIONAL HOUSING AND TOWN PLANNING COUNCIL
11 Green Street London W1

The National Housing and Town Planning Council was founded in 1900 as the National Housing Reform Council. In 1909 it adopted its present name. Its aim is to educate and stimulate public opinion so that the fullest possible use may be made of existing housing and planning legislation. It advocates the use of better and cheaper methods of local development and house building, particularly in the public sector of housing.

Papers

The Council houses, in its library, its minute books from May 1906 to the present. These minute books also contain details of important correspondence received as well as records of deputations undertaken by the Council. There are packets of older correspondence, but only current correspondence is systematically kept. In addition, the Council has retained all its annual reports as well as copies of its journal, *Housing and Planning Review*. The Council also holds a copy of *National Housing Manual* by Henry R. Aldridge (1923), which is now out of print.

Availability

On written application to the Secretary-General. The correspondence is generally not available.

NATIONAL LABOUR MUSEUM
Limehouse Town Hall Commercial Road London E14

The Walter Southgate Foundation Trust was established in April 1966 with the ultimate aim of providing a history centre and museum where visual documentary and printed sources for labour history might be collected and exhibited. This aim was achieved with the establishment of a museum in the London Borough of Tower Hamlets in 1973.

The material which forms the basis of the Museum's collection was originally gathered by the Socialist History Group, which operated in Surrey during the 1950s and early 1960s. Out of this developed the Trades Union, Labour, Co-operative-Democratic History Society (T.U.L.C.), which promotes interest in the records of the British Labour movement.

The Museum has an excellent collection of banners, insignia and other items reflecting the visual history of the British Labour movement, from which frequent displays and exhibitions have been mounted. The material includes relics of individuals active in the Labour and Radical movement, of early Socialist movements such as the *Social Democratic Federation* (q.v.) and of trade unions. In addition, several manuscript collections have been deposited with the Museum, together with books, pamphlets, etc.

Personal items in the collection include a grant of the Freedom of the City of Norwich to George Southgate, March 1818; an agreement, W. J. Southgate with Aberdeen Quill Co., to serve as quill pen cutter, *c.*1878; a Certificate of the Ragged School Union, 1867; school reports, occasional letters, scrapbooks, and daily journals of public events kept by Walter Southgate (seven books).

Manuscript and printed material includes: a balance sheet of the Peckham and Dulwich branch of the Social Democratic Federation, 1893; a minute book of the Wallasey branch of the Independent Labour Party, 1894-1900; a minute book of the Oxted branch of the Labour Party, 1919-26; records of a *Daily Herald* union chapel; and printed and other material relating to the Clarion Cycling Club, including a minute book of the North East London Section, *c.*1912. Enquiries concerning the collection should be directed to the curator of the Museum at Limehouse Town Hall. Enquiries regarding the work of T.U.L.C. should be directed to the Secretary, 31 Chartfield Road, Reigate, Surrey.

NATIONAL LABOUR PARTY

The party was formed in 1931 from the group of former Labour M.Ps. who supported J. R. MacDonald and the National Government. The party wound itself up just before the 1945 election.

Papers

The papers of J. R. MacDonald are obviously an indispensable source. However, the relevant material is disappointingly small. These papers are at present not available while David Marquand, M.P. is preparing a biography of MacDonald. They will eventually be deposited in the Public Record Office. Godfrey, Lord Elton, Hon. Political Secretary of the National Labour Committee, retained certain correspondence and diaries which throw light on the period. These papers are in the care of his heirs, and are not generally available.

Elton edited the National Labour journal, *The Newsletter*, and this is a useful source.

The 9th Earl de la Warr, a Labour Minister who supported MacDonald's formation of a National Government in 1931, is believed to have retained no papers.

NATIONAL LIBERAL CLUB
Whitehall Place London SW1

The Club was founded in 1882, and has acted since then as a focus for Liberal social and political activities.

Papers

The records of the Club itself are bulky, but at present unsorted and uncatalogued. A large number of minute books survives, covering the activities of the various committees. Of these, the records of the N.L.C. Political Committee would seem to be of chief interest to scholars.

The Library of the Club (the Gladstone Library) has a number of other collections relating to the activities of the Liberal Party. These include:

(1)   *T. Fisher Unwin Papers (1848-1935).* These consist of a fairly large metal box of correspondence, etc., totally unsorted, but with material on L.C.C. affairs, the Boer War and other turn-of-century events. Fisher Unwin was Chairman of the Political and Economic Circle of the National Liberal Club and founder of the Unwin publishing house.

(2)   *Alfred Austin Papers.* Relating to a leader writer on the *Evening Standard*, again late 19th and early 20th century. There are several box files, quite well catalogued. These contain some important correspondence, since he was in contact with many political leaders of his time (e.g. Bright).

(3)   *G. Leveson-Gore Papers.* Private Secretary to W. E. Gladstone. Two scrapbooks which include letters, etc.

(4)   *Liberal Central Association Papers.* Four minute books of the L.C.A. from
      c. 1880-1914. If other M.B.s survive, they are not in the Library. Dates
      covered are:

      Vol. I   1883
      Vol. II   1883-96
      Vol. III   1896-1911
      Vol. IV   1911-14

(5)   *Liberal Council Papers.* These consist only of two volumes of minutes of
      the Executive Committee of the Liberal Council from Jan. 1927 to June
      1939. Again, if other material survives, it is not in the Library.

(6)   *Women's National Liberal Federation Papers.* This collection is at present
      unsorted.

(7)   *Mirfin Papers.* A miscellaneous collection of papers for the period *c.*
      1958-62 concerning the National League of Young Liberals, the New
      Orbits Group and Radical Action. (Derick Mirfin was Liberal candidate in
      the 'Profumo' Stratford-upon-Avon by-election.)

(8)   *Fothergill Papers.* This collection consists only of a large unsorted bundle
      of agency press cuttings.

(9)   *Sir Geoffrey Mander.* A small collection has been deposited, including
      some correspondence and an incomplete autobiography.

(10) *Viscount Thurso.* A typescript memorandum of an interview between
      Thurso and Neville Chamberlain, 28 Aug. 1939, is a recent addition to the
      Library's holdings.

The Library has rich book and pamphlet material on the history of the Liberal
Party, including a run of the *Liberal Agent.* In particular, the Library has a very fine
collection of election addresses.

Availability

Applications should be made to the Librarian.

Note

Certain papers, including two minute books, 1920-25, relating to the Coalition
group of members of the Club are contained in the T. J. Evans Collection, National
Library of Wales.

NATIONAL LIBERAL PARTY

The origins of the party lay in the breakaway of 23 M.P.s from the Liberal Party
in October 1931 over the question of support for the National Government. The
Liberal National Group (later Party) continued to support the Government after
the 'Samuelite' Liberals left it over the Ottawa Agreements in 1932. Its increasingly
close relations with the Conservative Party were regulated by the Woolton-Teviot
agreement, in May 1947, which urged the combination of Conservative and Liberal
National constituency associations, and in 1948 the party adopted the name of
National Liberal Party. By the late 1960s the party had become an integral part of
the Conservative Party.

Papers

The surviving records of the party itself are at present in the possession of Lord
Drumalbyn. Most of the papers were destroyed in World War II, and many of the
remaining records were subsequently lost. The records passed on to Lord

Drumalbyn were therefore few in number, and they chiefly relate to the actual formation of the Liberal National Party.

In the absence of full records, reference should be made to the personal papers of prominent individuals.

Availability

At present the records of the party are not available.

NATIONAL MINORITY MOVEMENT

The Movement was set up in 1924, developing out of the British Bureau of the Red International of Labour Unions (R.I.L.U.). It was a Communist-led organisation of Left-inclined trade unionists working towards a 'United Workers' Front', with the aim of advancing a more militant industrial policy than that pursued by the T.U.C. During the General Strike it advocated the establishment of Councils of Action, but in the new climate after the Strike it emerged more disciplined but also more isolated. Its effectiveness had disappeared by 1932, but it survived until 1935.

Papers

Records at the Marx Memorial Library include much pamphlet material and reports of the annual conferences, Aug. 1924-Aug. 1929.

At Nuffield College, Oxford, the papers of Jack Tanner provide the most important single source for the history of the Movement. The Tanner Collection includes accounts of the N.M.M.'s organisation, as well as information bulletins, copies of speeches, reports and resolutions of R.I.L.U. Congresses, letters to members from the Executive, Conference circulars, resolutions, statements, as well as minutes of the Executive Bureau meetings, and material relating to the National Metalworkers' Minority Movement, shop stewards' and workers' committees, the Railway Workers' Minority Movement, and the National Transport Workers' Minority Movement.

Although not strictly a part of the Minority Movement, the London Busmen's Rank and File Movement which organised the Central London Bus Strike of May 1937 should be mentioned here. Certain papers relating to the Strike and to the Rank and File organisation are available at B.L.P.E.S.

Availability

Applications should be made to the relevant Librarian.

NATIONAL PARTY

The party was founded in September 1917 by a small group of Conservative M.P.s led by H. Page Croft (later Lord Croft). Its politics were pro-Imperialist, but most of the members drifted back to the Conservative Party and in 1921 the separate parliamentary group was dissolved.

Papers

The papers of Lord Croft have been deposited in the Library of Churchill College, Cambridge.

Availability

Applications should be made to the Archivist, Churchill College, Cambridge.

NATIONAL PEACE COUNCIL
29 Great James Street London WC1

The Council was established on a permanent footing in 1908, following the 17th Universal Peace Congress held in London in July-August of that year. An informal N.P.C. existed for some four years before that. For the period 1923-30 the name of the Council was changed to the National Council for Prevention of War. The Council brings together representatives of a number of national voluntary organisations with a common interest in peace, disarmament, international relations and racial problems. Its main function is to provide a forum for consultation and discussion and to help create an informed public opinion in order to influence government policy. The N.P.C. is closely connected with the United World Trust, an independent research and education organisation which it founded, and the Danilo Dolci Trust.

Papers

The records of the N.P.C. up to 1950 have been deposited in B.L.P.E.S. Records, since 1950, are retained at the offices of the N.P.C.

Those deposited include six minute books of the Council from 1908-50 containing duplicated signed minutes. Minutes of the Executive Committee are contained in seven volumes covering the years 1916-41. One volume, for the period 1930-37, is missing. Two further minute books cover the work of the 'London and Greater London Council for Prevention of War', 1924-32. Annual reports have also been deposited, running from 1931-59. Financial records include a minute book of the Finance Committee, 1918-33; a cash book, 1936-45; an expenditure book, 1935-43; and donations journals, 1946-50.

Availability

For records up to 1950, application should be made to the Librarian, British Library of Political and Economic Science.

NATIONAL SECULAR SOCIETY
698 Holloway Road London N19

The Society was founded in 1866 by Charles Bradlaugh, M.P. It works to promote secularism or humanism, i.e. the belief that this life is the only one of which we have knowledge and that human effort should be wholly directed towards its improvement.

Papers

The Society has retained records dating back to its inception. These are at present in store and no detailed examination could be made. Many records were destroyed during World War II. However, extant records include correspondence of Charles Bradlaugh, at present being microfilmed, minute books and annual reports. The Society also retains copies of various free-thought journals, including copies of the *National Reformer* from the 1860s, the *Secular Almanack* from the 1870s, and the Society's journal, *Freethinker*, dating back to 1881. A collection of pamphlets also survives.

Availability

These records are not at present available. Enquiries should be directed to the General Secretary of the Society.

NATIONAL SERVICE LEAGUE

The League was active in the first half of this century in advocating universal military service in Great Britain.

Papers

Mrs Dorothea Macleod, the widow of the League's last Secretary, has retained in her possession a substantial collection of papers, including minute books and related material. These are at present unsorted.

Availability

These papers were not available at the time of writing. Enquiries as to their availability should be directed to the National Register of Archives.

NATIONAL SOCIETY FOR THE PREVENTION OF CRUELTY TO CHILDREN
1 Riding House Street London W1P 8AA

Formed in 1884, the Society has worked for the prevention of private and public wrongs to children or corruption of their morals.

Papers

The Society has kept its records from foundation. The main series of papers are minute books, annual reports and branch reports, and individual case histories. The journal, *Child's Guardian*, dates from 1887.

Availability

Only the printed reports are open to researchers, since case papers are still regarded as confidential. Applications should be addressed to the Public Relations Officer.

NATIONAL SOCIETY FOR PROMOTING RELIGIOUS EDUCATION
69 Great Peter Street London SW1

The Society was founded in 1811 to promote a religious education under the auspices of the Church of England. Until the advent of a state system from 1870 onwards, the Society was a pioneer in providing schools and education for the masses. Since the 19th century the role of the Society has been to promote religious education within the state system, while at the same time supporting Church schools and training colleges. The National Society is an integral part of the Church of England and works closely with the Education Board of the General Synod.

Papers

The National Society has an excellent archive, dating back to its foundation, of both manuscript and printed material. Besides the minutes of the Society's various committees, the bulk of the manuscript material consists of some 15,000 files of correspondence. The majority of these files concern individual schools and training colleges and contain correspondence and administrative material from the 19th century to the present day. Other files deal with matters of policy, correspondence with the Education Department on religious education, submissions to government committees, etc. The more recent material, particularly that concerning personalities who are still alive, is generally not available for research purposes. Papers concerning the Society's work in the formation of the religious provisions of the 1944 Education Act have unfortunately been lost. However, the 'external' aspects of the Society's work are recorded in its annual reports, dating from foundation, in the *Monthly Paper*, published by the Society, 1847-75; and in the *School Guardian*, the continuation of the latter in an enlarged form, from 1875. In addition, the Diocesan National Society's reports covering the first half of the 19th century are a useful source for individual early Church schools; and the Diocesan Inspectors' Reports from 1875-1919 give general information on the inspection of religious knowledge in schools.

Other National Society material exists in the form of a small but interesting collection of sermons, tracts, pamphlets, petitions, etc., published by the Society, its members, supporters and opponents on a number of 19th-century education issues.

The National Society also has a useful collection of miscellaneous published educational and other writings, including, for example, material of other education societies. A history of the National Society has been published by H. J. Burgess, *Enterprise in Education* (N.S.P.R.E./S.P.C.K., 1958). H. J. Burgess has also, with P. A. Welsby, written *A Short History of the National Society* (N.S.P.R.E., 1961).

Availability

Students should write for an appointment to the General Secretary, giving some indication of their field of research. The Reading Room is open Monday to Friday 10 a.m. to 1 p.m., 2 p.m. to 4.30 p.m.

NATIONAL SOCIETY OF BRUSHMAKERS AND GENERAL WORKERS
20 The Parade Watford Herts.

The Society was established in London in 1747, as the United Society of Brushmakers. It appears to have been a linking together of societies which had been formed in various towns, such as Manchester and Bristol, with London as the head Society. In 1917 it amalgamated with the Amalgamated Society of Brush Makers (established in 1889) and the name was changed to its present form.

Papers

Records of the National Society are retained at its head office. These include minutes of the General Council, Executive Council and annual conference from 1917; other records include annual accounts, wage agreements, etc., all from 1917.

In addition, older records survive, including many records of the United Society of Brush Makers. Minutes of the London Society run from 1829-43, 1866-73, together with a report of the London conference, 1886; a report of the Executive Council survives for 1901, and an annual report and balance sheet for 1909. A cash book of the London General Society runs from 1814-26. An important set of records is a set of circulars issued by the various societies which make up the United Society, and dealing with all aspects of the societies' work. They are dated but not numbered, and cover a period from the 1820s to the 1890s. Certain correspondence, wage agreements, etc., also survive, as do some branch records, including a minute book of the Bristol Society, 1859-82, and the Bradford Society, 1900-28.

Miscellaneous other papers include minutes of proceedings of the Committee on Production, before which the National Society appeared, Aug. 1918; correspondence and press cuttings relating to William Kiddier and his book *The Old Trade Unions*, 1920-23, 1930-34; a typescript Bicentenary Souvenir, 1947; and various mementos, insignia, etc., of the Society and its predecessors.

The only surviving records of the Amalgamated Society of Brushmakers are rules for 1908 and a report of the Executive Council, 1901.

Certain other 19th-century records have been deposited in the Library of the *Trades Union Congress* (q.v.).

Availability

Records held by the National Society are made available on application to its General Secretary. Applications to consult records at the T.U.C. should be made to the Librarian.

NATIONAL SOCIETY OF CHILDREN'S NURSERIES

The society was founded in 1906 as the National Society of Day Nurseries. Until 1928 it was closely linked with the National League for Physical Education and Improvement (founded in 1905, and known from 1918 to its dissolution in 1928 as the National League for Health, Maternity and Child Welfare). The N.S.C.N. merged with the Nursery School Association in 1973 to form the British Association for Early Childhood Education.

Papers

The Society has deposited its records at B.L.P.E.S. These include minutes of the Council, 1928-70; minutes of Annual General Meetings, 1930-48; and minutes of the following: Advisory Board, 1941-4, 'Representatives', 1921-39; the Executive Committee, 1935-73; Creche Committee, 1908-34; Editorial Committee, 1947-58; Finance Committee, 1919-39; Examiners' Meeting, 1943-6; Lecture and Training sub-committee, 1942-4; Training Committee, 1944-6. Other material includes Financial Ledgers, 1948-64; Petty Cash books, 1954-66; Register of Members; Press cuttings album, 1940-1; Attendance Book, 1970-3; and a file marked 'Earlier documents', 1914-40s.

The N.S.C.N. also deposited in B.L.P.E.S. office copies of its Annual Reports and its journal, known as *The Creche*, 1907-10, *The Creche News*, 1915-32, *The Day Nursery Journal*, 1932-42, *The Nursery Journal*, 1942-73.

Availability

All enquiries concerning these records should be directed to the Librarian, B.L.P.E.S.

NATIONAL SOCIETY OF CONSERVATIVE AND UNIONIST AGENTS

The Society was founded in 1891. It works to advance the Conservative cause, to protect and promote the interests of agents, and to examine problems relating to political organisation, registration and related matters.

Papers

The following records have been deposited in the Archives Department, Westminster City Libraries: four volumes of minutes, 1895-1949, the latter volume including a list of Chairmen and Hon. Secretaries, 1891-1962; and a letter book, 1891-94, with index. Later records are kept by the current Secretary.

Minute books of the Metropolitan Society of Conservative Agents have been deposited in B.L.P.E.S., and these supplement the above.

Availability

Application should be made to the Archivist, Westminster Archives Department, and to the Librarian, B.L.P.E.S.

NATIONAL SOCIETY OF OPERATIVE PRINTERS, GRAPHICAL AND MEDIA PERSONNEL
Caxton House 13-16 Borough Road London SE1 0AL

The Society was formed in 1889 as the Printers' Labourers' Union. The name was changed in 1899 to the Operative Printers' Assistants' Society, in 1904 to the National Society of Operative Printers' Assistants, and in 1912 to the National Society of Operative Printers and Assistants. Among unions which amalgamated with NATSOPA were the Revisers' and Readers' Assistants' Society in 1916, and the London Press Clerks' Association in 1920. In 1966 it amalgamated with the National Union of Printing, Bookbinding and Paper Workers to form the Society of Graphical and Allied Trades. The two unions resumed their independent existence in 1972 as the National Society of Operative Printers, Graphical and Media Personnel, and the *Society of Graphical and Allied Trades* (q.v.). In 1972 the Sign and Display Trades Union (founded in 1918 as the National Union of Sign, Glass and Ticket Writers and Kindred Trades) amalgamated with NATSOPA.

Papers

Minutes of what became NATSOPA date from 1901 and reports and balance sheets run from 1904 to date. Other records include rules; partial membership records from 1900; role of honour, 1914 to date; records of agreements, 1901 to date. There is a complete run of the *NATSOPA Journal* from 1917. No records of the early affiliates of NATSOPA appear to survive. However, records of the Sign and Display Trades Union (Section) date from 1918 and include minutes, reports, memoranda, correspondence and *Newsletters*, 1939 to date.

Availability

Applications should be directed to the General Secretary.

NATIONAL TRADE DEVELOPMENT ASSOCIATION
42 Portman Square London W1H 0BB

The organisation was founded in 1888 as the National Trade Defence Fund; in 1900 it became the National Trade Defence Association, and after World War II adopted its present name. In its early days the Association saw its task as the defence of the brewing trade against attack. Now its task is generally to promote goodwill concerning the trade.

Papers

The records retained by the Society at its offices include minutes from the year of foundation and also the Manager's annual report on the activities of the Fund. These reports are extremely full and include correspondence, etc., to major figures.

In addition to this material there are some 80 or 90 letter books of correspondence, mainly for the period 1908-10; there is one file of correspondence for the early 1920s, probably of little use to scholars, whilst virtually all other correspondence seems to have been lost. There are, however, several volumes of evidence, etc., given to Committees and Royal Commissions, e.g. the 1902 Licensing Act. Finally, there is a very interesting book of questionnaires returned by candidates in the 1906 General Election for the Eastern area of the country, indicating M.P.s' and candidates' views on questions asked them by the Fund.

Availability

Application should be made in writing: each application will be considered individually and on its merits by the Association.

NATIONAL UNEMPLOYED WORKERS' MOVEMENT

The movement grew out of a series of local committees of the unemployed which developed in the years after World War I. A Council of Delegates established the National Unemployed Workers' Committee Movement in 1921, with Walter Hannington as National Organiser. The word 'Committee' was later dropped from the title. The Movement, which had strong links with the Communist Party, led campaigns against the Government over its policies towards the unemployed and demanded provision of work by the state with the alternative of full maintenance. During the 1930s it sponsored a number of 'hunger marches' to dramatise the plight of the unemployed, although the first such march had been held as early as 1922. Its functions largely ceased after the outbreak of World War II, and the Movement was officially wound up in 1945.

Papers

A considerable amount of relevant material is contained in the Hannington papers at the *Marx Memorial Library* (q.v.). This includes:

(1)   The agenda and conference reports of the N.U.W.M. for 1923, 1924, 1929, 1931 and 1939.
(2)   A few minutes, but mainly reports of the National Administrative Council (N.A.C.) of the N.U.W.M.
(3)   Assorted local publications of N.U.W.M. area and branch organisations. In nearly all cases, only odd issues were ever published.
(4)   An important collection (11 files) of letters and documents formerly belonging to W. Gallacher, concerning unemployment benefit cases which he raised in the Commons.
(5)   Printed bulletins of the Unemployed Research and Advice Bureau.

Copies of reports of the meetings of the National Administrative Council have been deposited in the University of Hull Library.

Relevant material may also be found in the Home Office files at the Public Record Office, and in the Metropolitan Police records for the period.

Availability

Applications should be made to the relevant Librarians. A Reader's Permit is needed for users of the Public Record Office.

NATIONAL UNION OF AGRICULTURAL AND ALLIED WORKERS
Headland House 308 Grays Inn Road London WC1X 8DS

The union was founded in 1906 as the Eastern Counties' Agricultural Labourers' and Small Holders' Union. It changed its name in 1912 to the National Agricultural Labourers' and Rural Workers' Union, and in 1920 to the National Union of Agricultural Workers. In 1966 it adopted the present title.

Papers

Many records held by the union have been deposited on loan at the Institute of Agricultural History, University of Reading (q.v.). These include records of the National Union, 1906-72, the National Agricultural Labourers' Union, 1873-1890s, and the Agricultural Wages Board (England and Wales), 1917-22.

National Union records include Executive Committee minutes, 1907-45; Finance and General Purpose Sub-committee minutes, 1913-41; Organising Sub-committee minutes, 1946-50; various branch minutes, 1906-49; General Council meeting and conference reports, 1913-47; annual reports and balance sheets, 1962-71; lists of officers and members, 1906-20; files containing correspondence, drafts of articles, proofs, etc., chiefly relating to the union journal, *The Labourer*, 1915-18; miscellaneous administrative material, 1930-72; and other 'social and personal' material, including historical notes, press cuttings, and social and personal ephemera. The Institute also holds a file of *The Landworker*, 1921-71. Later material is to be deposited at regular intervals.

Records of the National Agricultural Labourers' Union include minutes of the Yetminster branch, Dorset, 1873-77, and diaries of Joseph Arch, 1876 and 1892. A M.B. (1872-79) of the Oxfordshire Agricultural Labourers' Union is in the G. D. H. Cole papers at Nuffield College Oxford.

Records of the Agricultural Wages Board (England and Wales) consist of minutes, 1917-21, and the *Wages Board Gazette*, 1918-21. Reg Groves, *Sharpen the Sickle!* (1959) is a study of the farm workers' union which uses original material.

Availability

Enquiries should be directed to the Institute of Agricultural History.

NATIONAL UNION OF BANK EMPLOYEES
Queen's House 2 Holly Road Twickenham TW1 4EL

N.U.B.E. was founded in 1918 as the Bank Officers' Guild. It became N.U.B.E. in 1946 when the Bank Officers' Guild merged with the Scottish Bankers' Association.

Papers

Although the formal records of N.U.B.E. activities are very full, the collection as a whole is a small one. When the union moved its headquarters from Central London to Twickenham in 1964 much correspondence was destroyed. Most of the surviving material is contained in paper wallets and is not systematically catalogued. It includes a complete run of Annual Delegate Meeting minutes from 1919 to the present, and Executive Committee minutes from 1919 to the present. Similarly, records have been retained for both the Finance Committee and the General Purposes Committee. In addition, there is miscellaneous correspondence with various banks, and correspondence relating to the Cameron Inquiry. All the membership figures from the union's inception to the present are available. In addition, N.U.B.E. has kept all its circulars from head office since 1962, and has some that go back beyond that date. N.U.B.E. has kept copies of all its procedure agreements with banks and also copies of circulars from bank headquarters from 1920. The research files have been kept from 1962. The union publication was *The Bank Officer*, a magazine published quarterly from 1919-70, when it became a newspaper, *N.U.B.E. News*, which is published monthly. All copies of this journal have been bound and kept.

There is a 1,300-page unpublished history of the union, covering the period 1917-46, as well as one published and several unpublished theses and dissertations.

Availability

All the material of N.U.B.E. prior to 1960 is available on application to the Research Department of the union. Subsequent material is only available on application to the General Secretary.

NATIONAL UNION OF BLASTFURNACEMEN, ORE MINERS, COKE WORKERS AND KINDRED TRADES
93 Borough Road West Middlesbrough Teesside TS1 3AJ

The Cleveland Association of Blastfurnacemen, founded in 1878, was the predecessor of the present union. A similar Cumberland organisation was founded in 1887, and together the two formed the National Association of Blastfurnacemen in the same year. In 1892 this Association combined with several other district Associations to form the National Federation of Blastfurnacemen, Ore Miners and Kindred Trades. The separate district organisations thus federated finally combined in 1921 under the present title.

Papers

Records retained at the offices of the National Union are incomplete. However, records of the National Federation survive from 1909, and are continued by the National Union minutes to date. Reports cover the same period. Also retained are branch (lodge) and district minute books.

Availability

Applications should be made to the General Secretary.

NATIONAL UNION OF DYERS, BLEACHERS AND TEXTILE WORKERS
National House Sunbridge Road Bradford BD1 2QB

The union was established in 1936. Amalgamated unions include the Operative Bleachers', Dyers' and Finishers' Association, the National Union of Textile Workers, and the Amalgamated Society of Dyers, Bleachers, Finishers and Kindred Trades.

Papers

The union has retained a considerable amount of records, particularly a large number of minute books covering the history of the National Union and its predecessor organisations. These minute books have not been sorted and it is not at present possible to provide further details. These have now been deposited in Bradford Central Library, Prince's Way, Bradford.

Applications to consult these papers should be directed to the City Librarian in Bradford.

NATIONAL UNION OF GENERAL AND MUNICIPAL WORKERS
Ruxley Towers Claygate Esher Surrey

The union was formed in 1924 by an amalgamation of the National Union of General Workers (founded in 1889 as the National Union of Gasworkers and General Labourers of Great Britain and Ireland), the National Amalgamated Union of Labour (founded in 1889 as the Tyneside and National Labour Union), and the Municipal Employees' Association (founded in 1894). Since then the union has absorbed, among others, the Plumbers, Cumberland Ore Miners, Saw Grinders, Welsh Artisans, Elastic Web Weavers, and Scottish Operative Glaziers. It is the second largest British general union.

Papers

Records of the union, and of certain predecessor organisations, survive at the union headquarters. Executive Council minutes, half-yearly and Congress reports of the N.U.G.M.W. survive from 1924 to date. In addition there are copies of rules since 1924, and of wage agreements. There are a variety of miscellaneous items, the more interesting of which include a 'Report relating to the Action of Communists and the National Minority Movement, to be presented to the Second Biennial Delegate Conference, 1928'; and press cuttings, pasted in volumes for the years 1922-34.

More recent press cuttings date back only a few years, as does correspondence, which is not generally kept beyond what is currently necessary. There is a complete run of the union's journal from 1924. The union also retains a small collection of regalia, including sashes, armbands and badges. Branches retain their own records, but the union has a minute book of the Baths Employees (No. 24), 1933-54.

The records of the following unions are also at the N.U.G.M.W. headquarters:

(a) *National Union of Gasworkers and General Labourers.* Reports and balance sheets survive for 1889-1915 (bound in nine volumes), as do certain records of wage negotiations, agreements, and a book of press cuttings on various strikes in the late 1890s.

(b) *National Union of General Workers.* Again bound reports and balance sheets survive, covering the period 1916-23, together with miscellaneous other items, concerning wage agreements, etc.

(c) *Tyneside and National Labour Union.* Minutes of the Executive Council meetings survive for 1893; annual reports and financial statements and agenda and reports of the Delegate Assembly cover the years 1890-93. There are also sets of rules for 1890 and 1892.

(d) *National Amalgamated Union of Labour.* 31 volumes of minutes of the Executive Council date from 1894-1924, and reports and balance sheets, quarterly and (from 1901) annually, cover the same years. There are reports for 1895, 1896, and agenda and reports, 1900, 1903, 1905, 1915, 1920.

(e) *Municipal Employees' Association.* Annual reports and balance sheets survive for 1909-13, 1914-18, rules for 1904, 1907, 1909, 1912, 1916, 1920.

(f) *Cleveland Miners' and Quarrymen's Association.* There are minutes of the Council, Executive and Joint Committee meetings, 1873-88, 1889-98, and rules, financial statements, wage negotiations and agreements, etc., cover the same years.

(g)   *National Federation of General Workers.* This was established in 1917 and dissolved in 1924. Unions affiliated included the Amalgamated Society of Gas, Municipal and General Workers, the Dock, Wharf, Riverside and General Workers' Union, the National Union of General Workers, and the Workers' Union.

The records include the minutes of the Executive Council, of General Meetings from 1918-22, together with reports and balance sheets for the same year. Additional material includes manuscript minutes of the Association of Gasworkers, 1887, and of the Gasworkers and General Labourers, 1889-92.

It is believed that since the survey of records was conducted, removal of offices has led to the disappearance of certain of this material.

Availability

By personal application to Research Office.

NATIONAL UNION OF GOLD, SILVER AND ALLIED TRADES
District Office 203 King's Cross Road London WC1X 9DB

The National Union incorporates the Society of Goldsmiths, Jewellers and Kindred Trades, which has retained a full collection of records. This Society was established in 1893, as the London Society of Goldsmiths and Jewellers, the name being changed to its later form in 1925. The members of the Diamond Workers' Union joined on being dissolved in 1926, and became a section of the Society. This transferred its engagements to the National Union of Gold, Silver and Allied Trades in 1969.

Papers

The records of the Society of Goldsmiths are to be deposited at the Library of the Trades Union Congress. The collection includes minute books of general and committee meetings, 1892-1969; annual reports, 1893-1969, and quarterly reports, 1903-24. In addition, there are rule books from 1893, and miscellaneous membership cards. Only one minute book, 1927-29, and a special membership card for Dutch and Belgian workers, 1944, have survived from the records of the Diamond Workers' Section. Of the old London Diamond Workers Union, only the minute books for 1908-26 have been kept.

Availability

Researchers wishing to use the records should apply to the Librarian, Trades Union Congress.

NATIONAL UNION OF JOURNALISTS
Acorn House 314 Gray's Inn Road London WC1X 8DP

The union was formed in 1907.

Papers

An extensive collection of records is located at the Union's headquarters. The annual reports of the National Executive Council are available from 1907. These give details of the union's membership. A series of rule books from 1907 is preserved, together with the typescript minutes of the N.E.C. Reports of Annual Delegate Meetings are available in bound volumes of the union journal, published from 1908. A.D.M. agenda, conference reports and N.E.C. reports are preserved in box files. Only current correspondence is kept, except in exceptional cases where files have been maintained for record reasons. Details of wage agreements, negotiations, etc., can be followed in the files. Documentation also covers legal proceedings regarding salary during sickness (Manchester County Court, 1907), radius agreements (High Court and Court of Appeal, 1909), and entitlement to pension of employees withdrawing labour (High Court, Belfast, 1970). A record of the attempted amalgamation with the Institute of Journalists is available on file and in the union histories, which include *Gentlemen of the Press* by F. J. Mansfield, and *The National Union of Journalists: A Jubilee History, 1907-1957*, by C. J. Burdock.

A set of continuous branch minutes of the Cardiff and District branch (formerly South Wales and Monmouthshire) is deposited in Cardiff Public Library, and records of the Nottingham branch are in the City of Nottingham Public Library. The F. J. Mansfield Memorial Library, consisting of publications on the history of the press and journalism, formerly at Acorn House, has been donated to the John Rylands Library, University of Manchester.

Availability

The archives are open to scholars on request to the Research Officer or the Administrative Officer.

NATIONAL UNION OF MINEWORKERS
222 Euston Road London NW1

The union was founded in 1944 by various regional coal-mining unions, formerly affiliated to the Miners' Federation of Great Britain. The Federation itself had been established on a permanent basis in 1889.

Papers

Many records of the Miners' Federation of Great Britain and the National Union of Mineworkers were destroyed by war damage, and some were lost during the transit of offices. The records remaining at National Office are therefore minimal. The most important source is the annual volume of proceedings of the M.F.G.B., 1889-1944. These contain the minutes of the Executive Committee, proceedings of annual and special conferences. verbatim reports of deputations to Ministers, joint meetings with coal-owners, etc. In addition, circulars and financial statements are retained. Annual reports and minutes of the N.U.M. are retained from 1944. The National Office also holds reports and minutes of Area organisations. Certain correspondence is retained on a permanent basis. Press cuttings are various but incomplete, fuller for the recent period. Bound copies of journals are also retained.

Availability

Enquiries should be directed to the General Secretary.

Area Records

The following Area organisations have provided information regarding their records:

Cumberland
6 Nook Street Workington CA14 4EG

Records retained in the Area Office include minute books from 1910 and a certain amount of correspondence, though this has been diminished by frequent changes of address.

Derby
Saltgate Chesterfield

Records retained at the Area Office include Derbyshire Miners' Association, minutes of Council and Executive Committee meetings, 1886-91, 1893-96, 1908-26; Derbyshire Miners' Conference, minute book, 1887-90; and account books, letterbooks, reports of deputations, etc.

Durham
P. O. Box No. 6 Red Hill Durham

Records retained in the Area Office include minutes of the Durham Union from 1878, and M.F.G.B. minutes and reports from 1913; records of Durham Area Council meetings from 1878, and annual reports from 1947; an old letterbook *c.* 1900, and files of departmental correspondence dating back to the 1950s; press cuttings, 1920-21; certain branch records; and a considerable amount of printed material such as journals and printed histories.

Leicester
Miners' Offices Bakewell Street Coalville Leics. LE6 3BA

Many of the older records were destroyed or lost when the Leicestershire Miners' Association split after the 1926 strike. The records retained are therefore all fairly recent.

Midlands
c/o Administrative Offices 12 Lichfield Road Stafford

The Area has retained records of the old Midland Miners' Federation, including minutes, 1928-49.

Northumberland
Burt Hall Northumberland Road Newcastle-upon-Tyne NE1 8LD

The following records have been deposited with the Northumberland Record Office: Northumberland Miners' Mutual Confident Association, Executive Committee minutes, 1873-1940; Council minutes, 1898-1923; Wage Committee, Conciliation Board and other committee minute books and reports, 1898-1911; letterbooks, 1896-1920; Secretary's and President's diaries, 1898-1908; account books, 1863-93; miscellaneous papers, 1898-1935. In addition, annual volumes of Northumberland Miners' minutes, 1875-1970, have been deposited at the Record Office.

North Staffordshire
Park Road Stoke-on-Trent

The Area has retained a substantial collection of records dating from 1892.

North Western
Miners' Offices Bridgeman Place Bolton BL2 1DL

Minutes and reports of the Lancashire and Cheshire Miners' Federation, and of the present Area, are retained, dating from 1894. In addition, minutes of the

Lancashire Miners' Federation cover the period 1886-88, and the minutes of the Ashton-under-Lyne Miners' Association survive for 1895. No correspondence of historical value survives.

Nottingham
Miners' Offices Berry Hill Mansfield Notts.

The minutes of the following are retained at the Area Offices: Nottingham Miners' Association, 1894-1913; Nottingham and District Miners' Federated Union, 1939-45; the Nottingham Area, 1946 to date; M.F.G.B., 1893-1944; N.U.M., 1946 to date.

Scotland
Various records of the Scottish Area, and its predecessor unions, are deposited in the National Library of Scotland. Records of the Fife Area cover the period 1918-63 and include a considerable amount of correspondence, with minutes, 1929-32, of the Secretary, President and various departments, 1946-59; of the various members of the National Coal Board, 1948-51; of the Consultative Committee, 1948-57; general correspondence, 1953-59, and branch and pit correspondence, 1944-60. Minutes and reports of the Area date from 1933-53; Pit and Consultative Committee minutes, 1947-60; records of Dispute Committees, 1940-60; correspondence, pit meeting minutes, agreements, etc., 1930s to 1960; and financial statements and statistical information date back to the 1930s; general miscellaneous administrative papers cover the period 1918-63. Records of the Lothian Districts are for 1894-1946. These include minutes of the West Lothian District, 1899-1946; the Mid and East Lothian Districts, 1894-1943; the Scottish Miners' Federation, 1894-1907; the Scottish Coal Trade Conciliation Board, 1900-11.

Permission of the Secretary, N.U.M. (Scotland), is needed for access to the records.

Somerset
Records of the Somerset Miners' Association are deposited in Bristol University Library. They include minute books, 1888-1952; records of individual collieries, areas, etc., 1890-1952; accounts, 1889-1964; records of disputes, conditions of employment, strikes and wages, welfare provisions, accident and compensation claims, industrial diseases, 1888-1958; papers relating to political matters, 1868-1956; and miscellaneous correspondence, papers, etc., 1880-1957.

South Wales
Records of the South Wales Miners' Federation and of the South Wales Area of the N.U.M. have been deposited in the Library of University College, Swansea. They consist of the following:

S.W.M.F. Executive Council minute books (both printed and MSS.), 1908-40; South Wales Area, minutes and conference reports, 1953, 1954-68; notes on minutes, 1900-53; conference agenda, 1942-43, 1944-45, 1945-47, 1949-55, 1957-58.

M.F.G.B. Executive Council and conference minutes, 1905, 1907-09, 1912-14, 1916-20, 1922-23, 1926, 1929-33, 1936, 1938-44; conference agenda, 1933, 1939.

N.U.M. Annual reports and proceedings, 1945, 1947, 1949, 1950-54, 1956-57, 1959; conference agenda, 1946, 1948, 1952, 1963. Also minutes of the following: Joint Standing Disputes Committee, 1918-26, 1928-33, 1943-44; minute books and records of the Board of Conciliation for the Monmouthshire and South Wales Coal Trade, 1903-18.

Financial Records. A full collection of account books, etc., some dating back to 1901.

Correspondence with lodges and areas, 1933-48, and office correspondence dealing with particular issues from the 1940s.

Lodge and Area. Various records, including those of Forest of Dean Miners' Association, Abercynon, Caerau, Cefncoed, Clydach Merthyr, Coegnant, Darren, Emlyn, Gellyceidrim, Mountain Ash, Mynydd Newydd, Onllwyn, Parc and Dare, Rhos Lodges.

Printed material. A large collection dating from 1910-69, including Acts of Parliament and parliamentary papers relating to the coal-mining industry, official and union reports, regulations, circulars, statistics, and accounts of legal cases and official enquiries.

A South Wales Coalfield Research Project, financed by the Social Science Research Council, has succeeded in preserving much other relevant material in the Library of University College, Swansea.

Yorkshire
Miners' Offices Barnsley ST0 2LS

The following records are retained at the Miners' Offices: South Yorkshire Miners' Association, minutes, 1858-80; Yorkshire Mineworkers' Association, minutes, 1882 to date (with gaps 1886-91); M.F.G.B. minutes, 1892 to date, and conference reports, 1896 onwards.

NATIONAL UNION OF PUBLIC EMPLOYEES
Civic House Aberdeen Terrace London SE3

The union was founded in 1888 as the L.C.C. Employees' Protection Association. The name was changed in 1894 to Municipal Employees' Association. This split in 1907, one section retaining the title M.E.A. (and absorbed into the National Union of General and Municipal Workers in 1924), the other creating the National Union of Corporation Workers. This changed its title to National Union of Public Employees in 1928.

Papers
These are retained at the union's headquarters and include minutes of the union; certain documents on the 1907 split; reports from 1912 to the present; and various rules, membership records and wage agreements back to the 1930s, etc. There is a run of N.U.P.E.'s journal from 1930 and certain branch records.

N.U.P.E. (Scottish Region)
Records, 1920-62, are deposited in the National Library of Scotland and include Divisional Officer's correspondence with head office and branches, 1929-57; head office correspondence and papers, 1928-52; papers on National Joint Industrial Councils, 1937-62; on conferences, 1937-54; similar correspondence and papers relating to the activities of the Scottish Office branch records, 1933-60, including minutes, have also been deposited.

Availability
The records in London are not available at present for research. Applications to use the material in the National Library of Scotland should be addressed to the Librarian.

NATIONAL UNION OF RAILWAYMEN
Unity House Euston Road London NW1

The union was formed in 1913 by the amalgamation of the Amalgamated Society of Railway Servants (established 1872), the United Pointsmen's and Signalmen's Society (established 1880), and the General Railway Workers' Union (established 1890).

Papers

Records at Unity House are those of the A.S.R.S. and the N.U.R.; records of other constituent unions do not appear to have survived. These records include: bound volumes of proceedings and reports, including Executive Committee minutes, General Secretary's reports, A.G.M. agenda and decisions, reports and financial statements, Orphan Fund reports, 1873 to date; certain correspondence from 1872, including an undated letter book; rules from 1875, membership records (including those of amalgamated unions) from 1873; a variety of cash books; circulars issued to members from 1875, with a complete run from 1924 to the present; records of wage negotiations and agreements from 1909; records of legal cases, including the Taff Vale Case and the Osborne Judgement; various documents on accidents. Miscellaneous items include the Parliamentary Expenses Book of G. J. Wardle, Feb. 1906-Dec.1907, a variety of membership cards, assorted pamphlets, etc. Copies of the *Railway Express* run from 1890-92, and of the *Railway Review* from 1880 to date.

Availability

Application should be made to the General Secretary.

NATIONAL UNION OF RATEPAYERS' ASSOCIATIONS
47 Victoria Street London SW1

The National Union of Ratepayers' Associations was formally established in 1938 with the dual aim of promoting the interests of ratepayers at national level, and maintaining economy and efficiency in local government. Previous to this it had been a loose federation of ratepayers' associations closely connected with the *London Municipal Society* (q.v.).

Papers

The National Union has retained some of its records, including minutes from 1938 and annual reports. Several boxes of recent unsorted material also survive.

The *Ratepayer* was the journal of the ratepayers' associations, 1921-48. From 1948 this was incorporated in the *Londoner*.

Availability

Enquiries should be directed to the Secretary.

NATIONAL UNION OF SCALEMAKERS
2 St. John Street London EC1

The Society was formed in Manchester in 1909, as the Amalgamated Society of Scale Beam and Weighing Machine Makers. The name was changed in 1923 to the Society of Scale Beam and Weighing Machinists, and in 1930 to its present form.

These are housed at the union's headquarters and include: the annual report and balance sheet, 1937 to date; monthly letter to members, 1930 to date; rules, membership records, 1909 to date; financial records from 1910; wage agreements from 1928; circulars to branches, 1927 to date; and a London branch contribution book, 1877-96. Certain miscellaneous records, such as balance sheets, also survive for the 1870s-1890s.

Availability

Application should be made to the General Secretary.

NATIONAL UNION OF SEAMEN
Maritime House Old Town Clapham London SW4

The union was founded in Sunderland in 1887 as the National Amalgamated Sailors' and Firemen's Union of Great Britain and Ireland. In 1894 it went into voluntary liquidation, and was reformed as the National Sailors' and Firemen's Union. The name was changed in 1926 to the National Union of Seamen. The Hull Seamen's Union was absorbed in 1922.

Papers

These are housed at the union headquarters. Records of the N.A.S.F.U. include a minute book from the inaugural meeting, Aug. 1887-Dec. 1890, an annual report for 1891, and minutes of the evidence given by J. H. Wilson to the Royal Commission on Labour, 24 Nov. 1891.

The records of the N.S.F.U. (later N.U.S.) date back to the end of the 19th century. The report of the A.G.M. for 1890 survives, as do reports from 1915 to date. Other records include rules for 1916 and 1926 to date; membership information from 1943 (previous records having been destroyed during the war); statements of accounts, receipts and expenditure for years between 1897 and 1912; agreements with the National Maritime Board, 1917 to date.

In addition, there are minutes and proceedings of the General Executive Council of the Amalgamated Marine Workers' Union, 8 June 1925, and of the A.G.M., 9 June 1925. Published material includes leaflets and a run of the union's journal, the *Seamen*, from 1911 to the present.

Also at the headquarters of the National Union of Seamen are minutes of the Hull Seamen's Union from Jan. 1891 to Dec. 1895, and a minute book of the Hull Sailors' Mutual Association.

Availability

Applications to see these records should be made in writing to the General Secretary.

Branches

In November and December 1970 the Union conducted a survey of branch records through a questionnaire from head office. This revealed a considerable amount of interesting material in branch offices. Some of this has now been transferred to Maritime House. What follows is a brief summary of the results of this survey.

'N.U.S. H.Q.' indicates that records have been transferred to Maritime House.

Aberdeen. Minutes, ledgers and other papers from 1926-51 have been deposited in Aberdeen University Library, King's College, Aberdeen. More recent records are still in branch hands.

Antwerp. Branch minutes 1921-22, N.U.S. H.Q.

Avonmouth. Branch minutes 1921-48, N.U.S. H.Q.

Belfast. Minutes are recent (1960 to date) and no records are earlier than 1948.

Cardiff. Branch minutes 1948 to date.

Douglas, I.O.M. Branch minutes 1927-49, N.U.S. H.Q.

Dover. Minute books cover the period from 1947; A.G.M. reports date back to 1954 and account books to 1952.

Falmouth. The minutes of the branch run from 1933 to the present but annual reports are of more recent vintage (1947 to present). There are also branch financial accounts for 1929-31 and 1937 to date.

Glasgow. Branch minutes from 1953.

Goole. Branch minutes 1927-60, N.U.S. H.Q.

Greenock. The local branch of the National Sailors' and Firemen's Union has deposited its minutes for 1918-56 in the National Library of Scotland.

Grimsby. Minutes survive from 1928 to date; reports of A.G.M.s and accounts date from 1948.

Harwich. Branch minutes 1945-58, N.U.S. H.Q.

Heysham. This branch has minutes from 1949, annual financial statements from 1951 and other material from the 1960s.

Holyhead. Branch minutes 1934-44, N.U.S. H.Q.

Hull. Reports of the A.G.M. of the branch date from 1944. The branch also has reports of the Sailors' and Firemen's Union for 1915 and 1920.

Leith. Branch minutes 1945-60, 1964-67, N.U.S. H.Q.

Liverpool. Branch minutes from 1966.

Malta. Minutes, reports, financial statements, etc., date back to 1918.

Manchester. Branch minutes 1956-68, N.U.S. H.Q.

Methil. This branch has recent records only.

Middlesbrough. Branch minutes 1907-58, N.U.S. H.Q.

Milford Haven. Records are recent only.

Newcastle. Branch minutes 1939-66, N.U.S. H.Q.

North Shields. Branch minutes 1919-65, N.U.S. H.Q.

Plymouth. Branch minutes 1919-68, N.U.S. H.Q.

Southampton. Branch minutes 1919-23, N.U.S. H.Q.

South Shields. Reports of A.G.M.s date from 1938; other records date from the 1960s.

Sunderland. Branch minutes 1887-90, 1908-13, 1930-47, 1962-68, N.U.S. H.Q.

Swansea. Minutes date from 1949, and A.G.M. reports from 1946.

Tilbury. Branch minutes 1927-65, N.U.S. H.Q.

West Hartlepool. Branch minutes 1931-66, N.U.S. H.Q.

Weymouth. Branch minutes 1961-71, N.U.S. H.Q.

NATIONAL UNION OF SMALL SHOPKEEPERS
Westminster Buildings Theatre Square Nottingham NG1 6LH

The organisation was founded in 1943 to enhance and protect the interests of the small independent retailer.

Papers

Minutes, reports, memoranda and branch records are confidential; correspondence is not retained beyond ten years. Owing to the comparatively recent formation of this organisation, it is not considered by the organisation that the records could be classed as historical documents.

NATIONAL UNION OF TEACHERS
Hamilton House Mabledon Place London WC1H 9BD

Formed in 1870 as the National Union of Elementary Teachers, it changed its name in 1889 to the National Union of Teachers.

Papers

These are retained at union headquarters. Committee and Executive minutes are retained, some of which have been microfilmed. These are not generally available, and enquiries should be directed to the Organising Secretary. Other records are retained in the Library of the N.U.T., including annual reports, 1871 to date, conference agenda and minutes, 1890 to date, copies of *Schoolmaster* (the *Teacher* from 1963) from 1871, and *Higher Education,* 1936-70, known as *Secondary Education* from 1970.

Availability

With the exception mentioned above, enquiries should be directed to the Librarian of the Union.

NATIONAL UNION OF TEXTILE AND ALLIED WORKERS
Cloth Hall 150 Drake Street Rochdale Lancs.

The union was founded in 1886.

Papers

The union has retained many of its records since its formation, and these include a full run of minutes and reports and certain administrative records.

Availability

By appointment at the offices of the union.

NATIONAL UNION OF THE FOOTWEAR, LEATHER AND ALLIED TRADES
'The Grange' Earls Barton Northampton NN6 0JH

The union was established in 1971. The following unions transferred engagements to the new union: the National Union of Boot and Shoe Operatives (founded 1874), the Amalgamated Society of Leather Workers, the National Union of Leather Workers and Allied Trades, and the National Union of Glovers and Leather Workers.

Papers

The records of NUFLAT have been retained since 1971. Records of the National Union of Boot and Shoe Operatives date back to the 19th century. These include minutes, 1895-1903 (handwritten to 1903, printed thereafter); conference reports, 1920-71; circulars, 1931-71; memoranda, 1961-71; and correspondence on various administrative, industrial, educational, political and legal affairs. Press cuttings survive for the period 1909-12, and copies of the union's journal cover the whole period from 1874.

Certain records of the other predecessor unions also survive. These include minutes of the Amalgamated Society of Leatherworkers, 1939-71; minutes of the National Union of Glovers and Leather Workers, 1920-71, and of its Milborne Port branch from 1915.

Availability

Records may be consulted at the central office after authorisation by a General Officer of the union.

NATIONAL WOMEN CITIZEN'S ASSOCIATION
'Sylvanhoe' Warren Road Purley Surrey CR2 1AE

The Association was established in 1918 to develop 'educative work on women citizenship, and on the methods of using the new voting power given to women'. In 1946 the National Council for Equal Citizenship, and in 1949 Women for Westminster, became incorporated with the Association.

Papers

A small unsorted collection of papers is deposited in the Fawcett Library. No further details are at present available. The *Six Point Group* (q.v.) has retained records of Women for Westminster.

Availability

Enquiries should be directed to the Librarian, Fawcett Library, and to Mrs. Hazel Hunkins-Hallinan of the Six Point Group.

See also: *National Council of Women; Six Point Group; Women's Suffrage Societies.*

NAVY LEAGUE
Broadway House Broadway Wimbledon London SW19 1RL

The League was founded in 1895 as a strictly non-political organisation to urge upon the government and the electorate the paramount importance of an adequate navy as the best guarantee of peace. It founded the Sea Cadet Corps in 1899 and affiliated the Girls' Nautical Training Corps in 1963, and the support of these is now its main object.

Papers

Bound volumes of the Governing Body minutes from 1895, and of the monthly magazine (*Navy League Journal*, 1895-1943, thence *The Navy*) are housed at the League's offices. Correspondence has not been systematically retained, and there was a considerable 'clear-out' in 1970 when the League moved from its Central London offices. Some departments do hold files on particular matters, some of which go back as much as thirty years.

Four boxes of papers in the Hannon collection at the Beaverbrook Library relate to the Navy League. Sir Patrick Hannon was a member of the N.L. Executive, 1910-11 and 1918, General Secretary and editor of *The Navy*, 1911-18. These papers include the following: committee papers and agenda (Grand Council, Executive Committee, Finance and General Purposes Committee, Overseas Relief Fund), *c.* 1918-22; miscellaneous pamphlets and annual reports; correspondence, 1911-22.

Availability

Applications should be addressed to the League's Director-General. Persons wishing to see the Hannon papers should apply to the Director of the Beaverbrook Library.

NEW COMMONWEALTH SOCIETY

Founded in 1932 by Lord Davies of Llandinam, the Society was a voluntary international organisation for the promotion and maintenance of justice, law and order in the world, through the establishment of an International Tribunal and an International Police Force. In 1952 the Society was succeeded by the *David Davies Memorial Institute of International Studies* (q.v.).

Papers

Some records of New Commonwealth remain at the David Davies Institute. These concern matters that were current when the Institute was founded, e.g. submissions to Parliament, evidence on the Atomic Energy Bill. The bulk of the New Commonwealth records, however, are in the Lord Davies of Llandinam Collection at the National Library of Wales, Aberystwyth. The large quantity of material consists mainly of correspondence and memoranda rather than formal office records. This is now being sorted, and listed alphabetically by correspondent within each year. The material covers the period from the early 1930s to 1952.

Availability

Enquiries should be addressed to the Institute's Secretary and to the Librarian at the National Library of Wales.

NEW FABIAN RESEARCH BUREAU

The Bureau was founded in 1931 to undertake Socialist research on the lines of the Fabian Society in its heyday. Its early membership overlapped with that of the *Society for Socialist Inquiry and Propaganda* (q.v.), but it continued independently when that organisation was absorbed into the Socialist League. G. D. H. Cole was Hon. Secretary, and John Parker, M.P., became General Secretary. In 1939 it joined with the Fabian Society, retaining the traditional name, which adopted the N.F.R̊.B.'s 'self-denying ordinance' that no policy was to be put forward in the name of the Society, but only in the names of the individuals or groups which prepared it.

Papers

The Fabian Society archive at Nuffield College, Oxford, contains relevant records of the New Fabian Research Bureau. These include two minute books, 1931-38, a number of files containing research and other papers, and material relating to the amalgamation of the N.F.R.B. and the Fabian Society. This consists of various draft rules and amendments, and correspondence, 1937-38.

The Cole Collection, also at Nuffield College, is a further important source. It contains correspondence, circulars, etc. John Parker, M.P., was General Secretary of the Bureau, but he has retained no relevant records.

Availability

Applications to use the Fabian Society papers and the Cole Collection should be made to the Librarian, Nuffield College.

NEW PARTY

Founded in March 1931 by Sir Oswald Mosley as a party of action, based on youth, which would mobilise energy, vitality and manhood to serve and rebuild the nation. It wanted to introduce into government men who were not primarily or necessarily politicians. It had a youth movement which was 'to meet violence with violence in order to defend free speech'. The membership was varied and included members of both political parties. In 1932 the party was absorbed by the *British Union of Fascists* (q.v.).

Papers

No formal records of the party have been located. The papers of Harold Nicolson are at Balliol College, Oxford. The John Strachey papers, now with Mrs. Strachey, are not available. Sir Oswald Mosley has retained some of his papers.

See also note on the *Radical Right and Patriotic Groups*.

NEWMAN ASSOCIATION
Newman House 15 Carlisle Street London W1V 5RE

Founded at a meeting of the University Catholic Federation of Great Britain in 1942, the Newman Association and the Union of Catholic Students were successors to the U.C.F.G.B. The Association provides a forum for Roman Catholic graduates to meet and study on subjects relating to their faith and work. It is a member of the International Catholic Association for Intellectual and Cultural Affairs.

Papers

Most of the formal papers of the Association survive at Newman House. These include annual reports and minutes since 1942, together with bound volumes of the Association's main journals, *Unitas* and the *Newman Bulletin*. There are also records of summer schools, etc., and box files of correspondence on main topics.

Availability

The records may be seen by arrangement with the Secretary.

NEWSPAPER PUBLISHERS ASSOCIATION
6 Bouverie Street London EC4Y 8AY

Founded in 1906 as the Newspaper Proprietors Association, it is a trade organisation representing all national daily and Sunday papers.

Papers

All records, apart from minutes, previous to 1940 were destroyed during World War II. The minutes, and other material dating from 1940, are regarded as confidential and are not available for research purposes.

NEXT FIVE YEARS GROUP

Founded at All Souls College, Oxford, in 1934, by Clifford Allen (Lord Allen of Hurtwood), Harold Macmillan and other men and women of all political parties, the Group was concerned to plan a practical programme of action to deal with immediate and urgent needs. In 1935 appeared the Group's book, *The Next Five Years*, on

205

economic policy and international relations. All the members agreed on the need for some machinery 'by which a design and plan could be substituted for improvisation and the tradition of muddling through'. Although the Group had much in common with Lloyd George's *Council of Action* (q.v.), the two bodies were separate in form and purpose. One was a political movement, the other a group of individuals from all parties, agreeing upon a general programme and hoping to give a lead to public opinion as a whole. Early in 1936 the Next Five Years Group was reformed as a pressure group. In addition to occasional publications, the Group undertook research, set up committees for consultation with other similar bodies, arranged meetings and lectures, and deputations to Ministers and local authorities. The Group was formally dissolved in November 1937.

Papers

A monthly journal, *New Outlook*, was published (1936-37), in addition to the books *The Next Five Years* and *A Programme of Priorities*. Harold Macmillan deals with the N.F.Y. Group in his memoirs, but as yet the Macmillan papers are closed. Lord Allen of Hurtwood's papers are in the Library of the University of South Carolina.

1944 ASSOCIATION

This was established in 1944 as an organisation of businessmen sympathetic to the Labour Party.

Papers

A small group of records survives in the Labour Party archive at Transport House. This consists of one volume of signed minutes, 1944-8; and a folder and box file of unlisted material, together with a file of Morgan Phillips' during his membership of the Committee. The latter includes notices, minutes, reports on mortgages, personal letters, lists of members, a bank statement, and cashed cheques for 1953. The bulk of this collection, apart from the minutes, relates to the Labour Party's relations with the Committee, and are not the records of the Committee itself.

Availability

Application should be made in writing to the Librarian of the Labour Party.

NO CONSCRIPTION FELLOWSHIP

The Fellowship was founded in November 1914 by individuals likely to be called upon to undertake military service in the event of conscription, who subscribed to a statement of faith that they would 'refuse from conscientious motives to bear arms, because they consider human life too sacred'. It organised opposition to conscription during World War I and many of its members were imprisoned during 1916-18. It was dissolved in November 1919. Three committees were established to carry out residual activities: (1) the Anti-Conscription committee; (2) the Pacifist committee; (3) the committee to oppose military training in Schools.

Papers

The papers of Clifford Allen, later Lord Allen of Hurtwood, are deposited in the Library of the University of South Carolina. A selection of these papers has been published in Martin Gilbert (ed.), *Plough my Own Furrow: the story of Lord Allen of Hurtwood as told through his writings and correspondence* (1965).

The Bertrand Russell papers, which are available at McMaster University, Hamilton, Ontario, Canada, contain relevant material. Russell was a prominent member of the Fellowship, and editor of its journal, the *Tribunal*. The papers in this collection include correspondence, 1916-18, with officials and branch secretaries of the Fellowship, draft circulars, leaflets, material on court cases, etc.

The papers of Catherine Marshall, Parliamentary Secretary and later Hon. Secretary of the Fellowship, are available in the Record Office, The Castle, Carlisle.

The collection includes boxes of correspondence and papers, 1914-18 (including Clifford Allen and Bertrand Russell), and files on conscientious objectors, 1915-21. Certain of these records are on microfilm. As yet no detailed list of the papers is available.

Records of the Willesden branch of the No Conscription Fellowship are deposited in Hull University Library. This collection includes correspondence and other papers, 1916-17, relating to some 43 correspondencs and cases.

Copies of the Fellowship's journal, the *Tribunal*, 1916-20, Nos. 1-182, should be noted. They are available in major libraries, including B.L.P.E.S.

Reports about the treatment of conscientious objectors are contained in a small collection of National Council of Civil Liberties material deposited by Raymond Postgate at the International Institute of Social History, Amsterdam, in 1959. The collection can be consulted on request at the International Institute of Social History, Herengracht 262-266, Amsterdam-C, Netherlands.

NO MORE WAR MOVEMENT

The Movement was founded after World War I as the British Section of the *War Resisters' International* (q.v.) and was active as an absolute pacifist group until its merger with the *Peace Pledge Union* (q.v.) in 1937.

Papers

One minute book only survives, and this is in the care of Mrs. Mabel Eyles-Monk, 30 Southwood Park, Highgate Village, London N6 5SG. Mrs. Monk was Office Secretary of the Movement at the time of its amalgamation, and Hon. Secretary to the Trustees of the Movement, who formed the Pacifist Research Bureau and operated from Mrs. Monk's home in London.

The Pacifist Research Bureau published pamphlets as thought necessary, the three most important being *Why Were They Proud?*, *War and Colonies*, and *New Tendencies in Colonial Policy*. The Committee of the Pacifist Research Bureau did not meet during the war but has maintained contact unofficially until the present time.

A resolution of the General Purposes Committee, 11 Feb. 1937, reveals the fate of the other records then extant: this arranged, among other provisions, that correspondence files, all sub-committee minute books and all National Committee minute books were to be destroyed, with the exception of that in use, i.e. the surviving volume. This volume covers the period 1932-39, beginning with the 10th financial statement, for 1931, and ending with the Pacifist Research Bureau meeting minutes for 24 June 1939.

Availability

Applications should be made in writing to Mrs. Mabel Eyles-Monk.

NONCONFORMITY AND POLITICS

From 1854 onwards there was a Religious Equality Parliamentary Committee, more or less sponsored by the *Liberation Society* (q.v.), for consultation between Nonconformist M.P.s on ecclesiastical legislation and liaison with extra-parliamentary groups. The Nonconformist Political Council, intended to be a more forceful body, was established in 1898 on the initiative of R. W. Perks, a Wesleyan M.P., lawyer and financier for transport undertakings. Its object was to co-ordinate the various Nonconformist pressure groups, now including the Wesleyan Committee of Privileges, and the *National Education Association* (q.v.). Although it had Lloyd George as a vice-president, the Council lost all impetus in the early stages of the South African crisis. Distinctive Nonconformist pressure was mounted through the Aggressive Education Committee (1901) in the Commons against the Education Act of 1902, and after 1906 there were regular meetings of a Nonconformist committee of M.P.s under R. W. Perks, which negotiated with the other parliamentary sectional interests over the Liberal Government's successive educational measures.

There is a Religious Equality Parliamentary Committee minute book for 1901-03 in the archives of the Liberation Society deposited by the *Free Church Federal Council* (q.v.) at the Greater London Record Office, which contains correspondence of R. W. Perks with Lord Rosebery. The Rosebery papers at the National Library of Scotland are the chief source for the Nonconformist committee. Relevant material is also in the Viscount Gladstone papers at the British Library and in the W. J. Rowland Collection at Dr. Williams' Library, Gordon Square, London WC1. See also: William Evans and William Claridge, *James Hirst Hollowell and the Movement for Civic Control in Education* (Manchester, 1911); Denis Crane [W. T. Cranfield], *The Life-Story of Sir Robert W. Perks, Bart., M.P.* (1909), and *Sir Robert William Perks, Bart.* (1936).

A number of Socialist Groups was active within the Nonconformist movement. These included the Christian Socialist Society, formed in 1886, and the Socialist Quaker Society (see under *Society of Friends*). The Free Church Socialist League (1909) was the counterpart of the *Church Socialist League* (q.v.). Its founder, the Rev. Herbert Dunnico, became a Labour M.P. and was Secretary of the Peace Society and Warden of the Browning Settlement, Walworth. His son, the Rev. H. Rathbone Dunnico, is now Warden of the Settlement and Secretary of the *International Peace Society* (q.v.). All enquiries regarding papers should be addressed to him.

NUFFIELD COLLEGE ELECTION ARCHIVE

This archive consists of the records accumulated in the preparation of the successive Nuffield College Election Studies after 1945. These records include election addresses, biographical details concerning candidates, reports from selected areas, campaign notes, press cuttings, party pamphlets and a variety of correspondence for each General Election. There is also certain material on by-elections after 1948.

Most of this material is available for general inspection on application to the Librarian, Nuffield College. Certain material gathered on a confidential basis can only be seen or quoted after consultation with Dr. David Butler, who may be contacted at the College.

PALESTINE EXPLORATION FUND
2 Hinde Mews London W1M 5RH

Founded in 1865, the P.E.F. pioneered the work of exploration and archaeological excavation in Palestine. The aim of the Fund has been to obtain and disseminate through publication information regarding the land and peoples of Palestine.

Papers

A substantial archive is held at the Fund's office. At present a detailed calendar of the papers is being prepared. Minute books date from 1865 and in the early years contain copies of official correspondence and circulars. The rest of the material comprises a great volume of 'private' correspondence, notes, etc., prepared in the field by members of P.E.F. expeditions, and manuscripts of articles. The important work of the P.E.F. included the surveys of western and eastern Palestine in the 19th century, and the survey of southern Palestine in 1913-14. The War Office co-operated in providing Royal Engineers for ordnance survey work, and Kitchener (of Khartoum) took part in expeditions. The P.E.F. archive contains interesting letters from Kitchener for the period 1875-77 and the mid-1880s. The Negev survey of 1913-14 under T. E. Lawrence and C. L. Woolley again enjoyed War Office co-operation. Naturally, working in an area of such political sensitivity and involving most Englishmen prominent in Middle Eastern affairs, the P.E.F. has papers of wide-ranging interest. Among the Fund's founder members was Walter Morrison, M.P. up to 1900, and the archive includes an assortment of letters by him. From 1869 the Fund has published a quarterly.

Availability

Applications should be addressed to the Executive Secretary.

Note

Much related material may also be found in the Central Zionist Archives at Jerusalem.

PARENTS' NATIONAL EDUCATIONAL UNION
Murray House Vanden Street London SW1H 0AJ

The Parents' Educational Union was founded by Charlotte Mason in 1887. 'National' was added to the title in 1892. The P.N.E.U. exists to propound the educational views of Charlotte Mason and supports a number of schools which employ Charlotte Mason methods. Until the early 1960s the teaching work of the Union was concentrated at the Charlotte Mason College at Ambleside. Now all such work is concentrated in London.

Papers

The records of the P.N.E.U., together with the papers of its founder, Charlotte Mason, have been deposited in the University of London Library.

(1) *P.N.E.U.* Seven minute books cover the work of the various committees of the P.N.E.U., together with Council and ordinary meetings. These are not continuous, however: they cover the years 1899-1902, 1923-51, 1952-60. A file of loose Executive minutes covers the period 1951-59 and from 1960 to date.

The work of the 'Ambleside Council' (consisting of representatives of the Council of the Charlotte Mason College, the Practising School and the Parents' Union School) is covered in three minute books, 1923-30, 1931-42, 1943-51, and of its successor, the Charlotte Mason Foundation, in one volume, 1951-59. A volume of minutes of the Finance Sub-committee covers 1894-99 and of the Northern Ireland branch 1921-31. Other records include an attendance book for Executive meetings, 1915-61; a series of letters, 1926, on the training of students; reports of visits to P.N.E.U. schools, 1934-39; a volume of first enquiries, 1964-67;

two account books, 1956-59; together with various administrative records, correspondence on schools and courses, lecture notes, questionnaires, etc. Bound volumes of annual reports run from 1897-1921. Later reports can be found in the *Parents' Review*, of which there is a complete run, 1890-1966, in 77 volumes, and its successor, *P.N.E.U. Journal*, 1966 to date.

(2) *Charlotte Mason Papers*. These consist of five boxes of material:
  (i)   Letters to and from Charlotte Mason;
  (ii) Letters to and from Charlotte Mason and other correspondents;
  (iii) Constitutional affairs, conference material, press cuttings, memoirs;
  (iv) Manuscripts of Charlotte Mason's writings;
  (v)   Proofs and printed copies of Charlotte Mason's writings, Mothers' Education Course, P.N.E.U. Reading Course, examination results, books, prompt copy of *As You Like It.*

Availability

Application should be made to the Archivist, University of London Library.

PARLIAMENTARY RECRUITING COMMITTEE

This was founded in 1914 to encourage recruitment into the armed services.

Papers

Minutes of the Committee, 1914-16, are deposited in the British Library (Add. MSS. 54,192). Further minutes, 1915, are to be found in Newark Central Library, Castlegate, Newark-on-Trent.

Availability

Applications should be made to the Keeper of Manuscripts, British Library, and to the Librarian at Newark.

PEACE PLEDGE UNION
Dick Sheppard House 6 Endsleigh Street London WC1H 0DX

This was the British Section of the *War Resisters' International* (q.v.). The Peace Pledge Union was founded in 1934 by the Rev. 'Dick' Sheppard, as a non-party pacifist organisation. It works to promote pacifism by means of individual rejection of war, and by encouraging individuals to sign the pledge: 'I renounce war and will never support or sanction another'.

Papers

The society retains in its offices its annual reports and minute books from its inception. The minutes are those of the National Council, the Executive Committee and the various *ad hoc* committees which came into existence. Virtually no correspondence has survived. In addition, there survive four minute books (covering the period 1939-42) of the London Area of the Peace Pledge Union. Records of the Cambridge branch of the P.P.U. are deposited in Cambridge University Library.

Availability

Application should be made to the General Secretary, and to the Cambridge University Library.

PEOPLE'S BUDGET

In June 1909 the Budget Protest League was formed under the Presidency of Walter Long, Unionist M.P. and former Minister. The organisation spearheaded the campaign against Lloyd George's proposals for a People's Budget. The League won support especially in the City. Also founded in June 1909, at a House of Commons meeting with Winston Churchill as President, the Budget League conducted a vigorous campaign in the constituencies in support of the Chancellor's policy.

Papers

For material on these pressure groups, recourse should be made to the main collections of private papers: for example, the Lloyd George papers in the Beaverbrook Library; the Balfour papers at the British Library; the Churchill papers at Churchill College, Cambridge; the Long papers at the Wiltshire Record Office; and some papers of Sir Henry Norman at present with his daughter, Lady Burke, at Chiddingfold, Surrey.

PEOPLE'S CONVENTION, 1940-41

A People's Vigilance Committee was founded in July 1940 to campaign for friendship with the U.S.S.R. and for a 'people's government' and a 'people's peace'. The Convention itself met in January 1941. It had strong Communist Party and radical support.

Papers

A package of material relating to the Convention is deposited at the *Marx Memorial Library* (q.v.).

Availability

Enquiries should be directed to the Librarian, Marx Memorial Library.

PERSONAL RIGHTS ASSOCIATION
31 Parkside Gardens London SW19

The Association was founded in 1871 and has as its aim: 'The maintenance and development of Personal Rights and Liberties, with particular criticism of state interference with the free development of money'.

Papers

According to Mr. Henry Meulin, the present Hon. Secretary of the Association, minutes of meetings were kept up to the mid-1930s, but had disappeared by the time he became Secretary in 1937. Since 1937 the activities of the Association have been confined to the production of its journal, *The Individualist*. Complete bound volumes of this journal survive in the Association's offices, dating back to 1926, with a few odd copies reaching back to 1921.

PHARMACEUTICAL SOCIETY OF GREAT BRITAIN
17 Bloomsbury Square London WC1A 2NN

The Society was founded in 1841 and has as its main aims the advancement of chemistry and pharmacy; the promotion and application of pharmaceutical knowledge; and the safeguarding of the interests of members, former members and their dependants.

Papers

The Society has retained a complete set of minutes of the Society's Council and of its committees and sub-committees since its formation in 1841, its annual reports, and various unsorted miscellaneous papers, memoranda, and correspondence of recent years. The bulk of the earlier records of the Society appears to have been destroyed in the 1940s, but a group of records for the period 1880-1920 does survive. This is an assorted collection, containing certain manuscript minutes, e.g. of the 'Scotch Board', the Law and Parliamentary Committee, the Library Committee, bundles of letters and documents on various topics, such as the National Health Insurance Bill of 1911, and emergency matters during World War I.

Availability

Application should be made to the Librarian.

PLAID CYMRU (WELSH NATIONAL PARTY)
8 Queen Street Cardiff

The party was founded at the Pwllheli Eisteddfod in 1925 as a result of the union of two smaller groups based on the University Colleges at Bangor and Aberystwyth.

Papers

A large amount of material relating to its activities has been deposited by Plaid Cymru, over the past twenty years, in the National Library of Wales. The records have not been catalogued but it is possible to give a description of their general scope. The bulk of the records comprises correspondence and copy replies, dating from 1924 to the 1960s. These are arranged largely in monthly bundles, although there are some regional and subject divisions, as in the case of the correspondence of the first Organiser of the party, H. R. Jones: these are sorted according to writers, 1925-29. The collection includes membership forms, 1924; lists of party members, 1925-27; minutes of the Ladies' Committee, 1934-37; draft reports of party meetings, early 1930s; reports from county and regional committees, 1937-39; correspondence and minutes of the activities of the party in Caernarvonshire, 1930-35; correspondence relating to the activities of the London branch, 1929-30; correspondence and accounts of 'Y Clwb Cinio Difiau' (Thursday Dinner Club), 1936-40; correspondence of the Advisory Board, 1939-40; manuscript and typescript essays, articles and addresses on Welsh nationalism by H. R. Jones and others; a report by H. R. Jones to the annual conference, 1927; account books, 1925-34, and miscellaneous vouchers, 1927-31; a ledger of sales of *Y Ddraig Goch* and the *Welsh Nationalist*, 1930-36, and record cards of subscribers, 1936-46; balance sheets and accounts of sales of party literature, 1936-41; posters, leaflets, canvass books, lists of electors, correspondence, etc., in connection with parliamentary and local government elections, from 1929; circulars, lists of subscribers, accounts and printed matter in connection with special funds and campaigns from the early 1930s; correspondence, accounts and printed matter relating to the party's summer schools, 1933-39; and undated manuscript and typescript copies of contributions to *Y Ddraig Goch* and the *Welsh Nationalist*. The office correspondence, however, is the most important guide to the activities of the party.

This is being supplemented at periodic intervals by further deposits made by the party. *These papers are not generally available and application should be made to the General Secretary, Plaid Cymru.*

Certain other relevant records have been deposited by private owners, e.g. records of the Cardiganshire Regional Committee of Plaid Cymru, 1939-49, have been deposited in the National Library, as have miscellaneous papers relating particularly to the Fishguard branch.

Other papers relating to Plaid Cymru are available at the University College of North Wales, Bangor.

POLITICAL AND ECONOMIC PLANNING
12 Upper Belgrave Street London SW1X 8BB

Political and Economic Planning (P.E.P.) was founded in 1931 and now aims to contribute to more effective planning and policy-making by government and industry by studying selected problems and publishing the results. Its original purpose was to outline and advocate a National Plan at a period when such a concept was novel and controversial.

Papers

P.E.P. has retained a considerable collection of papers, which were recently sorted and listed. These papers are divided into three groups:

(1)   Administrative papers.

(2)   Research papers.

(3)   Press cuttings.

(1) The *administrative papers* consist of minutes and miscellaneous papers, including correspondence, accounts, reports, trustee papers, etc. The collection of minute books does not appear to be complete. Minutes of the following committees survive: Directorate, 1931-33; Publicity, 1933; Executive Committee, 1933-64; Council, 1936-47; Trustees, 1938-61; War, 1941-42; the P.E.P. Club, 1934-55; Finance and General Purposes, 1957-58; Finance, 1955.

The early administrative papers also contain some research papers from a period before research and administrative functions were clearly separated.

(2) The *research papers* have been divided into four groups: working groups up to World War II; publications, broadsheets and reports since 1937; post-war studies; and unprinted papers from 1937.

The working groups' material cover a wide variety of topics: economics, employment, industry, permissive legislation, distribution, transport, gas, local government, regional development, agriculture, social assistance, health, education, building and housing, international trade, physical planning, etc.

Similar interests are reflected in the published broadsheets and reports, and in the papers relating to post-war studies. The latter reflect particularly the changing directions in social and economic policy, with, for example, studies in the mental health services and the Common Market. The material includes minutes and correspondence of the various study groups, particularly for the earlier period, as well as drafts and discussion papers.

The unprinted papers cover the whole period from the 1930s, and include miscellaneous war-time research papers, and ten folders of notes and drafts on a historical survey of the work of P.E.P.

These research papers are particularly good for the 1930s; some later papers appear not to have survived. Work on the major projects, however, is unusually well documented.

(3) The *press cuttings* generally consist of press comments on P.E.P. activity, particularly reviews of publications. They are in a fragile condition.

Availability

Access to these records may be granted on application to the Director (Finance and Administration) at P.E.P. These papers are generally restricted by a ten-year rule. Certain classes of papers, however, have reserve periods of twenty-five or fifty years. A list of the papers is available at P.E.P., and at the National Register of Archives.

POST OFFICE ENGINEERING UNION
Greystoke House Hanger Lane London W5 1ER

The P.O.E.U. was formed in 1887 as the Postal, Telegraph and Linemen's Movement. In 1896 a related union was formed, the Amalgamated Association of the Postal Telegraph Department, which in 1901 joined with the Postal, Telegraph and Linemen's Movement to become the Post Office Engineering and Stores Association. A further amalgamation occurred in 1915 with the Amalgamated Society of Telephone Employees (which was formed in 1904 from the National Association of Telephone Operators and the National Society of Telephone Employees. Not all members joined: the clerks from A.S.T.E. went to form part of the Civil Service Clerical Association, now the Civil and Public Services Association; other grades, such as the inspectors, formed their own union, the Post Office Inspectors' Association, now the Society of Post Office Inspectors.) The current name of the P.O.E.U. was adopted in 1919. There have been two secessions from the P.O.E.U.: in 1896 when the Telegraph Mechanics became the Mechanicians' Union; and in 1948 when senior grades became the Engineers, Officers and Technicians' Association. Both have now rejoined the P.O.E.U.

Papers

The P.O.E.U. has retained most of its minutes. Only correspondence of an official nature (e.g. with the T.U.C. and the Post Office) is retained. Also kept at Greystoke House are details of pay claims made to the Post Office. A continuous run of the journal has been kept from 1896; these contain digests of branch activities, *c.* 1914-25. In addition, the P.O.E.U. has been tape-recording the memoirs of former officers and Presidents of the Union. An official history is being prepared by Professor Bealey.

Availability

On written application to the General Secretary.

PRESS ASSOCIATION LTD.
85 Fleet Street London EC4P 4BE

The Association was founded in 1868 at a meeting of proprietors of daily provincial newspapers, and the shares are still held by such newspapers. The aim was, and is, to provide accurate and objective news and ancillary services by subscription and otherwise.

Papers

The Association's records are in two principal categories. Those relating to the business meetings and company administration matters are intact, principally as minutes of board meetings and such occurrences. Apart from the published accounts they are necessarily of a mainly private nature, and are not available for research purposes.

On the other hand, as the national news agency they are abreast of political institutions in so far as they come into their daily reports. There is a full editorial library of news extracts, which preserves its continuity by continually adding and shedding, and the records therefore tend to be ephemeral.

PRIMROSE LEAGUE
Abbey House Victoria Street London SW1

The League was founded in 1883, to commemorate the work of Benjamin Disraeli particularly within the Conservative Party. It has as its declared aim the 'maintenance of religion, the Monarchy and Constitution, the unity of the Commonwealth and improvement of the conditions of the people'.

Papers

In general, all the formal records have survived from the earliest days of the League, and they are fullest for the first forty years of its existence. However, virtually nothing of an informal nature is kept more than a few years, and so there is no old correspondence.

Grand Council minutes date from 1883, and are very detailed. The minutes of Council meetings themselves are in manuscript form, and are quite brief and formal, but there are substantial duplicated reports for each meeting, presented to the Grand Council by the Finance, Executive, Agency and Publications Committees. These give very full records of publications produced, income and expenditure, local organisation, and the arrangement of political meetings.

Ladies Grand Council minutes date from 1885, and are also kept in continuous series to the present day. These too are equally full, and include an informative copy of the printed annual report presented to the A.G.M. There are no sub-committee reports in these minutes. Finance and General Purposes Committee minutes are only for more recent years, but these are less informative and less interesting to the historian. They tend to deal more with routine matters and to work only within the framework of policy laid down by the Grand Council.

The *Primrose League Gazette* has also been kept during the whole time of its existence. It was usually published monthly from 1887, but was only quarterly during World War I and just after. This contains a large and varied amount of news on the activities of the League, such as:

(a)   reports of meetings, both central and local;
(b)   cartoons, news and articles on current politics;
(c)   pictures and news from local branches;
(d)   the accounts of the League as in the Grand Council minutes;
(e)   biographical articles on prominent Conservatives.

Other miscellaneous items have survived, such as a large collection of badges which were used in the inter-war years. There are no collections of pamphlets or posters, except in the few cases where these were put into the minutes, as were the League's election manifestos.

Primrose League, Scottish Branch, records are sparse. Scottish Grand Council and sub-committee minutes are complete, in two bound volumes (2 Oct. 1885-23 Nov. 1904 at the Glasgow offices of the Conservative Party; 13 Dec. 1904-11 May 1920 at Edinburgh). Financial records consist of a ledger (26 Sept. 1885-20 Oct. 1917), the final (sixth) cash book (1 June 1910-11 May 1920) and the ledger of Habitation 271 of Edinburgh (20 Nov. 1884-1895), all at the Edinburgh offices.

Applications should be made to the Secretary of the League.

PRINTING AND KINDRED TRADES FEDERATION

The Federation was founded in 1901 on a national basis to represent the interests of all printing workers in negotiations with employers concerning questions of national or widespread application. Its object is 'to secure unity of action amongst the various affiliated unions'. The Federation was officially dissolved on 30 April 1974.

Papers

Records dating from 1901 include annual reports, reports of conferences, and copies of the *Printing Federation Bulletin*, 1923-58. Copies of rules may be found in the annual reports. Non-current records are now in the care of the Modern Records Centre, University of Warwick Library.

Availability

Applications should be made to the Archivist, Modern Records Centre.

PROGRESSIVE LEAGUE

Albion Cottage Fortis Green London N2

The society was founded in 1932 under the title Federation of Progressive Societies and Individuals by a group of progressives under the inspiration of H. G. Wells. Its declared objectives were to combine the efforts of progressive societies to avert the then growing menace of Fascism and reaction at home and abroad. The efforts to federate progressive societies had little success and in 1940 the society's title was changed to the Progressive League. It now consists of individual members, and has grown into an organisation working towards 'the fullest development of human potentialities'.

Papers

Various records are retained by the League and consist of minutes of the Council, Oct. 1936-Jan. 1939; the Executive Committee, Dec. 1936-Feb. 1947; the General Purposes Committee, Dec. 1937-Mar. 1940; miscellaneous Executive minutes, 1943-48; and volumes for 1947-51, 1952-55, which also include minutes of special General Meetings and A.G.M.s. A file of A.G.M. minutes covers the period 1941-52, and other records of this period include a minute book of the Administration Sub-committee, 1951-54, a volume of conference arrangements, 1937-41, and a file of minutes and papers of the committee preparing evidence for the Home Office Committee on Homosexuality and Prostitution, 1954-55.

A series of seven minute books covers the work of the League from 1955-68, and includes minutes of Council, sub-committees and annual meetings. Four parcels of files relate to the work of the now defunct Man-Woman Committee. A file marked 'Plan Bulletins' covers 1939-42; and there is a complete run of the League's journal, *Plan*, 1934 to date (the journal was not published 1940-43).

Availability

Applications should be made to the Secretary of the League.

PROTESTANT ALLIANCE
112 Colin Gardens London NW9 6ER

The Alliance was founded in 1845 by the 7th Earl of Shaftesbury. It has as its aim the 'maintenance of Protestantism'.

Papers

The Protestant Alliance has retained many of its records, including minute books, account books and copies of its publications. These records at the time of writing were in store, pending re-development of the Alliance's offices, and no inspection was possible.

The official organ of the Alliance is the *Reformer*.

Availability

The records are not available at the time of writing. Enquiries should be made in writing to the Secretary of the Alliance.

PROTESTANT REFORMATION SOCIETY
Lawn Mansions High Street Barnet Herts.

Formed in 1827 by a group of eminent clerics and laymen, the Society was originally called the British Reformation Society and is a recognised Church of England society. It aims for the spiritual welfare, the conversion and instruction of Roman Catholics and 'nominal members' of the Church of England, and to promote actively the religious principles of the Reformation.

Papers

Minutes for most years from 1827 have been preserved. These include hand-written (1827-1926) and typescript (from 1926) series, and minutes of A.G.M.s in printed annual reports (approximately 1828-1958, with gaps). There are no printed histories, no published journal, and correspondence has either been destroyed or was incorporated in the private papers of the Society's officials.

Availability

Applications should be addressed to the Society's Secretary.

PUSEY HOUSE
61 St. Giles Oxford

Founded in 1884 in memory of Dr. E. B. Pusey, one of the leading figures of the Oxford Movement, which attempted to revive English church life in the 19th century. It is a centre of theological study and pastoral work, with the purpose of promoting the understanding and practice of the Christian faith.

Papers

The Library has an excellent collection of books and pamphlets relating to theological matters. Some 20,000 pamphlets, relating chiefly to Anglo-Catholic controversy since the 19th century, have been collected and these are an essential source for scholars. The pamphlets represent a full record of the various controversies within the Church and are probably difficult to obtain elsewhere. A guide has been published as *Nineteenth Century Pamphlets at Pusey House* (1961). The

Library also holds a valuable series of magazines and journals of various organisations which were active in the Church.

In addition to these printed sources, there is a very full archive of manuscript material, most of it relating to 19th and early 20th-century religious figures. For example, the papers of Dr. E. B. Pusey survive in bulk, as do the records of other leading churchmen. There is, for example, a considerable amount of correspondence from people such as W. E. Gladstone and Cardinal Manning who were closely involved in the Angl∪-Catholic revival at various stages. There is an index of all the names in the archive collection to which research workers should refer.

Several groups of records might be mentioned:

(1) *Church Union.* There are about six packing cases and a number of parcels of assorted, uncatalogued papers.

(2) *Christian Social Union.* The papers consist of one file box of annual reports and occasional letters, 1905-13, three file boxes of records of the Oxford University branch, including reports, lists of members and pamphlets, and three volumes of minutes of the Oxford branch, 1889-1923 (known as the Industrial Christian Fellowship, 1920-23).

A recent acquisition of the Library has been certain records of the Guild of St. Alban, a society of Anglican laymen active in the late 19th and early 20th centuries, which had various branches, particularly in South East England. These records include a run of the journal, the *Guildsman*, 1882-1929, and one minute book of the Folkestone branch, 1885-1930.

In addition to these various collections, Pusey House also retains its own records: the minutes of Chapter and of the Governors' Meetings since 1884, lists of lectures and courses, etc. A manuscript history of the House, 1884-1919, in the care of the Library, is a further useful source.

RADICAL RIGHT AND PATRIOTIC GROUPS

Few archival records have been located for the numerous parties and pressure groups which stood on the right wing of the British political spectrum. Certain organisations have been included in the main body of this guide, viz. the *Anglo-German Fellowship*, the *Anti-Socialist and Anti-Communist Union*, the *Economic League*, the *Link*, the *New Party* and the *Social Credit Movement* (qq.v.). Even in these cases, no official archive of the organisation is described, and the student is directed to particular collections of private papers and to the organisations' published records. For other right-wing groups, an exhaustive search for records has not been attempted. However, the following notes may be of interest to researchers.

British Union of Fascists and National Socialists

Founded by Sir Oswald Mosley, Bt., in 1932, the B.U.F. incorporated the remnants of the *New Party* (q.v.) and of several pre-1930s right-wing groups. Its aims were to propagate a programme for economic and political reform; to have a party built on youth and action which would further the ideals of nationalism, anti-Communism, anti-Semitism and anti-political élites. The party worked for the establishment of a corporate state, and put up candidates in local and national elections to gain endorsement for their views. Its meetings were punctuated by violent outbursts, and were stewarded by Eric Hamilton Piercy's National Defence Force which had been amalgamated into the B.U.F. The party ceased operations in May 1940 when its leaders, including Mosley, were interned. It is believed that the B.U.F. records were seized in 1940 by the Home Office and closed for one hundred years. In his autobiography *My Life* (1968), Sir Oswald Mosley says that his early papers were lost during World War II and that he wrote the book mostly from memory. However, Sir Oswald does retain some material at his home in France. In time the papers will be deposited in some suitable library, but at present they are not available.

A former Labour M.P. and important figure in the B.U.F. was John Beckett (1894-1964), most of whose papers were destroyed but who left some material, including an unpublished autobiography and a collection of pamphlets, with his family. No papers of William Joyce ('Lord Haw Haw') have been located. Records do survive, however, for Major-General J. F. C. Fuller (1878-1966), the military historian, expert on tank warfare and Fascist crusader in the 1930s. Most of Fuller's papers have been deposited at Rutgers State University, New Jersey, U.S.A. These include letters received, 1893-1965, diaries, notes and drafts for published works. Other Fuller papers are available at the Centre for Military Archives, King's College, London. C. R. Burn (later Sir Charles Forbes-Leith of Fyvie, Bt.), one of the B.U.F. founders, left no papers.

In the absence of much archival material, scholars have relied heavily on the publications of the B.U.F. and its members. The main periodicals include *Action* (1936-40), *Blackshirt* (1933-39), *Fascist Week* (1933-34), *Fascist Quarterly* (1935-36) and *British Union Quarterly* (1937-40). Robert Benewick, in his book *Political Violence and Public Order* (1969), provides a very useful bibliography of Fascist publications and of material relating to Sir Oswald Mosley's career.

British Brothers' League

Founded in 1902, the League aimed to restrict alien immigration under the slogan 'England for the English'. Its activities were largely confined to the East End of London, where large numbers of Eastern Europeans, particularly Jews, were settling. No papers of its founder, Captain William Shaw, or of its parliamentary spokesman, Major Sir W. Evans Gordon (1857-1913), Conservative Member for Stepney (1900-07), have so far come to light. The League, however, did give evidence to the Royal Commission on Alien Immigration, 1903.

British Empire Union

Founded in 1915 as the Anti-German Union, the organisation aimed for British influences to be overriding, for the use of British labour and British goods, for an end to 'so-called peaceful picketing', and the revision of the 1906 Trades Disputes Act. By the 1930s the Union's main work was to counter Communist propaganda, and also Fascism. Published works survive, for example copies of *Empire Record*, and relevant material may exist in the private papers of some of its prominent members (see Benewick, op. cit, p. 40).

British Fascisti (later British Fascists)

Founded in 1923 by Miss Rotha Lintorn-Orman to uphold the ideals of brotherhood, service and duty, the group published the *British Lion* (1926-29), *British Fascism* (1930-34) and other literature. Miss Lintorn-Orman's papers have not been traced.

British People's Party

Founded in 1938 by John Beckett and the Marquis of Tavistock (12th Duke of Bedford), the party was anti-Socialist and propounded selective pacifism. It also incorporated many of the proposals for monetary and parliamentary reform of the *Social Credit Movement* (q.v.) in which the Marquis of Tavistock had been active. The party fielded candidates for public office, as did the B.U.F. Few records survive apart from the journal *People's Post* and an assortment of pamphlets. The present

Duke of Bedford and his sister Lady Daphne Russell know of no papers, but a collection of miscellaneous pamphlets of the 12th Duke of Bedford is available at the Wiener Library. Harry St. John Bridger Philby (1885-1960), the Arabist, was in 1939 a prospective parliamentary candidate for the British People's Party. His papers at the Middle East Centre, St. Antony's College, Oxford, include several boxes of material relating to his role in British politics.

The Britons

Founded by Henry Beamish in 1918, this was an anti-Semitic organisation which sought to eliminate aliens from British industry and politics. Miscellaneous pamphlets and leaflets, and material published by the Britons and Britons Publishing Society, are available. Beamish was also involved with the Silver Badge Party of Ex-Servicemen.

Imperial Fascist League

Founded in 1924 by Arnold Leese, who advocated a 'true democracy' elected on a restricted franchise, it was a nationalist body seeing the Jews as a threat to British society. It believed firmly in the principles of Fascism which it described as a patriotic revolt against democracy. It was anti-Socialist and anti-Communist, and rejected government intervention in the economy. The periodical the *Fascist* appeared from 1929-39, and the League's numerous books and pamphlets are available. Arnold Leese died in 1956, and his widow's representative knows of no papers.

Middle-Classes Union (National Citizens' Union)

Founded in 1919, it concerned itself with combating the growth of Socialism and Communism and with organisation for the maintenance of essential supplies in case of an emergency.

National Fascisti

Founded in 1924 as a breakaway movement from the British Fascists, its aims were the maintenance of the monarchy, and preservation of the Empire with greater ties and preferences; the government to be one of experts with a governing executive of men of British birth and breeding who had both the will and the power to govern. Some published material is available.

National Socialist League

Founded in 1937 by William Joyce and John Beckett, it adopted many of the economic principles of the Imperial Fascist League. It was an organisation which supported the Empire, and was openly anti-Semitic. It also propounded an alliance between Great Britain, Italy and Germany. Its publication was called the *Helmsman*.

Organisation for the Maintenance of Supplies

This was founded in 1925 to maintain essential supplies in the event of any 'civil unrest', particularly a general strike. The main thrust of its campaign and fund-raising was directed against the power of trade unions. It became an official government body during the General Strike of 1926. Papers relating to the O.M.S. are available at the Public Record Office. Other material can be found in the papers of Viscount Davidson at the Beaverbrook Library. Geoffrey Drage (1860-1955) was Chairman of the O.M.S. Finance Committee, and his papers are retained at Christ Church, Oxford.

At the *Public Record Office* (q.v.), most of the papers assembled by government departments and relating to Fascist activities and to political organisations are probably included in the classes of Home Office, Metropolitan Police and other files which are closed for a hundred years. Some material, however, may be found in the open classes of these departmental papers, and in the Cabinet records and Premier class papers. Researchers should consult the hand list in the Search Rooms at the Public Record Office.

The *Labour Party* (q.v.) archive at Transport House includes some very interesting reports and information about the political Right in the 1930s. For example, the National Organisation subject files contain material labelled 'anti-fascist activity, 1933-37' and a questionnaire on Fascist activity, 1934.

The papers of the *National Council of Civil Liberties* (q.v.) at Hull University Library also contain some important material on the 1930s Fascist movement. Some 60 files relate to Fascist activities and anti-Semitism, 1939-1960s, to events in London's East End during the 1930s, to anti-Fascist demonstrations, 1937-38, and to campaigns organised to counter anti-Semitic activities. The records of the *Board of Deputies of British Jews* (q.v.) are again a most valuable source. Of the main library holdings, the British Library and the Wiener Library are of particular importance. Certain material relating to Fascism after 1945, assembled by the 43 Group of Jewish Ex-Servicemen is available at B.L.P.E.S.

RAILWAY CLEARING HOUSE

The Railway Clearing House was originally constituted as a voluntary organisation in January 1842. Its organisation and functions were subsequently developed by the Railway Clearing House Act of June 1850 and further Acts in July 1873, June 1874 and July 1897. Its aim was to give the various railways the character of a uniform system as far as through traffic was concerned. It was dissolved in 1955.

Papers

Records are held by the British Transport Historical Commission, Porchester Road, London NW1. The records consist of several hundred volumes of minutes and reports. Among many varied items are a register of weekly wages staff, 1888-1915, an excursion fares book, 1900-12, volumes relating to the English and Scottish Traffic Rates Conference, and a variety of volumes on arrangements relating to rates for coaching traffic, regulations on goods classifications, etc.

Availability

A Public Record Office reader's ticket is required to use the above material.

RAILWAY COMPANIES ASSOCIATION

The Association grew out of a temporary committee formed in March 1854 of certain railway company directors arising from the Select Committee Report of 1853. In June 1867 a new organisation, the United Railway Companies Committee, was formed. In May 1869 this organisation became the Railway Companies Association. It ceased to function after the nationalisation of the railways, following the Transport Act of 1947.

Papers

Records are housed at the British Transport Historical Commission, Porchester Road, London NW1. Minutes of the organisation exist, complete from 1867; there is also one volume for the period 1858-61. In addition, there are voluminous minutes for a variety of sub-committees, the most important being the Parliamentary Committee, which survive from 1884. Little correspondence survives, although there are reports on planning and policy for the 1940s. In addition, there are certain papers for the period 1942-46 of the Southern Railway Co. relating to nationalisation.

Availability

A Public Record Office reader's ticket is required to use the above material.

RAINBOW CIRCLE

This was a small group of Liberal politicians, economists and publicists formed in the 1890s to discuss the 'new Liberalism'. Among its prominent members were J. A. Hobson, Herbert Samuel and Charles Trevelyan. J. R. MacDonald was for a short time associated with the group.

Papers

The minute book appears to have been destroyed in 1940. The only surviving record is an album in the care of the Sir Richard Stapley Educational Trust, 121 Gloucester Place, London, W1. This contains photographs and a number of cuttings only. Applications to see this album should be made to the Secretary of the Trust. The Circle founded the short-lived journal, *Progressive Review*, in 1896, and this should be consulted.

A few surviving papers of J. A. Hobson are in Hull University Library, some Viscount Samuel papers are in the House of Lords Record Office, and the Trevelyan papers are in the Library of the University of Newcastle-upon-Tyne.

RATIONALIST PRESS ASSOCIATION LTD.
88 Islington High Street London N1 8EW

Known as the Propagandist Press Committee, 1890-93, the Rationalist Press Committee, 1893-99, and by its present title since 1899, the Rationalist Press Association is the chief publishing organ of the humanist movement.

Papers

The Rationalist Press Association has retained many of its records. These include minute books dating from 1899, annual reports from 1902, and certain correspondence. The Association also retains copies of its publications. The *Agnostic Annual* was published 1883-1900, *Agnostic Annual and Ethical Review*, 1900-06, continued as the *R.P.A. Annual and Ethical Review*, 1908-26, and the *Rationalist Annual*, 1927-67. Its successor, *Question*, has been published annually since then. The journal of the R.P.A. is *New Humanist*. Its predecessor *The Literary Guide: A Rationalist Review* was published 1885-1955, followed by *The Humanist*, 1956-73.

Availability

Enquiries concerning these records should be directed to the General Secretary.

REFORM CLUB
Pall Mall London SW1Y 5EW

The Reform Club was formally instituted in 1836, four years after the passing of the great Reform Act.

Papers

Records have been retained in the Club offices and in the Library. The main series of records are the General Committee minutes, which date from 1844, the minutes of A.G.M.s and Extraordinary General Meetings from 1837, and annual reports from 1836. An assortment of the minutes and reports of various committees and sub-committees have also survived; for example, rough minutes concerning the operations of the Club from the period 1836-40, minutes of the Building Committee, the Wine and Cigar Committee, the House and Finance Committee and the Political Committee. Correspondence has not been kept, except for a few souvenir letters from original members such as Cobden, John Bright and Henry James. Other interesting items include a scrapbook on the 1941 centenary celebrations, applications from members and new members' nomination forms, and lists of members. An official history of the Club is now being prepared by Professor George Woodbridge. Louis Fagan's *The Reform Club: Its Founders and Architect* appeared in 1887, and a pamphlet *The Reform Club* by J. Mordaunt Crook was published in 1973. The papers of W. M. Eagar (1884-1966), secretary of the Liberal Land Inquiry (1923-27) and Liberal Industrial Inquiry (1926-28) are now in the care of the Reform Club.

Availability

The records are not generally open for inspection by members of the public. However, persons wishing to see the papers should write to the Secretary, who will submit individual applications for consideration by the Committee.

ROAD HAULAGE ASSOCIATION LTD.
Roadway House 22 Upper Woburn Place London WC1H 0ES

The Association was formed in December 1944, drawing together in amalgamation some 16 local road hauliers' organisations. Before 1944 these local associations were joined in the National Road Transport Federation, which also embraced those interested in passenger and freight transport. In 1944 the Federation divided into the Road Haulage Association, the Passenger Vehicle Operators' Association and the Traders' Road Transport Association (now the Freight Transport Association). The Road Haulage Association aims to protect the interests of individuals and firms engaged in the transport of goods by road for hire or reward; to promote consideration, discussion and legal reform of all questions affecting the road haulage industry, providing a channel for communication with the legislative and other bodies; to promote the settlement of industrial disputes by conciliation or arbitration; to undertake research, publishing and charitable works. The Memorandum of Association provides that nothing should be done which would make the R.H.A. a trade union.

Papers

A full collection of records exists at the offices of the Association. These include minute books of the National Council and of all boards and committees established by the Council, dating from before 1944, when a steering committee was formed to arrange the amalgamation, to the present day; annual reports; correspondence,

1944 to date (these papers are divided into bundles according to subject-matter). The Association also retains its Memorandum and Articles of Association, and copies of *Roadway* (the journal of the R.H.A.), published monthly. *The Royal Road*, by Robert Allan (1946), provides a brief history of the road haulage industry.

Availability

The unpublished records are not available for general use by the public, but specific enquiries from scholars, particularly in relation to the period before 1951, may be answered. Application should be made to the Secretary of the Association.

ROUND TABLE
18 Northumberland Avenue London WC2

Founded in 1910 by Lord Milner and other members of his 'kindergarten' (in particular, Lionel Curtis and Philip Kerr, later Lord Lothian), the Round Table was a co-operative enterprise conducted by people who dwelt in all parts of the British Empire. Members aimed to publish quarterly a comprehensive review of Imperial policies and developments, entirely free from the bias of local party issues. The journal analysed major international developments and later was increasingly involved in describing events leading to the establishment of independent nations from former British colonies. In 1966 the journal opened its columns to signed articles from independent contributors. Under its sub-title of *The Commonwealth Journal of International Affairs*, the journal covers the whole range of issues of international concern, and pays particular attention to developments which bring out the continued significance of the Commonwealth.

Papers

Records of the Round Table are kept at the editorial offices. They are uncatalogued and unsorted, but consist in the main of minutes of meetings of the group, and correspondence of members among themselves and with outside contacts. Unfortunately the first minute book, covering the time from the organisation of the London group to Jan. 1913, has been lost, and the surviving minutes are for the most part very brief records of matters discussed. A complete set of issues of the *Round Table* journal from 1910 is available. A fairly extensive collection of the privately published memoranda which were circulated among members of the group is housed in the Library of the Royal Commonwealth Society. Of persons who were connected with the Round Table, the Lothian papers are at the Scottish Record Office, the papers of Lord Brand are with his son-in-law, Sir Edward Ford and the papers of Lionel Curtis are in the Bodleian Library.

Availability

Applications should be addressed in the first instance to the Hon. Secretary of the Round Table.

ROYAL AERONAUTICAL SOCIETY
4 Hamilton Place London W1V 0BQ

Founded in 1866, the Royal Aeronautical Society is the world's oldest aeronautical association. The Society incorporates the Institution of Aeronautical Engineers and the Helicopter Association of Great Britain. The Engineering Sciences Data Unit is a subsidiary organisation which produces a wide range of critically evaluated design data.

From the beginning, the Society was concerned not only with balloons, kites and bird flight, but aimed at heavier-than-air flight. The Society aimed 'for the advancement of Aerial Navigation and for observations in Aerology connected therewith', and recent activities include the organisation of conferences and lectures.

Papers

A substantial archive covering the records of the Society and its branches is deposited in the Library at 4 Hamilton Place. Minute books date from the Society's foundation in 1866, and the correspondence has been assembled and indexed. The Library holds copies of the annual reports, which were issued until 1897 when the journal was launched. The minutes and annual reports of the various provincial and overseas branches are preserved, together with the annual reports of a number of sections and groups. These include an Agricultural Aviation Group, the Astronautics and Guided Flight Section, the Air Law Group, the Air Transport Group, the Historical Group, Management Studies Group, Manpowered Flight Section, etc. The Society also holds a large collection of unpublished papers on aeronautics. In addition, there is a large photographic collection and a considerable number of albums of press cuttings. The Library is furthermore a depository for several collections of private papers.

During the war an advisory committee which met at the R.A.S., under the chairmanship of Sir Roy Fedden, worked in close consultation with the Ministry of Aircraft Production. The records of this committee are not available.

Availability

The Library is intended primarily for use by members of the Society, but other persons may have access to the collection on written application to the Librarian.

ROYAL AFRICAN SOCIETY
18 Northumberland Avenue London WC2N 5BJ

Founded in 1901 in memory of Mary Kingsley as the African Society, the Society's present name was adopted in 1935. Founder members included the Marquess of Ripon (President), Sidney Buxton, Sir Harry Johnston and Brigadier-General Sir F. D. Lugard. A non-political organisation, the R.A.S. aims to develop public interest in African problems and conditions and to serve among other objects as a link between the peoples of the United Kingdom and Africa.

Papers

The offices of the Society received severe bomb damage during the last war, and very little archival material has survived. Some papers have now been deposited in the Library of the *Royal Commonwealth Society*. These comprise notes, reports, items of correspondence, photographs, draft articles and maps. Most of the material, including journals (various periods c. 1905-29), were accumulated by Dr. Cuthbert Christy (1863-1932). The Society publishes a quarterly journal entitled *African Affairs*.

Other papers relating to the African Society are included in the Chancellor Collection at Rhodes House Library, Oxford. Sir John Chancellor (1870-1952) was Governor of Southern Rhodesia, 1923-28, and later High Commissioner in Palestine. The papers (1924-40) include the constitution and rules of the Society (1906), correspondence (1924), leaflets relating to the Society's work, correspondence with R. Nicholson (1933-36), Chancellor's speeches on Southern Rhodesia

(1928), agenda and minutes of R.A.S. meeting (8 June 1936), and a file marked 'African Circle'. This comprises correspondence, circulars, minutes and memoranda (1932-33). Chancellor was Chairman of the Circle, formed in Jan. 1933 as a revival of the Chatham House 'African Group'.

Availability

Enquiries should be addressed to the Librarian, at the *Royal Commonwealth Society* (q.v.).

ROYAL AGRICULTURAL SOCIETY OF ENGLAND
35 Belgrave Square London SW1
and
National Agricultural Centre Kenilworth Warwicks.

The Society was founded in 1839. It exists to promote the development of British agriculture.

Papers

Records dating from the late 18th century have been deposited by the Society in the Institute of Agricultural History, University of Reading. These consist of manuscript material relating to the Old Board of Agriculture, 1793-1822, manuscript material relating to the Society, 1838-1970, and some periodical literature dating from the early 19th century.

The records of the Old Board of Agriculture include minutes of various committees, 1797-1819; a register of members, 1793-1819; a register of letters received, 1793-1822; letter books, 1793-1822; financial records, 1794-1820; and copies of agricultural surveys and reports, 1802-20.

The records of the Royal Agricultural Society include minutes of the Council, 1840-1932; of the Finance Committee, 1890-1932; the Show Committee, 1843-1948; Research and Scientific Committees, 1843-1948; the Education Committee and the National Dairy Examinations Board, 1865-1948; the Journal Committee, 1855-1939; the House Committee, 1844-1903; the Selection of Officers Committee, 1867-1938, together with records of other subsidiary committees; agenda books, 1841-1922; financial records, 1838-1970; printed reports of Council, 1874-97; and various other administrative and legal records.

The Society published a journal, 1838-51; and from 1924.

Availability

Applications should be made to the Keeper of Records at the *Institute of Agricultural History* (q.v.).

ROYAL ASIATIC SOCIETY OF GREAT BRITAIN AND IRELAND
56 Queen Anne Street London W1M 9LA

Founded in 1823, the Society undertakes the investigation of subjects connected with and for the encouragement of science, literature and the arts in relation to Asia.

Papers

A considerable mass of records and other papers relating to its various activities is housed in the Society's Library. The collection is largely unsorted but falls into

226

three main categories. Committee minute books are available, together with an assortment of correspondence, often fragmentary but including letters to and from many eminent figures. For the general history of the Society, the *Transactions*, published from 1827, and the *Journal*, from 1834, should be consulted, also the Centenary and (forthcoming) Sesquicentenary Commemorative Volumes. A very important collection of Oriental manuscripts is also housed in the Society's Library. Finally, several collections of the private papers of Society members have been deposited in the Library. Some papers relate to British administrators of the 18th and 19th century, e.g. B. Houghton Hodgson, the first British Resident in Nepal, and Major-General Sir Henry Rawlinson, M.P.

Availability

Occasional use of the Library can be arranged, but persons seeking regular access should pay a membership subscription. All papers may be seen by appointment with the Librarian.

ROYAL AUTOMOBILE CLUB
83-85 Pall Mall London SW1Y 5HW

Formed in 1897 as the Automobile Club of Great Britain, the Club is a national motoring authority for the encouragement of motoring and motor sport.

Papers

The R.A.C. confidential minutes have been kept intact through the years, but otherwise the archive comprises for the most part bound volumes of R.A.C. publications, paintings, photographs and cartoons, together with some models and relics.

Relevant material relating to the foundation of the Club, together with correspondence and other items, 1898-1908, can be found in the F. R. Simms papers in the University of London Library. The R.A.C. archive also includes a box of papers presented by Simms which supplements the above material.

Availability

The Club has under consideration a project to organise the archives in detail. For the moment, their unpublished records remain closed to scholars.

Permission to consult the Simms papers must be obtained from the Veteran Car Club, 14 Fitzhardinge Street, Portman Square, London W1. Enquiries should be directed to the Archivist, University of London Library.

ROYAL BRITISH LEGION
48-49 Pall Mall London SW1Y 5JY

The Royal British Legion developed out of several ex-Servicemen's organisations founded during the 1914-18 War: the National Association of Discharged Sailors and Soldiers (founded late 1916), the National Federation of Discharged and Demobilised Sailors and Soldiers (founded April 1917), the Comrades of the Great War (August 1917), and the Officers' Association (January 1920). These united to form the British Legion in 1921, with the aim of promoting the welfare of ex-Servicemen and women and their dependants. A left-wing body, the National Union of Ex-Servicemen, stood aloof from this unification, but had a limited life-span thereafter. The Royal prefix was granted to the British Legion during the 50th anniversary year, 1971.

Papers

Very full records of the Legion have been retained dating back to 1921 and include: minutes and verbatim records of the annual conferences, bound volumes of reports on action taken resulting from these conferences, annual conference reports, volumes of monthly and special circulars, and a complete set of the *British Legion Journal* from July 1921. Minutes of the Executive, Finance and Standing Committees have also been retained and these contain reports of various deputations to governments over the years. These records, however, are confidential. Correspondence is not retained, and records of the Legion's eleven Areas are retained at the Area offices.

Of the organisations that united to form the Legion, few records survive. The Legion has certain records in its care, chiefly the records of the National Federation of Discharged and Demobilised Sailors and Soldiers. These include minutes of the Executive Council and the more important committees, 1917-21; three minute books of the Central branch, 1917-20; miscellaneous handbooks, rules, leaflets and agenda of conferences, 1918-20; verbatim reports of deputations to Ministries, 1919-20; balance sheets; circulars, 1918-21; the *Bulletin* of the Army Ranker Officers' Association, 1923-25; and copies of the Federation's official organ, *D.S.S. Bulletin*, 1919-21.

Note

The ex-Servicemen's organisations displayed a variety of political opinions. The National Federation was a Liberal-oriented pressure group founded with the aid of J. M. Hogge, a Scottish Liberal M.P., while the Comrades was a more Conservative response. The National Union of Ex-Servicemen had close left-wing affiliations, and the International Union of Ex-Servicemen, founded in Glasgow in May 1919, took a fully revolutionary position. With these clear political affiliations at a time of social unrest, close security surveillance was maintained on the ex-Servicemen's organisations. For this reason, in the absence of full records of these organisations, useful sources of information are the reports produced by the Special Branch and the Directorate of Intelligence at the Home Office: 'Fortnightly Reports on Pacifism and Revolutionary Organisations in the U.K. and Morale Abroad', and 'Reports on Revolutionary Organisations in the U.K.' These are found in Cabinet papers (Cab. 24) at the Public Record Office. Useful journals include the *Daily Herald* and *Workers' Dreadnought* (see Stephen R. Ward, 'Intelligence Surveillance of British Ex-Servicemen, 1918-20', *Historical Journal*, XVI, 1 (1973) pp. 179-88). For a more general survey of the Royal British Legion and its predecessors, see the *Official History* by Graham Wootton (1956).

Availability

With the exception of the committee minutes the records may be consulted with prior permission from the General Secretary.

ROYAL COMMONWEALTH SOCIETY
Northumberland Avenue London WC2N 5BJ

Founded as the Colonial Society in 1868 to provide a focal point for persons interested in the Empire and its promotion, the Society offers members a study centre and social facilities, and disseminates information about the Commonwealth. During its lifetime, the Society has been known as the Royal Colonial Institute, the Royal Empire Society and, since 1957, by the present name.

Papers

The Society's own records include Council Minute books from foundation, and the minutes of several committees (e.g. education, library, emigration, Finance and General Purposes). Until 1909, reports, papers, etc. were published annually in the Society's *Proceedings*, and since that date a monthly (now bi-monthly) journal has been produced under various names, originally *United Empire* and now *Commonwealth*. Much of the Society's early correspondence has been destroyed, but recent letters are retained. The surviving old correspondence is mostly nineteenth-century, but interesting files include material relating to Rider Haggard's work in the Dominions (1916) as representative of the Royal Colonial Institute in connection with the post-war settlement of ex-servicemen.

Apart from the records of the Society, the Library also acts as a repository for other manuscript collections. These papers include some papers deposited by the *British Association of Malaysia* (q.v.) and the *Royal African Society* (q.v.); some papers (1913-16) of Sir Edward John Harding; papers relating to Sir Frederick Young (1817-1913) and Imperial Federation; and Lt. Col. P. B. Bramley's correspondence with British Government Departments on the problems of security in Palestine and the Middle East (1923-5).

Availability

A fifty year rule at present generally applies on the Society's Minutes and Correspondence. Other records may be seen on application to the Librarian.

ROYAL GEOGRAPHICAL SOCIETY
Kensington Gore London SW7 2AR

The Society was founded in 1830 to promote the advancement of geographical science.

Papers

The Society has retained records dating back to its foundation. These include Council minutes from 1830 to the present, and committee minutes from 1841. Correspondence, on a selective basis, has been retained from 1830. Other manuscript material includes field books and records of scientific observations, originals of papers submitted for publication in the *Geographical Journal*, and manuscripts received through gifts or bequests, such as diaries, maps from expeditions, collections of photographs, sketches, news cuttings, etc.

The Library of the Society has complete sets of the journal, *Proceedings*, supplementary papers and other occasional publications of the Society.

Availability

Access to the archives is generally restricted to Fellows of the Society. Other persons may seek permission for access by applying in writing beforehand to the Director and Secretary.

ROYAL INSTITUTE OF INTERNATIONAL AFFAIRS
Chatham House 10 St. James's Square London SW1Y 4LE

Founded in 1920, the Institute is an unofficial body which encourages and facilitates the scientific study of international questions.

The Press Library is of great value. It contains reports from British and foreign newspapers of speeches made by leading British politicians since 1924. These reports are filed by subject, and there is an index to speeches since 1932. Also available is biographical material on leading British politicians published in the daily press since 1924.

The general archives of Chatham House, which are being reorganised, contain material of great potential value to historians concerned either with the making of British foreign policy or with the development of British thinking about the study of international affairs over the last fifty years.

Availability

Persons wishing to use the Press Library should apply to the Press Librarian. The material in the general archives is mainly of a confidential character and is not open to researchers. Enquiries should be addressed to the Director.

RUSSIAN ÉMIGRÉ GROUPS IN GREAT BRITAIN

The most important and influential organisation active before 1917 was the Society of Friends of Russian Freedom, founded in 1890 by S. Stepniak and Robert Spence Watson. One of the main collections of source materials for the group are the personal papers of David Soskice, one of its active members and father of Lord Stow Hill, and the published journal *Free Russia*. The Soskice papers have recently been handed over to the Historical Manuscripts Commission for listing.

The records of the Society have not been located, nor have the papers of J. F. Green, editor of *Free Russia* and the Society's Secretary. Stepniak's papers were sold to the Soviet Government by his widow and are now in the public archives at Moscow, together with certain other émigré records. The papers of another S.F.R.F. member, Felix Volkhovsky, are now deposited in two sections, at the Hoover Institution, Stanford, California, and in the Harvard University Library. Volkhovsky's correspondents included J. Ramsay MacDonald, Tom Mann, J. Keir Hardie and Sir Charles Dilke. Manchester University Library holds the papers of another less active S.F.R.F. member, A. F. Aladin.

Stepniak, Volkhovsky and others formed in 1891 the Fund of the Russian Free Press, a small publishing company in London intended exclusively for supplying Russian subjects with literature prohibited within the boundaries of Russia. It was active in the 1890s, but appears not to have involved English sympathisers.

In November 1895 the Russian Reformation Society was founded to promote 'a better mutual understanding between the inhabitants of Great Britain and Russia, and the encouragement, in the first instance, of Russians who are striving for freedom of conscience in their native country, and for such reforms as have been accomplished in the States of Western Europe'. Its founder and guiding spirit was Jaakoff Prelooker (1860-1935) and its organ the *Anglo-Russian* (1897-1914). Many of Prelooker's books were acquired for the Bodleian Library by Mr. J. S. G. Simmons, now of All Souls, Oxford. A 'literary society' which brought Russian and English conservatives together at this time was the Anglo-Russian Literary Society, formed in 1893.

Arising out of the activity of members of the S.F.R.F. there were several short-lived groups, committees and societies which brought Russian radicals and their English sympathisers together. The Memorial to the Duma Committee in the House of Commons (1906) and the Parliamentary Russian Committee may be mentioned. The latter body, formed originally in 1908 and enlarged and put on a more permanent basis in 1909, had C. P. Trevelyan as its first Chairman. Initially its members were all M.P.s but in 1909 it came to include others, and later officials included Lord Courtney of Penwith (President), Arthur Ponsonby (Chairman), G. M. Trevelyan and A. MacCallum Scott (Secretary). The following collections of private papers may therefore be useful:

> Courtney MSS., B.L.P.E.S.;
> Ponsonby MSS., Bodleian Library;
> C. P. Trevelyan MSS., University of Newcastle Library;
> G. M. Trevelyan MSS., Trinity College, Cambridge.

The Committee published a series of bulletins on Russian affairs. The Russian Political Prisoners and Exiles Relief Committee was formed in June 1915 by G. V. Chicherin and Mrs. Bridges Adams. Some of the Committee's papers are now with Mrs. Bridges Adams's grandson, and other correspondence (1916-17) is included in the Bertrand Russell papers at McMaster University, Ontario, Canada. Philip Snowden was for a time Chairman, and Robert Williams of the National Transport Workers' Federation its Treasurer, and other M.P.s, notably Joseph King, were important 'agents' of the organisation, During World War I, Georgii Chicherin was active in various other Russian émigré groups, the Russian Anti-Conscription League being one example. Several other groups organised in 1917 dealt with the problems of repatriation following the February Revolution.

Of the post-1917 groups, the list is headed by the Russian Liberation Committee founded in 1918 and publishing a journal, *New Russia.* The records of this organisation were discovered several years ago in the British Library and have now been catalogued. The major part of the documents consists of the personal archives of Harold Williams, well-known journalist and expert on Russian affairs and his Russian-born wife, Ariadna Tyrkova-Williams, author and publicist, and the papers of the Committee. Their contacts were extensive and correspondents include Samuel Hoare and Rex Leeper of the Foreign Office, Sir Bernard Pares, General Denikin, the diplomat Konstantin Nabokov and numerous scholars and writers. For the Committee for the Relief of Russian Intellectuals, the Soskice papers are again useful. Sir Paul Vinogradoff chaired this Committee, to which J. F. Green and Soskice were secretaries. The Committee included several pre-1917 Russian émigrés and English M.P.s. The political centre of the post-1917 emigration was Paris and its intellectual centre (at least in the early 1920s) was Berlin. Many émigré groups flourished in France and Germany in the inter-war period, but there was nothing comparable in Great Britain. The S. P. Melgunov Collection at the B.L.P.E.S. relates to Russian emigrés in the post-1917 period.

SALVATION ARMY
International Headquarters 101 Queen Victoria Street P. O. Box 249 London EC4P 4EP

Founded among the destitute poor of London in 1865 by the Rev. William Booth, the organisation was first styled the Christian Mission but developed in 1878 into the Salvation Army. The Army has undertaken work all over the world 'for the benefit of the submerged, starving, vicious and criminal classes'.

Papers

Nearly all records were destroyed by bombing action during World War II. However, a good collection of published material has been assembled in the library (Literary Department). This includes bound volumes of the *East London Evangelist*

(1868-69), the *Christian Mission Magazine* (1870-78), the *Salvationist* (1879), the *War Cry* (from 1879), *All the World* (1884-), the *Young Soldier [Little-Soldier]* (1881-), the *Deliverer* (1889-) and the *Officer* (1893-). In addition, there are bound copies of the *Official Year Book* from 1905.

Availability
Applications should be addressed to the Assistant Literary Secretary.

SAVE EUROPE NOW

Save Europe Now was a campaign launched at the end of World War II to help alleviate the distress and disruption caused in Central Europe by the war. Relief schemes were launched, food and clothing collected and appeals made for funds. Victor Gollancz was Chairman. Amongst the distinctive features of the campaign was the sending of food parcels to Germany, beginning in 1946. A 'Memorial', a petition to the Government concerning the repatriation of Italian prisoners in Britain, was successfully launched in 1947. The campaign was wound up in 1948.

Papers
No central collection of records relating to the campaign has been located. Victor Gollancz Ltd, the publishers, have no knowledge of surviving papers.

Correspondence relating to the campaign can be found in the papers of Bertrand Russell, who was sponsor. These are deposited in McMaster University, Hamilton, Ontario, Canada.

Mrs Peggy Duff, Secretary of 'Save Europe Now', published a pamphlet by that title (1948) which is a useful source, as is her autobiography, *Left, Left, Left* (1971).

The appropriate Departmental files at the Public Record Office will also be of value to the researcher.

SCIENTIFIC ORGANISATIONS

The great majority of scientific organisations do not fall within the scope of this survey. However, reference should be made here to the work of the History and Social Studies of Science Division of the University of Sussex (c/o Physics Building, The University, Falmer, Brighton BN1 9QH). In particular, mention must be made of the surveys of the papers of men of science conducted with financial aid from the Social Science Research Council and the Royal Society. The results of these surveys were published as *Archives of British Men of Science* (Mansell Information Ltd, London, 1972), published in microfiche with printed introduction and index. The Division also holds some records of the Association of Scientific Workers (see *Association of Scientific, Technical and Managerial Staffs*).

Other relevant organisations include:

(1) *British Association for the Advancement of Science* (q.v.).

(2) British Science Guild; founded in 1905 by Sir Joseph Lockyer, it amalgamated in 1936 with the B.A. No surviving archive has so far been traced, and it appears unlikely any substantial archival material is left.

(3) Rather different in scope, but of significance to historians, are some records of the Pugwash Conferences, deposited in Cambridge University Library.

SCOTTISH COLLIERY ENGINEMEN, BOILERMEN and TRADESMEN'S ASSOCIATION

From 1877 to 1912 the Association was known as the United Engine Keepers' Mutual Protective Association of Scotland; from 1912 to 1933, the Scottish Colliery Enginemen and Boilermen's Association; and thereafter by the above name.

Papers

Records 1877-1965 have been deposited in the National Library of Scotland. These include: minutes of the Executive Committee, 1878-1955; the Secretary's expenditure book, 1948-65; records of the Lochgelly branch, 1903-66, the Hamilton branch, 1875-1942, the Clackmannan branch, 1901-52, Bathgate branch, 1949-65, Cardenden branch, 1956-67, Coalburn branch, 1892-1907, Prestonpans branch, 1914-63; and minutes of the National Federation of Colliery Enginemen, Boilermen and Mechanics, 1926-30.

Availability

Applications should be made to the National Library of Scotland.

SCOTTISH LANDOWNERS' FEDERATION
26 Rutland Square Edinburgh EH1 2BT

The Scottish Land and Property Federation was founded in 1906. It amalgamated in 1947 with the Scottish Mineral Owners and the Argyll Lands Association. In 1950 it adopted its present title.

Papers

The Federation has retained full records dating back to 1906. These include minutes and accounts, but in addition files and letter books have been retained. These have now been listed by N.R.A. (Scotland).

Availability

Access is restricted. Enquiries should be directed to the Secretary of the Federation.

SCOTTISH NATIONAL PARTY
14A Manor Place Edinburgh EH3 7ES

The party was founded in 1928 as the National Party of Scotland. It merged in 1933 with the Scottish Party (founded in 1930) and then adopted its present title.

Papers

The Party has retained many of its records, and also deposits material at regular intervals with the National Library of Scotland, which also has a considerable amount of other material relating to the Nationalist Movement in Scotland. In particular reference should be made to the papers of the *Scottish Secretariat* (q.v.), of R. E. Muirhead and of James Porteous.

Availability

Enquiries should be directed to the National Library of Scotland and to the National Register of Archives (Scotland) which has useful references to the Scottish Nationalist Movement.

See also: Appendix III. (pp. 308-9).

SCOTTISH SECRETARIAT

The Secretariat was founded in 1929 to promulgate information about the Scottish nationalist movement.

Papers

A substantial collection of papers, 1929-63, was bought by the National Library of Scotland in 1964. The main section consists of general correspondence (about 1,400 files) and personal correspondence (about 800 files) of the Director, R. E. Muirhead. The papers include an extensive collection of newspaper cuttings relating to Scotland, and also material concerning other nationalist groups, including the *Scottish National Party* (q.v.), the Scottish Congress and the Scottish Home Rule Association.

Availability

Application should be made to the National Library of Scotland.

SCOTTISH TRADES UNION CONGRESS
12 Woodlands Terrace Glasgow G3

Papers

A microfilm of the S.T.U.C. minute books, 1897-1939, has been deposited at the National Library of Scotland. The microfilm includes the minutes of the Parliamentary Committee, 1899-1923; the Scottish Workers' Parliamentary Elections Committee, 1900-02; the Scottish Workers' Representation Committee, 1903-07; and the Labour Party (Scottish Section), 1907-09. The minutes of the women's groups, 1926-52, and of the Youth Advisory Council, 1938-50, are also included.

In 1968 the General Secretary deposited fourteen collections of minutes and correspondence of the S.T.U.C. with various local Trades Councils at the National Library. These papers cover the years 1948-66.

Availability

Permission is required from the General Secretary of the S.T.U.C. General enquiries should be directed to the National Library of Scotland.

SIX POINT GROUP

Founded in 1921 by Lady Rhondda, it is a non-party organisation, wishing to establish equality — economic, legal, moral, social, occupational and political — for women.

Papers

The records of the group are in the care of Mrs. Hazel Hunkins-Hallinan, 45C Belsize Park Gardens, London NW3. They are being used in the compilation of a history of the Group. It has been tentatively arranged that they should eventually join other collections of suffrage papers at the London Museum. The papers include:

(1) Minutes and miscellaneous leaflets of the Women's Committee for Political Planning (now discontinued).
(2) Minutes, etc., of the now defunct organisation of the World War II period, 'Women for Westminster'.
(3) Minutes of the Six Point Group from 1921 to the present day.
(4) Its quarterly newsletter for the whole period for which it has been published.
(5) Records of deputations and appearances before official bodies for the last thirty years.

Availability

Applications should at present be addressed to Mrs. Hunkins-Hallinan at the above address.

See also: *National Council of Women; National Women Citizen's Association; Women's Suffrage Societies.*

SOCIAL CREDIT MOVEMENT

The ideas of Social Credit are based on the theories of Major C. H. Douglas (1879-1952). In 1919 he published *Economic Democracy*, and developed his ideas in a number of other books and articles. The main contention was that goods were left unsold because of the discrepancy between the final costs of the goods and the money distributed as wages, salaries and dividends during their production. The remedy was either periodic repayment to consumers in the form of citizens' dividends or their sale at a fraction of their cost, retailers being compensated by payments from national credit created for that purpose. Essential to the Douglas scheme was a transference of the monopoly of credit creation from the commercial banks to a National Credit Office, charged with the duty of creating interest-free credit as and when required. Its supporters came chiefly from the professions, among whom it was hoped that a way had been found to solve the problems of the post-war depression. In the early days of Social Credit controversy A. R. Orage, editor of the *New Age*, became an enthusiastic follower of Douglas, and the early development of Social Credit ideas may be traced in the columns of this journal.

The movement displayed various and often conflicting tendencies from the start. Any discussion of records of the movement must therefore begin with a discussion of its complex development. In fact, the history of the movement must be largely traced through its publications.

Douglas agreed to the establishment of a Secretariat in the 1920s, of which he became Chairman with sole right to appoint directors. The Secretariat did not meet for general consultation. It issued a weekly journal, *Social Credit*, which was subscribed to by the study groups then springing up throughout the country. A more ambitious monthly journal, of mixed economic and literary flavour, the *Fig Tree*, appeared in the 1930s but was short-lived.

The study groups were most numerous and active in the Midlands and North. That of Coventry was remarkable for its lead. During the 1930s the ideas of Social Credit also spread abroad, and took root particularly in Canada, Australia and New Zealand.

Dissensions in the Secretariat lead to Douglas's resignation as Chairman in 1938. He repudiated its activities, and issued a new paper, the *Social Crediter*. The disruption of the former united movement followed.

Members of northern study groups met in conference in Derbyshire and founded the Social Credit Co-ordinating Centre. This is now based at Montague Chambers, Mexborough, Yorks. The Centre retains many early records of the movement, and publishes a journal, *Abundance*, originally based in Glasgow. The *Social Crediter* is also published under its auspices.

The Social Credit Secretariat still survives and regards itself as the legitimate guardian of Social Credit ideas. No information concerning its records is available.

The Kibbo Kift, founded in 1920 by John Hargrave as a youth movement, became associated with the movement during the late 1920s. By 1927 it had adopted Social Credit as its policy, and in 1935 became the Greenshirt Movement for Social Credit. This published a *Broadsheet*, and a journal, *Attack*. During the late 1930s the Greenshirts transferred their movement into the Social Credit Party of Great Britain. Annual reports of the Greenshirt Movement and of the party are retained at the British Library. On the question of a separate party the movement was divided. Douglas, in his writings, had declared against party politics; strict Douglasites would have nothing to do with a Social Credit Party.

SOCIAL DEMOCRATIC FEDERATION

Founded in 1881 by H. M. Hyndman as the Democratic Federation, it was reorganised as a clearly Socialist organisation in 1883 when it adopted its traditional name. The S.D.F. introduced a distinctive Marxist approach into British politics but never succeeded in becoming a mass movement and was subject throughout its existence to various schisms. Towards the end of 1884 the *Socialist League* (q.v.), led by William Morris, broke away, and the early 20th century saw further splits which led to the formation of the *Socialist Labour Party* and the *Socialist Party of Great Britain* (qq.v.). In 1911 the Socialist Democratic Party, as it had become in 1909, provided the major constituent of the British Socialist Party.

A group led by H. M. Hyndman broke away from the B.S.P. in 1916 over the latter's opposition to the war, and formed the National Socialist Party. After the war this re-adopted the name of Social Democratic Federation and as an affiliate of the Labour Party survived into the 1930s. The British Socialist Party survived until 1920 when it provided the largest constituent of the new *Communist Party of Great Britain* (q.v.).

Papers

No single large collection of S.D.F. records has survived. Several libraries, however, have important collections which illuminate the history of the S.D.F.

1. *B.L.P.E.S.*

This library has a set of annual conference reports from 1894-1910, with gaps. A microfilm of the reports, and including agenda and rules, supplements this set. The reports of the British Socialist Party run from 1912. The Library also has a small one-volume collection of British Socialist Party papers, 1910-14, which includes a variety of manuscript and typescript material (largely letters, from among others Victor Grayson and Leonard Hall, press cuttings, receipts, telegrams, appeals, membership cards and programmes of meetings).

Journals in the Library include copies of *Justice*, 1884-1921, although there are gaps for the period 1904-21: a complete file, 1884-1914, is available on microfilm; and the *Social Democrat*, 1897-1911, succeeded by the *British Socialist*, Jan.-July 1912. There is also a complete file of the British Socialist Party's publication, *The Call*, available on microfilm, 1916-20.

2. *National Library of Scotland*

Post-World War I records for the S.D.F. have been deposited by J. P. M. Millar in the National Library. These include Executive Committee and trustees' minutes, 1931-41, associate members' register, 1930-39, and a cash book, 1925-45.

Also in Scotland, with Edinburgh Public Library, are the records of the Edinburgh group, 1919-27.

3. *Marx Memorial Library*

This has an extremely valuable collection relating to the British Marxist movement. Relevant material includes annual reports of the S.D.F. and B.S.P., 1894-1920; minute books of the S.D.F., Hackney and Kingsland branch, 1903-06; the B.S.P. North West Ham branch, 1917-19; and the S.D.F. London County Council Election Committee, 1907.

4. *International Institute of Social History, Amsterdam*

This is a major collection relating to the Labour and Socialist movements generally, with much useful material relating to the S.D.F., particularly in its early days. See also *Socialist League*.

SOCIAL SURVEYS (GALLUP POLLS) LTD.
202 Finchley Road London NW3 6BL

The British Institute of Public Opinion was established in 1937, and took its present name in 1952. Poll findings were published in the *News Chronicle* until 1960, and from then in the *Sunday Telegraph* and *Daily Telegraph*.

Papers

Much unpublished and supplementary material relating to the surveys and polls conducted by the organisation is filed at headquarters. The material provides much more additional information for the historian than can be obtained from the published findings. Poll findings and analyses are published from time to time, for example, in H. Cantril (ed.), *Public Opinion, 1935-46* (1951), and in the monthly Gallup Political Index available since 1960.

Availability

Applications should be addressed to the Director.

SOCIALIST CLARITY GROUP

This was founded in 1936 by various people, including Austen Albu, Patrick Gordon Walker and William Warbey. The Group was dissatisfied with the various opposition groupings within the Labour Party and decided to publish a journal outlining alternative policies. After three years the first of the journals appeared under the heading *Labour Discussion Notes*. This continued publication until the group disbanded around 1945. The group held discussions on war-time policy and called themselves the 'Loyal Opposition'. Many of the *Labour Discussion Notes* deal with Labour policy to be pursued after the war.

Papers

In the papers of Austen Albu (in his own possession) there are three boxes of files dated Aug. 1936-1939, 1939-41, 1941-45. These consist of correspondence within the group and some press cuttings. In addition, there is a folder of *Labour Discussion Notes* from 1939-45.

237

SOCIALIST FELLOWSHIP

The Fellowship is the successor to the Socialist Sunday Schools Movement, the first branch of which was formed in Battersea in 1892. The movement aimed to provide, through a Socialist education, an ethical alternative to Christianity for young people, and attempted to inculcate a morality which would make Socialism more than just a series of administrative changes. It adopted its present title in 1965.

Papers

The records of the Fellowship have been collected by Mrs. Ivy Tribe (formerly National President of the organisation) at her home, 7 Frank Beswick House, Clem Attlee Estate, London SW6.

There is a complete set of minutes of the National Council of the Socialist Sunday Schools from 1926. There are also conference minutes for a similar period (except for 1940, when no conference was held). These minutes are informative both for financial and membership details.

Surviving correspondence of the society is relatively small, arranged at present in subject order (e.g. festivals, international contacts, legacies left to the movement). There is, however, a useful set of press cuttings. There is also a complete run from 1901 of the magazine of the movement, *Young Socialist*.

Branch records are sparse. There are, however, minutes of the Yorkshire Union complete from 1912 to 1957 (3 vols.), together with minute books of the Fulham branch (Nov. 1903-1925, 2 vols.), Huddersfield (1923-34) and Halifax (1905-14). Minutes of the Edinburgh Socialist Sunday School (1905-31) are in the National Library of Scotland, and those of the Southend School (1902-15) in the Marx Memorial Library.

Certain records have also been deposited in the Mitchell Library, Glasgow. These include annual conference minutes of the Scottish Union, 1911-32, with a treasurer's cash book, 1906-32; and records of the Glasgow and District Union, some dating back to 1911.

In addition to these records, Mrs. Tribe has accumulated a varied collection of leaflets, membership certificates and memorabilia.

Note

In 1974 these papers were promised to the *National Labour Museum* (q.v.).

SOCIALIST LABOUR PARTY OF GREAT BRITAIN

The Socialist Labour Party (S.L.P.) developed out of the Scottish District of the *Social Democratic Federation* (q.v.). It was established as a separate organisation in 1903, advocating a more militant class-conscious policy. From the first it expressed support for the ideas of the American Socialist, Daniel De Leon, and in 1906 it adopted a policy of Industrial Unionism. During World War I the S.L.P. became involved in the Shop Stewards and Workers' Committee Movement and in 1916-18 adopted a pro-Bolshevik policy. The party split over support for Communist Unity proposals in 1920. Many members of the party entered the new Communist Party of Great Britain, but the rump of the S.L.P. continued as an independent group under the traditional name.

Papers

No comprehensive archive appears to survive. A minute book of the Executive Committee of the S.L.P., 1903-08, mainly in the hand of Neil Maclean, first

Secretary of the party, is deposited in the British Library (Add. MSS. 52,602). Personal interviews with members of the S.L.P. were used in the following: D. M. Chewter, 'The History of the Socialist Labour Party of Great Britain from 1902 until 1921, with special reference to the development of its ideas.' (Oxford B.Litt. thesis, 1966); R. Vernon, 'The Socialist Labour Party and the Working Class Movement on the Clyde, 1903-21' (Leeds M.Phil thesis, 1967).

Reference should also be made to C. Tzuzuki, 'The Impossibilist Revolt in Britain', *International Review of Social History* (1956). Certain relevant material may be found in the papers of and concerning John Maclean at the National Library of Scotland. Maclean was briefly a member of the S.L.P., 1920-21.

The S.L.P. published a journal, the *Socialist*, from 1902. The Leith branch of the S.L.P. founded the (British) Advocates of Industrial Unionism in 1906. This published from 1908 a journal, *Industrial Unionist*, and this organisation became known as the Industrial Workers of Great Britain in 1909. An Industrial League, opposed to political activity, was founded in 1908 by dissident members of the S.L.P. and this published the *Industrialist*. In the absence of a full archive, reference should be made to these journals.

SOCIALIST LEAGUE (1884-1891)

The League was founded towards the end of 1884 as a breakaway from the *Social Democratic Federation* (q.v.) dominated by H. M. Hyndman. The League, of which William Morris was the leading personality, objected to elements in Hyndman's personal dominance of the S.D.F. and the opportunist politics it pursued. But during its brief existence the League displayed fissiparous tendencies, with elements moving from Marxism towards anarchism. After Morris's break with the League in 1890 he founded the Hammersmith Socialist Society, which survived until 1896. The League itself faded away in the early 1890s.

Papers

The archives of the Socialist League are deposited in the International Institute of Social History, Amsterdam. They formed part of the collections amassed by the German historian, Dr. Max Nettlau, who had saved these archives from the pulping machines to which they had already been sent. The archive contains the papers of the Council of the League, 1885-90, and includes: copies of the rules drawn up at the League's foundation; annual conference reports; minutes of General Meetings of London members; records of Council meetings, including agenda, minutes and notes of minutes, lists of members present, reports from officers and committees, resolutions and motions; records of the Ways and Means Committee; various office and financial records; and papers relating to the production of *Commonweal*. Among other records are a number of branch records, records of committees formed by the League and other Socialist bodies, various correspondence, and copies of printed matter issued by the League.

Minutes of the Hammersmith branch of the Social Democratic Federation and the Socialist League, and the Hammersmith Socialist Society, 1884-96 are in the British Library (Add. MSS. 45,891-4). The William Morris papers at the British Library comprise letters of Morris to his family, lecturers, diaries and other documents.

Availability

Written application should be made to the director of the Institute for the records of the League.

SOCIALIST LEAGUE (1932-1937)

The League was founded in October 1932 as an amalgamation of the National I.L.P. Affiliation Committee, which had opposed the Independent Labour Party's disaffiliation from the Labour Party, and the Society for Socialist Inquiry and Propaganda (S.S.I.P.). It was composed of Socialists who desired to work out Socialist policies for the Labour Party, whilst remaining firmly loyal to it. The title commemorated William Morris's earlier Socialist League. Among its leaders were E. F. Wise, G. R. Mitchison (later Lord Mitchison) and Stafford Cripps. G. D. H. Cole and Ernest Bevin, prominent members of S.S.I.P., withdrew their early support. In 1937 the League supported the Socialist United Front campaign with the Communist Party and the I.L.P. As a result, the League was proscribed by the Labour Party and dissolved itself.

Papers

It has not proved possible to trace the formal records of the Socialist League. Two literary executors were appointed when the League was dissolved, Frank Horrabin and G. R. Mitchison. Horrabin's second wife, who survived him, retained no relevant papers; the papers of his first wife, Winifred, are now deposited in Hull University Library, but these also appear to contain no relevant records. Lady Mitchison informs us that the papers of her husband were destroyed during various moves. It is likely, therefore, that none of the League's own records has survived. In the absence of such records, recourse is necessary to private collections.

The Cole Collection, in the Library of Nuffield College, Oxford, contains correspondence concerning the negotiations of the S.S.I.P. and the I.L.P. Affiliationists over the foundation of the League. Also at Nuffield College are papers of Sir Stafford Cripps and the Fabian Society. The latter collection includes papers of the S.S.I.P. The papers of Sir Stafford Cripps are disappointing with regard to his involvement with the League, but contain correspondence. No large corpus of E. F. Wise papers appears to have survived. His daughters have few papers, and the remaining papers are with Wise's son in Canada. No information on these is available.

Certain papers relating to the last years of the League, including minutes and reports, are retained by Mr. R. Groves, 7 Heathfield Road, London SW18. Records of the Gateshead Socialist League, 1932-36, are available in Gateshead Public Library, and there is also a relevant subject file in the Labour Party archive (LP/SL/35/1-60). The League published pamphlets and a journal, the *Socialist Leaguer*, and these inevitably provide an invaluable source in the absence of a comprehensive archive.

SOCIALIST MEDICAL ASSOCIATION
3rd Floor Cornwall House 31 Lionel Street Birmingham B3

The Association was founded in 1930 and has as its aim: 'To work for a fully socialised and comprehensive national health service, both preventive and curative, of the highest possible standard for the community.'

Papers

Records of the S.M.A. have been deposited in Hull University Library. These include: minutes of A.G.M.s, with reports of the Executive Committee, 1931-39; signed minutes of the Council and Executive Committee, 1946-63; further files of Executive minutes, 1941-69, and Council and sub-committee minutes, 1946-68; Policy Committee minutes, 1946-56; Social Committee minutes, 1947-53; General Practitioner Sub-committee minutes and papers, 1948-51; Campaign (Propaganda) Committee minutes and papers, 1950-51; Mental Health Sub-committee records, 1950-54; and a file of papers of various other sub-committees, 1944-46.

Also in the collection are various files relating to the Association's work, 1941-66; membership and finance records, 1953-61; S.M.A. circulars, 1930-60, and copies of *Branch Bulletin*, 1946-50; assorted press cuttings, 1938-65; and miscellaneous items which include notes on the history of the S.M.A., circulars from other organisations, an S.M.A. committee attendance book, etc.

The Association itself has retained copies of its journal since 1938, at first called *Medicine Today and Tomorrow*, now known as *Socialism and Health;* and has retained copies of pamphlets published by the S.M.A.

Availability

Enquiries should be directed to the Librarian, Hull University Library.

SOCIALIST PARTY OF GREAT BRITAIN
52 Clapham High Street London SW4 7UN

The Socialist Party of Great Britain (S.P.G.B.) was founded on 12 June 1904 with a provisional committee of twelve people in order to work for 'the establishment of a system of society based upon the common ownership and democratic control of the means and instruments for producing and distributing wealth by and in the interest of the whole community' (Declaration of Principles, 1904). Its founders broke away from the Social Democratic Federation 'to establish a genuine Socialist organisation'.

It is opposed to all other political parties in this country, but works in close harmony with companion parties abroad based on the same principles as its own, e.g. Canada. The Declaration of Principles adopted in 1904 has not been changed. It is reproduced in all publications.

Papers

There is a substantial archive at the S.P.G.B. headquarters, since there is a policy to throw away only the most routine of correspondence. However, it is sorted only in a rough manner, and the pressure of space necessarily means that some of the records are either lost or mislaid. In addition to retaining all the material, archival and printed, the headquarters receives the past records of branches that cease to exist. The following is a brief selection of the records held:

(1) *Minutes.* Executive Committee minute books, most of them handwritten, survive from inception to date, except one inadvertently destroyed during World War I.

(2) *Annual Conference Reports.* A full set, also a full set of delegate meetings (where delegates can recommend but not mandate the E.C.).

(3) *Correspondence.* Most of the routine correspondence is destroyed owing to pressure of space. However, most of the main correspondence is retained. There is a 'letters in' book for 1942 stating sender and contents of each letter received. The S.P.G.B. has a complete file of correspondence of its dealings with the British Broadcasting Corporation charting its attempts to receive some time on the air. Also of interest is a file ('Special File') containing publications from, and communications with, the following: British Humanists, Rationalist Press Association, Ethical Union, National Secular Society, South Place Ethical Society. This file was established in accordance with Article 7 of the Declaration of Principles and the particular rule in the rule book under which a member shall not belong to any other political organisation. The correspondence also includes files on complaints laid against members (post-1951) and correspondence dealing with general membership questions. Additionally there are copies of E.C. correspondence with companion parties.

241

There are several account books relating to headquarters receipts and expenditure, mainly from 1942 to date, although there are earlier ones. There are also several branch accounts at headquarters, e.g. Manchester dues book, 1952-57, and annual financial statements, although certain years are missing. In addition, records of the Finance Committee survive from 1942 to date. Much material was destroyed, however, when the head office was bombed in April 1941.

(4) *Membership Records.* These are kept mainly in the Library in a steel trunk; they are filed alphabetically and are from foundation to date. There are also 'Forms F', 1932 to date, giving reasons for individuals leaving the party.

(5) *Published Material.* Headquarters has a literature room which contains copies of its journal *Socialist Standard* from 1904 to date. Also it contains the various pamphlets published by the S.P.G.B. as well as catalogues of those of companion parties, e.g. *Western Socialist* of the American party. There are also printed copies of *Discussions on Crisis.*

(6) *Other material.* There are several occasional notebooks by unknown authors, some of them on Socialist personalities such as William Morris.

The S.P.G.B. has periodic polls of its members on policy and keeps the ballot papers, normally for a period of three months, although there are some past collections, e.g. 1956, still intact. There are some election addresses, for the General Elections since 1945. These are also reproduced in *Socialist Standard.*

(7) *Histories.* The Jubilee edition of the *Socialist Standard* (Sept. 1954) provides a historical survey of the S.P.G.B.

Availability

This is normally granted on written application to the General Secretary.

SOCIETY FOR CULTURAL RELATIONS WITH THE U.S.S.R.
320 Brixton Road London SW9

The Society was founded in 1924 to promote mutual understanding between the British and Soviet peoples through cultural relations.

Papers

The Society has retained records dating back to its foundation in 1924. They are at present unsorted. The Society hopes to study the records, with a view to publishing an account of its work for its 50th anniversary.

Availability

These records are not at present available. Enquiries should be directed to the Secretary.

SOCIETY FOR PROMOTING CHRISTIAN KNOWLEDGE
Holy Trinity Church Marylebone Road London NW1

The S.P.C.K. was founded in 1698.

Papers

The records of the Society have been retained at Holy Trinity Church. Much correspondence and other documentary information is preserved only in the printed annual and quarterly reports (the former beginning with the first Annual Account of the Charity Schools, 1704), of which there are complete series in the

S.P.C.K. archives. There is, however, a substantial collection of papers, dating from the early 18th century. The Home Correspondence covers series of original letters and early documents, 1698-1860. The records of District and Diocesan Committees comprise various series of minutes, only some of which extend into the 20th century. Similarly, the available records relating to education and finance are mostly 18th and 19th century. Minutes of the General Board and of other functional committees, however, continue to date.

The S.P.C.K. also retains records relating in one way or another to every Anglican diocese in the world where it has been active.

Another important source is the full collection of S.P.C.K. topical pamphlets and tracts, and forms of service for special occasions or special needs, including many issued during the two world wars.

Availability

Applications should be made to the Archivist and Librarian, S.P.C.K.

SOCIETY FOR THE PROTECTION OF SCIENCE AND LEARNING LTD

3 Buckland Crescent London NW3 5DH

The Society was founded as the Academic Assistance Council in 1933, and adopted its present title in January 1937. It was established shortly after Hitler came to power in Germany to help scholars displaced from university teaching or research positions for reasons of racial origin, political or religious opinion. The Society offered research grants and gave personal comfort, to those who had lost their positions, and helped scholars to find new posts. In these ways the Society has helped, for example, refugees from Fascist and other countries in the 1930s, from war-torn Europe in the 1940s, and from Hungary, Czechoslovakia, Poland, South Africa, Greece, and other countries in Asia, Africa and South America, during the post-war period.

Papers

Records from 1933-51 have been deposited in the Bodleian Library. These have not yet been sorted. The material, however, is extensive, filling a number of large filing cabinets and chests. Papers are filed according to subjects (e.g. physics, philosophy) and persons, with a special series covering relations with the Home Office. The bulk of this material is correspondence. Five annual reports were issued up to 1946, but none has appeared since then. Minute books since 1933, and all other papers since 1951, are retained at the offices of the Society.

Availability

For records up to 1951 permission should be obtained from the Bodleian Library, and from the Society. Enquiries concerning the later records should be made to the Secretary, S.P.S.L. Ltd.

SOCIETY FOR SOCIALIST INQUIRY AND PROPAGANDA

The Society was founded in early 1931 by a group of Socialists led by G. D. H. and Margaret Cole, who sought a new direction in Labour Party policy. With Ernest Bevin as Chairman, members became known as 'loyal grousers'. Towards the end of 1932 the S.S.I.P. joined with the pro-Labour Party group of the Independent Labour Party to form the *Socialist League* (q.v.).

Papers

Certain relevant records are contained in the archive of the Fabian Society at Nuffield College, Oxford. These include: Reports of S.S.I.P. conferences, 1931-32; minutes of meetings, 1931, 1932 (one file, one book); discussion notes and drafts, *c*. 1931; circulars, rules, notices of meetings, 1931-32; and correspondence, chiefly concerning the formation of a new journal, with, among others, Ponsonby, Cripps, B. Webb, D. N. Pritt, Malcolm MacDonald, Sankey, Dalton, *c*. 1931.

The Cole Collection at Nuffield College also contains valuable material. This includes correspondence, circulars and notes, minutes of discussion meetings, etc. A complete set of *S.S.I.P. News*, 1931-32, has also been retained in this collection.

The Ernest Bevin papers are deposited at Churchill College, Cambridge, but they contain little of relevance on S.S.I.P.

SOCIETY OF CERTIFIED AND ASSOCIATED LIBERAL AGENTS

The chief functions of the Society were the promotion of knowledge of electoral law, particularly among Liberal agents; and the promotion of the interests and welfare of Liberal agents.

Papers

Records of the Society, 1895-1951, have been deposited in the Sheepscar Library, Leeds. These include six volumes of Society minutes, 1895-1945; one volume of the minutes of the Yorkshire District, 1910-34 (including a register of subscriptions, 1911-28); and three volumes of accounts, 1893-1951.

An incomplete run of the *Liberal Agent* is available at the *National Liberal Club* (q.v.).

Availability

Enquiries should be directed to the Archivist, Sheepscar Library, Leeds. There are restrictions on the publication of the deposited material.

SOCIETY OF FRIENDS (QUAKERS)
Friends House Euston Road London NW1 2BJ

The Society of Friends is a body of Christians commonly called Quakers. Its worship, fellowship and its work of service in the fields of peace, relief from distress, etc., display the Society's emphasis on the priesthood of all believers, the inward light and the importance of personal experience. Founded by George Fox (1624-91), Quakerism arose in Great Britain out of the religious ferment of the mid-17th century and represents the extreme left wing of the Puritan movement.

Papers

The supreme governing body of the Society of Friends in Great Britain is London Yearly Meeting. Minutes are extant from 1672 and printed *Proceedings* from 1857 contain documents presented to or issued by the meeting, reports of committees and (from 1876) a summary of proceedings of Meeting for Sufferings, the standing representative meeting of London Y.M. A printed index to *Y.M. Proceedings* to 1906 is available; from 1907 two typescript indices are available in the Library.

Minutes of Meeting for Sufferings are available from 1676 onwards; there is no cumulative index for the 20th century. Minutes are also extant for most (though not all) of the standing committees of Yearly Meeting and Meeting for Sufferings. Many of these have their origin in independent bodies set up in the 19th century: Friends Tract Association (1813), Friends First Day School Association (1847), Friends Temperance Union (1850), Friends Foreign Mission Association (1868). The administrative history of many of these bodies is complex and the Library maintains an organisational guide for the use of students. The range covered may be illustrated by the existence of committees on Peace (1888-1965), South Africa (1899-1928), Anti-slavery, largely devoted to work in Pemba (1894-1918), Slavery and Native Races, later Race Relations (1928-72). Opium Traffic (1903-31), Armenia (1924-38), Indian Affairs (1930-34), Palestine (1934-41, 1944-51), the Far East (1932-34), Betting and Gambling (1902-36), War and the Social Order, later Industrial and Social Order, later Social and Economic Affairs (1915-71), Penal Reform, later Penal Affairs (1920-72), Education (1902 to date), Vagrancy (1929-40), Industrial Crisis, later Allotments (1926-51).

The Council for International Service (1919) was united with Friends Foreign Mission Association in 1927 to form Friends Service Council. C.I.S. had itself absorbed in 1923 the residual work of Friends War Victims Relief Committee (1914) which sponsored work in Holland, France, Russia, Poland, Germany and Austria. F.S.C., besides continuing some work in many of these countries, was also responsible for service in India, China, Madagascar, Pemba, the Middle East and (from 1936) Spain. During World War II a new Friends War Victims Relief Committee (1940, later Friends Relief Service) undertook work at home among evacuees, especially old people, later working in France, Greece, Germany, Austria and Poland. F.R.S. also took over responsibility for work in this country with refugees and (later) internees of the Germany Emergency Committee (1933, later Friends Committee for Refugees and Aliens). Friends Service Council took over the residual work of F.R.S. in 1948. During both world wars there was an unofficial Friends Ambulance Unit: that set up during World War II was involved in relief operations, particularly in India, China, Greece and North West Europe. Reports, memoranda and correspondence exist in addition to minute books for F.W.V.R.C.-F.R.S. (both world wars), C.I.S., F.F.M.A., F.S.C. and F.A.U. (World War II).

For the Socialist Quaker Society (1898-1924) two minute books survive for the years 1898-1913. The journal *Ploughshare* (1912-19) and the Society's published tracts are also useful. The Friends Social Union was a more moderate and respectable rival to S.Q.S., founded in 1904. Only its printed reports and pamphlets (1904-15) are available at Friends House. Among the other interesting papers which are retained are the records of the India Conciliation Group (see *India in British Politics*).

The Quaker peace testimony led to the establishment of a Service Committee (1915-20) and Visitation of Prisoners Committee (1916-20), for both of which correspondence as well as official minutes are extant. In World War II there was a Conscription Committee (1939-45), but much work was done through the Central Board for Conscientious Objectors for which minutes, tribunal reports, correspondence, etc., survive. There are, too, several private collections of papers relating to conscientious objectors; for example, the correspondence of R. B. Murdoch, M.P., Arnold S. Rowntree, M.P., and T. E. Harvey, M.P. Friends House Library maintains indexes listing all Quakers who were members of Meeting for Sufferings or of standing committees of that Meeting or of Yearly Meeting during the period covered by this Guide.

The Library acts as a repository for the private papers of individual Quakers. These collections include the papers of a number of public figures and persons active in politics: for example, the papers of Henry T. Hodgkin (1877-1933), a missionary in China and prominent figure in the *Fellowship of Reconciliation* (q.v.); Alexander C. Wilson (1866-1955), relating to the temperance question, abolition of slavery and the peace movement; Catharine L. Braithwaite (1864-1957), a co-founder of the Emergency Committee (which helped aliens resident in Britain throughout World War I). An important feature of the Library is its typescript Dictionary of Quaker Biography, and other compilations such as the Index of Quaker Members of Parliament.

Availability

The Library may be used by arrangement with the Librarian. A fifty-year rule operates but it may be waived at the discretion of the Library Committee.

SOCIETY OF GRAPHICAL AND ALLIED TRADES
74 Nightingale Lane London SW12 8NR

SOGAT in its present form was established in 1972. This is the present name of the organisation known as the National Union of Printing, Bookbinding and Paper Workers until 1966. In that year the National Union amalgamated with the National Society of Operative Printers' Assistants to form the Society of Graphical and Allied Trades. This amalgamation was dissolved in December 1971, and the old N.U.P.B.W. resumed its separate existence under the present title.

The National Union had been founded in 1921 as the National Union of Printing, Bookbinding, Machine Ruling and Paper Workers, as an amalgamation of the National Union of Bookbinders and Machine Rulers (established as a result of amalgamation in 1911) and the National Union of Printing and Paper Workers (established in 1914, again as a result of amalgamation). The older predecessors of the Paper Workers had histories, particularly the London societies, dating back to the 18th century. Since 1920s a number of other unions has joined with the larger union, including in 1963, the Monotype Casters' and Typefounders' Society.

Papers

The national organisation has retained its records dating back to about 1910. These include Executive Committee minutes; these, however, are regarded as confidential and access is not granted. Similarly, the bound financial records of the union are not made available. Records of the Biennial Delegates Council date from 1912 and these may be consulted. The national organisation of SOGAT also retains copies of its rule books and bound copies of the *Paperworkers' Journal* and its successor, *SOGAT Journal.*

The union has grown through a long series of amalgamations. Many of the amalgamated unions have become separate branches of SOGAT, and have retained their records. The following collections are particularly important:

(1) *London Society of Bookbinders.* A very important collection of papers, largely collected by John Jaffrey, covering the period 1796-1919 is deposited in the British Library (Add. MSS. 57,618-57,620). These include minute books of the Society and of lodges, registers, accounts, correspondence, etc.

(2) *Monotype Casters' and Typefounders' Branch*, Natsopa House, 46-47 Blackfriars Road, London SE1. This became part of the N.U.P.B.W. in 1963. It had been established in 1889 as the Amalgamated Typefounders' Trade Society, and changed its name in 1937 to the Monotype Casters' and Typefounders' Society. Records include minutes from the 1890s, reports and balance sheets.

(3) *Edinburgh Branch.* A substantial collection of material, much of it on microfilm, covering 150 years, 1822-1972, has been deposited in the National Library of Scotland. These include minutes and other papers of the Union Society of Journeymen Bookbinders of Edinburgh, 1822-61; the Bookbinders, Paper Rulers and

Pocket Book Makers of Edinburgh, 1862-72; the Edinburgh branch of the Book-binders' Consolidated Union, 1869-86; the Edinburgh branch of the Bookbinders' and Machine Rulers' Consolidated Union, 1886-1911; the Edinburgh branch of the National Union of Printers, Bookbinders, Machine Rulers, and Paperworkers, 1914 to the 1950s; together with records of the Scottish District Council of the union. Various banners and regalia of the branch are deposited in Huntley House Museum, Canongate, Edinburgh.

Availability

General enquiries should be directed to SOGAT national office in Nightingale Lane. Other enquiries should be directed to the relevant libraries and branches.

SOCIETY OF LABOUR LAWYERS
9 King's Bench Walk Temple London EC4

The Society was founded in 1948, to work particularly for law reform. It is affiliated to the Labour Party.

Papers

Records of the Society have been deposited in B.L.P.E.S. These include formal records, such as Executive Committee minutes, correspondence, arrangements for meetings; A.G.M. papers; membership enquiries, rules, etc. The bulk of the collection, however, relates to the Society's work for law reform, consisting of a considerable amount of correspondence, papers of working parties, submissions, etc.

Availability

Enquiries should be directed to the Librarian, B.L.P.E.S.

SOCIETY OF LITHOGRAPHIC ARTISTS, DESIGNERS, ENGRAVERS AND PROCESS WORKERS
Slade House 55 Clapham Common South Side London SW4 9DF

The Society was established in Manchester in 1885 as the National Society of Lithographic Artists, Designers and Writers, Copperplate and Wood Engravers. The present form of the name was adopted in 1924.

Papers

The series of minutes covering the Executive Committee, the National Council and delegate meetings run from 1885 to date. The set of annual reports is also complete, as are details of the Society's rules. The annual reports include balance sheets and accounts, and lists of members for the period 1885-1953. Recent membership records are kept on a card index. There are records of wage negotiations and agreements from 1916 to date. The Society also holds copies of the *Process Journal*, founded in 1929 by a small group of newspaper members; from 1938 the *Journal* became the official organ of the Society. A history of the Society has been produced, *A Record of Fifty Years, 1885-1935*, with 'Additional Notes', written in 1945.

The Arthur Ebenezer Cooke Collection at B.L.P.E.S., contains typescript and printed material concerning the Union and related organisations, 1885-1935 (37 vols.).

Availability

Availability

Researchers should apply to the Society's General Secretary for permission to use the archives; and to the Librarian, B.L.P.E.S., for the Cooke Collection.

SOCIETY OF MOTOR MANUFACTURERS AND TRADERS LTD.
Forbes House Halkin Street London SW1X 7DS

The Society was founded in 1902 to represent and promote the interests of the motor industry.

Papers

The Society has retained its formal records since 1902, including minutes of the Council, the standing committees and sub-committees. These are treated as confidential, as is correspondence, and are not generally available. Copies of annual reports since 1903 have been retained, and are available, as are copies of catalogues of the Motor Shows organised by the Society, at Crystal Palace, Olympia and now Earls Court.

The Press and Public Relations Department acts as an information centre and can deal with particular enquiries. Copies of the *Newsletter*, the now defunct *Journal*, and statistical and trade information published by the Society, are also available.

Availability

Enquiries should be made to the Secretarial Manager.

SOCIETY OF ST. VINCENT DE PAUL
24 George Street London W1H 5RB

Founded in France in 1833 by Frederic Ozanam, the Society extended its work to Britain in 1844. The S.V.P. is a Roman Catholic international charity seeking to help the needy by practising Christian love in all spheres of life.

Papers

A selection of records is housed at the George Street offices. Unfortunately they are as yet unsorted and uncatalogued. The Society is at present preparing a catalogue of its records. However, some details of the collection can be given. Among the assorted minute books, the interesting items include: Superior Council, minutes, 1844-1927, with gaps; London Council, minutes, 1857-65; East London Particular Council, minutes, 1923-38; Islington Conference, minutes, with some correspondence, food tickets, posters and rules, 1878-92; Catholic Seamen's Home, minutes, 1937-48; London Council Committee for the Patronage of Boys, minutes, 1857-80. Annual Reports go back to 1844, and the records of annual meetings are available. Correspondence files exist but have not been sorted. Much of this material relates to cases and individuals dealt with by the Society. Some Council and Conference records are kept locally.

Availability

Application to see the records should be addressed to the Secretary. Access to the individual case records would not usually be allowed.

SOUTH PLACE ETHICAL SOCIETY
Conway Hall 25 Red Lion Square London WC1R 4RL

The Society was founded in 1793 and has provided a continuous congregation since then for those who have rejected conventional religions. It defines its aims as the study and dissemination of ethical principles and the cultivation of a rational religious sentiment. It does this by means of meetings, forums, lectures, etc.

Papers

The Society has an important Library containing a great deal of published material relating to the humanist movements from the end of the 18th century onwards. The Library holds, among other important items, the manuscript of G. J. Holyoake's autobiography. The history of the Society itself is recorded in bound volumes of the lectures and tracts of W. J. Fox, 1817-52, and M. D. Conway; in minutes, some dating back to the 1850s; in annual reports; and in copies of the *Ethical Record* (formerly the *Monthly Record*) dating back to 1895. Correspondence has not generally been retained (except for recent years), but a small collection of items of historical importance is kept on the premises.

Availability

The Library is open to readers. Enquiries should be directed to the General Secretary.

SPANISH CIVIL WAR

Many individuals and a wide variety of organisations in Britain were involved in the affairs of Spain during the 1930s. Archival material is scattered through numerous collections of the private papers of statesmen, campaigners and volunteers; for example, the George Orwell papers (University College, London), the papers of Lord Chatfield (National Maritime Museum) and Oliver Harvey (British Library).

Naturally, the files of government departments, especially the Foreign Office, at the Public Record Office are of primary importance. Also valuable are the Labour Party, the Communist Party and Trades Union Congress archives. The South Wales Miners' Federation (see under *National Union of Mineworkers*) was just one union closely involved in Spanish affairs. Unfortunately the papers of Victor Gollancz are believed not to have survived (see under *Left Book Club*). Quaker work during the war is recorded in the files of the Friends Service Council, Spain Relief Committee, 1936-40 (see under *Society of Friends*), and the records of other pacifist and relief organisations should also be consulted. Of printed literature, pamphlets and leaflets, a good collection is housed at B.L.P.E.S. This material includes runs of periodicals, *War in Spain* and *Voice of Spain*, news-sheets, pictures, and official propaganda produced by each side. Further material is available in the Press Library at Chatham House (see under *Royal Institute of International Affairs*) and at the *International Institute of Social History* (q.v.).

Of the many organisations, the following may be mentioned:

Formed in Sept. 1936, the Non-Intervention Committee (later known as the International Committee for the Application of Non-Intervention in Spain) was an official body mainly concerned with the restriction of arms supplies to opposing sides in the Spanish Civil War and with the withdrawal of foreign volunteers from Spain. Assorted papers of the Committee (1936-39) are available at the Public Record Office (Cab. 62 and F.O: 849). Other records of the Council's work, 1936-49, are included in the Francis Hemming Collection at Corpus Christi College,

Oxford. Hemming was Secretary to the Spanish Non-Intervention Committee, and to the Spanish Non-Intervention Board, 1937-39. The papers include: press cuttings on the Spanish situation, 1937-38; Chairman's Sub-committee memoranda and papers, 1936-38; Technical Advisory Sub-committee's notes of proceedings, agenda papers, 1936-39, reports, 1936-38, official records of proceedings (meetings 1-93), 1936-39; Advisory Sub-committee to the Secretary, minutes, 1936-39; notes, memoranda, etc., 1936-54; Non-Intervention Board, index to Secretary's memoranda, 1937-39; conclusions of meetings 1-4, 1937; typescript of journal, Jan.-Dec. 1938; gazettes, 1938-39; circulars, 1938-39; diaries, covering various periods, 1938-39, interleaved with assorted letters regarding Spanish affairs (correspondents include members of the Foreign Office and foreign ambassadors in London); assorted papers, covering such subjects as accounts, the Sea Observation Scheme, reports from the Franco-Spanish frontier, evacuation of foreign volunteers; report dated 27 July 1949 to the A.G.M., and a letter of 25 July 1949, from A. S. Pankhurst to Francis Hemming, with (a) a short report on the activities of the Non-Intervention Council since the outbreak of war in 1939, and (b) a brief for the A.G.M. Applications should be made to the Librarian at Corpus Christi College, Oxford.

Formed in London in March 1937, the Labour Spain Committee aimed to persuade the National Executive of the Labour Party to adopt a tougher attitude to the British Government's policy of non-intervention in Spain and to organise aid for the Spanish Republican Government. The Committee ceased to exist about April 1939. The records are deposited at Churchill College, Cambridge, and comprise letters and papers arranged chronologically in nine folders, prefaced by a historical note on the Labour Spain Committee. Some of the papers are not yet open to general inspection, but application to see any of them should be made to the Archivist at Churchill College.

The International Brigade Association was founded in 1939, with the aim of continuing the 'struggle against Fascism' (i.e. to continue the struggle against the regime of General Franco) 'on other fronts' (i.e. after the return to their own countries of the members of the International Brigades). When the Brigade offices closed in the early 1950s most of the files were dispersed. The present Secretary inherited no papers when she took over in 1961, and has been unable to trace any. However, the Marx Memorial Library contains a complete set of the publications of the Association, including the periodical *Volunteer for Liberty*, later renamed *Spain Today*.

SYNDICALISM AND INDUSTRIAL UNREST, 1910-21

In the absence of any major collection of records, the following notes attempt to bring together information on the history of the industrial unrest, together with information concerning the major publications and major collections of relevant papers. From 1910 to the outbreak of World War I a chief element in the industrial unrest that was a characteristic of British politics during this period was labelled 'Syndicalism'. This had found its earliest expression in Britain in the *Socialist Labour Party* (q.v.) and its dependent body, the British Advocates of Industrial Unionism. The early Industrial Unionists stressed the importance of building up new unions on industrial lines, to replace the existing craft unions. Tom Mann, already an Industrial Unionist, declared in 1910 that Syndicalism (or Industrial Syndicalism as it was more widely known) would suit British conditions better (see *Industrial Syndicalist*, July 1910). The emphasis henceforth was on influencing existing union structures rather than building new ones.

The result was the foundation of the Industrial Syndicalist Education League at the end of 1910, 'to educate Trade Unionists and the workers generally in the principles of industrial Syndicalism for the purposes of conducting the class struggle on non-parliamentary lines'. The League was a loose body whose main activity was propaganda for industrial unity and involvement in strikes. There appear to be no surviving records. Papers of its chief propagandists, Tom Mann and Guy Bowman, have not been located. The League published the *Industrial Syndicalist* from July 1910 to 1914 and this is a useful source. Manifestations of Syndicalism in the trade unions may be traced in their records, e.g. in the records of the *National Union of Railwaymen* (q.v.), the prototype of the new industrial union. A journal entitled the *Syndicalist Railwayman* was published by Syndicalists in the industry. The Unofficial Reform Committee of the South Wales Miners' Federation, based in Rhondda, published the *Miners' Next Step* (1912), which was an important text of the movement, and a journal, *Rhondda Bomb*. Records of the South Wales Miners' Federation are deposited in University College, Swansea. (For other records of the miners' organisations, see under *National Union of Mineworkers.*) Reference should also be made to records of its predecessor organisations now held by the *Transport and General Workers' Union* (q.v.). The National Transport Workers' Federation was established to co-ordinate activities of unions in the transport industries. Ben Tillett and Tom Mann were instrumental in setting this up. A journal, *Transport Worker*, propagated the new ideas in the industry during the Liverpool strikes of 1911-12.

The Triple Alliance of Railwaymen, Miners and Dockers (1914-21) was an important example of cross-union alliances. Minutes of the Alliance may be found in the annual volumes of proceedings of the Miners' Federation of Great Britain. After 1913 Syndicalism as such became less prominent and more emphasis was placed on industrial reorganisation and the building of what became known as 'rank and file' movements. Between 1910 and 1917 an Amalgamation Committee Movement, an unofficial rank and file movement, was particularly active in the engineering industry. A Federation of Amalgamation Committees was established in 1913 (and the *Syndicalist* became the *Syndicalist and Amalgamation News*). After the disintegration of the Industrial Syndicalist Education League the Federation became the Industrial Democracy League which published a journal, *Solidarity*. This ceased publication on the outbreak of the war. The Amalgamation Committee in the engineering industry became the Metal Engineering and Shipbuilding Amalgamation Committee (M.E.S.A.C.) in 1913. This again was affected by the outbreak of war. In November 1915 Tom Mann and others started *Trade Unionist* (1915-16), and early 1916 saw the revival of the amalgamation movement. From mid-1915 the series of National Rank and File Conferences acted as a focus for the new mood of militancy in industry. In January 1918 the Rank and File Movement merged with the Shop Stewards' and Workers' Committee Movement.

The formation of the Clyde Workers' Committee in the summer of 1915 marks the beginning of the Shop Stewards' Movement. Strikes on the Clyde in 1915 and 1916, in Sheffield in 1916, and the engineering strike of 1917 marked the spreading influence of the movement. It had no main centre, and local differences were manifest, but it was firmly rooted in the engineering workshop. *Solidarity*, founded in 1916, became an organ of the movement, and from 1918 the *Worker*, based in Glasgow, fulfilled a similar function.

At the conference of August 1917 23 Workers' Committees were represented, and in 1921 the movement changed its name to National Workers' Committee Movement. It was dissolved in 1922; no central collection of papers survives.

The Clyde Workers' Committee is the best documented of the movement. No records of the Committee itself, apart from its journal, the *Worker*, are extant, but its history may be traced in the minutes of the Glasgow Trades Council at the Mitchell Library, Glasgow; miscellaneous papers and legal correspondence of the Clyde Workers' Defence Committee, 1919, also at the Mitchell Library; the P. J.

Dollan-'Gibson'-Broady Collection in Glasgow University Library; the records of the Ministry of Munitions at the Public Record Office in London; and the Beveridge Papers at B.L.P.E.S. Reference should also be made to the John Maclean papers at the National Library of Scotland.

Few of the main participants in the various movements seem to have retained their papers. The papers of Robert Smillie, President of the Miners' Federation of Great Britain, have been destroyed, though Nuffield College, Oxford, has a collection of largely printed material that belonged to him. The Tanner Collection, also at Nuffield College, has material on Jack Tanner's involvement in Syndicalism. Tanner was a shop steward in Sheffield during World War I.

The industrial unrest between 1910 and 1921 evoked a considerable response, particularly on the left of British politics, which may be traced in various collections of papers: the Cole Collection at Nuffield College, Oxford; the Passfield Papers at B.L.P.E.S.; and the records of the *Fabian Society* (q.v.), the *Labour Party* (q.v.), *Labour Research Department* (q.v.), *National Guilds League* (q.v.) and the *National Council of Labour Colleges* (q.v.). Lord Askwith, who as G. R. Askwith was Chief Industrial Commissioner, 1912-19, seems to have left no relevant papers. The only records in the care of his daughter are personal diaries of his wife.

The impact of the unrest during the war may be traced in such records as Cabinet papers, the Ministry of Munitions papers, in the Lloyd George papers at the Beaverbrook Library, London, and in the Beveridge Munitions Collection, B.L.P.E.S.

It should be noted that the *Daily Herald* (known as the *Herald*, 1914-19) carried sympathetic coverage of the industrial unrest and the various movements associated with it throughout the period. Further information can be obtained from B. Pribicevic, *Shop Stewards' Movement and Workers' Control* (Oxford, 1959); J. Hinton, *The First Shop Stewards' Movement* (1973); and Walter Kendall, *The Revolutionary Movement in Britain, 1900-21* (1968).

See also *National Minority Movement*.

TARIFF COMMISSION

The Commission was established in 1903 by Joseph Chamberlain. It consisted of a cross-section of businessmen, and had the task of investigating the conditions of British industry and of recommending how tariffs might be used to promote production, discourage unfair competition, and develop Imperial trade. H. A. S. Hewins was Secretary of the Commission, 1903-17, and Chairman, 1920-22.

Papers

A substantial collection of papers relating to the Commission has been deposited at B.L.P.E.S. These are at present unsorted and are not easily available for research purposes. However, certain printed material, including a considerable amount of memoranda, is readily available at B.L.P.E.S.

Availability

Enquiries should be directed to the Librarian, B.L.P.E.S.

TARIFF REFORM LEAGUE

The League was established in mid-1903 on the initiative of Joseph Chamberlain. Originally intended as a propaganda organisation for Chamberlain's advocacy of Imperial Preference, it became a focal point for protectionist feeling, and a movement in favour of moderate protection for British industry. From the early 1920s, however, its propagandist role was increasingly assumed by newer organisations, e.g. the *Commonwealth Industries Association* (q.v.).

Papers

The chief sources for the League are in a variety of collections of private papers. The Joseph Chamberlain papers at Birmingham University Library are an important source, of course. Also at Birmingham are the papers of Sir Austen and Neville Chamberlain. The papers of J. L. Garvin, a prominent press supporter of Chamberlain are at the University of Texas; and the papers of W. A. S. Hewins, Director of the London School of Economics and later an M.P. and Secretary of the Tariff Commission, have been deposited at Sheffield University Library. The papers of James Parker Smith (who was Joseph Chamberlain's private secretary) are in the Glasgow City Archives. L. S. Amery was prominent in the Tariff movement throughout its history, and his papers are in the care of his son, the Rt. Hon. Julian Amery, M.P.

Copies of the League's leaflets, annual reports, 1905-14, and of the *Tariff Reformer and Empire Monthly*, 1917-19, are available at B.L.P.E.S.

TEMPERANCE

A good deal of material, both manuscript and printed, relating to the activities of the Temperance movement survives, in libraries and in the possession of the surviving Temperance organisations. The United Kingdom Alliance and the British National Temperance League (see below) have very substantial collections of printed material, including reports of Temperance organisations, pamphlets, circulars, journals, etc. Several libraries have comparable collections: the Rochdale Public Library, which holds a valuable collection of pamphlets and manuscripts in its Local History Department; the University of London Library, which holds the James Turner Temperance Collection; and the British Library of Political and Economic Science, which has a collection of translations of foreign works and extracts relating to the Temperance movement, *c.* 1895-1915 (15 vols.: Arthur James Sherwell Collection). These collections provide a valuable supplement to the manuscript material described below.

I. National Organisations

British National Temperance League
Livesey-Clegg House 44 Union Street Sheffield S1 2JP

The League was established under its present title in 1952, as the result of the amalgamation of the British Temperance League (founded 1834) and the National Temperance League (founded 1856), incorporating the Medical Abstainers' Association (founded 1876).

Papers

A substantial set of records, both of the British National Temperance League since 1952 and of its original constituents, is retained in the Library of Livesey-Clegg House.

1. *British Temperance League*

These include: minutes of the General Purposes Committee, 1859-61, 1863-77, 1898-1931; minutes of the Executive Committee, 1847-59, 1878-1943; a book kept by Samuel Sims, with autobiography, personal diary and records of meetings, 1854-66; minutes of the annual congress, 1845-64; agents' reports, 1884-88; report of a ministerial conference on temperance, 1874; annual report of the Executive Committee, 1879; account books, 1903-21; Medical Abstainers: members and correspondents of League, 1905; twelve notebooks containing lists of names of possible supporters of the League, in a number of towns and counties, 1911-30; a day book for the 1930s; conference reports 1925, 1926, 1928, 1929, 1930, 1931, 1933, 1935, 1936.

2. National Temperance League

Records comprise minutes of committee, 1845-46, 1896-1906; annual reports, 1857-1950, with 1893-94 and 1897-98 missing.

3. Sheffield Temperance Association

This set of records includes minutes, 1856-61, 1863-64, 1874-1916; minutes of the Indoors Committee, Buildings Committee, Hall Committee and New Year's Festival Committee, 1905-18; minutes of the Outdoor Committee, 1904-12; correspondence book, 1921-27; subscription book, 1899-1918; account book, 1899-1919; annual report, 1919; rules, 1910.

In addition to the above records, the League's library contains annual reports of many other local and Temperance associations.

Availability

Records are available for consultation in the library during normal office hours.

Church of England Council for Social Aid
Church House Deans Yard London SW1P 3NZ

The parent bodies, the Church of England Temperance Society and the National Police Court Mission, were founded in 1872 and 1876 respectively. The present name was adopted in 1967 to indicate the practical breadth of the Council's work. The Society works in particular (1) to promote temperance and higher standards of moral life in the individual, the family and the community; (2) to rehabilitate the intemperate, the delinquent, the drug addict and others in need of help; and (3) to relieve the distress or suffering arising from delinquency, intemperance or addiction. The Council maintains homes and hostels and undertakes educational work in this field.

Papers

Assorted records of the Church of England Temperance Society have been deposited at Lambeth Palace Library. They include: Council minutes, 1880-1950, and Auxiliary Committee minutes 1930-39; minutes of board meetings, 1883-93; Executive Committee minutes and miscellaneous papers, agenda, etc., 1885-1919; minutes of the Central Executive Committee, 1935-49; Legislative Committee minutes, 1884-91; minutes of the Secretaries' Consultative Committee, 1923-39; Finance Committee minutes, 1893-1914; and the Central Finance Committee, 1927-29. Other series of papers and minute books relate to the Central Women's Union Board, 1892-1947; the Central Juvenile Board (later the Central Education Board) and its sub-committees, 1910-66; the Deafwork Committee, 1924-39; and the Anti-Betting and Gambling Sub-committee, 1937-38. With these papers are also some records of the Police Court Mission: for example, minutes of the Guild of Police Court Missionaries Executive, 1923-38; minutes of the Central Police Court Mission Committee, 1927-38; minutes of the National Police Court Mission Council, 1938-42. Other records at Lambeth Palace relate to certain of the homes run by the Society.

Applications should be addressed to the Archivist at Lambeth Palace Library.

National British Women's Total Abstinence Union (Incorporated)
Rosalind Carlisle House 23 Dawson Place London W2

Formed in 1876 as the British Women's Temperance Association, in order to further the control and ultimate suppression of the liquor trade, the Association changed its name in 1893 to the National British Women's Temperance Association, a name it retained until 1926 when it federated to the World's Women's Christian Federation and adopted the title National British Women's Total Abstinence Union (Incorporated).

Papers

The Union has retained almost the entirety of its records, including 35 volumes of Executive Committee minutes from 1876 to the present. In addition, all the annual reports from the date of foundation to the present have been retained. The Union has also kept issues of its journal, formerly the *British Women's Temperance Journal*, later the *Wings*, and now the *White Ribbon*, from 1886 to the present. Some recent correspondence has also been kept.

Availability

These records are available on written application to the General Secretary.

United Kingdom Alliance
Alliance House 12 Caxton Street London SW1H 0QS

The Alliance was founded in Manchester in 1853 by Nathaniel Card with the aim of suppressing the liquor traffic and has had an active existence ever since. Its aim is now defined as 'the elimination of the drink evil from the life of the nation'. Its educational work was taken over in 1942 by the newly registered company, United Kingdom Temperance Alliance Ltd. The Alliance works in association with the Christian Economic and Social Research Foundation, which produces annual statistical reports on drunkenness, etc. In the 1960s the Alliance absorbed the National Commercial Temperance League. It is a member of the National Temperance Federation.

Papers

These are housed in Alliance House and consist of the following:

(1) General minute books, 1871-1923, together with a minute book of the U.K.A. Agency Committee, 1908-25.
(2) *Alliance Reports*, bound volumes of the annual reports, 1853 to date.
(3) *Alliance Year Book*, a mainly statistical compilation of information (e.g. on the incidence of drunkenness) from its first edition in 1910 to its last in 1952.
(4) Receipts, 1860's, 1929-30.
(5) *Alliance News*, a complete run of this journal since its inception.
(6) Scottish Temperance League, register for 1916, plus three volumes of S.T.L. Tracts, Nos. 1-614.
(7) National Commercial Temperance League, three general minute books, 1894-1924; minutes of the Publishing Committee, 1924-38; of the General Purposes Committee, 1924-33; of the London Division, 1899-1910,

1923-39; plus a book containing leaflets and posters of the League, 1917-29. There is also a run of the League's journal, *Outlook*, 1925-67.

(8)   National Temperance Federation, certain recent reports.

(9)   In addition to these, the United Kingdom Alliance has a large collection of printed and duplicated material related to the Temperance movement and similar interests. These include books, pamphlets, articles, reports, etc., all of which have been listed by Dr. Brian Harrison, Fellow of Corpus Christi College, Oxford. A copy of his list is available in the Alliance's offices.

Availability

The records are available for research by prior arrangement with the General Secretary.

II. Local Organisations

Aberystwyth Women's Temperance Association

Minutes, 1900-52, and assorted other material, are deposited in the National Library of Wales.

Flintshire United Temperance Association

Five minute books, 1909-60, are deposited in the National Library of Wales.

Glasgow Temperance Society

Records, 1872-92, are deposited in Glasgow City Archives.

Mere Temperance Society

The records of the Society are in the care of Miss Joyce Rutter, Newport House, Mere, Wiltshire (to whom all enquiries should be addressed). They consist of five minute books: 1860-74, 1874-79, 1879-90, 1890-1905, 1935-46 (the minute book for 1905-35 is missing). In addition the papers include: rules; the Receiver-General's monthly pay book, 1886-93, 1894-1901; accounts, 1867-70; an account book, 1923-39; a copy of *A Short History of Mere Temperance Society* (1890) by John Farley Rutter; and a bound edition of *Mere Temperance Society Monthly Visitor*, 1907-11; together with more ephemeral material.

Newport Temperance Society

Minute books, 1885-1963, accounts, 1889-1961, and an incomplete set of reports, 1906-59, are deposited in Monmouthshire Record Office.

North of England Temperance League

Papers of Guy Hayler, one-time Secretary of the League, are deposited in the Memorial Library, University of Wisconsin.

Reading Temperance Society
Palmer Hall West Street Reading RG1 1UD

The Society was founded in 1832 and has had an active and continuous history ever since.

A very good collection survives at Palmer Hall. These include a complete run of minute books, an incomplete but useful set of annual reports, and other, more recent reports, including correspondence, press cuttings, etc. These records may be seen by appointment with the Secretary.

Rochdale Temperance Society

The following records are deposited in Rochdale Reference Library: annual reports of the Society, 1891, 1900-01, 1906-07; reports of the Rochdale and District Temperance Union, 1889-1910; of the Band of Hope Union, 1882 and 1886; and minutes of the Rochdale Auxiliary Society, 1832-53.

South Wales Temperance Union

The records of the organisation have been deposited in the National Library of Wales. The records include a minute book for the period 1931-66, a volume containing accounts of meetings, etc., chiefly press cuttings, 1931-57, with a number of printed annual reports, etc.; a register of church subscriptions, private donations, branch fees, etc., 1916-59; a cash book containing a list of church subscriptions, 1936-59; an account book relating to the literature and badges section, 1923-56; names and addresses of officers, delegates, etc., c. 1931-57; a list of contributions to the Miss Maglona Rees testimonial fund, 1956-57; two small account books, 1949-66, 1953-65; two minute books of the Swansea and District branch of the Union, 1933-49, 1950-57; and a minute book of the Pontardawe branch, 1958-61.

Ulster Women's Christian Temperance Union

Records are deposited in the Northern Ireland Public Record Office.

THE TIMES
P.O. Box 7 New Printing House Square Gray's Inn Road London WC1X 8EZ

Papers

The Times archive consists of a considerable amount of material relating to the history of the newspaper. Besides the usual records of a business organisation, it contains a large amount of material emanating from the editors and correspondents of the paper. These records are extremely valuable to the historian but are not, in a strict sense, personal collections. They are, rather, collections of papers which derive their importance from the central role of *The Times*, both in journalism and politics, and consist of confidential briefings, correspondence and memoranda, as well as more normal editorial material.

Material in the archive dates back to 1785, but there was no systematic policy of preservation of documents in the various departments of *The Times* until they were gathered together before World War II for the compilation of *The History of the Times* (published in 5 vols., 1935-52). Since then an attempt has been made to maintain a comprehensive archive, and editorial and other papers are deposited there at regular intervals.

The records are filed in boxes, and a subject and persons index gives easy guidance to their contents. No detailed itemisation has been attempted. The boxes are arranged in two series:

(1) An A-Z arrangement of 'Subjects and Countries'.

(2) A-Z arrangement of individuals.

(1) The material in this series ranges from advertising copy to unpublished material about the Abdication. Countries and subjects are juxtaposed alphabetically. The larger subjects fill whole boxes, other subjects have single files. Within each box the material is roughly sorted. A box on Egypt, for example, covers the period from Disraeli buying Suez Canal shares to commercial arrangements of *The Times* in the 1950s, and includes memoranda, etc., on the Suez crisis. Similarly a

box devoted to Ireland has material from *c.* 1912 to the 1940s,and includes for the earlier period letters from Sir Edward Carson, Horace Plunkett and Tim Healey. Additional material on these countries, and others, can be found in the boxes of correspondents' papers, while more contemporary papers are filed but remain closed at present. Other topics covered include: company affairs from 1885 to the present, with correspondence, legal documents, balance sheets covering the whole period which are particularly important for the Northcliffe takeover, and the Astor-Walter arrangements of 1922-23; boxes on the book clubs and shops, Litigation, office site, publication of the *History*, printing presses, staff lists and salaries, typography, etc.

Material on the Royal Family includes three boxes of cuttings books, some dating back to the reign of William IV, and a considerable amount of still confidential material on the Abdication, including unpublished letters to the Editor from all over the world. Of particular importance are five boxes of material concerning the Parnell libel case and special commission covering the period 1886-89. These contain a mass of correspondence, including copies of the 'Parnell Letters' which gave rise to the case.

(2) The 'personal' papers consist of the confidential memoranda of correspondents, background briefings, etc., and the papers of editors and managers. They again vary in bulk from the single file to a considerable number of boxes. The more important groups are listed below:

Lord Astor of Hever (Proprietor)

Two boxes of papers, one of which includes appointments diaries of Lord Astor of Hever, 1944-62.

R. M. Barrington-Ward (Editor, 1941-48)

Papers include engagement books, private memoranda and letters.

Thomas Barnes (Editor, 1817-41)

Papers consist of two boxes of miscellaneous material dating from the 1830s.

C. F. Moberly Bell (correspondent in Egypt and later Managing Director)

Four boxes of material covering the period 1865-1910. Bell had the habit of writing correspondence from his home, and this has been lost.

H. S. O. de Blowitz (correspondent in Paris during Franco-Prussian war)

A small but very useful collection.

J. D. Bourchier (correspondent in the Balkans)

One box of material.

G. E. Buckle (Editor, 1884-1912)

Buckle made a habit of destroying his correspondence, so little survives apart from one box of miscellaneous material.

Geoffrey Dawson (Editor, 1912-19, 1922-41)

Dawson's papers concern the period 1906-40 and include a press cutting book covering his career, and correspondence. The correspondence, relating chiefly to his second term as Editor, is important in illustrating his relationship with public figures. He had the habit also of writing memoranda of events and interviews and these provide a useful guide to his attitudes to major events, e.g. the Abdication. Certain private papers are in the possession of his family and a microfilm of these is in *The Times* archive.

John Thadeus Delane (Editor, 1841-77)

A very important collection of letters to Delane from all the important personalities of his period: Peel, Palmerston, Russell, Gladstone, Disraeli, etc. The letters are bound in 27 volumes. The first 22 contain the general correspondence in approximate order of date; vols. 23 and 24 contain letters to Delane from John Walter III, the proprietor, and vols. 25-27 contain letters thought at the time of binding to be of minor importance, or to which not even an approximate date could be given. There are also some unbound letters.

Editors' Diaries

Delane began the practice of keeping an office diary in 1857, and this has been continued to the present. The information contained in these is small; they are valuable in that they provide the names of writers of leaders and certain other important articles.

Foreign Department

Letter books exist up to 1910, and include out-letters to Moberly Bell (Cairo), Blowitz (Paris), Bourchier (Balkans), Chirol (Berlin), Saunders (Berlin), Steed (Berlin, Rome, Vienna), Stillman (Rome). Valentine Chirol, head of the Foreign Department 1899-1910, like Bell, conducted his correspondence from home, and this has generally been lost.

Manager's Letter Books

From his appointment as Manager in 1847, Mowbray Morris kept copies of the letters he wrote and this practice was continued by his successors. They are kept in letter books, press-copied from manuscript. For the early years the collection appears to be incomplete. From 1893 the typewriter was used but it was ten years before Bell had his correspondence typewritten and correspondence was press-copied until 1915, when it was superseded by copying by carbon.

G. E. Morrison (correspondent in the Far East)

One box of correspondence, etc.

Northcliffe (Proprietor)

This is a major grouping, covering the period 1889-1922. It provides a prime source for Northcliffe's journalistic policies, particularly through the large collection of notes headed 'communiqué', 'memoranda' or 'message', which began in 1912 in the form of typewritten letters to Dawson. At a later stage copies were circulated, sometimes as many as 25. The surviving 'messages' cover all aspects of journalism: ink, paper, typographic printing, advertising, recountment, style of writing, etc., as well as occasionally touching on political matters.

Sir William Howard Russell (war correspondent)

This collection consists of books of letters to Russell, together with a box file of miscellaneous correspondence. The diaries of Russell covering the period from the Crimean War are on permanent loan to *The Times*. At present access to these is restricted.

Henry Wickham Steed (Editor, 1919-22)

As Foreign Editor and Editor, Steed was a prolific correspondent, and much of this survives. A considerable amount of his memoranda and notes as correspondent in Rome and Vienna, with his confidential memoranda from Versailles in 1919, are also deposited in the archive.

Sir Donald Mackenzie Wallace (Foreign Editor)

Three boxes of his office papers are in the archive. The bulk of his papers has been deposited in Cambridge University Library.

Walter Papers

These papers of the chief proprietors for much of the period date back to the 1780s and are a vital source for the history of *The Times*.

These collections are a selection only from the considerable mass of material at New Printing House Square. Others that might be mentioned are certain papers of Liddell Hart; correspondence between Lord Irwin (the Earl of Halifax), as Viceroy of India, and Dawson in the late 1920s; memoranda from W. B. Harris, correspondent in Morocco, and A. L. Kennedy, correspondent in Nazi Germany. Such collections will complement the material contained in the files under the relevant country heading.

The Times also has a useful collection of memorabilia, including portraits, posters and ancillary advertising and museum pieces.

In addition to these records in the Archives, note should be made of *The Times* Cuttings Books. These form a most valuable collection covering all the major events of the century. They are organised on the following lines: 'Geographical', 'Second World War' (46 vols.), 'International' (53 vols.) and by subject, e.g. 'Aircraft Accidents to Women', and covering all variety of topics. These books have been microfilmed, and as this has been done the originals are destroyed. Reprints of the microfilms are available. Further information may be obtained from Information Services Manager, Times Newspapers Ltd.

Availability

Most papers are available to accredited students for the period covered by *The History of the Times* (1785-1948). The exceptions are those papers which deal with sensitive matters, such as the Abdication, or the personal records of employees. Enquiries should be made to the Archivist at *The Times*.

TOBACCO WORKERS' UNION
218 Upper Street London N1

The union was founded in 1834, and incorporates the National Cigar and Tobacco Workers' Union.

Papers

Records are retained at the union's national office. Nothing survives prior to 1881, but since then minute books and miscellaneous other material survives.

Availability

Applications should be made in writing to the General Secretary of the union.

TOWN AND COUNTRY PLANNING ASSOCIATION
17 Carlton House Terrace London SW1Y 5AS

The Association was founded in 1899 as the Garden City Association and adopted its present name in 1941. The Association advocates and promotes an understanding of national and regional planning policies that will improve living and working conditions, safeguard the best countryside and farmland, enhance natural, architectural and cultural amenities, and advance economic efficiency.

Papers

Records have been retained at the offices of the Association. These are, however, by no means complete: periodic changes of office, and wartime destruction, have diminished the quantity of records, and those that survive are at present unsorted. The minutes of the Executive Committee and the Council are almost complete and records of certain sub-committees survive, e.g. the Educational Propaganda Committee, the Country Towns Committee, the Dispersal Policy Committee. The Association has retained full sets of its journal, now known as *Town and Country Planning*, since 1904.

Availability

Applications should be made to the Director of the Association.

TRADES UNION CONGRESS
Congress House Great Russell Street London WC1

Apart from the records of the more important committees, few records of the T.U.C. survive for the period before 1918-20. Since then, however, a systematic filing policy has resulted in what amounts to a comprehensive archive at Congress House, covering the whole gamut of the T.U.C.'s activities. Since the mid-1920s the records have been filed under subject headings, arranged by a decimalised classification system:

000-099: Trade Unionism, T.U.C., T.C.s' Organisation
100-199: Labour (conditions), National Insurance, Industrial Injuries
200-299: Labour-Capital Relations, Agreements, Disputes
300-399: Capitalism, Trusts, Companies
400-499: Finance, Banking, Insurance
500-599: Trade, Production and Economics, Nationalisation
600-699: Industries and Services
700-799: Politics and Publicity
800-899: Social Questions
900-999: International, Europe, Asia, Africa, America and Australia

The most coherent body of records are the minutes and papers of the various committees through which the work of the Congress is carried out. Minutes of the Parliamentary Committee (after 1921 the General Council) date back to 1888, the records from 1888-1911 being kept in a fireproof box. Later records are filed in transfer boxes. In addition to minutes, agenda, notices and correspondence are also extant. Minutes and papers of other committees date from the 1920s, for example:

Finance and General Purposes Committee, 1923 to date;
Economic Committee, 1929 to date;
International Committee, 1923 to date;
Workmen's Compensation Committee, 1924-47;
Standing Advisory Committee on Social Insurance, 1928-47, and Social
    Insurance and Industrial Welfare Committee, 1947 to date;
Education Committee, 1922 to date.

During the early 1920s particularly, a number of joint Labour Party-T.U.C. committees, e.g. on International Affairs, Research, Press and Publicity, Legal and Finance matters, had an active existence, and these records are also in Congress House. Similarly the records of other joint committees, such as the Trades Councils Joint Consultative Committee, joint Government-T.U.C. committees, etc., survive, as do the records of the Women's Advisory Committee. Another coherent grouping consists of the records of the numerous *ad hoc* committees active during the 1926 General Strike, viz. those dealing with Food and Essential Services, General Purposes, Intelligence, Mining and the Mining Joint Campaign Committee, Mining Joint Financial Committee, Negotiating Committee, Powers and Orders Committee, Propaganda Committee, Publicity Committee, Special Industrial Committee and the Strike Organisation Committee. It would be safe to assume that the records of all the T.U.C. committees are extant since at least the early 1920s.

Records of the National Joint Council of the T.U.C. and the Labour Party, now the National Council of Labour, are also housed in Congress House. These include minutes, correspondence, agenda and other documents, including papers on the inclusion within the Council of the Co-operative Union, and regular reports from each section of the Council. A complete set of Congress annual reports is housed in the T.U.C. Library. Papers concerning arrangements for Congress are destroyed periodically as being of no historic interest.

261

A file is kept for every trades council, dealing with administrative matters; affiliation, membership, etc. Particular issues brought up by a trades council would be filed under the relevant subject heading. Similarly, files are kept for each member trade union.

The growing involvement of the T.U.C. in British public life is reflected in the increasing bulk of material concerned with this expanding activity. Subjects covered range from purely organisational matters, dealing with personnel, internal financial matters, and the construction of Congress House, to the increasing contacts with successive governments, and relations with foreign trade unions, the International Federation of Trade Unions, and the International Confederation of Free Trade Unions. Particular issues covered include inter-union relations and disputes, the development of wages and employment policies, relations with the Labour Party and other political movements, particularly the Communist Party. In addition there are valuable files on the *Daily Herald.*

In summary, the T.U.C. archive is an extremely valuable collection of records of the labour and trade union movement.

Availability

There is no general access to these papers. Enquiries should in the first case be made to the Assistant General Secretary, and each application will be treated on its merits.

The Library

The nucleus of the Library was formed with the setting-up in 1915 of the Labour Party Information Bureau. A Joint Library of the Labour Party and the T.U.C. remained in existence until 1956, when the T.U.C. left Transport House to move to new premises at Congress House. They took the greater part of the original stock with them.

The bulk of the collection of printed material consists of reports, pamphlets and government publications. Much of this material dates from the 1920s, although some earlier pamphlets date back to the 19th century. While the Joint Library existed an extensive press cuttings service was provided. The Labour Party maintains this service, and the party retained the back files of clippings when the Library was split up. The major part of T.U.C. press cuttings files, therefore, date back to the 1950s only, though some files go back as far as 1911.

The John Burns Collection should also be mentioned here. This was given to the T.U.C. Library on permanent loan in 1954 by the Amalgamated Engineering Union. This contains a collection of 18th and 19th-century books and bound pamphlets in the field of labour history, including the almost complete works of Robert Owen and William Cobbett. The collection includes sets of all the important labour journals of the late 19th century, and certain manuscript material also survives.

The Library also holds several important archive collections. The Gertrude Tuckwell collection covers the last decades of the 19th century and the early years of this century. This consists of notes and press cuttings currently arranged under Gertrude Tuckwell's own filing system.

The papers of the *Women's Trade Union League* (q.v.) on microfilm include committee minutes, 1895-1921; annual reports, 1875-1921; and journals, 1877-1921. Minutes of the *National Society of Brushmakers* (q.v.) have also been deposited.

The Library also holds the minutes, reports and press cuttings of the London Trades Council. The collection includes minute books, 1860-1953; annual reports from 1873; press cuttings, 1885-86, 1930-47; minutes of the Central Workers' Committee on Unemployment, 1905-07; and an account book, 1860-74.

The Library exists primarily to service the staff of Congress House. Access is granted to accredited research workers on written application to the Librarian. See also *Bishopsgate Institute*.

TRANSPORT AND GENERAL WORKERS' UNION
Transport House Smith Square London SW1
The union was established in 1922, as the result of an amalgamation of 14 unions on the initiative of the Dock, Wharf, Riverside and General Workers' Union, in association with the National Union of Dock Labourers. Since 1922 the T.G.W.U. has amalgamated with a large number of other unions, big and small. The more prominent of these are listed below.

Papers

For most of the predecessor unions the Transport and General Workers' Union has no records. It has been suggested that this may be accounted for partly by the fact that many of the unions did not affiliate by ballot, but were dissolved, the members joining the T.G.W.U. individually. The list that follows is not definitive, but should be regarded as a guide to the records that survive. Enquiries should be directed to the National Secretary, Education and Research Department, T.G.W.U.

(1)   *T.G.W.U.*
The Union has retained full records, including minutes of the General Executive Council, annual reports and balance sheets, rules and membership records, and wage agreements, since 1922, reports of the Biennial Delegate Conference since 1925, the All-Ireland Delegate Conferences and the Scottish Delegate Conferences since 1948, copies of the *Record* since 1921, and handwritten minutes of the meetings of M.P.s who were members of, and representatives of, the Political and International Department of the union, 1922-27. In addition, correspondence and minutes of the Manchester branch are deposited in the Archives Department, Manchester Central Library.

(2)   *Amalgamated Society of Watermen, Lightermen and Watchmen of the River Thames*, from 1910 known as *Amalgamated Society of Watermen, Lightermen and Bargemen* (founder member of T.G.W.U.)
Records include: minutes of Delegate Meetings, 1890-1914; annual reports, 1890-1914; reports and accounts, 1893-1921; various financial records for the 1890s; and copies of the *Dockers' Record*, 1901-11, 1920-21.

(3)   *National Union of Docks, Wharves and Shipping Staffs*, founded as *Port of London Docks and Wharves Staffs Association* (founder member of T.G.W.U.)
Copies of *Quayside and Office*, 1919-20, survive.

(4)   *United Vehicle Workers* (founder member of T.G.W.U.)
Minutes of the Executive Council run from 1920-21, as do annual reports and annual conference material; and copies of the *Record* run from 1919-21.

(5)   *Amalgamated Association of Tramway and Vehicle Workers*
Established in 1889 as the Amalgamated Association of Tramway, Hackney Carriage Employees and Horsemen in General, the name was changed in 1902. In 1919 it amalgamated with the London and Provincial Union of Licensed Vehicle Workers, to form the United Vehicle Builders.
Annual reports run from 1896-1918; quarterly reports from 1897-1902; reports of Annual Delegate Meetings run from 1911-19; and copies of the *Tramway and Vehicle Workers* for 1905.

(6)   *London and Provincial Union of Licensed Vehicle Workers*
   Established in 1894 as the London Cab Drivers' Trade Union, its name was changed in 1911. It amalgamated in 1919 with the Amalgamated Association of Tramway and Vehicle Workers to form the United Vehicle Builders.
   Surviving records are sparse, but include the report of the Special Delegate Meeting, 21-24 Nov. 1916; copies of the *Cab Drivers' Record,* 1897-1908, and the *Licensed Vehicle Trades Record,* 1913-17, 1919.

(7)   *National Union of Enginemen, Firemen, Mechanics, Motormen and Electrical Workers*
   Established in 1889 as the National Amalgamated Union of Enginemen, Cranemen and Boilermen, it was reorganised in 1895 as the National Amalgamated Union of Enginemen, Cranemen, Hammer-Drivers and Boilermen. In 1900 it became the National Amalgamated Union of Enginemen, Cranemen, Hammer, Steam and Electric Tram Drivers and Boiler Firemen; in 1902, the National Amalgamated Union of Enginemen, Firemen, Mechanics and Electrical Workers; in 1913 it adopted the above title; and in 1926 it became the Power Workers' Group of the Transport and General Workers' Union.
   Records include the minutes of the Executive meetings, 1900-06; reports of annual conferences, 1892, 1896-1908; statements of income and expenditure, 1895-97.

(8)   *Workers' Union*
   The Union, founded in 1898, joined the T.G.W.U. in 1929. Records are few, but include annual reports and statement of accounts, 1905-28. Records of the Midland Region are deposited in Birmingham Central Library. Reference should also be made to Richard Hyman *The Workers' Union* (1971).

(9)   *National Transport Workers' Federation*
   Established in 1910, it was dissolved in 1927. Surviving records include: reports of General Council meetings, 1911-22; of the Special Councils, 1919; and of the National Councils, 1924-27; and a report of the Special Amalgamation Conference, 1914; and of the Reorganisation Conference, 1924, when the T.G.W.U. withdrew.

(10)   *National Federation of General Workers*
   Established in 1917, it was dissolved *c.* 1924. Minutes of the Provisional Executive Council, and of the monthly meeting of the Executive Council, 1917-22, survive.

(11)   *Records at T.U.C. Library*
   In addition to the records at Transport House, certain other records, chiefly reports and journals, of the T.G.W.U. and of unions which have amalgamated with it are held by the Trades Union Congress Library. The unions involved include: the T.G.W.U.; the Dock, Wharf, Riverside and General Workers' Union; the National Amalgamated Labourers' Union; the National Union of Docks, Wharves and Shipping Staffs; the North of England Trimmers' and Teemers' Association; the North of Scotland Horse and Motormen's Association; the United Vehicle Workers; the Amalgamated Association of Tramway and Vehicle Workers; the London and Provincial Union of Licensed Vehicle Workers; the National Union of Dock, Riverside and General Workers; the National Union of Millers; the North Wales Craftsmen and General Workers' Union; the North Wales Quarrymen's Union; the Weaver Watermen's Association; the National Amalgamated Union of Enginemen, Firemen, Mechanics, Motormen and Electrical Workers; the Workers' Union; the National Association of Builders' Labourers; the National Winding and General Engineers Society; the North of England Engineers and Firemen's Amalgamation; the National Glass Workers' Trade Protection Association; the Glass Bottle Makers of Yorkshire; the Liverpool and District Carters' and Motormen's Union. These records are by no means complete but are a useful addition to those of the T.G.W.U. itself.

(12) *National Union of Vehicle Builders*

The union was born as the United Kingdom Society of Coachmakers in 1834. It transferred its engagements to the T.G.W.U. in 1971. Its records now form part of the T.G.W.U. archive. No details are available.

Three of the more important collections of amalgamated unions are itemised separately below.

National Association of Operative Plasterers

The Association was established under the above name in 1860, as the result of the fusion of a number of local societies. The name was changed in 1919 to the National Association of Plasterers, Granolithic and Cement Workers, but reverted to the original form in 1932. The Association was later amalgamated with the T.G.W.U.

Papers

The archives retained include the following: rules and regulations, as suggested by the Central Committee of the London Society of Operative Plasterers, 28 Mar. 1860, and from 1872; individual membership records, in reports for 1876-1924, and on a card index for 1924 to date; minute book, 1862-65, and auditors' report, 1864-66; Annual reports, 1876-1931, and monthly reports, 1886-1931, with some oddments from the earlier period; quarterly and annual reports from 1932. The records cover details of wage negotiations and agreements, for example 1904 and 1913, and the National Joint Council for the Plastering Industry, minutes, 1928-30, etc. There are also miscellaneous 19th-century documents and series of papers, and the minutes of the International Council of Operative Plasterers (1925-35). Certain 19th-century local plasterers' societies have some records in the union archives, and minute books of the Birmingham Branch, 1876-84, 1888-1927, have been preserved.

North Wales Quarrymen's Union

The union became part of the T.G.W.U. in 1923.

Papers

Manuscript volumes and files of papers of the union, making a very full collection, have been deposited in the National Library of Wales. These include minute books, 1891-1933; two cash books, 1885-1914; two ledgers, 1907-22; 76 letter books, 1896-1939; three books of letters to the union's solicitors, 1922-27; volumes relating to particular lodges; volumes relating to strikes; papers relating to the non-union activities of R. T. Jones, the union's General Secretary, particularly his parliamentary candidature; material relating to the union's headquarters and to the slate industry generally; particulars of output, 1909-25; correspondence relating to the miners' crisis, 1925-27; correspondence relating to individual quarries, etc., and printed material including reports, balance sheets, and programmes of the union's conferences, 1898-57.

Availability

Application should be made to the Librarian, National Library of Wales.

Scottish Commercial Motormen's Union

The Scottish Carters' Association was founded in 1898; it became the Scottish Horse and Motormen's Association in 1908, and the Scottish Commercial Motormen's Union in 1964. In 1971 it became part of the T.G.W.U.

The records of the union have been deposited in the National Library of Scotland. They include minutes of the Executive Committee from 1902; of the Convalescent Home Committee, 1923-63; records of the Plantation branch, Glasgow, 1898-1907; of the Glasgow branch, 1919-29; the Aberdeen branch, 1929-51; and the Edinburgh and Leith branch, 1931-60; together with a volume of newspaper cuttings concerning the activities of the union, 1918-36.

Availability

Application should be made to the National Library of Scotland.

TRANSPORT SALARIED STAFFS' ASSOCIATION
Walkden House 10 Melton Street, London NW1

The Association was founded at Sheffield in 1897, as the National Association of General Railway Clerks. The name was changed in 1898 to the Railway Clerks' Association, and in 1951 to its present form.

Papers

Records are retained at Walkden House and include: minutes of the annual and special delegate conferences, 1900 to date; annual reports, 1899 to date; wage agreements from 1920; membership records from 1897; and circulars from 1939. There are runs of the union's journal: the *Railway Clerk*, 1904-18; *Railway Service Journal*, 1919-51; *Transport Salaried Staff Journal*, 1951 to date. The union also has press cuttings and miscellaneous papers relating to the Railway Nationalisation League, 1893-1900.

Many of these records were deposited in the Modern Records Centre, University of Warwick in 1974.

Xerox copies of certain documents relating to the Railway Clerks' Association's work in Scotland have been deposited in the National Library of Scotland. These include papers relating to the Scottish Salaries Movement, 1912, and recognition struggles, 1918-19; Scottish Advisory Council papers, 1921-29; minutes of the Scottish Advisory Council, 1924-48; minutes of the Scottish Conference Special Committee, 1926.

Availability

Application should be made to the Research Department of the Association or, where relevant, to the National Library of Scotland, and the Modern Records Centre, University of Warwick.

TROTSKYIST RECORDS

The Trotskyist movement in Britain during this period was relatively weak. For the origins of the 'Left Opposition' in Britain reference should be made to Reg Groves, *The Balham Group* (1974), which traces its break with the *Communist Party of Great Britain* (q.v.) in the early 1930s. He has used much original material, still in his care.

The Maitland-Sara Collection, mainly comprising printed material and ephemera, in the University of Warwick Library and Modern Records Centre, is a source for the history of the Trotskyist movement, especially it origins in the 1930s.

UNDEB CYMRU FYDD (NEW WALES UNION)

The society grew out of the Council for the Preservation of Welsh Culture, and was formally established in 1941 under the inspiration of the late T. I. Ellis. Its primary function was to act to safeguard the position of the Welsh language and to promote the cultural life of Wales. From 1967, when it became a charitable foundation, it worked to promote the study of the Welsh language. The society has not undertaken any public activities since the end of 1969.

Papers

An extensive collection of records has been deposited in the National Library of Wales. A catalogue, in Welsh, may be consulted in the Library. The records include minute books of the Council, 1939-60; numerous files and volumes from 1939 containing memoranda and evidence submitted to committees on matters of Welsh cultural and educational interest, correspondence and accounts of sub-committees and joint committees, office account books and vouchers, etc.; a minute book of the Llanelli branch of the Committee for the Preservation of Welsh Culture, 1947-57; accounts, etc., relating to the Pontypridd branch, 1945-49; minute books, 1940-45, of the Council for the Preservation of Welsh Culture, South Cardiganshire branch; minutes, files and correspondence, 1936-44, of the Merioneth branch.

Availability

Applications should be made to the National Library of Wales.

UNION OF CONSTRUCTION, ALLIED TRADES AND TECHNICIANS

9-11 Macaulay Road London SW4

UCATT was formed in 1971. Previous to this, in 1970, the Amalgamated Society of Woodworkers had amalgamated with the Amalgamated Society of Painters and Decorators to form the Amalgamated Society of Woodworkers and Painters. The Association of Building Technicians joined this union later in 1970. This new Amalgamated Society joined with the Amalgamated Union of Building Trade Workers to form UCATT in 1971.

Papers

UCATT at present holds the records of various of its predecessors at its headquarters in London.

1. *Amalgamated Society of Woodworkers*

The A.S.W. records include: minutes of the Executive Council, 1921 to date, and of the Proceedings of the General Council, 1922 to date; annual reports and monthly *Journals,* from 1921, and conference reports from 1947; rule books and membership records from 1921.

Details of wage negotiations and agreements can be followed in various papers; for example, correspondence and reports relating to the piece-work issue, 1941-45, and papers relating to the shipbuilding and engineering disputes of 1922 and the national building dispute of 1924. Minutes of meetings in 1920, and 1921-22, document the amalgamation of the A.S.C.C.J. with the General Union, and the proposed amalgamation with the Amalgamated Society of Woodcutting Machinists. Miscellaneous papers include certain 19th-century records of early woodworkers' associations, for example, the Belfast Cabinetmakers and the Preston Joiners' Society.

Records of the Amalgamated Society of Carpenters (Cabinetmakers) and Joiners (estd. 1860) include minutes of the Proceedings of the General Council for various years, 1871-1921 and of the Executive Council, 1915-20; annual and monthly reports, 1860-1920; rule books, membership records and accounts books. Other series of papers cover wage negotiations, disputes and agreements made by the Society. There is also a good assortment of 19th-century branch records. Among the records are papers relating to the original Friendly Society of Carpenters and Joiners (c. 1868), the Mersey Ship Joiners' Association and the United Brothers of Joseph, or the Regular Carpenters of Dublin.

The Associated Carpenters and Joiners of Scotland was formed in 1861 and amalgamated with the A.S.C.J. in 1911. Surviving papers include assorted minute books and reports, membership and branch records, a rule book, 1880, and correspondence relating to disputes, 1866-75.

The Amalgamated Union of Cabinet Makers was established in 1833 and amalgamated with the A.S.C.J. in 1918. Annual and monthly reports are supplemented by branch records, rule books and a local amalgamation agreement of 1876.

A similar assortment of records survives relating to the General Union of Carpenters and Joiners which was formed in 1827.

2. Amalgamated Union of Building Trade Workers of Great Britain and Ireland

The Union came into being in 1921 through the amalgamation of the Operative Bricklayers' Society of London and the Manchester Unity of Operative Bricklayers. In 1942 amalgamation was effected with the Building and Monumental Workers' Association of Scotland, and in 1952 with the National Builders' Labourers' and Constructional Workers' Society.

The union's records date from 1921 and include the following: monthly and quarterly reports, 1921-27; quarterly and annual reports, 1928 to date; reports of the National Delegate Conference, 1922 to date; rules from 1921 to the present; nine volumes on membership of amalgamated societies, 1921; registers of members and admission forms, 1921 to date; financial records chiefly for the 1920s and 1930s; records of wage agreements since 1921; and miscellaneous items including papers relating to new offices, 1935; a fire-watching record book, 1941-45; and a file of 'interesting items'.

In addition, there are runs of the *Building Worker*, 1947-59, and of *Builders Standard* from 1960.

A minute book of Box Lodge of the Operative Stone Masons' Friendly Society survives for 1873-1905, and there is a run of the Operative Stone Masons' *Journal*, 1911-20. Other records of this Society include annual accounts, 1843-60; the annual audit, 1863-1920; fortnightly returns, 1834-1910 (with the years 1852-56 missing); and the constitution books of Constantine Lodge, 1847-1921, of Box Lodge, 1858-87, and Reading Lodge, 1906-21. Additionally, there are miscellaneous documents, 1852-62, and the report and financial statement of the Central Disputes Committee, 1914.

Accounts and contributions for 1837-40, and annual reports and fortnightly returns, 1838-45, have been retained concerning the United Operative Masons' Society.

Rules for 1840-60 (one volume), and a subscription book, 1832-38, survive relating to the Warrington Operative Stone Masons' Society.

The records of the Operative Bricklayers' Society of London include annual reports, 1867-1920; annual and quarterly reports, 1862-66; trade circulars and monthly reports, 1861-1920; Metropolitan Central Committee reports, 1895-96, 1901, 1904-07, and Annual Moveable General Council Minutes, 1896-1918; membership records, 1860-1921; quarterly balance sheets, 1908-20; general office accounts, 1919-20; yearly return of members' Payments, 1871-1920; benefit records, 1900-21; and the Metropolitan Central Strike Committee report, 1892.

Reports of the Friendly Operative Bricklayers' Trade Protection Society (later the United Operatives' Building Trade Protection Society of Great Britain and Ireland) cover the period 1902-21.

Quarterly reports of the Manchester Unity of Operative Bricklayers run from 1907-18, contribution registers from 1883-1920, and rules from 1881.

Certain papers of the Amalgamated Slaters, Tilers and Roofing Operatives' Society, which was incorporated into the A.U.B.T.W., are preserved in the Library at the University of Hull. The papers comprise: minutes of the Hull branch, 1891-1943, with gaps; minutes of the Yorkshire District Committee, 1938-55; letter book (Hull), 1899-1909; income and expenditure account books (Hull), 1909-17, 1937-42; *Journal* of the Society, 1965 etc.; report of conference, 1967.

Availability

The main body of records may be seen on application to the General Secretary of UCATT. In 1974, these records were promised to the Modern Records Centre, University of Warwick Library.

UNION OF DEMOCRATIC CONTROL

The U.D.C. was founded in September 1914 with the aim of securing a new course in diplomatic policy. Among prominent members during the war were J. R. MacDonald, J. A. Hobson, Norman Angell and, as Secretary, E. D. Morel. The U.D.C. demanded the ending of the war by negotiation, no annexations, open and democratic diplomacy, and disarmament. The latter aims continued to be the guidelines of its activities in the years after 1918.

Papers

Substantial records of the Union of Democratic Control have been deposited in Hull University Library. These include minutes of the General Council from 1914; a file of minutes and associated papers relating to the General Council, 1914-16; minutes of the Executive Council, 1915-54; minutes of the General Purposes Committee, 1936-37; minutes of the Management Sub-committee, 1954-56, and of the Publications Sub-committee, 1955; financial records dating from 1927-61; a number of files dealing with administrative offices, publication of pamphlets, staff matters, international matters and relations with other bodies; and certain correspondence, circulars to members, etc., chiefly for the late 1950s and 1960s.

A variety of other material includes papers of E. D. Morel, 1910-35; correspondence with founder members, 1918-24; annual reports of the U.D.C.; and documents relating to the various activities of the Union, both in relationship to home affairs (e.g. documents on the British Union of Fascists and the Royal Commission on the Munitions Industry) and foreign affairs (e.g. papers on Portugal, Greece, Algeria, South America, the British colonies, etc.).

Certain papers in the E. D. Morel Collection at B.L.P.E.S. are particularly relevant to the origins and early activities of the U.D.C.

Availability

Applications to use the U.D.C. papers should be made to the Librarian, Hull University Library. Enquiries concerning the Morel papers should be directed to the Librarian, B.L.P.E.S.

UNION OF POST OFFICE WORKERS
U.P.W. House Crescent Lane Clapham London SW4

The U.P.W. was formed in 1920, although there had been organised groups among postal workers from 1874. The main groups which made up the U.P.W. were as follows: the Postal and Telegraph Clerks' Association, which was formed as the Postal Telegraph Clerks' Association in 1880 and amalgamated with the United Kingdom Postal Clerks' Association, which was founded in 1886; the Fawcett Association, which was an organisation of postal sorters, inaugurated in 1890 after meetings held between 1887 and 1890; and the Postmen's Federation, founded in 1891 after four years of attempted organisation.

In addition, various small unions went into the U.P.W. in 1920, among them the Adult Messengers' Association, the Bagmen's Association, the London Postal Bagmen's Association (1906), the Central London Postmen's Association (1906), the London Postal Porters' Association (1902), the Tracers' Association (1892) and the Tube Staff Association (1903). In 1928 a secessionist group, the National Guild of Telephonists, broke away to form a separate union.

Papers

The U.P.W. has a very full archive dating back to 1875. There is an index to part of it. Records of particular interest are those of the Postmen's Federation, which has material going back to 1891, including 28 volumes of Executive Committee minutes. Also, there are U.K.P.C.A. records from 1892-1910, including ten volumes of Executive Committee minutes. P.C.T.A. records have survived back to 1875, as have the Fawcett Association Executive Committee minutes from 1890-1919. There is a collection of miscellaneous records, including annual reports, specific reports on conditions, and accounts. In addition, the U.P.W. has a collection of correspondence with the Postmaster-General, 1903-44, and the official reports of the Post Office from 1858 to the present. For many years the postal unions met in a National Joint Committee and the proceedings of that committee exist from 1908-19. The minutes of the U.P.W. run from 1919, three months prior to amalgamation, to the present.

There is also general material relating to the National Association of Postmen, 1930-44. The U.P.W. has an indexed run of its journal, the *Post*, which was formally the journal of the Fawcett Association from 1920, although there are some from its pre-U.P.W. days. Other journals in the Library include the *Postmen's Gazette*, which dates back to 1892. In addition, from 1963, the *Branch Officials' Bulletin* has covered conference decisions and actions taken.

The U.P.W. maintains a press cuttings system which covers five-yearly periods. At the end of each five-year period, only those considered most important are selected and retained.

Availability

Bona fide researchers only may apply to the General Secretary. It is hoped that the records will be microfilmed within the next few years.

UNION OF SHOP, DISTRIBUTIVE AND ALLIED WORKERS
'Oakley' 188 Wilmslow Road Manchester M14 6LJ

The union was formed in 1947 by the amalgamation of the National Union of Distributive and Allied Workers, formed 1921, and the National Amalgamated Union of Shop Assistants, Warehousemen and Clerks, formed 1898. These incorporated smaller unions of an earlier period.

The records of the present union, together with a collection of papers relating to the earlier associations, have been preserved. The records include the following: minute books: USDAW, from 1947; NUDAW, from 1921; and NAUSAW & C, from 1936. Reports: from 1947, 1921 and 1891 respectively. Rules: from 1947, 1921 and 1889. Membership records: from 1947, 1923 and 1938.

Files relating to the amalgamations are available, and details of wage agreements and negotiations from 1947 can be followed. Correspondence files date from 1962. and as early as 1936 in some cases. Recent press cuttings and papers relating to various legal cases have also been kept. Branch records date from 1947. The union also holds assorted minute books, account books, leaflets, photographs and documents of historical interest. Various journals have been published, including *New Dawn* (1921 to date), the *Shop Assistant* (NAUSAW & C, 1896-1938), the *Distributive Trades Journal* (NAUSAW & C, 1939-46), and the *Co-operative Employee* (Amalgamated Union of Co-operative Employees, 1908-20). A history of the NAUSAW & C, *They Also Serve,* appeared in 1949.

Availability

Persons wishing to have access to the USDAW archives should apply to the General Secretary of the union.

UNIONIST BUSINESS COMMITTEE

The Committee was established soon after the outbreak of World War I by Conservative Party supporters, with the aim of safeguarding the interests of British business against the effects of war. W. A. S. Hewins was Chairman.

Papers

Some records of the Committee are contained in the W.A.S. Hewins papers at Sheffield University Library. These include Committee minutes, 1915-16, 1919-21, and sub-committee minutes, 1915-16. The Hewins diaries throw additional light on the Committee's activities. No further records appear to survive.

Availability

Applications should be made to the Librarian, Sheffield University Library.

UNITED CHRISTIAN PETITION MOVEMENT

The Movement was founded by Robert J. Scrutton at the beginning of World War II with the aim of influencing public opinion against the war and the political and economic policies of the British Government.

Papers

A small collection of relevant material of Robert Scrutton (some 20 items) is included in the William B. Hamilton Collection at Duke University, Durham, North Carolina, U.S.A. This consists of letters, articles and broadsides of August and September 1941, concerning the work of the Movement and its allies. Most of the letters are those between Scrutton and the Duke of Bedford. There is also one from Admiral James Vandeleur Creagh.

Availability

Applications should be made to the Archivist, Duke University.

UNITED COMMITTEE FOR THE TAXATION OF LAND VALUES LTD.

177 Vauxhall Bridge Road London SW1

The Committee is a limited company of 100 members, and exists to propagate the ideas of Henry George, the American economist, whose *Progress and Poverty* was published in 1879. Its chief concern is with the taxation of land values as a principle of economic reform. It is linked with a policy of complete free trade, both at home and abroad. This means opposition to monopolies at home and exclusive economic unions abroad.

The present organisation developed out of a series of Land-Value Leagues established in the late 19th and early 20th centuries: the Land Restoration League in Scotland, and similar leagues in Yorkshire, Portsmouth, Edinburgh, Glasgow, Manchester, the Midlands and Wales.

The United Committee was formed originally as a meeting of delegates of these separate leagues. In the early 1920s it became an independent organisation, with its own funds, provided from legacies, etc. Under this were four distinct bodies:

(1)   *The Henry George School of Social Science.* A teaching organisation, begun in 1936, based in London with an autonomous branch in Glasgow. The Glasgow school is still extant. The school in London is in abeyance for the time being.

(2)   *Land and Liberty Press Ltd.* A publishing organ, producing *Land and Liberty*, a bi-monthly magazine, pamphlets, and books.

(3)   *Land-Value Taxation League.* This is the inheritor of three earlier bodies: the Liberal Liberty League, the Georgists, and the old English League. This exists on an *ad hoc* basis and has little formal existence.

(4)   *Rating Reform Campaign.* This represents the idea of the taxation of land values at local level, known as site-value rating.

Existing separately from these is the International Union for Land-Value Taxation and Free Trade, an autonomous body linking the independent bodies throughout the world, on a basis of individual membership.

There are personal links also with the *Free Trade League* and the *Cobden Club* (qq.v.).

Papers

A substantial collection of papers and pamphlets relating to the activities of the United Committee and its associated bodies survives. Much of the material is unsorted and there is no index. A great deal of the material was destroyed during the war-time bombing. It is housed at the headquarters of the United Committee.

Minute books are kept in a trunk in the basement. These include: minute books for the English League, 1906-18, 1941-62 (foundation of L.V.T. League); for the Manchester League, 1906-52 (with gaps); Yorkshire League, 1911-49; and for the United Committee, 1929-57. There are also certain account books extant.

There are also records surviving for the Commonwealth Land Party, established in the 1920s as a more political body, which fought elections particularly in Staffordshire.

These are open to students, but current minute books are closed.

A large collection of unsorted correspondence also exists. Of particular interest is a number of files of correspondence of Richard Stokes, M.P., who was a supporter of the movement. He gave these to the United Committee before his death.

A large collection of past conference papers has survived, as have papers (including correspondence) concerned with similar activities in the rest of the world. It is probable that a number of other categories are buried in the papers, but no systematic survey has been undertaken.

There is a large collection of pamphlets published by the Land-Value Taxation bodies dating back to the 1890s. These are filed, and indexed under subject and author headings.

The Committee retains a complete run of the *Georgite Magazine*, now known as *Land and Liberty* (previously *Single Tax* and *Land Values*), dating back to the 1890s, and bound copies of the *Standard* (ed. H. George) and the *League* for 1844. Certain tracts, leaflets and annual reports relating to the English Land Restoration League, the English League for the Taxation of Land Values and the United Committee itself, from c.1885-1970, have been deposited in the *Institute of Agricultural History* (q.v.).

Availability

All enquiries should be directed to the Secretary of the United Committee.

UNITED NATIONS ASSOCIATION OF GREAT BRITAIN AND NORTHERN IRELAND
93 Albert Embankment London SE1 7TX

The Association was founded in 1945 to support the work of the United Nations Organisation. It is the direct descendant of the *League of Nations Union* (q.v.).

Papers

A complete set of the Association's annual reports and of the minutes of the Executive Committee and Annual General Conference, together with other unsorted material, is kept in the head office.

Availability

Applications should be made to the Director.

UNITED SOCIETY FOR THE PROPAGATION OF THE GOSPEL
15 Tufton Street London SW1

The Society for the Propagation of the Gospel in Foreign Parts was founded in 1701. In 1965 it merged with the Universities' Mission to Central Africa (founded 1857) to form the United Society for the Propagation of the Gospel.

Papers

A very large archive is housed at the United Society's headquarters, the bulk of which relates to the work of the Society for the Propagation of the Gospel. In the Home Affairs series, there are Standing Committee (Executive) minutes, journals and accounts, from 1701-02. The Candidates Department has committee and sub-committee minutes, 1839-1938, correspondence and papers, mostly from the 19th century. The Medical Missions Department has its own series of minutes, 1908-36, and miscellaneous papers, including records of the formation of the Medical Mission Department, 1907-08, and correspondence with bishops, etc., c. 1930-50. Various series of committee minutes and assorted papers relate to Women's Work. The correspondence, minutes and reports of this department are largely filed according to geographical area, with series covering Africa, Asia, the Americas and the Middle East. Most series stop in the 1920s or earlier, but some extend to the 1950s.

The majority of the records relate to S.P.G. work overseas, and are filed according to particular mission areas. Papers relating to Asia are the most extensive. There are some 19th century general series covering the Far East, and Far Eastern reports and letters for 1941-45. Assorted minutes, reports and correspondence cover work in Borneo, Burma, China and Hong Kong, Japan, Korea, Thailand and Singapore, and there is a very large collection relating to India. There are similar series relating to Africa, in particular Madagascar, Mauritius, Seychelles, St. Helena, and West, South and Central Africa, and Tristan da Cunha. The American, West Indian, Australian and New Zealand series relate mostly to the Society's early work.

A few papers cover work in the Middle East, including Palestine and North Africa, Addis Ababa, and Constantinople.

The Universities' Mission to Central Africa was founded in response to Livingstone's call against slavery and for Christian mission. Records include runs of minute books from 1857, but the collection largely consists of letters from Africa, the bulk of which date from 1861-1925, after which they dwindle in quantity.

The Cambridge Mission to Delhi, founded in 1880, merged with U.S.P.G. in 1965. Certain of its records date back to 1857, but the core of the surviving collection dates from 1900.

The U.S.P.G. archive holds the records of the Gambia and Rio Pongo Mission, a West Indian mission to West Africa founded in 1855, the South African Church Railway Mission, and the Transvaal and Southern Rhodesia Mission. All these were active in the 20th century.

During the 19th century the S.P.G. had chaplaincies in Europe, and relevant minutes and files survive. In addition, a series of papers has been deposited by individuals, e.g. Roland Allen, A. S. Cripps, Bishop Macrorie of Maritzburg, L. B. Cholmondley.

Records of the United Society continue from 1965.

Availability

The Society generally exercises a forty-year rule regarding its records. Enquiries should be directed to the Archivist.

VOLUNTARY EUTHANASIA SOCIETY
13 Prince of Wales Terrace London W8

The Society was formed in 1936 by Dr. C. Killick Millard under the title of the Voluntary Euthanasia Legalisation Society, and changed its name firstly in 1960 to the Euthanasia Society, and in 1967 to the Voluntary Euthanasia Society. Its objects are to create a public opinion favourable to the view that an adult person suffering from a severe illness for which no relief is known, should be entitled by law to the mercy of a painless death if, and only if, that is his express wish — and to promote legislation to this effect.

Papers

There is a small collection of the Society's papers at their headquarters. It comprises about a dozen volumes of press cuttings from 1931 to the present, and some later press cuttings which are filed under subject-matter, e.g. arguments against euthanasia, manner of death, etc. There are various files of miscellaneous correspondence marked 'old correspondence' which contain letters from supporters and antagonists. Most of these are bundled into small files. There is a volume (1936-37) on the inauguration of the society, and a photographic record, *c.* 1950, of prominent supporters. From 1964, the original letters of support have been copied out into extracts, and the letters kept. One file deals with a similar American campaign and has sundry correspondence covering their dealings. The Society's

Executive Committee minutes from 1957 are in the office, and earlier minutes are available. Finally, the records contain plots of plays and short stories written around the subject of euthanasia.

Availability

The records are available to research students on written application to the Secretary.

WAR EMERGENCY WORKERS' NATIONAL COMMITTEE

The Committee was founded on 5 August 1914, arising from a conference of Socialist and labour organisations called by the Secretary of the Labour Party, Arthur Henderson. Its foundation must be seen in the light of the outbreak of World War I, and the resulting divisions in the labour movement; the Committee provided an arena for united action by both supporters and opponents of the war, and concerned itself with such issues as profiteering, unemployment, the equitable distribution and price restriction of scarce and essential commodities, and various welfare measures. The crucial importance of these in wartime inevitably led to many of the Committee's deliberations taking on a distinctly political tone.

Papers

The Secretary of the Committee was J. S. Middleton, Assistant Secretary of the Labour Party. As a result of this coincidence of posts the records of the W.N.C. are in the archives of the Labour Party at Transport House. They have been catalogued as part of the work of the Royal Commission on Historical Manuscripts at Transport House (see under *Labour Party*). Copies of the report can be seen at the Commission and at Transport House.

The main section of the W.N.C. papers consists of 35 box files, containing some 10,000 documents, which have been listed, together with an index. After this was completed, another group of W.N.C. records was discovered, and these have been listed and indexed separately. The bulk of the material consists of alphabetically arranged subject files, the titles of which, such as 'Air Raids and Children', 'Aliens', 'Food Prices', 'Labour After the War', 'Milk', 'Old Age Pensions', illustrate the type of problem the Committee was concerned with.

Many of the documents are basically groups of papers on particular issues, about matters on which the Committee was asked for advice or action. Others, such as the group relating to government contracts, in particular the construction of huts for the Army, consist of answers to enquiries put by the Committee to sympathisers in various parts of the country. Information on problems of national concern to the working class is thus mixed with and contained in data on local conditions and individual problems. The majority of the correspondents are not national figures, although they may have been prominent locally in trades and labour councils and the branches of trade unions or other Socialist organisations. The most notable exceptions to this are Sidney Webb, Robert Smillie and H. M. Hyndman, the latter being represented by a number of letters giving his views on policy and wider issues. The W.N.C. archive is also of interest for the material it contains, such as circulars and leaflets, from other organisations and pressure groups (whose own archives may not have survived or be accessible), for example in the fields of housing and town planning, opposition to conscription and the protection of civil liberties.

No complete file of the minutes of the W.N.C. itself has been found at Transport House. Copies of the minutes may be consulted, however, as the *Marx Memorial Library* (q.v.).

Availability

Application should be made to the Librarian, the Labour Party, Transport House.

WAR RESISTERS INTERNATIONAL
3 Caledonian Road London N1

Founded in 1921 in Holland, it was known as PACO until its transfer to Britain in 1924, when it adopted its present title. Its aim is to implement the declaration that war is a crime against humanity. Its work consists in the co-ordination and planning of support of national and international projects to achieve peace. The *Peace Pledge Union* and the *Fellowship of Reconciliation* (qq.v.) form the British sections of the W.R.I.

Papers

A substantial collection dating back to its foundation is housed in the offices of the W.R.I. These include a complete run of minute books of the International Council, the Executive Council, and of conferences since its headquarters were established in Britain. Translations of the earlier minutes are also in the possession of the W.R.I., and photocopies of the originals are soon to join the collection. In addition to these minutes, which may be used for research purposes by the serious student, the W.R.I. papers include a large amount of correspondence, which at present is not available. A considerable amount was destroyed during World War II, but the surviving material contains correspondence from various people involved in the international peace movement, as well as correspondence with national sections. It is unsorted and uncatalogued, and at present filed in a considerable number of parcels, some of which are labelled. It is hoped that in the fairly near future the W.R.I. will be able to have this correspondence catalogued.

In addition to these records, the W.R.I. has a large collection of publications from 1923 to the present day. For the most part these have been printed, although there is a considerable amount of duplicated material. A 'Catalogue of Publications, 1923 to May 1972' has been prepared by War Resisters International. This covers all known works published by W.R.I., and is arranged as follows: by subject; by author; conference papers (covering international, triennial and study conferences); periodicals.

The conference papers date back to the 1st International Conference in London, in July 1925. The periodicals include both English and foreign-language editions from 1923. A recent publication is the first of a proposed two volumes of W.R.I. 'Statements'. The period covered by the first volume is 1963-72.

The W.R.I. also has a specialised collection of documents on compulsory military service in all the countries of the world. This is probably a unique collection and includes correspondence and official statements. The W.R.I. has published the result of this work (edited by Tony Smythe and Devi Prasad).

WEST INDIA COMMITTEE
18 Grosvenor Street London W1X 0HP

The Committee was founded in the late 1770s as an association of the Society of West India Merchants and the Society of West India Planters and Merchants. Today its main aim is the development of trade and the fostering of relationships between the Caribbean countries and Britain.

The Committee has retained minute books of the Society of West India Merchants dating back to 1769, and of the Society of West India Planters and Merchants from 1785.

These early records are particularly important for the controversies concerning the slave trade. Minutes of the Committee, its executive body and various sub-committees, have also been retained, to provide a very full collection. However, because of the deteriorating condition of many of the minute books, an embargo on their use is in operation. The Committee hopes to repair these and possibly microfilm them.

The Committee's Library contains a very full collection of pamphlets, particularly on the anti-slavery campaign, the sugar duties debates and the opposition to bountied beet sugar in the late 19th century. Reports, Committee circulars, etc., have also been retained. Negotiations are in progress for the possible sale of this Library and its removal to a suitable location either in the United Kingdom or the Caribbean where it can be properly maintained and be readily available to West Indian students and historians. Enquiries should be directed to the Secretary of the West India Committee.

Records of the Liverpool West India Association have been deposited by Liverpool Chamber of Commerce in Liverpool City Library. These records include: minutes of the Board of Commissioners for the issue of Exchequer Bills, Liverpool, 1799-1800 and 1803 (one volume); a minute book of a Committee on Customs and Excise, 1824-28 (one volume); and a minute book of the Association, 1860-98. These records may be consulted on application to the City Librarian.

Records of the Glasgow West India Association, 1807-1935, are deposited in Glasgow City Archives.

WOMEN'S EMIGRATION SOCIETIES

A substantial collection of papers relating to women's emigration societies has been deposited in the Fawcett Library. These include:

1. *Female Middle Class Emigration Society* (1862-86)
   Annual reports, 1862-86 (1st to 6th); two letter books, 1862-76, 1877-82; three pamphlets published by the Society.

2. *United Englishwomen's Emigration Association* (1885-86)
   Finance Committee minutes, 1885-86, and a press cutting book, 1883-1915.

3. *United British Women's Emigration Association* (1886-1901)
   A volume of Council minutes, 1896-1901, including reports from sub-committees; minutes of the South African Expansion Committee, 1901; annual reports, 1888-1901; three volumes of press cuttings, 1883-1915, 1887-96, 1894-1901; and some correspondence and notes, 1891-1900.

4. *British Women's Emigration Association* (1901-19)
   Minutes of Council, 1915-19; Sub-committee for Diffusing Information, 1903-05; Factory Scheme Sub-committee, 1903-04; Hostel Committee, 1909-12; Advisory Committee, 1914; several papers of the Council meeting, Dec. 1919; annual reports, 1901-18; and several items of correspondence, 1909.

5. *South African Colonisation Society* (1903-19) (formerly South African Expansion Committee of B.W.E.A.)
   Minutes of the Executive Committee, 1902-19; Finance Committee, 1912-19; Shipping Committee, 1901-03; Rhodesia Sub-committee, 1901-22; Rhodes Hostel,

1908-11; Transvaal Sub-committee, 1901-09; Orange River Sub-committee, and Cape Colony Sub-committee, 1901-06; Natal Sub-committee, 1901-06; annual reports, 1903-19; two volumes of correspondence, 1902-04, 1907.

6. *Colonial Intelligence League* (1910-19)

Minutes of the Council, 1912-19; Executive Committee, 1910-19; Finance and Settlement Sub-committee, 1913-19; County Organisation Sub-committee, 1912-14; Literature Sub-committee, 1912-15; Canada, reference volume of extracts, 1912-14; annual reports, 1910-19.

7. *Joint Council of Women's Emigration Societies* (1917-19)

Minutes of the Joint Council, 1917-19.

8. *Society for the Overseas Settlement of British Women* (1920-62), renamed *Women's Migration and Overseas Appointments Society* (1962-64)

Minutes of Council, 1919-37; Executive, 1920-67; Finance Committee, 1919-64; various committees and Sub-committees, 1919-52, including those dealing with Africa, Canada, Australia and New Zealand. Annual reports of S.O.S.B.W., 1920-35, 1936-60; of Rhodesia Sub-committee, 1919-37; W.M.O.A.S., 1961-63. Other records include various correspondence files from 1907; and Lady Knox's diary, 1922-28.

WOMEN'S INTERNATIONAL LEAGUE FOR PEACE AND FREEDOM (BRITISH SECTION)
29 Great James Street London WC1N 3ES

Founded in 1915 by Jane Addams and Emily Greene Balch, among others, the League aimed to bring together women of different political and philosophical tendencies united in the determination to study, make known and abolish the political, social, economic and psychological causes of war, and to work for a constructive peace.

The primary objects of the League remain: total and universal disarmament; the abolition of violent means of coercion for the settlement of conflicts; the substitution in every case of some form of peaceful settlement; and the strengthening of a world organisation for the prevention of war, the institution of international law, and for the political, social and economic co-operation of people.

Papers

A large assortment of the League's records and other material relating to the peace movement has been deposited in the B.L.P.E.S. The records include Executive Committee minutes, 1918-21, 1929-54; most of the British Section's annual reports, 1915-61; many papers of the International Executive and of International Congresses; copies of the *Monthly News-sheet* up to 1951; a run of the monthly journal *Pax International* (June 1928 — Feb. 1940); and a large assortment of press cuttings, pamphlets and leaflets. Many papers collected by Catherine Marshall, one-time Secretary of the British Section, are of particular interest. They include League correspondence in the 1920s, a file on envoys' work in Berlin, Paris and London, 1922-23, and assorted notes and typescript reports. Files on particular subjects relate to China (1920s), Russia (1920s), the Baltic States, India (1930-36), Cyprus and Palestine.

Catherine Marshall's personal papers are deposited in the Record Office, Carlisle. These include correspondence and other material relating to the League, 1908-37.

Availability

The League's papers may be seen on application to the Librarian at B.L.P.E.S. Enquiries concerning the Marshall papers should be directed to the Archivist, the Record Office, Carlisle.

WOMEN'S LABOUR LEAGUE

The League was founded in 1906 as an organisation of women to work for independent Labour representation in connection with the Labour Party, and to obtain direct representation of women in Parliament and on local authorities. Margaret MacDonald was a prime instigator of the League, and among other women involved were Mary Middleton, Dr. Marion Phillips and Katherine Bruce Glasier. The W.L.L. ceased its separate identity after World War I.

Papers

The surviving records of the Women's Labour League are in the Labour Party archive at Transport House. These include signed minutes of the Executive Committee, 1908-18; of the General Purposes Committee, 1911; of meetings of the Central London branch of the League, 1908-18; and of the Executive of the Central London branch, 1906-18. A Treasurer's receipts and expenditure book covers the period 1917-18; a volume, 1911-17, contains names of subscribers to and purchasers of W.L.L. leaflets; and a further volume from 1910 contains brief notes about branches, in alphabetical order. In addition to these records, certain relevant correspondence has been deposited in the archive by Mrs. Lucy Middleton, widow of J. S. Middleton. Middleton's first wife, Mary Middleton, was Secretary of the League, 1907-11, and this group of papers is the surviving bulk of her correspondence. It largely covers the period 1906-08.

Correspondence relating to the W.L.L. may be found throughout the Labour Party archive. A file relating specifically to the Labour Party's relations with the W.L.L., 1908-15, includes papers on the formal relations between the two organisations, arrangements for attendance at annual conferences, for a financial grant to the W.L.L. by the party, and papers on the resultant discussions, 1914-15, on the better organisation of the W.L.L. so as to make it more effective in providing electoral assistance for the Labour Party.

Labour Woman was the official organ of the Women's Labour League.

Availability

Applications to use the records should be made in writing to the Librarian of the Labour Party at Transport House.

WOMEN'S SUFFRAGE SOCIETIES

The Women's Suffrage movement, most active from the 1860s to 1918 when the Representation of the People Act gave the franchise to women over 30, produced an extraordinary variety of organisations, and brought into political activity a large number of women of all classes.

Two organisations, the National Union of Women's Suffrage Societies, and the Women's Social and Political Union, were the most important in the decade before 1914, representing the constitutionalists and the militants respectively.

A number of other organisations, however, either under the umbrella of the N.U.W.S.S. or as breakaways from the W.S.P.U., pursued their own campaigns. As a result no central definitive collection of papers relating to the suffrage movement exists. The largest single collection is housed in the *Fawcett Library* (q.v.). The London Museum also has an important collection deposited by the Suffragette Fellowship.

Manchester Central Library, Archives Department, has an important collection of manuscript material, and the John Rylands Library, University of Manchester, has a collection of journals published by the various suffragette organisations, together with a large collection of relevant press cuttings. Other libraries have smaller collections, including the papers of various individual participants in the movement, e.g. the notebook of Olive Wharry, kept during her imprisonment at Holloway and Winson Green Prisons, 1911-14 (British Library, Add. MSS. 49,976); miscellaneous papers of Lady Clark (née Barbara Keen), 1912-20 (Bodleian Library); and a variety of other papers are still in private hands.

The list below attempts to bring together relevant information concerning the major suffrage organisations. Further information may be obtained from the Assistant Keeper, Manuscripts, at the London Museum; the Fawcett Librarian; and the various librarians indicated. Information concerning the other organisations active in the woman's movement may be found under the relevant headings, e.g. *Josephine Butler Society; British Vigilance Association; National Women Citizen's Association; Women's Emigration Societies.*

Artists' Franchise League

Drawings and posters and correspondence of the London society are deposited in the Fawcett Library.

Commonwealth Countries' League

This was founded in 1925 as the British Commonwealth League, and brought together women active in Commonwealth countries who were active in suffrage and related campaigns.

Papers

These are at present in the care of the Sadd-Brown Library within the *Fawcett Library* (q.v.). They include minute books, financial records, conference reports and chairmen's reports from 1925, together with earlier records of the British Dominion Suffragette Union, founded in the late 19th century.

East London Federation of the Suffragettes

See *Workers' Suffrage Federation.*

Fawcett Society
27 Wilfred Street London SW1E 6PR

The Fawcett Society is the successor body of a series of women's suffrage organisations dating back to the 1860s. The Women's Suffrage Petition Committee, founded in late 1865, became the Women's Suffrage Provisional Committee in the autumn of 1866, the Women's Society for Obtaining Political Rights for Women in July 1867, and the London National Society for Women's Suffrage a month later. In 1871 this split, one faction retaining the old name, and another becoming known as the Central Committee of the National Society for Women's Suffrage, which became the name of the reunited society in 1877. This split again in 1888, over the question of political affiliation, into the Central Committee of the National Society for Women's Suffrage (Central and East of England Society for Women's Suffrage, 1897) and the Central National Society for Women's Suffrage (Central and Western Society for Women's Suffrage, 1897). These were reunited in 1900 as the Central

Society for Women's Suffrage, known as the London Society for Women's Suffrage from 1907, the London Society for Women's Service from 1919 (when it absorbed the Committee for the Opening of the Legal Profession to Women), the London and National Society for Women's Service from 1926, and the Fawcett Society from 1953.

Papers

The surviving records of the predecessor organisations of the Fawcett Society housed in the Fawcett Library include the following:

(1) *Central Committee of the National Society for Women's Suffrage.* Executive Committee minute books from 1875-77, 1883-88, and including reports of annual and special general meetings, minutes of the Finance Committee, 1877-85, and circulars and leaflets, 1888-97.

(2) *Central National Society for Women's Suffrage.* Executive Council minutes, 1888-89 (a continuation of the above), 1890-92, 1894-95, and a ledger of the Lecture Campaign Fund, 1890-1900.

(3) *Central Society for Women's Suffrage.* Executive Committee minutes, 1903-07.

(4) *London Society for Women's Suffrage (Service).* Executive Committee minutes from 1912-41; minutes of the Junior Council Executive, 1929-31, 1939; Commerce and Business Group minutes, 1930-35; parties and debates, programmes, etc., 1927-39; Debating sub-committee minutes, 1928-32; Swimming Club minutes, 1930-35; Science Group minutes, 1933-39; Arts Group minutes, 1932-38; Political Sub-committee minutes, Feb, Mar, 1929, including questionnaires to the three political parties; Finance Committee minutes, 1918-20, 1930-39; Public Work Committee, minutes and reports, 1934-44; Employment Committee minutes, 1922-26, 1929-34.

Men's League for Women's Suffrage

The League was founded in 1907 as a constitutional supporter of the suffrage movement.

Papers

The chief sources would appear to be in collections of private papers. The H. W. Nevinson diaries at the Bodleian Library, Oxford, reflect Nevinson's involvement in the League, and the Bertrand Russell papers at McMaster University, Canada, are revealing for Russell's involvement in the suffrage movement. The papers of W. H. Dickinson (Lord Dickinson) at the Greater London Record Office contain a file on the suffrage question.

A good deal of useful information is also contained in a collection of press cuttings, pamphlets, leaflets and letters, mainly relating to the suffrage movement, formed and annotated by Maud Arncliffe Sennett. These are contained in 37 volumes, 1906-36, which are available at the British Library.

National League for Opposing Women's Suffrage

The Women's National Anti-Suffrage League was founded in 1908, largely through the inspiration of Mrs. Humphrey Ward, and under the Presidency of the Countess of Jersey. In July 1910 the Men's League for Opposing Women's Suffrage was founded, with the Earl of Cromer as President. The two Leagues amalgamated in January 1911 as the National League for Opposing Women's Suffrage. Lord Cromer became President, succeeded in 1912 by Lord Curzon and Lord Weardale. The League was dissolved in 1918. There was also a Scottish Women's National Anti-Suffrage League, which the Duchess of Montrose founded in 1910.

The chief sources for the movements opposing women's suffrage are probably the copies of the *Anti-Suffrage Review*, published monthly, 1908-18. The National League also published a series of leaflets and a speakers' *Handbook*, which are a useful source for its attitudes.

As regards private papers, reference should be made to the Curzon papers (India Office Library), the Cromer papers (Public Record Office), St. Loe Strachey papers (Beaverbrook Library), and the Harcourt papers (Bodleian Library).

The Curzon papers are particularly illuminating, consisting of copies of speeches; three bundles of letters, 1910-13; a bundle of papers appealing for subscriptions, 1910; a file, 1913-14; and a file, 1916-17, including letters from Cromer. A note by Curzon (Oct, 1918) indicates that he destroyed a vast amount of correspondence relating to his work in the National League.

National Union of Women's Suffrage Societies

This was established in 1897 as a federation of all the suffrage groups — some dating back to 1867 — then existing. Mrs. Fawcett was the President, and throughout the suffrage campaign the N.U.W.S.S. remained the chief constitutional organisation. Its members were referred to as 'suffragists'. After the Representation of the People Act was passed in 1918 the name was changed to National Union of Societies for Equal Citizenship, later the National Council for Equal Citizenship. In 1946 this was incorporated into the National Women Citizens' Association.

Papers

(1) Various records are deposited in the Fawcett Library. These consist largely of correspondence, including some letters with branches outside London. Correspondence of Dame Millicent Fawcett and some papers of Eleanor Rathbone for the later period are also housed in the Library. The records of the precursor organisations of the Fawcett Society are described above.

(2) Manchester Central Library, Archives Department, has records of the Manchester Women's Suffrage Society (later Manchester and District Federation of the National Union of Women's Suffrage Societies), 1867-1917. These include duplicated minutes of the N.U.W.S.S., 1913-18; papers of Dame Millicent Fawcett, 1867-1920; pamphlets, 1867-1919; and the autobiography of Hannah Mitchell.

(3) The Record Office, The Castle, Carlisle, has papers of Catherine Marshall which include correspondence and papers relating to the N.U.W.S.S., 1909-21 (8 boxes in all).

(4) A variety of smaller collections are deposited in local record offices, e.g. records of the Cambridge Women's Suffrage Association (later the Cambridge Standing Committee for Equal Citizenship), 1884-1939, and the Cambridge and District Women's Citizens Association, 1918-33, are deposited in the Cambridgeshire and Isle of Ely Record Office. Records of the Great Yarmouth Women's Suffrage Society are in the Great Yarmouth Borough Archives.

National Women's Social and Political Union

See *Women's Social and Political Union*.

St. Joan's Social and Political Alliance

Formerly the Catholic Women's Suffrage Society, the present title was adopted in October 1933.

Papers

Committee minutes run from 1911-44, and a diary covers the period 1914-28. These are deposited in the Fawcett Library.

Suffragette Fellowship

The Fellowship was founded to perpetuate the memory of the pioneers and outstanding events connected with women's emancipation and especially with the militant suffrage campaign, 1905-14.

Papers

A substantial collection of records has been deposited in the London Museum, including papers relating to the Fellowship itself and the work of former suffragettes after 1918; certain records of the W.S.P.U., the Women's Freedom League, and the Tax Resistance League; papers of various prominent suffragettes; and copies of circulars, speeches and pamphlets.

Votes for Women Fellowship

This was founded in 1912 by the Pethick-Lawrences as a breakaway from the W.S.P.U.

Papers

The papers of Lord and Lady Pethick-Lawrence are at present in private hands. It is expected that they will eventually be deposited in Trinity College, Cambridge.

Women's Emancipation Union

Letters from Mrs. Elizabeth C. Wolstenhome Elvey, Hon. Secretary of the Union, to Mrs. Harriet McIlquhar, are deposited in the British Library (7 vols: Add. MSS. 47,449-47,455).

Women's Freedom League

This was founded in 1907 as a breakaway from the *Women's Social and Political Union* (q.v.) by, among others, Mrs. Despard, Edith How-Martyn and Teresa Billington-Greig.

Papers

Records are deposited in the Fawcett Library. These include minutes of the National Executive, 1908-61; of the Political and Militant Department (later the Political Sub-committee), 1910-21; the Finance Sub-committee, 1907-09; the Press Sub-committee, 1908-10; the Social Committee, 1909, the *Vote Brigade*, a journal of rallies and poster parades, 1913-19; the Parliamentary Committee minutes, 1908; the Organisation Committee minutes, 1908-09, verbatim minutes of the annual conference from the 3rd (1908) to the 26th (1933); two minute books of the Middlesbrough branch are also extant.

Certain other papers, relating to the League's formation, constitution and policy, are among the Suffragette Fellowship papers at the London Museum, as are reports of annual conferences, 1908-12.

Women's Social and Political Union

The W.S.P.U. (founded in Manchester in 1903 by Emmeline Pankhurst) was the chief militant suffrage society, and remained so despite various splits and the establishment of new organisations: the *Women's Freedom League* (q.v.), 1907; the

Votes for Women Fellowship (q.v.), founded by the Pethick-Lawrences, 1912; and the East London Federation of the Suffragettes, founded by Sylvia Pankhurst in 1913, which in February 1916 became the *Workers' Suffrage Federation* (see below).

Papers

Records deposited in the London Museum by the Suffragette Fellowship are important sources for the history of the W.S.P.U. The papers there include diaries, correspondence, autobiographical notes of various suffragettes, relating their experiences in campaigns and in prison; letters from Mrs. Pankhurst, Mrs. Pethick-Lawrence, etc.; papers relating to Emily Davidson; letters and papers relating to demonstrations and political action; other, miscellaneous correspondence from supporters; programmes, tickets, souvenirs of the W.S.P.U.; press cuttings; a collection of pamphlets and papers relating to the W.S.P.U. constitution and policy; and a minute book of the Canning Town branch of the W.S.P.U., 1906-07.

Certain correspondence, 1906-21, of Jean Lawlie, one-time Organising Secretary of the W.S.P.U., is deposited in Baillie's Library, 69 Oakfield Avenue, Glasgow, W2 (23 items in all). Additional material can be found in the National Library of Scotland.

Women's Tax Resistance League

The League was established in 1909, growing out of the Women's Freedom League, and extending its tactic of organising tax resistance as a weapon in the suffrage campaign.

Papers

Minute books, 1909-18, are deposited in the Fawcett Library. Papers relating to the League, and to refusals to pay taxes in general, are deposited in the Suffragette Fellowship papers at the London Museum.

Workers' Socialist Federation

The East London Federation of the Suffragettes was established in 1913 by Sylvia Pankhurst as a breakaway from the Women's Social and Political Union. In 1916 it became the Workers' Suffrage Federation, and in 1918 the Workers' Socialist Federation.

Papers

The chief source for the Federation is in the Sylvia Pankhurst Collection at the International Institute of Social History, Amsterdam. This collection was given to the Institute by Dr. R. K. P. Pankhurst after his mother's death in 1960. Sylvia Pankhurst herself had given her file of the *Women's Dreadnought/Workers' Dreadnought* to the Institute in 1956, when she went to live in Addis Ababa.

The collection covers a long period, the oldest material dating from the 1860s, but there are large gaps.

The oldest part consists of papers of Dr. R. M. Pankhurst. There are books of newspaper clippings (1863-96, 8 vols.), some letters from Lydia Becker about suffrage matters and a few personal and family documents (late 1860s, early 1870s).

There are a few letters from Mrs. Jacob Bright to Mrs. Emmeline Pankhurst about suffrage matters (early 1890s). To this part also belong a number of family photographs, birth certificates, certificates of burial, school reports and diplomas of several members of the family, and some correspondence about legacies. There is hardly any personal correspondence.

The material of Sylvia Pankhurst herself can be divided roughly into three parts:

(1) Notes, manuscripts, typescripts, printed material and photographs used for her books and articles, some of them unpublished, and some correspondence connected with the collecting of material for them, as well as some material put together in connection with a lawsuit about the Home Front.

(2) Correspondence, leaflets, minute books, etc., connected with her various activities, e.g. the minute books of the East London Federation of the Suffragettes, later the Workers' Suffrage Federation, still later the Workers' Socialist Federation; correspondence about her membership of the Communist Party of Great Britain; notes about international congresses; material (mostly printed) about her involvement in various anti-Fascist activities, in particular her support of Ethiopia and its emperor and the publication of the *New Times and Ethiopian News*.

(3) A small amount of personal correspondence, *inter alia* with J. Keir Hardie, Emmeline Pethick-Lawrence, Dora Russell, Adela Walsh (née Pankhurst); some sketches and designs and photographs.

The collection is being arranged. It can be consulted on request, preferably by writing in advance to the England-North America Department of the International Institute of Social History, Herengracht 262-266, Amsterdam-C, Netherlands.

WOMEN'S TRADE UNION (MUTUAL AND PROVIDENT) LEAGUE

The League was founded in 1874 as a centre of propaganda and education for the promotion of trade unionism among women. Any trade union which allowed women as members was able to affiliate, and the policy of the League was to encourage women to join the men's societies. The National Federation of Women Workers was formed in 1906 for the purpose of organising women in miscellaneous trades not already organised. The League itself ceased its work in the early 1920s.

Papers

A microfilm of records of the Women's Trade Union League is available in the Library of the Trades Union Congress, Great Russell Street, London WC1B 3LS. The records include Executive Committee minute books, 1903-21; Congress Committee minutes, 1895-1921; and annual reports, 1875-1921. Copies of journals cover the period 1877-1921. The W.T.U.L. published *Quarterly Report and Review*, 1891, known as *Women's Trades Union Review*, 1891-1919.

Availability

The records may be consulted on prior application to the Librarian, Trades Union Congress.

WOOL (AND ALLIED) TEXTILE EMPLOYERS' COUNCIL
60 Toller Lane Bradford BD8 9DA

The Council was founded in 1919.

Papers

A complete set of minutes of the organisation survives from World War I. Apart from certain negotiating and other material, few other records survive.

Availability

Applications should be made to the Director.

WORKERS' EDUCATIONAL ASSOCIATION
Temple House 9 Upper Berkeley Street London W1H 8BY

The Association was formed in 1903 with the specific aim of promoting education for the working class. Its stated aim is 'to interest men and women in their own continued education and in the better education of their children'.

Papers

The association has retained a valuable collection of records which are preserved in its Library. These include:

(1)   All minute books of the national organisation since the foundation of the W.E.A. in 1903. There are also reports from the regional organisations, but these are not kept in the Library at Temple House. Minutes of the Oxford Joint Conference on the Education of Work-People, 1909, also survive.

(2)   There is very little correspondence that is separate from the general files contained in the Library. All relevant correspondence has been filed in the subject-matter files.

There are three files of Tawney correspondence:
(*a*)   1907-08 on early tutorial classes;
(*b*)   1913-14 on tutorial classes and matters of general policy;
(*c*)   1958-62 general correspondence.

All the annual reports have been kept since 1903. They include the reports of the National Conference with the resolutions.

The W.E.A. gives evidence to all the appropriate government committees. In some cases the evidence has been printed and is on the shelves, in other cases it was merely duplicated and is filed in steel cupboards in an adjoining room. The same cupboards contain files, in alphabetical order of subject, except for some files of sundry documents which are filed under date and indexed under subject.

Temple House contains all the material relating to the Central Joint Advisory Committee on Tutorial Classes from 1909-58. Also housed there is the material relating to the Secretariat of the International W.E.A. from 1947-68, when it moved to Düsseldorf. These records are available, subject to prior application to the Librarian.

Other records relevant to the growth of the W.E.A. are available at the University of Oxford, Department for External Studies, Rewley House, Wellington Square, Oxford OX1 2JA.

These include records of the University Extension Delegacy from about 1878, and associated records of the extension lecture movement which was important in the setting-up of the W.E.A. There are also records about the establishment of tutorial classes, and many records of the early tutorial classes and associated Summer Schools. These records are only roughly sorted. Applications as to their availability should be made to the Librarian at Rewley House.

Minute books of the North Staffordshire Miners' Higher Education Movement, 1911-20, are retained at Cartwright House, Hanley, Stoke-on-Trent.

WORKINGMEN'S CLUB AND INSTITUTE UNION LTD.
Club Union House 251-256 Upper Street London N1 1RY

More commonly known as the Club and Institute Union (C.I.U.), the organisation was founded on 14 June 1862 on the initiative of the Revd. Henry Solly. It is not a club but a union of clubs. Originating in London, its membership has grown from 710 in 1900 to over 4,000 in 1973. It is a non-political federation, acting in an advisory and defensive role to protect and further the interests of its members.

Papers

Some surviving records exist at the headquarters of the C.I.U. As a result of extensive clearances, in 1962 and again in 1973, no correspondence (except for current material) has survived. However, minutes of the Executive Committee (and a variety of sub-committees) have survived. For the early years, the Executive minutes are only a brief record of decisions made; they become fuller after 1900. In part, the lack of archive material is compensated for by a centenary history of the C.I.U. (*The First Century*, by George Tremlett) which used (and quoted) unpublished material. Annual reports (which include financial reports) are also extant.

In addition to this material, a collection of correspondence concerning the C.I.U. is to be found in the Henry Solly Collection at the B.L.P.E.S.

Availability

Applications to use the material at Club Union House should be made to the General Secretary. This will not normally be refused.

WORLD EDUCATION FELLOWSHIP
13 Kinnaird Avenue London W4

The Society was founded in 1921 as the New Education Fellowship. It adopted its present title in 1966 to emphasise its international scope. The Fellowship 'sets out to further educational improvement and reform throughout the world so that every individual — whatever his nationality, race, status or religion — shall be educated under conditions which allow of the full and harmonious development of his whole personality and lead to his realising and fulfilling his responsibilities to the community'.

Papers

The records of the Fellowship have been deposited in the Library of the University of London Institute of Education, 11-13 Ridgmount Street, London WC1E 7AH. They have not been catalogued at the time of writing and no detailed information is available. They appear to comprise a full set of records.

Availability

Enquiries should be directed to the Librarian of the Institute of Education.

YOUTH MOVEMENTS

A Youth Movement Archive was established at University College, Cardiff at the beginning of 1974. This reflected the growing interest in the development of youth movements, youth culture, and their social and political import, and the anxiety that records relating to the various British movements should not be lost. Many of the larger youth movements have, in fact, taken some care to preserve their records, and these are detailed below. There is a danger, however, that many of the records of the smaller, less formally organised, movements, will disappear. For this reason the Youth Archive has begun collecting both formal and personal records of the various movements, together with their periodicals and publications. The archives of particular organisations deposited in Cardiff are listed below, in the alphabetical list of youth organisations. In general terms, the Youth Archive has source material such as log books, diaries of members, teaching manuals, correspondence, arrangements for camps and schools, as well as the minutes, reports, circulars, pamphlets and journals, etc. of particular organisations. The Archive also holds a valuable collection of tape recordings relating to the work of the mass youth movements including interviews with pioneer members. This material may be consulted on application to the Social Sciences Librarian, University College, P.O. Box 96, Cardiff CF1 1XB. The list below describes the records of organisations which have been contacted, either by the survey or by the Youth Movement Archive.

Boys Brigade
Brigade House Parsons Green London SW6 4TH

The Brigade was founded in Scotland in 1883, as a predominantly Presbyterian youth organisation. It now embraces all the main Protestant denominations, and retains a fundamentally religious outlook.

Papers

The Brigade has retained various records of its activities, in both its London and Glasgow offices. These are at present unsorted but work is being undertaken to sort and list these records. They may be consulted on prior application to Brigade House.

British Apprentices Club

This was founded in 1921 by Katherine Mayo, the authoress.

Papers

The Katherine Mayo collection in Yale University Library includes much correspondence relating to the Club.

Church Lads' Brigade
58 Gloucester Place London W1

The Brigade was founded in 1891 and is attached to the Church of England. It was based on strong pro-Empire sentiments, and later affiliated to the British National Cadet Association for a brief period (1911-23).

Papers

Some older publications, including a unique souvenir publication, have been deposited in the Youth Movement Archive at Cardiff. A full range of publications and minutes is retained by the Brigade Headquarters.

Covenanters' Union
City Gate House Finsbury Square London EC2A 1RJ

Founded in 1930, the Union is an inter-denominational evangelical Christian movement for boys, which is essentially a voluntary association of Bible classes.

Papers

Records have been retained by the Union but these are not generally made available.

Crusaders' Union
St. Paul's Corner 1 Ludgate Hill London EC4M 7AB

This is a religious but non-denominational youth organisation.

All the Union's records are retained at its head office. These include Minutes of Meetings of the General Committee and various sub-committees but these are not generally made available. Each enquiry will be judged on its merits.

Girls' Friendly Society
Townsend House Greycoat Place London SW1P 1SL

The Society was founded in 1874, with the aim of bringing respectable young girls together within the ambit of the Church of England, and training them in religious principles and domestic duties.

Papers

The Society has retained extensive records covering its whole history. These are at present being listed and catalogued, and enquiries should be directed to the General Secretary.

Girl Guides Association
17-19 Buckingham Palace Road London SW1W 0PT

The Association was founded in 1910 by Lord Baden-Powell to give girls opportunities for education and recreation analogous to those which Scouting provided for boys.

Papers

Many records, dating from 1910, have been retained by the Association, including formal records, press cuttings and journals. Applications to consult these records should be made to the archivist.

Jewish Youth Movements

The Youth Movement Archive in Cardiff has collected a considerable amount of material relating to various Jewish Youth organisations that developed, particularly in Jewish communities in the East End of London, from the 1880s onwards. These include the Jewish Lads' Brigade as well as Youth Clubs. Apart from the material it holds itself, the Archive has a comprehensive guide to the whereabouts of other relevant material.

Kibbo Kift

See Social Credit Movement.

National Union of Students
3 Endsleigh Street London WC1

The Union was founded in 1922.

Papers

The National Union of Students has retained some of its earlier records, but these are at present unsorted. Four volumes of material relating to the pre-World War II period are available in the British Library.

Order of Woodcraft Chivalry

This was found in the 1920s by F. Ernest and Aubrey Westlake.

Papers

Aubrey Westlake has retained a substantial collection of records, including diaries, log books, correspondence and circulars. Some representative materials are to be deposited in the Youth Movement Archive.

Outward Bound Trust
34 Broadway London SW1H 0BQ

Papers

The trust has retained many of its records, including Council and Management Committee minute books and old files of material. These records may be made available to bona fide researchers.

Scout Association
25 Buckingham Palace Road London SW1W 0PY

The Boy Scout Movement was founded in 1908 by Lord Baden-Powell.

Papers

The Scout Association has retained many of its records. Enquiries should be directed to the Executive Commissioner (Administration) and Secretary.

Socialist Fellowship (q.v.)

Student Christian Movement

The organisation developed from the Student Voluntary Missionary Movement, founded in 1892.

Papers

The Movement has placed its records in the care of the Bodleian Library, Oxford. The archive consists of records of the Student Voluntary Missionary Movement from its foundation, of the S.C.M. itself, and the early records of other organisations which had close relationships with the Movement in earlier days, such as the National Union of Students and the World University Service.

Woodcraft Folk

See Co-operative Movement.
Further papers relating to the Folk are deposited in the Youth Movement Archive, University College, Cardiff. These include papers relating to the foundation of the Folk, early manuals, diaries, and journals.

Urdd Gobaith Cymru

See Appendix II: Archives in Wales.

Young Men's Christian Association
640 Forest Road Walthamstow London E17 3DZ

Founded in London in 1844 by George Williams, the Convenor of a religious group of drapers' apprentices, the Y.M.C.A. quickly spread throughout the country and abroad, embracing earlier organisations of a similar nature. The Y.M.C.A. remains an inter-denominational, active missionary organisation, which promotes the physical, intellectual and spiritual fitness, training and well-being of youth. The association's activities extend to the provision of social, cultural and educational services, and close relations are maintained with the Y.W.C.A.

Papers

The Association has retained extensive records. Minutes of the following committees have been retained:

National Council from 1882;

War Emergency Committee, May 1915;

Executive Committee from 1919;

Finance and General Purposes Committee from 1924; and Treasurers' Committee from 1928;

Community Services Committee, 1934-9;

War Emergency Committee, 1939-51;

Officers' Training and Nomination Committee, assorted from 1885;

Religious Work Committee, 1923-40, 1947-58;

Universities and Education Committee 1923-40, 1942-53.

Among the more interesting records available are a large number of files containing material relating to local Y.M.C.A.'s, for example, reports and letters etc., 1884-1921, of the South Midlands, Oxford County Federation. Much of the material consists of printed annual reports of the local associations, but this is an interesting collection. The letters, minutes and printed papers 1879-1908 of the London Metropolitan Organisation form a useful series.

Another significant series is the large collection of photographs and papers relating to aspects of the war work of the Y.M.C.A.

Most of the other material in the archives is made up of printed annual Reports, published lectures and books on Y.M.C.A. work, papers and mementoes relating to Sir George Williams. Finally a good assortment of the association's magazines is retained, for example: *Young Men's Monthly*, 1874; *YM*, 1915-17; *Red Triangle*, c. 1917-24; *British Y.M.C.A. Review*, c. 1936-71; War-time papers of the National Women's Auxiliary have been deposited with the Y.M.C.A. records.

Persons wishing to see the records should apply to the Secretary of the National Council.

Young Women's Christian Association of Great Britain
National Offices: Hampden House 2 Weymouth Street London W1N 4AX

In 1855 Miss Emma Robarts of Barnet founded a Prayer Union, which in time opened branches in all parts of the United Kingdom. In the same year, the Hon. Mrs Arthur Kinnaird opened a hostel in London for nurses en route to and from the Crimean War hospitals. This was continued after the war as a home for working girls, and other hostels were soon opened. in 1877 the Prayer Union and Lady Kinnaird's Homes were united in one organisation, the Y.W.C.A., with Lord Shaftesbury as President. The Association aims to promote world-wide fellowship and understanding of the Christian faith, and to advancing education and welfare, especially among young people.

Papers

A large collection of records has been deposited by the Association in the Modern Records Centre, University of Warwick. Local centres of the Association retain their own records. The national records include minutes of the Governing Body from 1884, and minutes and papers of numerous committees covering administration, financial affairs and the particular activities of the Association. Annual Reports from 1862 are also retained. Of special interest are the records of Y.W.C.A. work in the two World Wars, the files on 'Industrial Legislation' and on the schemes to help women emigrants, and papers relating to the organisation of Day Release Courses in the 1950s.

Note

Reference should also be made to the entries on the major political parties for reference to their youth movements.

THE ZIONIST FEDERATION OF GREAT BRITAIN AND NORTHERN IRELAND

Rex House 4/12 Regent Street London SW1

The Zionist Federation of Great Britain was formed on 16 March 1898, following the Clerkenwell Conference. It took its inspiration from the World Zionist Federation founded by Dr Theodor Herzl. The British branch included among its founders Sir Moses Montiefore, Bt., Albert Goldsmid and Israel Zangwill. Its declared object, embodied in its constitution is 'to create for the Jewish People a Home in Eretz Yisrael secured by public law'. This was amended by the twenty-third Zionist Congress held in Jerusalem to include as the task of Zionism 'the consolidation of the State of Israel, the ingathering of the exiles in Eretz Yisrael and the fostering of the unity of the Jewish people'. Further aims of the Federation include the encouragement of capital investment in Israel; the fostering of Jewish consciousness; the defence of Jewish rights and the mobilisation of public opinion in favour of Israel and Zionism. Until 1931 the Federation was known as the English Zionist Federation when its name was changed to the Zionist Federation of Great Britain and Ireland. In 1966, the present title was adopted. The Zionist Federation of Great Britain and Northern Ireland is affiliated to the World Confederation of General Zionists (which was situated in Britain until 1948).

Papers

While executive committee minute books from 1946 to date and annual reports from 1930 are held in Rex House, most of the archival material is sent periodically to the Central Zionist Archives, P.O. Box 92, Jerusalem, Israel. Records prior to 1948 were also transferred there on the outbreak of World War II. All policy correspondence is retained both in London and in Israel. Some archival material of an unspecified nature covering the years 1899-1914 was destroyed by fire. The Federation was responsible for fund-raising to help Jewish refugees. The minutes relating to this activity are held at the Central Fund headquarters at Woburn House, Upper Woburn Place, London WC1.

The Federation publishes an annual report which is circulated to members, copies of which are also held at Rex House. In addition, there are back numbers of the *Zionist Review* (founded 1923) which was published monthly. This was later supplanted by a weekly publication, the *Jewish Observer*.

Availability

The executive committee minutes are usually confidential although each request to consult them would be considered on its merits. Other material can be seen with prior permission of the General Secretary. For material held in the Central Zionist Archive, application should be made to the Director, P.O. Box 92, Jerusalem, Israel.

Appendix I
Archives in Ireland

In this section an outline is given of the extent of archives surviving for political organisations functioning in Ireland in the late 19th and early 20th centuries. The period dealt with is more or less determined by political events. No organisation which did not exist in one form or another at the beginning of the 20th century is dealt with, and the politics of the twenty-six counties established as the Irish Free State in 1922 are sufficiently divergent from the mainstream of British politics not to be included. This account is thus concerned with the records of Irish politics in its period of greatest involvement with the politics of Britain itself; a more thorough survey of the resources of Irish politics from a more specifically Irish point of view has yet to be done, but a volume such as this is not the most appropriate place for such a task.

The groundwork for an account of British political archives has now been fairly thoroughly undertaken, but in Ireland the situation is different. Fortunately very considerable advances are currently taking place in Ireland to assist the work of discovering and conserving records of all kinds. In particular, in November 1970 occurred the foundation of an Irish Society for Archives (*Cumann Cartlannaiochte Eireann*), a body devoting its energies to discovering and saving historical records and providing a focus for those wishing to press for new legislation to ensure the preservation of public records. The *Irish Archives Bulletin* is published twice yearly by this society and has already provided an important service in drawing attention to particular archives and in providing a forum for the discussion of Irish archival questions in general. This journal is now one of the most important means by which students interested in various Irish records, and most particularly local records, can keep abreast of new discoveries. The establishment of a diploma course in Archival Studies at University College, Dublin, is a further welcome development which should help to provide more expert knowledge for the handling of archives in Ireland. There have also been significant archival developments in Cork, where a Cork Archives Council has been set up under the auspices of Cork Corporation, Cork County Council, University College, Cork, and Cork Harbour Commissioners. This has led to the establishment of an archives centre in Cork Courthouse, where the County Library now has its first trained archivist. The announcement in 1971 that the records of Dail Eireann for the period 1919-22 were to be transferred from the Taoiseach's Department to the State Paper Office is an encouraging sign that the Irish Government may establish more satisfactory procedures for the preservation of public records in Ireland.[1] All these developments suggest that the

---

[1] See Owen Dudley Edwards, 'Procedure Needed for State Papers', *Irish Archives Bulletin*, I, 2 (Oct. 1971) 6-10.

historian's task of locating and using Irish historical records may become much more straightforward in future.

Quite separate difficulties exist in relation to the records of Irish political organisations, apart from the relatively undeveloped condition of archive preservation. Irish parties and pressure groups have tended to be expressions of current ideology and have passed out of existence with any radical change in the orientation of politics. Thus, in Ireland the chances are that the records of a particular organisation were either destroyed at the time or passed into the hands of an individual, being subsequently destroyed or lost. The papers of individuals are therefore specially important in Ireland, not only in themselves, but for the material in them which might otherwise have been preserved as organisational records. Much of what follows in this section is an attempt to point out the private collections in which such records have survived, albeit in some cases in a very fragmentary form. Yet another difficulty exists with Irish political records which is absent in Britain. Much of Irish political activity has taken place at the fringe of — or beyond — the accepted machinery of constitutional politics, with leading politicians liable to police prosecutions and often constantly on the move from place to place. Such an environment is unconducive to the preservation of written materials. For these reasons, any account of Irish organisational records must inevitably be more fragmentary, and less specific, than is possible with British records.

Although certain aspects of modern Irish archives are relatively uncharted, this should not lead the student to suppose that there are no existing aids to the location of manuscript sources. Indeed, for those manuscripts which have already been deposited in the larger national libraries and record offices there are particularly useful guides. The most important of all is undoubtedly the eleven-volume *Manuscript Sources for the History of Irish Civilisation* (Boston, 1965), edited by R. J. Hayes, the former director of the National Library of Ireland. This publication, produced by the photographic reproduction of index cards, contains detailed information of holdings, both in Ireland and other countries, of manuscripts relating to Ireland. It serves in effect as a catalogue of the National Library's own holdings, but is also the most comprehensive guide available to worldwide holdings of Irish material. Its contents are arranged under many different categories and a perusal of its many volumes is the most effective starting-point for a search for particular records available. It should be noted that an unpublished appendix of manuscripts catalogued in the National Library since the publication of Hayes, up to 1970, is now available.[1] It may be consulted in the manuscript room of the National Library in Dublin, and a copy is also available in the Bodleian Library, Oxford. The other major source of information about Irish records are the *Reports* of the Deputy Keeper of the Records in Northern Ireland, which are published at periodic intervals by the Northern Ireland Government and give detailed information about accessions of manuscripts in the Public Record Office, Belfast. It has in the past been difficult to locate and see the records kept by local government bodies in Ireland, but the new journal, the *Irish Archives Bulletin*, is ideally placed for providing information about developments in this field.[2] For certain periods of modern Irish history, published material provides the only available source; special importance therefore attaches to James Carty's two-volume *Bibliography of Irish History* (Dublin, 1936).

---

[1] See in particular P. J. White, 'Procedure Needed for Local Records Also!', *Irish Archives Bulletin*, I, 2 (Oct. 1971) 11-18, and Sean McMenamin, 'Board of Guardians Records', ibid., pp. 19-33.

[2] Shelflist of Additional MSS. catalogued since publication of *Manuscript Sources for the History of Irish Civilisation* (typescript, 1970), referred to hereafter as 'Shelflist of Additional MSS'.

Many of the most important manuscript collections are already in archive repositories in Ireland. The most important of these are the National Library of Ireland, the State Paper Office, and the Public Record Office — all in Dublin — and the Public Record Office of Northern Ireland in Belfast. The various university libraries in Dublin, Cork, Belfast and Galway also contain useful manuscript material, and the Linen Hall Library in Belfast and the Royal Irish Academy in Dublin also have manuscript holdings. In addition, the Public Record Office, London, holds a considerable quantity of Irish material, although some of this is subject to a special hundred years restriction. It should be noted that most official records of political significance which have been kept in Dublin are in the State Paper Office in Dublin Castle, and that there is little of political importance in the Public Record Office in Dublin, many of its records being destroyed in 1922.[1] Students wishing to use any of these institutions should write beforehand to enquire about conditions of access.

Irish Parliamentary Movement

The movement which, from the 1870s until 1918, attempted by means of involvement in Westminster politics to wrest from Britain a measure of Home Rule for Ireland consisted of no single or continuous organisation, although there were strong organisational and individual links which provided an element of continuity. The party led by Charles Parnell in the 1880s was a very different body from Isaac Butt's Home Rule party of the 1870s, while after 1890 dissensions among Parnell's followers led to a multiplication of different organisations, all ostensibly in pursuit of Home Rule. After 1900 the party led by John Redmond, although claiming a line of descent from Parnell, operated under quite new conditions and was in many respects a new body. There were also a number of splinter groups from the mainstream of the parliamentary party. The most important of these was the Cork-based All-for-Ireland League which, between 1910 and 1916, sought to find a basis of compromise between the parliamentarians, Sinn Fein and the Unionists. But for archival purposes these are all best dealt with in one category.

Very little survives in the form of actual office archives for the parliamentary party, but this deficiency is not a significant one because of the character of the material that passed into the hands of individual members of the party. The party never employed an extensive bureaucracy and so the most significant of its working papers were kept in the hands of leading politicians. There are a number of minute books for the party which are held by the National Library of Ireland, apart from the papers of individual politicians, but these are of little importance. They include three minute books of meetings of the party in the House of Commons between 1900 and 1918 (MSS. 12,080-82) and the minute book of the National Directory of the United Irish League, the party's national organisation, between 1904 and 1918 (MS. 708). But as the former of these consists almost entirely of newspaper reports of the party's meetings and the latter lists resolutions, but rarely gives the gist of discussion, they contain little information not readily available from other sources. It is from the papers of individuals that the more significant information is to be culled.

The biggest gap in the party's archive resources is for the period before 1890. The papers of Isaac Butt, chairman of the party in the 1870s, are in the National Library, but they consist principally of correspondence and personal papers. There are, however, no Parnell papers, and so there is little of an authoritative nature on the internal affairs of the party in the 1880s. Indeed, even the papers of Parnell's associates, often voluminous for later periods, contain very little for this earlier

---

[1] See Herbert Wood, 'The Public Records of Ireland before and after 1922', *Royal Historical Society Transactions,* 4th ser., XII (1930) 17-49; and Margaret Griffith, 'A Short Guide to the Public Record Office of Ireland', *Irish Historical Studies,* VIII (1952-3), 45-58.

period. The leaders of the party were at this time often in conflict with the police and the pattern of their lives was very unsettled; it is therefore not surprising that they left very few written records behind them.

It is after 1890, and especially after 1900, that the papers of certain key members of the party provide what amounts to a very full party archive. Of particular importance are the papers of John Redmond, leader of the Parnellite party in the 1890s and of the reunited party from 1900 until his death in 1917. This collection contains very extensive correspondence between Redmond, other Irish Nationalists, British politicians and Ministers, and many individuals and organisations throughout Ireland. The collection includes correspondence and papers relating to the day-to-day functioning of the Parnellite party before 1900, including assessments of the party's viability, both financially and in terms of political support. After 1900 the collection has very extensive material on the organisation of the whole party, including considerable correspondence before 1904 with Laurence Ginnell and John O'Donnell, who between them were largely responsible for the functioning of the Dublin office of the United Irish League, and important correspondence after 1907 with John Muldoon on party organisation. This collection is probably the most consistently comprehensive record of the party's history. It is held in the National Library of Ireland, and it can also be seen on microfilm in the Bodleian Library, Oxford. A detailed list of the collection is contained in the National Library's 'Shelflist of Additional MSS'.

The papers of John Dillon contain many significant party records for the 1890s, arising from Dillon's involvement with and eventual leadership of the anti-Parnellite section of the party. His papers contain many volumes of minutes and of other records of the party and of its various national organisations. These include the minute books of the Irish parliamentary party from 1886 to 1900; the minute book of the Executive Committee of the Irish National Federation, 11 March 1891 – 31 January 1899; the minute book of the Council of the Federation from its first meeting on 9 January 1893 until 19 January 1898; and the scrapbook containing press reports of the public meetings of the Federation from 16 November 1892 until 19 January 1898. The Dillon papers are also rich in correspondence and papers about the affairs of both the anti-Parnellite party in the 1890s and the reunited party after 1900, of which he became the last chairman for a brief period after Redmond's death. His papers are particularly valuable for administrative detail and for personal relationships within the party, and they reflect the crucial role that Dillon played in the party's affairs in the 1890s and up to 1918. The papers are still held by the Dillon family, and although they were readily made available for research purposes for many years by the late Professor Myles Dillon, they have now been temporarily restricted.

The papers of William O'Brien, a prominent figure in the Nationalist movement from the early 1880s until 1918, are a further indispensable source for the history of the parliamentary party and of the associated bodies in which he was active. O'Brien's papers were divided by his widow into two parts, one of which she gave to the National Library of Ireland and the other to the Library of University College, Cork. In the National Library is O'Brien's correspondence with more important national figures, as well as some selected, more general correspondence and papers. Included is his correspondence with Michael Davitt (MSS. 913-14), Lord Dunraven (MS. 8554), John Dillon (MS. 8555), T. M. Healy (MS. 8556) and John Redmond (MS. 10,496). There are also more general groups of papers, and a manuscript work by Mrs. Sophie O'Brien, 'Recollections of a Long Life' (MSS. 4213-17), contains many copies of O'Brien's letters. From an organisational point of view, however, the O'Brien papers in Cork are more significant. They include correspondence and papers relating to the history of the party in the early 1890s, including the Parnell crisis of 1890-91 and the disputes among the anti-Parnellites between 1892 and 1896; but their greatest importance lies in papers relating to the development of the United Irish League between 1898 and 1900. In eight boxes of correspondence for this period a detailed picture emerges of the origins and establishment of this new body, of its methods of organisation, the character of the agitation that it engendered, its relations with the established Nationalist politicians, and its eventual part in the reunion of the parliamentary party in 1900. The collection also contains material about the disputes among parliamentarians after 1903, the establishment and functioning of the All-for-Ireland League after 1910, and considerable information about the running of newspapers with which O'Brien was concerned, especially the *Irish People* and the *Cork Free Press*.[1]

J. F. X. O'Brien held central positions in the parliamentary party, and his papers reflect his administrative importance to the party. He occupied the position of treasurer of the parliamentary party and was also secretary of the party's organisation in Great Britain. His papers include minutes of the committee of the anti-Parnellite party, 1892-95 (MS. 9223), account books and ledgers relating to the party's parliamentary fund between 1886 and 1896, and two letter books containing copies of correspondence relating to the Irish National League of Great Britain and its successor, the United Irish League of Great Britain, 1896-1905 (MSS. 9224-25). There is also extensive correspondence between 1879 and 1905 relating to the administration and general affairs of the party.

The papers of other members of the party are also important sources for its activities. The papers of T. C. Harrington in the National Library contain material on the 1880s and are also particularly informative on the attempts to reunite the party in the late 1890s. The papers of Edward Blake in the Public Archives of Canada are particularly valuable for party discussions on the second Home Rule Bill and on the affairs of the anti-Parnellite party generally in the 1890s. A microfilm of this collection is held in the National Library. The papers of Michael Davitt also appear to be an important source for the history of the party from the 1870s onwards. They are in the possession of Professor T. W. Moody of Trinity College, Dublin, but are not yet available for research. The papers of T. P. Gill in the National Library (MSS. 13,478-526) contain material on the Plan of Campaign in the 1880s, on the Parnell crisis of 1890-91 and on more general political matters. The National Library also contains smaller collections and individual items belonging to other Nationalist politicians. A few papers of T. M. Healy have recently been placed in University College, Dublin.

Records of a kind not normally associated directly with a political party assume importance in the case of the Irish parliamentary party because of its special relationship to certain other institutions. In particular, the close association of the party with the Roman Catholic Church, especially in the 1880s, gives significance to certain ecclesiastical archives in relation to the administration and policy of the party. Particularly important are the papers of Archbishops Croke of Cashel and Walsh of Dublin, who were the two bishops most closely associated with the parliamentary party. The Croke papers, in the archiepiscopal archives at Cashel, are accessible, normally by means of microfilm in the National Library of Ireland. The Walsh papers, in the Dublin diocesan archives, have not generally been available for research, but it is now possible that they may be opened in a few years time, when adequate cataloguing has been done.

The unusual relationship of the Irish parliamentary party to government makes certain other records of importance to its history. The surveillance kept by the police and other government bodies over the activities of the party and of its

---

[1] For a description and list of this collection see P. J. Bull, 'The William O'Brien Manuscripts in the Library of University College, Cork', *Journal of the Cork Historical and Archaeological Society*, LXXV (1970) 129-41.

associated organisations resulted in the compilation of extensive files and records of great value to the historian. The most important of these are among the Chief Secretary's Office Papers in Dublin Castle and in the Irish Office Papers in the Public Record Office, London. The close liaison between the party and the Liberal Government after 1905 gives significance to the papers of various Ministers and administrators, particularly those of James Bryce in the Bodleian Library and the National Library and those of Sir Antony MacDonnell, Augustine Birrell and Sir Matthew Nathan, all in the Bodleian Library.

Finally, mention should be made of two important and largely untapped sources of information about the functioning of the Irish parliamentary party, especially in particular localities. Many Irish local newspapers, usually published weekly, had strong associations with the party or with one of its sections. They are therefore very useful for information about the activities of the party and its individual members in particular areas. In particular, such newspapers often give an indication of tensions and disagreements at a local level which often found more indirect expression in national politics. The parliamentary party also controlled, as a consequence of the Local Government (Ireland) Act of 1898, large areas of local government in Ireland. The records of the county councils and other local authorities have not been easily available in the past. However, such records could throw light upon the local character of the parliamentary party.

Sinn Fein and the Republican Movement

The body known after 1906 as Sinn Fein had its origins in the late 1890s among a group of Nationalists who, although defenders of Parnell, were disillusioned with the idea of parliamentary representation as a means of securing Irish independence and who sought to infect Irish nationalism with a stronger sense of Irish cultural developments. The principal architect of its policy was Arthur Griffith, who espoused what came to be known as the 'Hungarian policy', which envisaged a solution of Ireland's constitutional problems by means of a dual monarchy. Sinn Fein was not therefore Republican in policy and it was a quite separate organisation from the Irish Republican Brotherhood, which then represented the Fenian tradition in Irish politics. Moreover, the later development of revolutionary policies which emerged in 1916 was only indirectly connected with Sinn Fein. But after 1916 the destinies of Sinn Fein and the Republican organisation merged under the impact of the Easter Rising and subsequent events; they are therefore treated here together.

By the very nature of these organisations they have left very little in the way of institutional records, although the climate of opinion in Ireland has led to a careful preservation of items relating to the history of the revolutionary bodies. Manuscript relics of Sinn Fein, the Irish Republican Brotherhood, the Irish Volunteers, the Irish Republican Army and other bodies are therefore quite extensive, but fragmentary in character. Great importance therefore attaches to a close examination of various lists of manuscripts, especially Hayes' *Manuscript Sources for the History of Irish Civilisation*, which mentions under a number of different headings small items which together make up a moderately substantial archive for Sinn Fein and other revolutionary and Republican organisations.

The actual institutional records for Sinn Fein which have survived include minutes of the Standing Committee of Sinn Fein, January 1918 — March 1922; minutes of the Sinn Fein Publishing Company, 1906-12; and audited accounts for the Sinn Fein Publishing Company for 1912. All these records are in the National Library of Ireland, as are a number of other collections which contain significant material about Sinn Fein. In particular, a collection of letters, circulars, accounts and other papers relating to Sinn Fein, collected by Miss D. Barton and known as the Barton papers, contains considerable material on the Sinn Fein organisation, especially in Counties Wicklow and Wexford, and on Dail Eireann, 1917-27. The National Library also holds a number of miscellaneous items which have been collected from various sources and which relate to the activities of Sinn Fein; they include a miscellaneous collection of circulars and other documents, 1917 and later (MS. 10,916).

The Irish Volunteers, established in 1913 in response to the formation of the Ulster Volunteer Force, eventually provided the military basis for the revolution after 1916. The ranks of this organisation were split in 1914 when Redmond successfully gained control of the organisation in the interests of the parliamentary party and a minority of its ranks broke from the main body, retaining for themselves the original name of the Irish Volunteers. The majority, which became known as the Irish National Volunteers, were eventually superseded as an organisation with the decline of the parliamentary party, although many of its numbers and resources were merged with the by then ascendant Irish Volunteers. There is considerable archival material for the history of the Volunteers, much of which throws light on the activities of the more secretive Irish Republican Brotherhood, for which few records survive. The most important of these materials are in the papers of Colonel Maurice Moore, who was active in the Volunteers from its inception, became Inspector-General of the Irish National Volunteers, and maintained close contact with the military sector of the Republican movement in subsequent years. This collection is held by the National Library of Ireland and includes the following records of the National Volunteers: minutes of the National Committee, October 1914-March 1917, together with agenda for meetings; minutes of the General Purposes Committee, March 1916-June 1917, with agenda for meetings, May 1916-August 1917; and minutes of the Finance Committee, November 1914-July 1915 and March 1916-June 1917. The collection also contains a large quantity of general material, arranged mainly by county, consisting of letters, accounts, reports and similar papers relating to the organisation and equipment of the Volunteers, 1913-17, the 1916 rebellion, and other matters. There are also materials and drafts for a history of the Volunteers, an office diary (1916) and a petty cash book (August 1914-April 1917), which also serves as a partial register of outgoing letters. The papers of the O'Rahilly, still in private hands, contain material not only on the Volunteers, but also on Sinn Fein in general. A copy book of Miss Grace O'Brien in the National Library (MS. 4482) contains the names and particulars of dependants of Volunteers deported after the rising of 1916.

Material of importance to the history of the Volunteers, and the Republican movement in general, is contained in the papers of Bulmer Hobson in the National Library. They contain letters and papers relating to the Easter Rising and other subjects, and they include letters of Roger Casement, Eoin MacNeill, P. H. Pearse and others. Various miscellaneous items in the National Library relate to the Irish Republican Army. These include a group of general orders, circulars and memoranda of the I.R.A., 1920-21 (MS. 739), a collection of general orders from headquarters and documents relating to the Dublin Brigade of the I.R.A., 1918-21 (MSS. 900-3), and a roll-book of the 2nd battalion of the Dublin Brigade, 1919-20. There are also a number of personal collections of papers in the National Library which contain useful information on the Republican movement. The papers of Art O'Briain, who was envoy of Dail Eireann in London, contain correspondence with the British Government, including correspondence leading up to the Treaty; minutes, correspondence and other documents of the Irish National Relief Fund, London, 1916-22; and correspondence relating to Irish political prisoners in Great Britain, to the Irish Republican Prisoners' Dependants Fund, and to the Irish Self-Determination League, 1916-25. The papers of J. M. Plunkett contain considerable material on the Republican movement in general and on the organisation of Sinn Fein between 1917 and 1921 in particular. The papers of Roger Casement consist of family papers and documents on his Nationalist activities, including his journeys to the United States and to Germany, and his trial. Further material is contained in smaller collections of papers of Michael Collins, Diarmuid Lynch (a member of Dail Eireann and Sinn Fein Food Controller) and Eamonn Ceannt. The papers of Erskine Childers are still held by his family, although microfilm of some of them is held by the National Library. There is also material of interest about the Republican movement in the papers of Eoin Neeson, also privately held, but with microfilm in the National Library. The J. J. Hearn[1] papers, in the National Library, contain material about the Irish Republican movement in America in the 1920s.

The papers of the Dublin trade unionist, William O'Brien, which are in the National Library of Ireland, contain considerable material relevant to the history of the Republican movement. They include many of James Connolly's own papers and papers relating to many Republican bodies, to the Irish Citizen Army, the Irish Neutrality League, and to various events in the history of the Republican movement.

Irish Unionism

The most important repository of records relating to the history of Irish Unionism is the Public Record Office of Northern Ireland in Belfast. For this reason, a close perusal of the various *Reports* of the Deputy Keeper of the Records is the most effective way of obtaining up-to-date information on the records of Unionist organisations.

The Irish Unionist Alliance, known from 1885 until 1891 as the Irish Loyal and Patriotic Union, was most active among Unionists outside Ulster, although it was ostensibly an all-Ireland organisation. Many of its records are now in the Northern Ireland Public Record Office. They include minute books of its Executive Council, 1886-1920; Executive Committee, 1893-94; Organising Sub-committee, 1886; Speakers' Committee, 1893-94; Parliamentary Consultative Committee, 1894-1900; Special Committee on the Local Government Bill, 1898; Finance and other committees, 1907-12; and London Committee, 1919-39. There are also subscription books and annual reports. The collection includes correspondence with Sir Edward Carson, the correspondence and papers of J. M. Wilson, reports of Richard Dawson of the London Committee of the Irish Unionist Alliance, and papers relating to the split in the Alliance in 1918-19 and to incidents affecting Loyalists during the Anglo-Irish and civil wars.

The records of the Ulster Unionist Council provide the most important source for specifically Ulster Unionism; they are also held in the Belfast Public Record Office. The Ulster Unionist Council was established in 1905 to draw together disparate Ulster Unionist bodies and it eventually became the central policy-making body of the Northern Ireland Unionist Party. Minutes in this collection include those of the Ulster Day Committee, 1911-12; the Unionist Defence Fund Committee, 1912-14; the Business Men's Executive Committee, 1913-14; the Ulster Unionist delegates to the Irish Convention, 1917-18; and the Ulster Women's Unionist Council from 1911. There are also records relating to the gun-running in April 1914; the Unionist Clubs' Council, 1893-1919; the Unionist Association of Ireland, 1907-15; the Junior Imperial League, 1925-45; and the work of the Ulster Gift Fund, an organisation set up to assist prisoners-of-war, 1939-45.

Many of the records of the Ulster Volunteer Force are also held in the Public Record Office, Belfast. Some of these, including the minutes of the Headquarters Council, 1914-20, and the minutes of the County Down Committee, were among the records of the Ulster Unionist Council. Many other items were deposited in

---

[1] J. J. Hearn was, from October 1926, representative in the United States of the irregular 'Government of the Republic of Ireland'.

response to an appeal in 1961 by the late Viscount Brookeborough, then Prime Minister of Northern Ireland, for the preservation of papers relating to the Home Rule crisis, and particularly to the activities of the Ulster Volunteer Force. Lord O'Neill, for example, gave as a result of this appeal papers relating to the North Antrim regiment of the Force, while similar deposits were made for the South Down units. Colonel Frank Hall, who played a prominent part in the organisation of Unionist Clubs and the Ulster Volunteer Force, deposited a number of papers. The papers of Sir George Richardson relating to his connection with the Force and with the Ulster Division were also deposited, as were records relating to the organisation of the Force in County Fermanagh and the outward letter book of Colonel Fred Crawford, the gun-runner, for the years 1906-11.

Collections of private papers of various individuals are important sources for the history of Irish Unionism. In particular, the papers of Lord Midleton in the Public Record Office, London, contain material relating to his involvement in Unionist politics, especially in the south of Ireland. These papers are especially valuable for developments after 1916, and particularly for the growing divergence between southern Unionists and those of Ulster. The papers of John Henry Bernard and W. H. Lecky, in the Library of Trinity College, Dublin, should also be consulted for information about the activities of Unionists in general. On Ulster Unionism, the papers of Sir Edward Carson, Sir James Craig and Sir Wilfred Spender, all in the Public Record Office, Belfast, provide useful material.

There are many miscellaneous accessions to various repositories in Ireland which form an essential part of the archives of Irish Unionist organisations. The various lists issued by these institutions should be carefully consulted. This is particularly so of the Northern Ireland Public Record Office, which has acquired very considerable numbers of miscellaneous items, such as minute books, membership lists and photographs, relating to various local Unionist organisations. These include records of the Armagh constituency, together with records of Antrim. Similarly, the records of local government bodies in Ulster, which are generally becoming more readily available, could be useful in showing how Unionist-controlled councils operated.

Irish Labour Movement

The history of organised labour in Ireland has been a fragmented one. The trade union movement has been greatly affected by the bitter industrial disputes of the early 20th century, and the subsequent divisions between those following the more revolutionary traditions established by leaders such as James Connolly and James Larkin and those pursuing the more limited objectives of trade unionism; moreover, the division of Ireland politically, created by the establishment of Northern Ireland, has further fragmented both union activity and political action. Such a development has necessarily affected the extent to which records have been preserved, and it is still difficult to know how extensive such records are and where they are to be found. It is intended here to give only a general indication of the nature of the more readily available records and papers.

The most significant collection of papers for the history of Irish trade unionism and the labour movement in general are those of William O'Brien, the Dublin trade unionist, whose life was devoted to the service of the Irish Transport and General Workers' Union. After his death in 1968, O'Brien's papers were given to the National Library of Ireland. They include extensive material on his own political career, in the labour movement and in association with various Republican bodies. But many of the papers of James Connolly came into O'Brien's hands, and these are included in the collection; they are an important source for the earliest period of the Irish labour movement and of Irish Socialism in general. The O'Brien papers contain very extensive material relating to the activities and membership of the

Irish Transport and General Workers' Union. This includes a census of the member-ship of the union, together with lists of its branch officers, compiled in 1918, and O'Brien's diaries as union secretary, as well as several of his personal diaries. But a very substantial proportion of the general correspondence in the collection is intimately related to the activities of this union.[1]

The William O'Brien Collection also contains papers and records relating to other labour organisations. These include minutes of the Labour Representation Com-mittee of the Dublin United Trades Council (1911), a minute book of the Labour Representation Committee and Dublin Labour Party (1911-12), a minute book of the Pearse Street, Dublin, branch of the Irish Labour Party (December 1942-December 1943), letters relating to the formation of the National Labour Party in 1944, and papers relating to the Irish Women Workers' Union (1917-55), the Irish Co-operative Clothing Manufacturing Society (1904-21), the Amalgamated Society of Tailors (1904-22), the Irish Neutrality League (1914) and the Anti-Conscription Committee (1915). There is also a list of subscribers and a receipt book of the Irish Co-operative Labour Press, the publishers of the *Irish Worker* (1911-12). O'Brien's papers, including those of Connolly, also contain many records of early Socialist parties in Ireland. In particular, these include account books (1900-04) and minute books (1898-1904) of the Irish Socialist Republican Party and minute books (1904-08, 1910-12) of the Socialist Party of Ireland. There are also audited accounts of both these parties for various dates between 1900 and 1908. There is a minute book of the Independent Labour Party of Ireland (1912-14). Other organisations for which there are records in this collection include the Workers' Union of Ireland, the Irish Trades Union Congress, the Irish Labour Party, the Dublin United Trades Council and Labour League, the Dublin Trades Union Congress, and the Irish Citizen Army. The collection also includes the papers of the Commission of Enquiry set up by the Irish Trades Union Congress to con-sider the state of the trade union movement in Ireland (1936-39).

The National Library also holds other items of relevance to the history of the Irish labour movement. These include some further records of the Irish Transport and General Workers' Union, in particular relating to the annual conferences of the union (1922-39); there is also a roll book of the union from about 1915 (MS. 3097). The National Library also holds seven volumes of records of the Dublin Trades Council, 1893-1932 (MSS. 12,779-85) and miscellaneous fragmentary papers of Charles Diamond, an Irish trade unionist in Glasgow, 1919-23 (MS. 13,540).

The Northern Ireland Public Record Office holds certain items of interest to the history of the Irish labour movement. These include four volumes of diaries kept by R. McElborough, in which he comments on his experiences in the gas industry and his dealings with trade unions, 1884-1949 (D. 770), and the papers of Patrick Agnew, trade unionist and Labour M.P. for South Armagh in the Northern Ireland Parliament from 1938 to 1944, which include two minute books of the Armagh branch of the Northern Ireland Labour Party, 1933, 1946-47, two personal diaries, 1955-56, and correspondence (D. 1676).

Other Organisations

Certain organisations in Ireland, although not necessarily ostensibly political, have exercised considerable political influence in the 20th century and therefore deserve consideration here.

---

[1] A list of this collection may be found in 'Shelflist of Additional MSS'.

Gaelic League (Connradh na Gaedhilge)

The League was founded in 1893 with a twofold aim: to preserve Irish as the national language of the country and promote its spoken use; and to promote the study and publication of Gaelic literature, and to encourage a modern Irish literature. It was intended to be politically neutral, but this became difficult during the ensuing years. It split in 1915 over the question of Irish independence, and in 1918 was declared an illegal organisation, together with Sinn Fein. Since independence the League has continued its work to preserve and promote the Irish language.

Many of the earlier records of the League have been deposited in the National Library of Ireland. These provide an excellent source for the history of the League up to and beyond the establishment of the Irish State. They include the minutes of the Executive Committee, 1897-1926; the annual conference, 1908, 1919-22; the Business Committee, 1916-20; the Organisation Committee, 1902-20; the Finance Committee, 1902-20; the Education Committee, 1902-20; the Publication Committee, 1902-12; the Industrial Committee, 1902-11; and the Dublin District Committee. Other records include attendance and membership lists, 1892-1925; names and addresses of branch secretaries in England and Ireland, 1906-09; staff attendance books, 1907-11; letter books, 1903-09; post-books, 1903-22. Financial records, including account and cash books, survive from 1900. Other records of note are those relating to the publication of various League periodicals. These again date from the beginning of the century. There is also a copy letter book, 1917, and other items, 1910-19, of the Terenure branch of the Gaelic League.

Orange Order

This organisation, and various Lodges associated with it, provided for Ulster Unionism some of the organisational and cultural backing which for the Nationalists derived from the Gaelic League, the Gaelic Athletic Association and the Ancient Order of Hibernians.

The Northern Ireland Public Record Office holds a number of records of particular Orange Lodges. These include correspondence, accounts and pamphlets of Cookstown Orange Lodge and of County Tyrone Grand Orange Lodge, mid-19th century to 1944.

Irish Co-operative Movement

The co-operative movement in Ireland was very largely the creation of Sir Horace Plunkett, a moderate Unionist politician, who wished to resolve many of the problems of rural Ireland by means of co-operation. The movement's aims were mildly political in the sense that it was concerned with many of the same issues as were politicians, but its relations with politicians were not always easy.

The Horace Plunkett papers, which are at the Plunkett Foundation for Co-operative Studies in Oxford, are the most significant collection of papers, although these are not as comprehensive as they would have been had many of them not been destroyed by fire during the civil war in Ireland. They include Plunkett's diaries, with their detailed comments on his everyday activities in Ireland and on discussions with political leaders and others. There is also considerable correspondence, both with British politicians and with individuals in Ireland, and there are other records relating to the Irish co-operative movement.

T. P. Gill, at one time a Nationalist M.P., spent the greater part of his life in non-political activity in Ireland, most of this with the Department of Agriculture and Technical Instruction, of which Plunkett was for many years the head. Gill's papers at the National Library of Ireland contain considerable material on his work at the Department, intertwined as it was with the advocacy and establishment of co-operatives, especially in the dairying industry.

There are a number of records relating to various co-operative organisations in the papers of William O'Brien, the Irish trade unionist. These are in the National Library of Ireland and include papers of the Irish Co-operative Clothing Manufacturing Society (MS. 15, 650) and the Irish Co-operative Labour Press (MS. 15,651).

Irish Convention, 1917-18

The Irish Convention, convened by Lloyd George in an attempt to find an agreed solution to the problem of Irish government, was more widely representative of Irish opinion than any other political activity in Ireland's recent history. The Convention, under the chairmanship of Sir Horace Plunkett, has left a number of papers relating to its proceedings. These include the notes of J. P. Mahaffy, Provost of Trinity College, Dublin, which are in the Library of Trinity College, and agenda papers of the Convention which are in Trinity College and in the State Paper Office.

Irish Recess Committee

This body was representative of members of various political parties in Ireland and was set up in 1895, mainly on the instigation of Sir Horace Plunkett, as a forum for the discussion of matters of common agreement to all Irishmen.

Papers relating to the work of this committee may be found among the papers of many of the politicians who took part in its proceedings. This is particularly so of Plunkett's own papers at the Horace Plunkett Foundation for Co-operative Studies at Oxford. There is also in the National Library of Ireland a minute book of the Committee's proceedings, October 1895-April 1897 (MS. 4532).

Irish Land Conference, 1902-03

This conference of representatives of Irish landlords and tenants was instrumental in securing the most important advance in the resolution of the land problem in Ireland. Its report paved the way for the Land Act of 1903 which secured a massive transfer of the land of Ireland to peasant proprietorship.

The papers of William O'Brien, the Nationalist M.P., John Redmond and T. C. Harrington all contain important papers and correspondence about the work of the conference. In addition, there is a small group of papers relating specifically to the conference, particularly on the preliminaries on the landlord side, in the National Library of Ireland (MS. 10,907).

Irish Self-Determination League

An Irish Republican organisation established in 1919 for the purpose of furthering the Irish cause in England and Wales, this body sought to raise funds in England and also to function as a propaganda organisation.

The most important archive for this organisation is in the papers of its president, Art O'Briain, which are in the National Library of Ireland. They include account books for the organisation as well as extensive relevant correspondence.

Biographical Notes

Many of the persons mentioned in the text will be familiar to students of British history. However, the following details may be helpful to readers:

Bulmer Hobson. Member of the Irish Republican Brotherhood, active Republican journalist (founder of the *Republic*, assistant editor of the *Peasant* and editor of *Irish Freedom*), leading figure in the Irish Volunteers.

Eamonn Caennt. Member of I.R.B. Military Council, active in Gaelic League and Sinn Fein, founder member of the Irish Volunteers, of which he was Director of Communications, executed in 1916.

The O'Rahilly. Active in Sinn Fein and the Gaelic League, one of the founders of the Irish Volunteers, of which he was Director of Arms, although played part in attempt to avert Easter Rising, eventually killed while taking part in it.

Joseph Mary Plunkett. Active in literary circles, editor of the *Irish Review*, a founder of the Irish Volunteers, member of Irish Republican Brotherhood, Director of Military Operations, in which capacity he made the military plans for the rising of 1916.

Appendix II
Archives in Wales

The National Library of Wales, at Aberystwyth (Dyfed), which was established in 1908, is the most important repository of records relating to Wales and Welsh politics. Its holdings are described in its annual reports, and in 'Handlist of Manuscripts in the National Library of Wales', a supplement to the *National Library of Wales Journal*.

The relevant collections for the 20th century include both personal papers and records of various societies and institutions. In the former category are papers of a variety of prominent political figures, active both in Wales and at Westminster, including D. R. Daniel, Lord Davies of Llandinam, T. E. Ellis, A. C. Humphreys-Owen, Sir Hussey Vivian, Ellis Griffith, E. J. John, Herbert Lewis, David and Megan Lloyd George, Stuart Rendel, Lord Rhondda, J. Bryn Roberts, Thomas Jones and Clement Davies.

Many of these collections include a wide variety of material relating to the activities of various organisations, e.g. the Davies of Llandinam Collection includes papers relating to the activities of the Welsh Council of the *League of Nations Union* (q.v.) and *New Commonwealth* (q.v.).

The activities of Cymru Fydd, a Welsh cultural and political movement active during the last decade of the 19th century, may be traced in collections at the National Library. The papers of a later organisation, *Undeb Cymru Fydd* (q.v.), are also in the Library.

Plaid Cymru (Welsh Nationalist Party) (q.v.) has deposited many of its records in the National Library of Wales. Other organisations whose papers are in this Library include the North Wales Liberal Federation, the Parliament for Wales Campaign (papers of the Merioneth Committee, early 1950s), Urdd Gobaith Cymru, Urdd y Deyrnas (papers, 1918-57), Undeb y Cymru ar Wasgar (correspondence, 1947-67), and the Welsh Language Society (minutes and correspondence, 1885-1938).

The Library of the University College of North Wales, Bangor, also contains items relating to the activities of Plaid Cymru, as well as the personal papers of prominent Welsh figures, such as William Jones and W. J. Parry.

The campaigns for Disestablishment of the Church in Wales may be traced in the records of the *Liberation Society* (q.v.) and in many collections at the National Library. A microfilm of minutes of the Liberation Society is available in the Library of the University College of Swansea.

The central role of the coal-mining industry in Welsh industrial and social life has recently been recognised by a research project at the University College of Swansea, sponsored by the Social Science Research Council. This has undertaken to locate, preserve and collect material relating to the history of the South Wales coalfield. A specialist library for this material has recently been opened at the University

College. Relevant records at the University College include: records of the South Wales Miners' Federation and of various Miners' lodges; other collections relating to trade union and labour relations in South Wales; local records of political parties; records of Miners' Institutes; and papers of prominent personalities in South Wales life, including Arthur Horner and Will Paynter.

At the Cardiff Public Library the papers of the Bute family and Lord Pontypridd are useful. Carmarthenshire Record Office holds the papers of Lord Cawdor, and Caernarvonshire Record Office has materials relating to David Lloyd George.

Appendix III
Archives in Scotland

The Scottish Record Office, H. M. General Register House, Edinburgh EH1 3YY contains among its holdings of twentieth century material files of Scottish Departments of State and the Scottish Headquarters of United Kingdom Departments, the records of the Scottish Courts and of many local authorities. The Office also holds many private muniments containing relevant material, the most noteworthy being the papers of Philip Kerr, 11th Marquess of Lothian, and of Sir Arthur Steel-Maitland. The Annual Report of the Keeper of the Records of Scotland gives details of accessions, and the first volume of a *List of Gifts and Deposits* has been published giving details of private archives in the custody of the Office. A revised guide to the Scottish Record Office is in the course of preparation and will give details of all classes of records. The National Register of Archives (Scotland) is a branch of the Scottish Record Office which exists to record manuscript material in and relating to Scotland held in private hands or in non-governmental repositories. Copies of all lists prepared by the Register are furnished to the Scottish Universities, to the National Register of Archives, London, and to the Institute of Historical Research.

The Advocates' Library, Edinburgh, founded in 1682, became the National Library of Scotland in 1925. The Department of Manuscripts there has a large collection of material relevant to twentieth century politics. This ranges from the papers of the 5th Earl of Rosebery, which include records of the Liberal League (q.v.), to material deposited at the instigation of the Scottish Labour History Society. Papers in the National Library relating to Socialist and trade union activities include the records of the National Council of Labour Colleges (q.v.), the Scottish Trades Union Congress (q.v.), the Scottish Area of the National Union of Mineworkers (q.v.), and later records of the Social Democratic Federation (q.v.). Papers of Socialist pioneers such as Keir Hardie and John Maclean may also be consulted at the National Library of Scotland.

The Library has published a *Catalogue of Manuscripts* and *Accessions of Manuscripts*, detailing accessions since 1959. Previous to that accessions may be traced in the *Annual Reports* of the Library.

The Scottish National Party (q.v.) has retained many records. Certain records in the National Library of Scotland are useful for tracing the development of Scottish nationalism, e.g. the papers of R. E. Muirhead, and the collection of papers relating to the Scottish Secretariat (q.v.). Reference should be made to the following works:

Kenneth C. Fraser: *Bibliography of the Scottish National Movement 1928-58.* (Strathclyde University Scottish Nationalist Club, Glasgow, 1968).

H. J. Hanham: *Scottish Nationalism* (1969).

Records relating to the Labour Movement in Scotland are listed in Ian MacDougall (ed.): *An Interim Bibliography of the Scottish Working Class Movement* (Scottish Society for the Study of Labour History, Edinburgh, 1965). A further and fuller bibliography is forthcoming. These should be consulted for full details concerning Scottish trade unions and socialist organisations.

Important collections of records are deposited in various University Libraries, e.g. records of the Scottish Liberal Federation are held in Edinburgh University Library, and other local party records are available in the Library of King's College, University of Aberdeen.

The Mitchell Library, Glasgow, holds useful manuscript material, including a large body of Scottish trade union material and certain records of the Socialist Sunday School movement (see: Socialist Fellowship). Also in Glasgow, the City Archives Office has material which is relevant, including the papers of James Parker Smith, M.P., who was closely involved with the *Tariff Reform League* (q.v.).

See also: Conservative Party, Labour Party, Liberal Party.

Appendix IV
Selected Libraries
and Record Repositories

The following is an alphabetical list of libraries mentioned in the text. At the time of writing, the most up-to-date list of relevant libraries was that produced by the Royal Commission on Historical Manuscripts, *Record Repositories in Great Britain* (5th ed., H.M.S.O., 1973). Since this was published the reorganisation of local government areas (operative from April 1974) has resulted in a reorganisation of record and library authorities. This list has attempted, where possible, to provide the most up-to-date list of addresses. Where a now redundant name has been used in the text, this will be found in its alphabetical position, with the current title and address alongside it.

ABERDEEN, University Library.
Manuscript and Archives Section, University Library, King's College, Aberdeen AB9 2UB.
ARBROATH Public Library, Hill Place, Arbroath, Angus.
Archbishop's archives: WESTMINSTER DIOCESAN ARCHIVES, Archbishop's House, Westminster, London SW1P 1QJ.

BALLIOL COLLEGE, Oxford.
BANGOR, University College of North Wales. Department of Manuscripts, The Library, UCNW, Bangor LL57 2DG, Gwynedd.
BATH Record Office, Guildhall, Bath, Avon BA1 5AW.
BEAVERBROOK LIBRARY, 33 St Bride Street, London EC4A 4AY.
BIRMINGHAM Central (Reference) Library, Birmingham B3 3HQ.
BIRMINGHAM University Library, PO Box 363, The University, Edgbaston, Birmingham B15 2TT.
BISHOPSGATE INSTITUTE, 230 Bishopsgate, London EC2.
BODLEIAN LIBRARY, Oxford OX1 3BG.
BRADFORD Central Library, Prince's Way, Bradford BD1 1NN.
BRISTOL Archives Office, Council House, Bristol, Avon BS1 5TR.
BRISTOL University Library, Wills Memorial Library, Queens Road, Bristol, Avon, BS8 1RJ.
BRITISH ACADEMY, Burlington House, Piccadilly, London W1V 0NS

BRITISH LIBRARY, Department of Manuscripts, Great Russell Street, London WC1B 3DG.
BRITISH LIBRARY OF POLITICAL AND ECONOMIC SCIENCE (B.L.P.E.S.), London School of Economics, Houghton Street, Aldwych, London WC2A 2AE.
BROTHERTON LIBRARY, University of Leeds, Leeds LS2 9JT.
BURNLEY Central Library, Grimshaw Street, Burnley, Lancs.

CAERNARVONSHIRE: Gwynedd Record Office, County Offices, Caernarvon, Gwynedd LL55 1SH.
CAMBRIDGE University Library and Archives, West Road, Cambridge CB3 9DR.
CAMBRIDGESHIRE AND ISLE OF ELY: Cambridgeshire County Record Office, Shire Hall Castle Hill, Cambridge CB3 0AP.
CARDIFF Central Library, The Hayes, Cardiff, South Glamorgan CF1 2QU.
CARDIFF University College Library, PO Box 78, Cardiff, South Glamorgan CF1 1XL.
CARLISLE: Cumbria Record Office, The Castle, Carlisle CA3 8UR.
CARMARTHENSHIRE: Dyfed Archives, Carmarthen Record Office, County Hall, Carmarthen, Dyfed.
CENTRAL ZIONIST ARCHIVES, PO Box 92, Jerusalem, Israel.
CENTRE OF SOUTH ASIAN STUDIES, University of Cambridge, Laundress Lane, Cambridge.
CHESHIRE Record Office, The Castle, Chester CH1 2DN.
CHRIST CHURCH, Oxford.
CHURCHILL COLLEGE, Cambridge CB3 0DS.
CORK, University College Library, Cork, Eire.
CORNWALL County Record Office, County Hall, Truro, Cornwall TR1 3AY.
COVENTRY Record Office, 9 Hay Lane, Coventry CV1 5RF.

DERBY Central Library, Wardwick, Derby DE1 1HS.
DERBYSHIRE Record Office, County Offices, Matlock, Derbyshire DE4 3AG.
DEWSBURY Central Library, Wellington Road, Dewsbury, Kirklees, West Yorkshire WF13 1HW.
DONCASTER: South Yorkshire Industrial Museum, Cusworth Hall, Doncaster DN5 7TU.
DUBLIN University College Library, Archives Department, 82 St Stephen's Green, Dublin 2, Eire.
DUDLEY Public Libraries, St James's Road, Dudley, West Midlands, DY1 1HR.
DUKE University Library, Durham, North Carolina, U.S.A. 27706.
DUNFERMLINE Public Library, Abbey View, Dunfermline, Fife.
DURHAM County Record Office, County Hall, Durham DH1 5UL.
DURHAM University Library, Palace Green, Durham DH1 3RN.

EAST SUFFOLK: Suffolk Record Office.
EDINBURGH City Archives, City Chambers, Edinburgh EH1 1YJ.
EDINBURGH University Library, Department of Manuscripts, George Square, Edinburgh EH8 9LJ.

FAWCETT LIBRARY, 27 Wilfred Street, London SW1E 6PR.
FITZWILLIAM MUSEUM, Trumpington Street, Cambridge.
FLINTSHIRE: Clwyd Record Office, The Old Rectory, Hawarden, Deeside, Clwyd CH5 3NR.
FRIENDS HOUSE LIBRARY, Friends House, Euston Road, London NW1 2BJ.

GALWAY University College Library, Galway, Eire.

311

GATESHEAD Public Libraries, Central Library and Borough Record Office, Prince Consort Road, Gateshead, Tyne and Wear NE8 4LN.

GLAMORGAN County Record Office, County Hall, Cathays Park, Cardiff CF1 3NE.

GLASGOW City Archives Office, PO Box 27, City Chambers, Glasgow G2 1DU.

GLASGOW Mitchell Library, North Street, Glasgow G3 7DN.

GLASGOW University Archives, The University, Glasgow G12 8QQ.

GLASGOW University Library, The University, Glasgow G12 8QE.

GOLDSMITHS' LIBRARY, University of London Library, Senate House, Malet Street, London WC1E 7HU.

GREAT YARMOUTH Borough Records: transferred to Norfolk Record Office.

GREATER LONDON Record Office: (London Records), The County Hall, London SE1 7PB; (Middlesex Records), 1 Queen Anne's Gate Buildings, Dartmouth Street, London SW1H 9BS.

GUILDFORD Muniment Room, Castle Arch, Guildford, Surrey GU1 3SX.

GUILDHALL LIBRARY, Basinghall Street, London EC2P 2EJ.

HACKNEY Libraries Department, Archives Department, Shoreditch Library, Pitfield Street, London N1 6EX.

HAMMERSMITH Public Libraries, Archives Department, Shepherds Bush Library, Uxbridge Road, London W12 8LJ.

HAMPSHIRE Record Office, 20 Southgate Street, Winchester, Hants SO23 9EF.

HARINGEY Libraries Department, Bruce Castle, Lordship Lane, London N17 8NU.

HARVARD University Library, Cambridge, Mass. 02138, U.S.A.

HASTINGS Public Museum, John's Place, Cambridge Road, Hastings, East Sussex.

HERTFORDSHIRE County Record Office, County Hall, Hertford.

HOOVER INSTITUTION ON WAR, REVOLUTION AND PEACE, Stanford, California, U.S.A. 94305.

HOUSE OF LORDS Record Office, House of Lords, London SW1A 0PW.

HUDDERSFIELD Central Library, Princess Alexandra Walk, Huddersfield, Kirklees HD2 2SU.

HULL City Record Office, Guildhall, Kingston upon Hull, Humberside HU1 2AA.

HULL University Library, The Brynmor Jones Library, The University, Hull, Humberside, HU6 7RX.

IMPERIAL WAR MUSEUM, Department of Libraries and Archives, Imperial War Museum, Lambeth Road, London SE1 6HZ.

INDIA OFFICE LIBRARY, European Manuscripts Section, Foreign and Commonwealth Office, 197 Blackfriars Road, London SE1 8NG.

INSTITUTE OF AGRICULTURAL HISTORY and Museum of English Rural Life, University of Reading, Whiteknights, Reading, Berks. RE6 2AG.

INSTITUTE OF COMMONWEALTH STUDIES Library, University of London, 27 Russell Square, London WC1.

INTERNATIONAL INSTITUTE OF SOCIAL HISTORY, Herengracht, 262-266, Amsterdam, Netherlands.

IPSWICH Public Library, Central Library, Northgate Street, Ipswich, Suffolk IP1 3DE.

IPSWICH and EAST SUFFOLK: Suffolk Record Office, County Hall, Ipswich, Suffolk IP4 2JS.

ISLINGTON Public Libraries, Central Library, 68 Holloway Road, London N7 8JN.

JEWISH HISTORICAL SOCIETY, 33 Seymour Place, London W1.

KENT Archives Office, County Hall, Maidstone, Kent ME14 1XQ.
KING'S COLLEGE Library, University of London, Strand, London WC2R 2LS.

LAMBETH PALACE Library, London SE1.
LANCASHIRE Record Office, Sessions House, Lancaster Road, Preston, Lancashire PR1 2RE.
LEEDS Brotherton Library, University of Leeds, Leeds LS2 9JT.
LEEDS Metropolitan District Libraries, Sheepscar Branch Library, Chapeltown Road, Leeds LS7 3AP.
LEICESTER Museums, Department of Archives, The Museum and Art Gallery, New Walk, Leicester LE1 6TD.
LEICESTERSHIRE Record Office, 57 New Walk, Leicester LE1 7JB.
LIDDELL HART CENTRE FOR MILITARY ARCHIVES, King's College, Strand, London WC2R 2LS.
LINCOLNSHIRE Archives Office, The Castle, Lincoln LN1 3AB.
LIVERPOOL Record Office, City Libraries, William Brown Street, Liverpool, Merseyside L3 8EW.
LIVERPOOL University Archives, The University, Senate House, Abercromby Square, PO Box 147, Liverpool, Merseyside L69 3BX.
LIVERPOOL University Library, The University, PO Box 123, Liverpool, Merseyside L69 3DA.
LONDON MUSEUM, Kensington Palace, London W8.
LONDON University College Library, Gower Street, London WC1E 6BT.
LONDON UNIVERSITY Institute of Education Library, 11/13 Ridgmount Street, London WC1
LONDON UNIVERSITY LIBRARY, Senate House, Malet Street, London WC1E 7HU.

McMASTER University Library, Hamilton, Ontario, Canada.
MANCHESTER Central Library, St Peter's Square, Manchester M2 5PD.
MANCHESTER: John Rylands University Library of Manchester, Deansgate, Manchester M3 3EH.
MARX MEMORIAL LIBRARY, Marx House, 37A Clerkenwell Green, London EC1.
MERIONETH: Gwynedd Archives Service, County Offices, Y Lawnt, Dolgellau, Gwynedd.
MIDDLE EAST CENTRE, St Antony's College, 137 Banbury Road, Oxford OX2 6JF.
MITCHELL LIBRARY, North Street, Glasgow G12 8QQ.
MOCATTA LIBRARY, University College London, Gower Street, London WC1E 6BT.
MODERN RECORDS CENTRE, University of Warwick Library, Coventry CV4 7AL.
MONMOUTHSHIRE: Gwent County Record Office, County Hall, Newport, Gwent, NP7 5XJ.

NATIONAL LIBRARY OF IRELAND, Department of Manuscripts, Kildare Street, Dublin 2, Eire.
NATIONAL LIBRARY OF SCOTLAND, Department of Manuscripts, George IV Bridge, Edinburgh EH1 1EW.
NATIONAL LIBRARY OF WALES, Department of Manuscripts, Aberystwyth, Dyfed SY23 3BU.
NATIONAL MARITIME MUSEUM, Greenwich, London SE10.
NATIONAL REGISTER OF ARCHIVES, Historical Manuscripts Commission, Quality House, Quality Court, Chancery Lane, London WC2A 1HP.
NATIONAL REGISTER OF ARCHIVES (SCOTLAND), General Register House, Edinburgh EH1 3YY.
NEHRU MEMORIAL LIBRARY, Teen Murti House, New Delhi, India.
NEW COLLEGE Library, Oxford.

NEWARK Gilstrap Library, Castle Gate, Newark, Notts.
NEWCASTLE UPON TYNE University Library, Queen Victoria Road, Newcastle upon Tyne, Tyne and Wear NE1 7RU.
NEWHAM Public Libraries, Stratford Reference Library, Water Lane, London E15 3NJ.
NORFOLK Record Office, Norwich District Central Library, Norwich NOR 57E.
NORTHAMPTONSHIRE Record Office, Delapré Abbey, Northampton NN4 9AW.
NORTHERN IRELAND PUBLIC RECORD OFFICE, 66 Balmoral Avenue, Belfast BT9 6NY.
NORTHUMBERLAND Record Office, Melton Park, North Gosforth, Newcastle upon Tyne, Tyne and Wear NE3 5QX.
NORWICH Central Library, Bethel Street, Norwich NOR 57E.
NOTTINGHAM Archives Department, The Guildhall, Nottingham NG1 4BT.
NOTTINGHAM University Manuscripts Department, University of Nottingham Library, University Park, Nottingham NG7 2RD.
NOTTINGHAMSHIRE Record Office, County House, High Pavement, Nottingham NG1 1HR.
NUFFIELD COLLEGE Library, Oxford OX1 1NF.

OXFORD Central Library, St Aldate's, Oxford OX1 1DJ.
OXFORDSHIRE County Record Office, County Hall, New Road, Oxford OX1 1ND.

PARKES LIBRARY, Southampton University Library, Southampton SO9 5NH.
PETERBOROUGH Central Library and Information Service, Broadway, Peterborough, Cambridgeshire.
PONTYPRIDD Library, Rhydfelin, Pontypridd, Mid-Glamorgan.
POOLE Central Library, Arndale Centre, Poole, Dorset BH15 1QE.
PORTSMOUTH Record Office, Guildhall, Portsmouth PO1 2AL.
PRESTON, Harris Public Library, Preston, Lancs.
PUBLIC RECORD OFFICE, Chancery Lane, London WC2A 1LR.
PUBLIC RECORD OFFICE OF IRELAND, Four Courts, Dublin, Eire.
PUBLIC RECORD OFFICE OF NORTHERN IRELAND, 66 Balmoral Avenue, Belfast BT9 6NY.
PUSEY HOUSE Library, St Giles, Oxford.

QUEEN'S UNIVERSITY Library, University Road, Belfast 7, Northern Ireland.

READING: B.B.C. Written Archives Centre, Caversham Park, Reading, Berks. RG4 8TZ.
READING University Library, Whiteknights, Reading, Berks, RG6 2AE.
RHODES HOUSE Library, Oxford.
ROCHDALE Central Library, The Esplanade, Rochdale, Greater Manchester.
ROYAL COMMONWEALTH SOCIETY Library, Northumberland Avenue, London WC2N 5BJ.
ROYAL INSTITUTE OF INTERNATIONAL AFFAIRS, The Library, Chatham House, 10 St James' Square, London SW1Y 4LE.
ROYAL IRISH ACADEMY, 19 Dawson Street, Dublin 2, Eire.
RUSKIN COLLEGE Library, Oxford OX1 2HE.
RUTGERS STATE UNIVERSITY Library, New Brunswick, New Jersey 08903, U.S.A.

ST ANDREWS University Library, The University, St Andrews, Fife.
SCHOOL OF ORIENTAL AND AFRICAN STUDIES Library, University of London, Malet Street, London WC1E 7HP.

SCOTTISH RECORD OFFICE, PO Box 36, H.M. General Register House, Edinburgh EH1 3YY.
SHEEPSCAR LIBRARY, Leeds Metropolitan District Libraries, Chapeltown Road, Leeds, West Yorkshire LS7 3AP.
SHEFFIELD Central Library, Surrey Street, Sheffield, South Yorkshire S1 1XZ.
SHEFFIELD University Library, Western Bank, Sheffield, South Yorkshire S10 2TN.
SHROPSHIRE: Salop Record Office, Shirehall, Abbey Foregate, Shrewsbury, Salop SY2 6ND.
SMETHWICK District Library, High Street, Smethwick, Warley, West Midlands B66 1AB.
SOMERSET Record Office, Obridge Road, Taunton, Somerset TA2 7PU.
SOUTH CAROLINA, University of, Library, Columbia, South Carolina 29208, U.S.A.
SOUTHAMPTON University Library, Southampton, Hants. SO9 5NH.
STAFFORDSHIRE Record Office, Eastgate Street, Stafford ST16 2L2.
STATE PAPER OFFICE, Dublin 2, Eire.
STIRLING Burgh Public Library, Corn Exchange Road, Stirling.
STOCKPORT Central Library, Wellington Road South, Stockport, Greater Manchester SK1 3RS.
SUSSEX University Library, Brighton BN1 9QL.
SWANSEA University College Library, Singleton Park, Swansea, West Glamorgan SA2 8PP.
SWINTON and PENDLEBURY Public Library, Chorley Road, Swinton, Manchester M27 2AF.

TEXAS, University of, Library, Austin, Texas 78712, U.S.A.
THEOSOPHICAL SOCIETY Library, Adyar, Madras, India.
TRADES UNION CONGRESS Library, Congress House, Great Russell Street, London WC1
TRINITY COLLEGE, University of Dublin, Library, Dublin 2, Eire.
TYNE and WEAR County Record Office, 109 Pilgrim Street, Newcastle upon Tyne NE1 6QF.

WALSALL Public Library, Lichfield Street, Walsall, West Midlands.
WARWICKSHIRE County Record Office, Priory Park, Cape Road, Warwick CV4 4JS.
WEDNESBURY Public Library, Hollies Drive, Wednesbury, Staffs.
WELLCOME INSTITUTE of the History of Medicine Library, 183 Euston Road, London NW1 2BP.
WEST SUSSEX Record Office, West Street, Chichester, West Sussex PO19 1RN.
WESTMINSTER DIOCESAN Archives, Archbishop's House, London SW1P 1QJ.
WESTMINSTER City Libraries, Archives Department, Victoria Library, Buckingham Palace Road, London SW1W 9TR; Local History Library, Marylebone Library, Marylebone Road, London NW1 5PS.
WIENER LIBRARY and Institute of Contemporary History, 4 Devonshire Street, London W1N 2BH.
DR WILLIAMS'S LIBRARY, 14 Gordon Square, London WC1H 0AG.
WILTSHIRE Record Office, County Hall, Trowbridge, Wilts. BA14 8JG.
WISCONSIN, University of, Memorial Library, Madison, Wisconsin 53706, U.S.A.
WORCESTERSHIRE: Hereford and Worcester Record Office, Shirehall, Worcester WR1 1TR.

YALE University Library, New Haven, Connecticut 06520, U.S.A.
YORK Archives Department, Central Library, Museum Street, York, North Yorkshire YO1 2DS.

Index of Organisations and Societies

Italics indicate a main entry in the Guide

318

'Girls' Nautical Training Corps, 203
Glasgow Citizens' Union and Glasgow Ratepayers' Federation, 103
Glasgow Shipwrights' Society, 4
Glass Bottle Makers of Yorkshire, 264
Gold Standard Defence Association, 103
Greenshirt Movement for Social Credit, 236
Guardian, The, 104
Guild of Insurance Officials, 17
Guild of Loyal Women in South Africa, 109
Guild of St Alban, 218

Hammersmith Socialist Society, 239
Headmasters' Association, 123
Headmasters' Conference, 104
Health Visitors' Association, 105
Helicopter Association of Great Britain, 224
Henry George School of Social Science, 272
Hire Purchase Trade Association, 105
Hispanic Council, 33
History and Social Studies of Science Division of the University of Sussex, 232
Hong Kong Association, 36
Hospital and Welfare Services Union, 50
Hospital Saturday Funds, 26
Howard Association, 106
Howard League for Penal Reform, 106, 169
Hull Seamen's Union, 200

Imperial Alliance for the Defence of Sundays, 106, 158
Imperial and Commonwealth Affairs, 107
Imperial Commercial Association, 108
Imperial Fascist League, 220
Imperial Federation League, 108
Imperial South African Association, 108
Incorporated Association of Assistant Masters in Secondary Schools, 124
Independent Labour Party, 109, 162, 181
India Conciliation Group, 113
India Defence League, 111, *113*
India League, 111, *113*
India Society, 112
Indian Affairs: Societies and Organisations in Britian 1900-47, 111
Indian Empire Society, 111, *113*
Indian Home Rule League, British Auxiliary, 112, 113
Indian Reform Committee, 113
Indo-British Association, 112
Industrial Democracy League, 251
Industrial Participation Association, 114
Industrial Society, 114
Industrial Syndicalist Education League, 250
Industrial Welfare Society, 114
Infant Welfare Movement, 167
Inland Revenue Staff Federation, 115
Institute of Aeronautical Engineers, 224
Institute of Agricultural History, 116

Institute of Agricultural History and Museum of English Rural Life, 116
Institute of Directors, 117
Institute of Journalists, 117, 195
Institute of Mining Surveyors, 23
Instrument Makers' Society, 7
International African Institute, 108
International Bible Reading Association, 170
International Brigade Association, 250
International Catholic Association for Intellectual and Cultural Affairs, 205
International Committee for the Application of Non-Intervention in Spain, 249
International Committee of the Red Cross, 28-9
International Co-operative Alliance, 77, 78
International Council of Women, 176
International Ethical Union, 27
International Federation for the Abolition of State Regulation of Vice, 125
International Federation of Business and Professional Women, 26
International Institute of Languages, 108
International Institute of Social History, 117
International Missionary Council, 51
International Peace Society, 120
International Union for Land-Value Taxation and Free Trade, 272
International Women's Co-operative Guild, 77, 78
International Women's Guild, 78
International Workingmen's Association, 20, 161
Irish Convention, 304
Irish Co-operative Movement, 303
Irish Labour Movement, 301
Irish Land Conference 1902-03, 304
Irish Parliamentary Movement, 295
Irish Recess Committee, 304
Irish Self-Determination League, 304
Irish Society for Archives, 293
Irish Unionism, 300
Irish Unionist Alliance, 300
Iron and Steel Trades Confederation, 120
Ironfounding Workers' Association, 8
Italian Refugees Relief Committee, 121

Japan Association, 36
Jewish Dominion of Palestine League, 122
Jewish Organisations in Britain, 122
Jewish Welfare Board, 122
Jewish Youth Movements, 289
Joint Africa Board, 123
Joint Council of Women's Emigration Societies, 278
Joint East African Board, 123
Joint Executive Committee of the Associations of Headmasters, Head Mistresses, Assistant Masters and Assistant Mistresses, 123